TRADE ISSUES, POLICIES AND LAWS

CURRENT ISSUES IN INTERNATIONAL TRADE

METHODOLOGIES AND DEVELOPMENT IMPLICATIONS FOR THE WORLD ECONOMY

TRADE ISSUES, POLICIES AND LAWS

Additional books in this series can be found on Nova's website under the Series tab.

Additional e-books in this series can be found on Nova's website under the e-book tab.

TRADE ISSUES, POLICIES AND LAWS

CURRENT ISSUES IN INTERNATIONAL TRADE

METHODOLOGIES AND DEVELOPMENT IMPLICATIONS FOR THE WORLD ECONOMY

GOURANGA G. DAS, PH.D.
EDITOR

nova publishers
New York

Library of Congress Cataloging-in-Publication Data

ISBN: 978-1-63321-405-7

Published by Nova Science Publishers, Inc. † New York

Pluck this little flower and take it, delay not! I fear lest it droop and drop into the dust ---Rabindranath Tagore, Nobel Laureate Poet (India). In Gitanjali (Song-offerings), Poem No. 6. (1912).

To
The Fondest Memory of My Parents,
whose lifetime inspiration and blessings helped me to persevere,
and
To my wife Saswati, and son Sohom for their enduring love, and support

CONTENTS

Acknowledgments **ix**

Preface **xi**

List of Contributors (In Alphabetical Order) **xxi**

Part I: Current Scenarios of Global Trade and the Emerging Issues **1**

Chapter 1 The Global Recession and Developing Economies in Asia: Evidence from China and India **3**
Ananya G. Dastidar

Chapter 2 Development of Asia's Industrial Network and Cross-Pacific Trade **27**
Hongyul Han

Chapter 3 China-Africa's Trade Patterns and Potentials for Technology Upgrading in Africa **55**
Jean-Claude Maswana

Chapter 4 Structural Breaks and the Effect of Exchange Rate on India's Exports **71**
Ranajoy Bhattacharyya and Jaydeep Mukherjee

Chapter 5 Complementarities of India–Russia Economic Relations: Present Status and Future Prospects **87**
Sanjib Pohit

Part II: Analytical Frameworks to Model Selective Issues **109**

Chapter 6 International Trade, Gravity Equations and Tourism: An Application for Intra-Latin American Trade Flows **111**
Maria Santana-Gallego, Francisco J. Ledesma-Rodríguez and Jorge V. Pérez-Rodríguez

Chapter 7 A Factor Endowment Explanation for China's Emergence As an International Trading Power: Calibrating the Dornbusch-Fischer-Samuelson Model for China's Trade, 1968-2008 **127**
Roger White

Chapter 8	Trade Reform, Environment and Intermediation: Implication for Health Standard *Biswajit Mandal*	**151**
Chapter 9	Constructing Trade Barrier Index for Selected Countries of South Asia *Dripto Mukhopadhyay and Sanjib Pohit*	**161**
Part III: Methodologies and Policy Applications		**181**
Chapter 10	CGE Modelling As a Framework for Absorbing Specialist Information: Linking an Energy Model and a CGE Model to Analyse U.S. Energy Policies *Peter B. Dixon and Maureen T. Rimmer*	**183**
Chapter 11	When Modellers Behave Like Lawyers: Have We Lost the Plot? *Alan A. Powell*	**201**
Chapter 12	CGE-Based Analysis of Trade Policies: Capturing the "Devil" in the Details *Badri G. Narayanan*	**213**
Chapter 13	CGE Methodology and Trade-Technology Nexus Redux: Illustrations and Synthesis for Modelling and Policy Analysis *Gouranga G. Das*	**227**
Index		**261**

ACKNOWLEDGMENTS

I owe gratitude and debts to many. The book would not have been possible without generous and continuous support of the Nova Science Publishers and their team. I would like to convey my sincerest appreciation to Nadya Columbus, Donna Dennis, and Carra Feagaiga for being supportive when I was hard-pressed with commitments and slogging over editorial jobs in my hand. Last but not least, without constant encouragement from my family members this book would not see the daylight. I thank all of them; however, the remaining errors and omissions are mine.

PREFACE

"The notion that trade, free trade, unencumbered by government restrictions–is welfare-enhancing -is one of the most fundamental doctrines in modern economics, dating back at least to Adam Smith (1776) and David Ricardo (1816). But the subject has always been marked by controversy because the issue facing most countries is not a binary choice of autarky (no trade) or free trade, but rather a choice among a spectrum of trade regimes with varying degrees of liberalizations."

–Joseph E. Stiglitz and Andrew Charlton, in Fair Trade for All (2005), pg. 12, Chapter 2.

"Our understanding of global trade has improved immensely over the generations, as a result of countless efforts by scholars who used theory and empirical analysis to gain insights into the complex forces that mold foreign trade and foreign direct investment. Because the world economy has been continually changing, economists have had repeatedly to reexamine existing views on these issues, to modify analytical frameworks in view of new empirical findings, and to devise new ways for testing propositions that emerged from theory. This research enterprise has entailed a continuous race between a changing world economy and economists' adaptation of analytical and empirical frameworks to fit the changing circumstances."

---Elhanan Helpman, Understanding Global Trade (2011). Pg. ix-x, preface. The Belknap Press of Harvard University Press, Cambridge, MA.

The quotations opening this prelude highlight the significance of taking a broad-view of trade, economic growth and development as well as the need for improvising methodological innovation in order to capture those variable effects. Necessity of trade and exchange has been recognized since the days of Adam Smith and following him, Ricardo also extended support for productivity-based comparative cost principle. Historically, three distinct phases of globalization are: 1870—1914, 1945—1980, and 1980-2000. There were retreats in inter-war period during 1914—1950 (World Bank 2002). After the third-wave of globalization, we see the fourth wave aided by technological progress, E-commerce, and consequential trade facilitation. The last phase or 'new eave' continuing till now occurred due to emergence of new technologies, trade facilitation and geographical fragmentation or dispersion of production.

In order to understand the process of globalization and its pervasive impacts across the world economy, it is essential to comprehend the forces shaping trade, investment, migration, capital flows, as well as the factors beyond the domain of trade-variables, and covering macroeconomic factors. Genesis of the World Trade Organization (WTO) after dismantling of the GATT is a watershed in the historical evolution of trade pattern, and its impacts on the current global economy. Especially after the failure of the Doha round of trade negotiations (or, Doha Development Agenda), the recent conclusion of the Bali round of trade negotiations in February 2014 under the direction of Roberto Azevedo of Brazil, the newly appointed director-general of the WTO, trade liberalization is heading presumably to a new direction. Apparent failure of reaching an agreement in the Doha round did not change the course of trade negotiations and the Bali round in December 7th, 2013 was the first deal since WTO came into being in 1995. The main focus is on trade facilitation via streamlining customs procedure so as to increase annual global trade volume. Trade liberalization via say Trans-pacific partnership (TPP) or Trans-Atlantic Trade and Investment Partnership (TTIP) among others are debatable, but cutting customs-related impediments is the main focus. However, all these negotiations involve also the developing countries like India, China, Cuba and others as well, who are concerned with their macroeconomic effects. Thus, trade liberalization agenda is also part of a broader framework of development agenda. Whether trade is an engine or handmaiden of growth is a debate that interests academics and policy-practitioners alike. The debate is unsettled and contours change, as none could reach a unanimous convergence on this issue.

The question is: given that DD round had suffered a setback, which way trade and FDI are going to evolve and what are the implications for G-20 countries, emerging Southern Economies, and the relatively backward nations. Also, how can one explore such complex web of global interactions and what analysis could shed more light on future path of globalization-led growth and economic development? The contributions in this volume offer both factual and empirical analysis as well as methodological and theoretical angle for analyzing such empiricism.

Since history, trade and commerce has shaped the evolution of trade theory. In the 19th and 20th century, Ricardian and Heckscher-Ohlin trade theory explained trade in terms of comparative advantage with differences in productivity (technology) and factor endowments (resources) respectively. However, in early 1980s we saw the emergence of "New" trade theory based on product differentiation (monopolistic competition) and increasing returns to scale to substantiate empirical patterns of rise in trade in differentiated products within same industry (i.e., changes from inter-sectoral trade basis to intra-industry within a sector) and between countries at similar levels of economic development. As traditional resource and technology-based theories could not handle new phenomena, Krugman and Helpman, among others, pioneered this area of research. Following this new departure from orthodoxy there was trade based on agglomeration and geography or spatial advantage. We saw the emergence of intra-industry trade in manufactured or technology-intensive goods and that led to flourishing of research in areas of measurement (Grubel-Lloyd index of measuring such trade and its modifications) and empirical methods of accounting for such trade. After this, in last 20 years we saw another set of theoretical outpourings explaining empirical phenomena of trade in products by heterogeneous firms and multinational corporations spreading their wings to subsidiaries in foreign locations. All these show that trade theory (alike other disciplines and fields in economics) has been subject to state of flux. Right now, emergence of high performing Asian economies and penetration of electronic commerce thanks to new technology led by information and communication revolutions has triggered new vistas of research. Economic meltdown and its spillovers across globe have been shaping our views of trade, globalization, and their macroeconomic impacts.

Due to the onset of financial crisis (2008-2010 and continued thereafter), the focus of debate on world trade has undergone transformation. Researchers and policy analysts have engaged in evaluating the causes and consequences of such recessionary phase. With growth collapse and trade collapse (relative decline of manufacturing and rise of services), policymakers are redesigning trade and growth strategies. G-20 framework for strong, balanced, sustainable, and inclusive growth and development has shaped the contour of debate. As the quote by Stiglitz and Charlton reiterates, trade is important driver with lots of preconditions depending on 'behind the border' constraints as well as 'beyond the border' factors. Global cooperation is important for macroeconomic stability and trade relation is an important factor behind the coordination. With the rise of spaghetti bowl effects of regional trade agreements, the regional production networks in Asia and other parts of the world, and the emergence of India and China with product sophistication, trade theory needed a revisit and overhaul.

Regarding methodologies, we see proliferation of theoretical and empirical literature in explaining the old and new thematic issues in trade, growth and development area. In 1965, Ronald W. Jones wrote the famous paper on general structure of general equilibrium model in which famous Neo-classical trade theories and their variants based on Heckscher-Ohlin Theorem, Specific-Factor model, or even Ricardian model could be analytically explained. This was developed on the fundation of Kenneth Arrow and Gerard Debreu's 1954 seminal work on the proof of existence of competitive equilibrium based on Brouwer and Kakutani fixed point theorems. Herbert Scarf further advanced this to the computational method as a close approximation to equilibrium configuration of concerned variables. General equilibrium and its computational extension are useful for policy formation. However, it is not a strait-jacket and hence, methodological flexibility is important. With this principle in mind, this edited volume brings together scholarly contributions on various topics.

This collection of articles from contributors from different areas of specialization introduces a cornucopia of issues to the readers. Articles are organized into three broad themes, viz.: Part 1 dealing with emerging issues, whereas Part 2 combining chapters on some theoretical and empirical analytical framework for modeling such issues, and concluding Part 3 presents papers on especially computable general equilibrium (CGE) methodologies for trade policy analysis. Although each contribution focuses on specific themes, they offer an integrated canvas of issues and methodologies.

The severe recessions and debt crises during 2007 to 2009 in the US and the Europe, and spreading after that period, had adverse implications for many countries—emerging economies, as well as, in least-developed economies like Africa—via macroeconomic transmission through financial and trade channels. As Chapter 1 unfolds, we get a cogent analysis of the impact of financial crisis and debt crises on the emerging nations, viz., China and India—the dragon and the elephant, respectively. As the author argues, "By the end of 2013 signs of recovery in the Eurozone were signaling the worst seemed over and US recovery seemed on its way, yet growth in both China and India was not restored to pre-2007 levels, with no immediate prospects of a turnaround apparent." By carrying out a growth decomposition analysis and based on a Keynesian macroeconomic framework, the author shows empirically the importance of external factors as well as the factors underlying investment demand and investor confidence matter for growth performance of emerging economies. However, the author distinguished between the service-export-led growths in Indian context as compared to export-led or investment-led growth in China. By analyzing two probable scenarios—ex post contraction of capital flows to developing economies with less-than-adequate macroeconomic fundamentals and demand contraction and expectations of an impending currency crisis–of an external shock in the wake of the crisis, the author demonstrates that trade, FDI, investor confidence, and investment-GDP ratio are all important ingredients for growth recovery in post-2010 period in these Asian giants. External vulnerability of these countries due to trade with the US and Europe depends on extent of coupling or trade integration, and country-specific variables capturing economic uncertainty due to systemic crises.

Quite understandably, it could be envisaged that the quantitative and qualitative implications of the global economic and financial crises would be different as structural transformations of these Southern Emerging Engines (SEE) of growth are diverse during 2003—2008 and subsequently in the later period. China has developed her own dynamic comparative advantage in East Asia and it has spillover effects on Asia's industrial production. Continuing in that light, Chapter 2 explores the dimensions and extent of Asia's industrial network, regional production networks, fragmentation and value-chain slicing, to investigate the trade expansion in the Asia-Pacific and beyond. Specifically, it discusses the impact of emergence of China as a supplier of intermediate or high technology products (moving up the value-added ladder) on the trade between ASEAN countries, Japan, South Korea, and Taiwan. Evolution of a tripartite or triangular regional production networks among China, South Korea and ASEAN is an important development inducing a change in established 'flying-geese model' of industrialization in Asia. This accounts for the global imbalance or, accumulated surplus of China thanks to rise in China's value-added in U.S. and Japanese exports and decline in US and Japanese value-added in China's export. This is pointer to a shift from East Asia's sequential upgrading and industrialization. Role of constellation of hybrid policies, such as, technology policy, education policy, trade policy, as well as, the importance of land reform need to be emphasized for tracing the historical roots of development of the East Asian economies, which rose to pinnacles of success and created trade surplus with the US and Europe. The chapter emphasizes the importance of technology and industrial policy for rise of China. Next chapter further extends this discussion by highlighting the role of technology upgrading via Sino-African trade for Africa's industrial development.

A great deal of research has been done on the role of trade and technology diffusion for enhancing growth in the destinations. North-South trade flows and realizing the potentials for technology transfer or technology upgrading is essential for convergence and catching-up of the developing economies, especially the technologically laggards. By dint of product diversification, export sophistication, and investment in human and physical capital, China is moving up the value-chain and converted her into 'factory of Asia.' Production relocation and trade in manufacturing products intensive in skill and semi-skilled products, and high technology trade has transformed the image of the 'dragon' whereas the 'elephant' has harped mainly on software and IT-exports.

Two subsequent chapters in the volume deal separately with these two emerging economies in different contexts. Chapter 3 adds another dimension into the discussion by offering a view on technology upgrading in Africa via trade with China. The study concludes that the sectoral composition remains more or less the same, without significant technology upgrading or technical progress. Then, in Chapter 5, the analysis extends the discussion in the context of India-Russia with implications for trade relation with the U.S. It considers complementarities and potentialities in Indo-Russian merchandise trade with special reference to high technology trade. This promotes the scope of bilateral skill and technology transfer and realization of growth and development potentials. The CGE simulation using a global trade model of Neo-Classical variety shows that trade is gainful via allocative efficiency and need for trade logistics network. However, the emergence of free trade agreements of India with OECD nations reduces the scope of such trade prospects with Russia. Thus, growing importance of India's trade with the US and Europe as well as with Japan and South Korea would hinder such prospects unless India and Russia overcome the inefficiency in logistics trade networks and trade facilitation measures.

Trade and capital flows being dominant drivers for transmission channels of shock propagation, role of exchange rate movements for India's exports can no way be ignored and Chapter 4 presents an empirical study on such aspect by identifying structural breaks. Since 1991, India experienced extensive economic reforms affecting foreign exchange market and international trade. They have shown that for India trade liberalization policy shock breaks the long-run relationship between real effective exchange rate and gross domestic product and thus, affects the export supply function.

Part II is devoted to some modeling framework for analyzing issues related to emergence of China's trade, environment and health factors in trade matters, gravity model along with addressing some empirical phenomena of quantifying trade barrier. It opens with one of the most popular and widely used empirical analysis of trade model based on Gravity modeling approach.

In the empirical context of intra-Latin American trade flows spanning 1995-2010, Chapter 6 offers estimation of trade flows based on gravity equation on the basis of an important methodological approach, so that zero trade flows between non-participating countries do not cause information loss and biasedness in estimation. Not only that, the authors incorporate an important aspect ignored in traditional gravity models, namely, the arrival of tourists as a determinant of trade-costs (export costs). Their results in Latin American case shows that such omissions of zero trade for unrelated countries/regions and tourism services could result in biases in estimates. Based on a monopolistic competition model and assumption of variety-seeking Dixit-Stiglitz Utility function, they derive a firm selection equation as well as a gravity equation augmented by inclusion of tourism variables facilitating trade in diverse dimensions, such as, cultural ties, business habit synchronizations, language learning, communications, and mutual exchange of habits shaping commerce. According to the authors: "For instance, tourism may improve the knowledge about foreign culture and, as a consequence, about business habits and practices in other countries. Furthermore, tourism facilitates and stimulates to learn other languages, making bilateral trade easier. In addition, international tourism needs good basic facilities, services, and infrastructure such as transportation and communication systems that are also necessary for trade activity to function." Estimations of such equations with appropriate explanatory regressors showed that this method could capture impacts of transport costs, tourism factors, and omitted trading regions' indirect effects on estimated bilateral and multilateral trade volumes, by affecting extensive and intensive margin of trade.

Emergence of China as a global trading power and her concomitant robust economic growth is subject to analysis and debates among academics and hence, has led to profusion of research papers on U.S.-China trade as well as politico-economic relationships shaping the contour of international economic relations. The model in Chapter 7 offers a cogent analysis of evolution of trade pattern of China since her adoption of economic reforms in 1978 and its gradual unfolding, and based on this stylized empirical fact, employing data spanning the period from 1968 through 2008, the author extends a well-known seminal work in trade-theory to calibrate the Dornbusch-Fischer-Samuelson model of Ricardian comparative advantage. As per the author, "[We] examine changes in labor supplies, capital stocks, and technology as possible explanations for the rise of China as an international trading power. We then conduct a regression analysis, using data for the years 1972-2007, to explore corresponding labor market implications, in the form of trade-induced changes in industry-level employment and average wages, for both production workers and non-production workers in the United States manufacturing sector." The analysis shows that, quoting the author, "China has gained comparative advantage relative to the US and to the cohort of high income countries considered in this study. Even though US production has increased since 1968 at both the extensive margin and at the intensive margin, China's emergence as a trading power may have adversely affected US labor." The extent of labor market effects owing to burgeoning trade with China, the study estimates 'a series of dynamic regression models' for isolating the impacts of exports and import penetration. The analysis exhibits that greater import penetration from China into the U.S. has adverse effects on employment of both production workers and non-production workers, while increased exports from high-income nations to China does not favor significantly the average wages of non-production workers. These opposite effects are causes of concern domestically due to its impact on wage-inequality between skilled vis-à-vis unskilled workers.

Chapter 8 adds a different but pertinent discussion on issues related to trade and environment that is quite topical at this juncture. In this paper, the author argues that environmental quality is a determining factor for an economy's health standard, and also informal sector plays crucial role for maintaining such quality. In other words, taken from a less-developed country point of view the paper asks for tariff reform for use of abatement technology when informal sector does not conform to stringent environmental laws and regulations imposed by the government for formal sectors. Adopting a general equilibrium framework (common methodology in trade analysis), the paper derives conditions under which tariff cut could induce greater usage of abatement technology and shows that nexus between trade reform and issues such as environmental standards could be analyzed using a methodology capturing interlinkages among sectors and policy variables.

In order to do analysis of trade reform and resultant changes in the pattern and composition of trade, it is often essential to have notions about extent and magnitude of trade-orientation of the participating countries. Several indices for quantifying the magnitude of trade volume are prevalent in literature (one of which is oft-quoted Dollar's trade-openness index). Chapter 9 shows a methodology for construction of trade barrier index for South Asian countries, which are becoming an important trade partner of developed countries in the emerging global order when G20 countries are gathering momentum to become the centre of economic gravity. As India is one of the Southern Engines of Economic Growth (apart from the rise of Middle Kingdom of China) among BRICSAM nations and as India has established herself as an important trading partner for the North (especially, the U.S. and Europe), it is worthwhile to quantify the magnitude of trade-policy variables so as to comprehend the forces facilitating or inhibiting evolution of future trade dynamics. Given the fact the South Asian countries have regional cooperation agreements among themselves and the fact that these countries differ in terms of their levels of economic growth and development, the role of North-South trade-spillover for inducing economic development is interesting area of research. Although these nations have liberalized and became part of the globalization paradigm, still they have not gone full swing. Thus, the chapter measures external trade from South Asian countries and finds that one of the key determinants for this trend is trade barriers within the region, affecting adversely the inter and intra-regional trade. The study concludes that these trade barriers inhibit trade via escalation of transactions costs significantly in the form of bribery and damages.

Part III is devoted to methodological aspects and some policy analysis related to trade. Owing to the availability of large datasets and relatively easy access to data sources in public domain, modeling structures have evolved for academic research (focusing more on key parameters like elasticities, structural features, sensitivity analysis, etc.) and policy analysis for decision-making by practitioners in government, multinational agencies like the World Bank, International Monetary Fund (IMF), the World Trade Organization (WTO after GATT), and others in policy spheres. More importantly, it needs to be borne in mind that the analytical structures based on economic theory are underlying the quantitative policy analysis via numerical modeling. Thus, this part presents researches on such policy analysis based on CGE and econometric methodologies and shows the dependence of modeling exercise on structure, parametric specification, robustness, estimation of key parameters, and as well as on the ensuing policy-induced responsiveness of the key variables of interest.

The 10th chapter presents an alternative rigorous Computable General Equilibrium (CGE) methodological development from an integrated point of view. CGE model is used widely with plethora of applications in the field of international trade covering issues such as trade liberalization, welfare impacts, migration and poverty, technology transfer, land-use and climate change policy, as well as forest products trade, dynamic models of capital flows and FDI, E-commerce and trade facilitation, among others. Profusion of CGE models under North American and Australian modeling schools, differing in terms of modeling implementation methodologies, converge with respect to commonality of practical policy modeling and its plentiful applications. This makes such tools tremendously useful for trade policy analysis as well as for any kind of scenario simulations. In terms of solutions for variables, they differ in terms of ‘levels’, ‘linear’ or ‘mixed level and linear’ variables in system of equations, which are solved using specific software, namely General Algebraic Modeling Software (GAMS) or General Equilibrium Modeling Package (GEMPACK). Linearized representation of variables following Euler or Johansen methodology offers percentage change in endogenous variables of interest with respect to simulated shocks of exogenous disturbances or shocks relevant to the policy experiments. In this context, Dixon and Rimmer’s embedding of an energy model into a CGE model offer novelty in methodology. Chapter 10 is a sophisticated analysis of integrating an engineering and energy economics model (NEMS) into a large-scale applied general equilibrium model (USAGE) of the US economy. United States Applied General Equilibrium model (USAGE) is a multi-regional CGE model of the US economy developed at the US International Trade Commission (USITC) with the intellectual contributions of the leading CGE researchers at the leading CGE modeling institution at the Centre of Policy Studies (formerly located at the Monash University, Melbourne, Australia and currently housed in Victoria University, Australia after the relocation in February 2014). In this chapter, the methodological approach is novel as it integrates an energy model into a different genre of model for policy analysis. Without directly incorporating the features of the engineering-economic nexus model to a highly non-linear economy-wide model in the USAGE, the authors illustrates a mechanism to show the pathways of effect of an energy sector induced shock for the rest of the economy. By considering a business-as-usual as well as a policy run for long run period spanning 2010—2035, the authors show how to analyze complex simulated impacts in a general equilibrium framework of interlocked variables via back-of-the-envelope type calculations. The analysis is valuable in terms of methodological advancement in tracing effects on the trade-exposed activities like Aluminum smelting, Nitro-phosphorous fertilizer, coal, commercial fishing, education exports, and Construction. Given the herculean task of rapprochement of two genres of models, certainly this chapter demonstrates a methodological advance in passing energy-model results into a CGE model via transfer of variables, changes in macroeconomic environment through closure rule changes (swaps of naturally endogenous variables in the USAGE model into exogenous categories as informed by variable transfers from NEMS-model policy runs), and a scenario analysis of replacing fossil fuel consumption of coal by natural gas for electricity production. Further extensions plan leave rooms for researchers to engage in further real policy analysis with practical implications, such as in the context of climate change, clean technology, sustainable trade and development goals, and trade-environment nexus, to name a few.

On a different angle, Chapter 11 touches upon the debatable enigma of the modelers in terms of the contribution of quantitative economic modeling exercise—be it econometrically sophisticated analysis or, general equilibrium policy modeling—in informing the intelligentsia in academia and public policy discussions. This chapter's contribution is more into the basic foundational philosophy underlying the whole ballgame of model-making spree gripping academic scholars as well as the policy makers. The author, quite provocatively, argues—in the Australian public policy-making context—that we might lose the 'plot' of intellectual contributions and true policy analysis if the modellers are not impartial, rather biased advocators alike the lawyers. In this chapter, we learn that building analytical model and employing sophisticated methodology add value and serve the broader interest or, general welfare of society as long as those are pursued with integrity, honesty, seriousness, and deep philosophical value without dogmatic judgment. Judging the results of theoretical and empirical model is important and should be guided by questioning the validity, authenticity, and independent replication or, verification in the public domain. Failing this, the author apprehends that the modellers will be like 'hired guns' or, 'hired mouths'.

In a related concern for the importance of *verification and authentication* of models with wide-ranging parameter values and the black-box type framework, Chapter 12 suggests improvements on several grounds esp., in the context of CGE and detailed disaggregated analysis with sensitivity of results under alternative parametric specifications.

However, although methodologically sound, CGE analysis has been subject to criticism on several grounds, such as, non-transparency or black-box type underlying theoretical mechanism to explain results of policy simulations, estimation of parameters for demand (elasticity of substitution in production nest or demand nest, elasticity of transformation between joint products, Armington trade elasticity, etc. In fact, chapter 10 mentioned the plausibility of realistic result by reducing the value of elasticity of substitution for coal from 1.0 to near range of 0.0. Chapter 12 adds value to this pint of dissatisfaction. Where the author summarizes that: "CGE analysis has been criticized by policy analysts for its usually aggregated analysis, with sectors that usually comprise hundreds of sub-sectors that are of interest to practical policy specialists. Few CGE modelers have come up with tools and methods to address this issue." Thus, Chapter 12 reviews many new methods for disaggregating sectors, factors, household types and regions in typical CGE models. These methods are useful for conducting trade policy analysis of US with rest-of-the-world. Thus, the author gives succinct overview for the modelers by offering plethora of choice of the tools specific to issues under consideration. For example, he mentions employing nested partial and general equilibrium (PE-GE) models in conjunction with the TASTE tool, the input-output structure, using a software facilitating split of sectors based on social-accounting matrix or underlying input-output (SPLITCOM), using assumptions on production structure and consumption. As mentioned elsewhere and discussed in the context of Chapter 10, Centre of Policy Studies at the Victoria University in Australia (formerly at Monash University) is a leading center of Australian school for CGE methodology. They developed a TERM framework as a tool for disaggregating regions. Most of these tools and methodologies are reviewed with examples from US trade policy issues and emerging economies.

Although Chapter 12 emphasizes the absolute imperatives of carrying out disaggregated analysis to capture more intersectoral competition effects, intra-industry trade and specialization, and presents plateful of models and software-based techniques for implementation, the next and final chapter shows that even in a highly stylized aggregated 'macro' model, the scope of inter-regional as well as inter-commodity competition looms large due to trade competition and product differentiation based on geographical separation of production. Thus, Chapter 13 presents some evidences on trade patterns for countries at different levels of development, discusses general features of analytical framework of CGE model, and offers example from a global technology spillover model in a one-commodity-three-region set up to show trade between the US, European Union and the Rest-of-the-World. This chapter synthesizes common features of two prominent CGE models, viz., ORANI (Australian Regional Economic Model with multi-sectoral effects developed at Monash University, Australia and currently, moving to Victoria University, Australia) and GTAP (Global trade analysis project developed at Purdue University, USA). GTAP is based on predecessor ORANI-genre of models extended to account for trade linkages across the world divided into regions and therefore, they have structural symmetry. Based on results from previously published works, for illustration purpose, this chapter offers a synthetic view to highlight the significance of undertaking joint-venture of need-based adaptation /augmentation of existing methodologies influenced by predominance of issues as well as incorporating current developments into the analytical framework. In particular, it shows that with rise in trade in manufactured and industrial products trade-mediated technology diffusion is important for tracing the changes in price relativities across trading regions. Trade and welfare gains are prominent in the presence of total factor productivity gains and absorption of trade-embodied technology flows. Thus, as a 'macro' model could capture such detailed trade and growth effects quite insightfully, with a disaggregated methodology of CGE structure the model could offer more inter-sectoral dynamics of trade-technology and productivity effects. This chapter illustrates that, to research on analyzing issues in globalization and its many facets such as trade in middle products (product fragmentation or organization of production networks) or outsourcing (vertical specialization), its effects on factor markets or product space (e.g., labor markets and manufactures or services sectors), for intellectual and investigative excellence it is necessary to take a detailed segregated approach as well as an integrated view supplementing the separate issue-based analysis.

Given the globalization fever gripping all and sundry, no one doubts the significance of trade and its pervasiveness in the world economy. But there are plethora of analytical and empirical framework, and also a convex combination of both flavors enriching the discipline. In organizing this volume, I have constantly strived to keep focus on this trade-off: between emerging issues, and the usefulness and applicability of models (standard, conventional, computational, and newly built ones) for tractability of such themes. Questions and concerns are raised in the research community about the plausibility and practical relevance of results. Like all disciplines and more than the other areas of economic research, trade theory is constantly evolving as world is becoming more integrated and the contagion is not sparing anyone. As global trade has evolved over the years with gradual mutation and transformation of patterns, direction, and composition, the issues are more important than ever. Plethora of issues that we face need careful investigation and each issue deserves appropriate methodological innovation or 'newness' in approach in its own right. Often, the models fail to capture or accommodate several aspects fully (for instance, emergence of BRICSAM as major trading nations, or the disintegration of production into locations spatially separated offshore or outsourcing, or firm heterogeneity, and impacts on income inequality, to name a few). Challenges faced by conventional wisdom due to current evolution of trade patterns necessitate constant research on alternative methodologies and frameworks. This volume offers a platter of such economic delicacies that need to be spiced up with tools and techniques evolving constantly with continued vigorous research and exchange of ideas. The authors' contribution bears testimony to this effort. With great optimism, I believe this book would enable the readers to absorb the content with due intellectual curiosity.

Gouranga G. Das, Ph.D.
Hanyang University,
Erica Campus at Ansan,
South Korea

SELECT REFERENCES

1. Dixon P.B., and D.W. Jorgenson (2013) Handbook of Computable General Equilibrium Modeling (Amsterdam and New York: North Holland/Elsevier).
2. Dollar, David. (1992). "Outward-Oriented Developing Economies Do Grow More Rapidly: Evidence from 95 LDCs, 1976-85." *Economic Development and Cultural Change,* 40(3): pp. 523-44.
3. Jones, R.W. (1965) – The Structure of Simple General Equilibrium Models. Journal of Political Economy, 73, pp.557-572.
4. Stiglitz, Joseph and Andrew Charlton (2005). Fair Trade for All: How Trade can Promote Development. Oxford University Press.
5. World Bank (2002). Globalization, Growth, and Poverty: Building an Inclusive World Economy. Oxford University Press. Washington DC, USA.

List of Contributors
(In Alphabetical Order)

Alan Anthony Leslie Powell: Alan Powell is Emeritus Professor in the Department of Econometrics and Business Statistics, Monash University, Clayton, Melbourne, Victoria, Australia. He was foundation Professor of Econometrics at Monash University from 1968. He is a Member of the Order of Australia, a Fellow of the Academy of the Social Sciences in Australia, a Fellow of the (international) Econometric Society, a recipient of the Research Medals of the Royal Society of Victoria and of the Australian Modelling and Simulation Society. He is listed in Who's Who in Australia and in the 1999 edition of Who's Who in Economics. In 1972 he was a visiting Economist at the Development Research Center, World Bank, Washington, D.C. In 1998 he received the Distinguished Fellowship Award of the Economic Society of Australia. In recognition of his outstanding contributions to GTAP, the Center for Global Trade Analysis, Purdue University, USA has established the Alan A. Powell Award.

Email: Alan.Powell@monash.edu

Ananya Ghosh Dastidar: She has been an Assistant Professor at the Department of Business Economics, University of Delhi South Campus, New Delhi, India since 2004, where she has taught graduate courses on Econometrics, Macroeconomics and Global Finance. She has worked on issues related to trade openness, income distribution, poverty and education and has consultancy experience with the Indian Planning Commission and UNDP.

Email: agdastidar@gmail.com

Badri Narayanan Gopalakrishnan.: Badri Narayanan is a Research Economist at the Center for Global Trade Analysis, Purdue University, USA. He earned his PhD from Indira Gandhi Institute of Development Research, Mumbai, 2007. He has several refereed publications in journals such as Applied Economics, Applied Economics Letters and Economic Modelling. He contributes to the Global trade analysis project's GTAP trade model and its database development and the GTAP software, nemly, General Equilibrium modeling Package (GEMPACK) software in collaboration with the Centre of Policy Studies (COPS) at Victoria University, Melbourne, Victoria, Australia (formerly at Monash University, Australia).

E-mail: badri@purdue.edu

Biswajit Mandal: Prof. Biswajit Mandal is an Assistant Professor of Economics in Visva-Bharati University, Santiniketan, India. He earned his Ph. D from Centre for Studies in Social Sciences Calcutta, India and also received National Scholarship from Government of India and Junior Research Fellowship by University Grants Commission. He has been honoured with Japan Society for the Promotion of Sciences (JSPS) Fellowship to visit Kobe University, Kobe, Japan, and C V Raman Fellowship to visit University at Albany-SUNY, New York, USA. Journals like the Review of Development Economics, Economic Modelling, International Review of Economics and Finance, International Journal of Economic Theory, Economics Bulletin, etc. are among the journals that have published Prof. Mandal's research. He also made a few contributions in edited volumes and conference proceedings. He has attended about 35 conferences in different countries to present his research work.

Email: biswajiteco@gmail.com

Dripto Mukhopadhyay: He is associated with applied economic and consumer research for more than 18 years. His education was from Faculty of Management Studies (Delhi University), Jawaharlal Nehru University, New Delhi and Kolkata University. Currently he is leading the research division of Indicus Analytics, one of the leading economic research organizations in India. Before joining Indicus in 2008, Dripto worked with National Council of Applied Economic Research (NCAER), New Delhi for about 12 years. He has worked in more than 150 studies across different domains in applied economics, development sector and consumer market related research. Dripto has authored more than 50 publications in various journals and books in form of research papers and chapters. His major research interests are evaluation studies, demand estimation and forecasting, consumer segmentation and locational studies, indexation, environment and tourism economics.

Email: dripto.mukhopadhyay@gmail.com

***Francisco J. Ledesma-Rodríguez*:** Francisco J. Ledesma-Rodriguez is Associate Professor in the Department of Economics, University of La Laguna, Spain. He teaches Microeconomics and International Economics. His main research areas are Tourism Economics and International Economics.

E-mail: fledesma@ull.es

Gouranga Gopal Das: He is a Professor of Economics at the Department of Economics, Hanyang University, South Korea. Prior to this appointment, he worked as a Visiting Professor of Economics at Kyungpook National University, Korea and as a Post-Doctoral Research Fellow at the University of Florida. He obtained his M.Phil and PhD in Economics from Jawaharlal Nehru University, India and Monash University, Melbourne, Australia respectively. He has been a visiting researcher in the International Monetary Fund (IMF) at Washington DC, University of Antwerp, Belgium and United Nations University-World Institute of Development Economics Research (UNU-WIDER) at Helsinki, Finland. Primary fields of his research focus on Trade and Development, Computable General Equilibrium Modeling, Technological Change, Outsourcing. Since 2009, in appreciation of his contribution he is enlisted in the Marquis Who's Who in the World (published from New York, USA). He serves as editor of some international journals.

Email: ggd@hanyang.ac.kr , dasgouranga@gmail.com

Hongyul Han: Professor of Economics at Hanyang University, Erica Campus. He is a specialist in the area of Regional Trade Agreements and APEC. He is the chairman of Korea Consensus Research Center, Seoul Korea.

Email: hyhan@hanyang.ac.kr

Jaydeep Mukherjee: Jaydeep Mukherjee is a assistant professor at the Indian Institute of Foreign Trade, Delhi Campus. Before this he was Lecturer at the Department of Economics, Sreerampore College. His field of specialization is open economy macroeconomics.

Email: jaydeep@iift.ac.in

Jean Claude Maswana: A native of the Democratic Republic of the Congo, Professor Maswana, received a PhD in International Development from Nagoya University in Japan. After serving at Kyoto University, JICA-Research Institute and the University of Tokyo, he has joined Tsukuba University's MBA program in Tokyo. His research interests are in the broad areas of development economics and international business. Within those areas, he has published on the topics of financial system development, finance and trade nexus, growth-effects of China-Africa's trade and investment, economic growth empirics in non-linear frameworks, sources of the recent African growth performance. These articles have been published in outlets such as Global Economic Review, Applied Econometrics and International Development, Journal of Chinese Economics and Finance, The Chinese Economy, the Journal of Policy Analysis and Management as well as book chapters, conference proceedings, and numerous international keynotes (such as the OECD China-Africa Study Group reports).

Email: maswana@mbaib.gsbs.tsukuba.ac.jp

Jorge V. Pérez-Rodríguez: Jorge V. Pérez-Rodríguez is Associate Professor in the Department of Quantitative Methods for Economics and Management, University of Las Palmas de Gran Canaria. He teaches Statistic, Operational Research and Econometrics. His main research areas are Financial Econometrics and Tourism Economics.

E-mail: jvperez@dmc.ulpgc.es

Maria Santana-Gallego: María Santana-Gallego is Assistant Professor in the Department of Applied Economics, University of the Balearic Islands, Spain. She teaches Macroeconomics and Tourism Economics.

E-mail: maria.santana@uib.es

Maureen Rimmer: Maureen Rimmer is a Professor in the Centre of Policy Studies at Victoria University. She is the author and co-author of 55 scholarly published articles, appearing in mathematics and economics journals and edited volumes. Her main area of expertise is in model development and application. With Peter Dixon she is the co-developer of the MONASH model of the Australian economy and the co-author of the MONASH book which was published in 2002 in North-Holland's Contributions to Economic Analysis. In the last ten years Professor Rimmer has been a key contributor in the development, application and documentation of USAGE, a 500-industry, dynamic model of the U.S. economy. The model is used in Washington by the U.S. International Trade Commission and the U.S.

Departments of Commerce, Homeland Security, Agriculture, Energy and Transport. Maureen hold the position of Professor in the Centre of Policy Studies at Victoria University Australia.

Email: maureen.bleazby@vu.edu.au

Peter Bishop Dixon: Peter Dixon was a student of Nobel-prize winning economist W. Leontief at Harvard University, USA. Dixon led the teams that created Australia's ORANI and MONASH models in the 1970s and 1990s. ORANI was the world's first detailed (100+ industries) computable general equilibrium model regularly used in policy analysis. MONASH was its dynamic successor. He is pioneer in CGE analysis and published several books, book chapters, and more than 100 articles in reputed journals. In recent years Dixon developed the USAGE model of the U.S. which is used by the U.S. International Trade Commission and the Departments of Agriculture, Commerce, Energy, Transportation and Homeland Security. Dixon was elected a Fellow of the Academy of Social Sciences in 1982. In 2003, he was awarded the Distinguished Fellowship of the Economic Society of Australia and in 2006 he was appointed Sir John Monash Distinguished Professor at Monash. In 2013, Elsevier published its two-volume Handbook of Computable General Equilibrium Modeling edited by Dixon and Dale Jorgenson, Harvard University, USA. In 2014 Dixon took up his present position as Professor in the Centre of Policy Studies at Victoria University.

Email: peter.dixon@vu.edu.au

Ranajoy Bhattacharyya: Ranajoy Bhattacharyya is a professor at the Indian Institute of Foreign Trade, Kolkata Campus. Before this he was Reader in the Department of Business Management, Calcutta University. His field of specialization is applied international trade theory.

Email: ranajoy@iift.ac.in

Roger White: Associate Professor, Whittier College, Department of Economics. September 2012-present. Professor, Sinoway International Education (SIE) Summer Program in China: Nanjing University, Nanjing, China. June-August 2012 and June-August 2013. Foreign Expert, China One Thousand Foreign Experts Project: Beijing Information Science & Technology University, School of Economics and Management, Beijing, China. October 2012-present.

Email: rwhite1@whittier.edu

Sanjib Pohit: Dr. Sanjib Pohit is presently working as Professor, AcSIR and Senior Principal Scientist, at CSIR-National Institute of Science, Technology & Development Studies since Aug. 2010. Previously, he held research position (Senior Fellow/Chief Economist) at National Council for Applied Economic Research, New Delhi), Indian Statistical Institute and was a visiting scholar to University of Michigan (Ann Arbor, USA) and Conference Board of Canada. He has been member of several committees of Government of India), a Council Member of Gerson Lehrman group. He has been a Consultant to various national and international bodies, including The World Bank, Asian Development Bank, The Energy & Resource Institute (TERI), OECD, Price Waterhouse Coopers, ICRIER and RIS (New Delhi). Dr. Pohit is an experienced modeler in the area of trade and environment with 20 years of modelling experience. He has co-authored 6 books, and has published about 100 articles in journals/books. Email: spohit@nistads.res.in, spohit@gmail.com

PART I: CURRENT SCENARIOS OF GLOBAL TRADE AND THE EMERGING ISSUES

In: Current Issues in International Trade
Editor: Gouranga G. Das
ISBN: 978-1-63321-405-7

Chapter 1

THE GLOBAL RECESSION AND DEVELOPING ECONOMIES IN ASIA: EVIDENCE FROM CHINA AND INDIA

Ananya G. Dastidar *

Department of Business Economics,
University of Delhi South Campus, New Delhi, India

ABSTRACT

This paper analyses the impact of the global financial crisis on selected developing economies in the Asian region, focusing especially on China and India, two of the largest emerging economies in the developing world. Both countries were expected to weather the crisis relatively smoothly based on the strength of their domestic markets. However, it is becoming evident that India and China did not remain 'de-coupled' from the global downturn, despite the large size of their domestic economies. This paper examines the channels through which the impact of the global crisis, originating in the USA and Europe, was transmitted to these large Asian economies.

The framework of analysis, based on a Keynesian macro-theoretic approach, attempts to characterize the various channels of transmission of the economic shock from the OECD to developing countries. The global recession affected both international trade and capital flows; as such both trade and financial channels are considered within the analytical framework. This is followed by an empirical analysis aimed at gauging the impact of the downturn on the economies of China and India.

First, a data analysis is carried out to characterize salient structural characteristics of these economies and capture various dimensions of their engagement with the world economy. This is followed by a growth decomposition exercise from the demand side; changes in the main components of aggregate demand are quantified with a view to capture the demand side adjustments observed in these developing countries, especially in the aftermath of the crisis.

* Department of Business Economics, University of Delhi South Campus, Benito Juarez Road, New Delhi – 110021, India, Email:agdastidar@gmail.com

The main findings indicate that apart from external causes, factors affecting investment demand and investor confidence may hold the key to growth performance in these economies.

Keywords: Financial Crisis, Global Recession, Developing Economies, Growth Decomposition

INTRODUCTION

This paper analyses the impact of the global financial crisis on selected developing economies in the Asian region, focusing especially on China and India, two of the largest emerging economies in the developing world. Both countries were expected to weather the crisis relatively smoothly based on the strength of their domestic markets. However, it is becoming evident that India and China did not remain 'de-coupled' from the global downturn, despite the large size of their domestic economies. This paper examines the channels through which the impact of the global crisis, originating in the USA and Europe, was transmitted to these large Asian economies.

The framework of analysis, based on a Keynesian macro-theoretic approach, attempts to characterize the various channels of transmission of the economic shock from the OECD to developing countries. The global recession affected both international trade and capital flows; as such both trade and financial channels are considered within the analytical framework. This is followed by an empirical analysis aimed at gauging the impact of the downturn on the economies of China and India.

The paper is structured as follows. In what follows, we briefly outline the contours of the crisis as it unfolded in the US economy and deepened, as banking and debt crises ravaged the Eurozone. In this context we review the main arguments provided in the literature regarding the implications of the crisis, especially for developing countries. Then we present our framework of analysis that draws on this literature and attempts to characterize the various *channels* through which the crisis could have affected emerging market economies.

Thereafter, a data analysis is carried out mainly to characterize the sheer magnitude and various dimensions of China and India's engagement with the world economy. We essentially try to highlight the main changes that took place, especially in the external sector of these economies corresponding to major events that marked the timeline of the global crisis. This is followed by a growth decomposition exercise from the demand side which attempts to characterize the process of adjustment in these economies in the post-crisis phase. Changes in the main components of aggregate demand are quantified with a view to capture the demand side adjustments observed in these developing countries, especially in the aftermath of the crisis.

Finally the paper concludes with a discussion on the policy implications of the main findings and with a few pointers on directions for future research.

THE GLOBAL CRISIS : IMPLICATIONS FOR DEVELOPED AND DEVELOPING COUNTRIES

In what follows, first we outline briefly the contours of the crisis and examine its implications for the world economy in general; this is followed by a review of the main implications for developing economies identified in the literature so far. The arguments and analyses in this Section are based on a review of the existing literature on this topic.

The Crisis and Developed Economies

A large body of literature has emerged on the contours and causes of the global recession which, as is well recognized now, had its origins in the US sub-prime crisis of 2007 (see Gorton and Metrick, 2012 and Lo, 2012 for a recent survey of this literature). The problem of insolvency in a single sector (real estate) of the American economy soon spread across the financial sector of the world's largest economy, bringing down financial giants like Lehman Brothers and Merrill Lynch and assuming crisis proportions within months. The financial meltdown that followed severely disrupted credit flows which are the lifeline of business investments and led to the most severe recession since the Great Depression.

The financial crisis with its origin in the US essentially unfolded from 2007 to 2009 (see, e.g., Gorton and Metrick, 2012 for a review of major events marking the timeline of the crisis). It is now well recognized that it all started with the collapse of the housing bubble in the US and the ensuing sub-prime crisis in early 2007. The spate of defaults on housing loans had a cascading effect, dealing a severe blow to the financial architecture across developed market economies. Collapse of financial giant Lehman Brothers in September, 2008 created massive financial panic and contagion in the financial sector. As the banking system was affected, disrupting crucial linkages between savings and investment flows, growth slowdown ensued in the real sector with the US unemployment rate peaking at 10 percent by mid-2009. By this time the Eurozone sovereign debt crisis had begun to unfold; the International Monetary Fund (IMF) bailed out Greece and Ireland by the end of 2010 and Portugal by the middle of 2011. With contagion spreading through the Eurozone in 2012, its very existence and stability faced a stiff challenge, with the banking sector in advanced economies of Spain, Italy, even France, reeling under pressure. In 2013, although "end" of the crisis is still not in sight, 'green shoots of recovery' in the US economy are clearly evident; yet developments in the Eurozone and potential effects of "QE tapering" (cutback of 'quantitative easing' by the US Fed) continue to send emerging financial markets into a tizzy.

As we go over the factors responsible for the sheer scale of the crisis, the importance of developments within the financial sector come to the fore (see for instance, Bernanke, 2010; Krugman, 2008 etc.). The nineties and first half of the 2000s decade witnessed growth of a largely unregulated 'shadow banking' sector. This comprised financial institutions that essentially performed same functions as banks and faced similar risks (like, e.g., maturity mismatch), but unlike the banking sector did not come under the purview of a regulatory authority such as the central bank. As monetary policy of the US Fed in the Greenspan era lowered returns on safe government assets to near zero levels, financial markets searched for high returns elsewhere and took on associated high risks, encouraging growth of the *shadow banking* sector in the process. Enabled by advances in technology, financial innovations led to evolution of increasingly complex financial instruments whose risk implications could not be easily assessed, leading to accumulation of hidden systemic vulnerability to shocks, which were finally exposed when the real estate bubble burst in the US.

Detailed empirical analyses by Reinhart and Rogoff (2009) highlights the critical role played by the banking and real estate sectors in context of economic crises. The authors show, a collapse of a housing bubble can lead to prolonged downturn, even recessionary conditions, especially when it coincides with (or causes) a crisis in the banking sector. The implications of the crisis essentially flow from its underlying causes and drivers. Financial contagion spread across the developed countries in Europe mainly through the banking sector, with virtual collapse of the asset side of banks' balance sheets, marked by exposure to similar lending portfolios. A liquidity crisis ensued as banks collectively tried to sell assets at 'fire sale' prices, to meet depositors' demands, driving down asset prices further, which in turn led to further deterioration of banks' balance sheets. Possibility of a banking *crisis* loomed large in the horizon, compelling governments to intervene and bail out banks to prevent large scale bank failures, not witnessed since the days of the Great Depression.

Banks and similar financial institutions play the key role of channelizing savings towards investment activities, the investment rate being of paramount importance for economic growth. As such, collapse of the banking sector could adversely affect investor confidence and deepen an economic downturn. To prevent such a possibility bailing out financial institutions was considered a priority by most governments even though they faced mounting fiscal deficits. With a deep recession under way, growth rates collapsed and unemployment grew across the developed world, and their governments had to step up spending at the cost of widening deficits and mounting sovereign debt.

The Crisis and Developing Countries

What were the implications of the global crisis for developing countries? We now discuss some of the main implications that emerge from the literature for developing countries in general and for China and India in particular.

To understand the consequence of the recession for developing countries in general it's important to briefly delve into the background against which their integration with the world economy occurred over the past few decades. The eighties and especially the nineties decades saw globalization sweep across the developing world and widespread emergence of market based policies, while strengthening of the WTO as a major international institution, fostered a move towards freer trade. The collapse of communism in Russia and success of market based policies in China added momentum to these pro-market capitalist forces operating in the world economy; and developing countries across Asia and Latin America abandoned inward orientation and import substituting policies, lowering tariff and non-tariff barriers and restrictions on international capital flows.

Just as these gave firms in developing nations greater incentive to engage in production for the world market, so also it gave developed country enterprises (especially giant multi-national firms) greater access to markets in poorer countries. The era of globalization also saw a revolution in transport and communications technologies that brought about dramatic reduction in costs and greatly facilitated trans-border mobility of capital and of goods.

Consequently this period witnessed break-up of the global value chain especially in manufacturing production with capital re-locating from the developed world to take advantage of cheap labour in developing countries; international trade especially in manufactured goods saw tremendous growth as a result. The era of globalization also witnessed cross-border capital flows on a massive scale like under the age of gold standard, although unlike that phase in history, mobility of labour remained relatively restricted. Developments in communications and transport technology as well as several other factors fostered this growth in capital mobility (see Obstfeld and Taylor, 2004 for a discussion).

The global slowdown was preceded by a fairly long period of buoyancy, through the 1990s and the first half of the twenty-first century. Interest rates remained low in the US in the Greenspan era and finance capital looked for higher returns elsewhere, especially in emerging markets, that were opening up to trade and capital flows. The pre-crisis period also saw relatively stable financial environment, especially in the Asian region which, barring the Asian crisis of 1997, experienced no other major financial upheaval. Further, financial de-regulation and emergence of booming stock markets in emerging economies provided international finance capital with newer avenues for earning high returns.

The flow of international finance took the form of portfolio flows into asset markets as well as flows of FDI into the real sector of the developing economies. FDI flows, especially in the tradables sector, played an important role in fostering growth in manufacturing capacity especially for exports. Capital flows leading to business process offshoring and outsourcing also made a major contribution to the growth in export of services from countries like India. However, with rising capital flows into asset markets also came greater volatility of asset returns which showed systematic linkages with ebbs and flows of international portfolio investment flows made by Foreign Institutional Investors or FIIs. In fact, the volatility and disruptive effects associated with international capital flows was demonstrated during the Asian crisis, the speculative attack on Hong Kong's currency by international hedge funds and time and again with the incidence of currency crises in Latin American economies like Mexico and Argentina (see Krugman, 2008; Obstfeld, 1998; Obstfeld and Taylor, 2004; Reinhart and Rogoff, 2009 etc.). These episodes clearly indicated that international capital flowing into the non-tradables sector had the capacity to create an asset bubble which, when it burst, could have a devastating impact on the banking and overall financial system; the consequent linkages between financial and real sector could usher in prolonged recessionary conditions.

Against this backdrop the world economy saw phenomenal rise in trade and capital flows between developed and developing nations especially in the 2000s decade; the resultant increase in inter-dependence between national and world economies, it is argued, would make it virtually impossible for developing nations to remain unaffected for long, from the effects of the deepest recession the world economy has witnessed since the Great Depression. The literature on this topic is still evolving. Some studies focus on specific country experiences (see for instance, Mc Nally (2008), Whalley et al. (2009) on China; Kim (2012) on Korea; Nagaraj (2013), Ram Mohan (2009), Ghosh and Chandrasekhar (2009) etc. on India); while others seek to characterize trends either for developing countries in general or for a specific set of nations such as BRICS (Brazil, Russia, India, China and South Africa) (see e.g., Akyuz 2013a and 2013b; Aloui et al., 2011; Massa et al., 2012; Nayyar, 2011;UNCTAD, 2009 etc.). The central issue addressed in this literature is the nature of the impact of the sharp recession in the developed world on developing countries and the relative importance of various channels of transmission.

Initially, as the global recession originated and spread across the developed world, developing countries, especially large economies like China, India and Brazil remained relatively unaffected (see, e.g., Nayyar, 2011). In fact, the debate on whether developing economies were 'de-coupled' from the world economy was revived (see for instance, Park, 2011). With growing intra-regional trade (especially among EMEs in Asia, led by China) and owing to the advantages conferred by demographics, growing incomes and size of domestic markets, it was argued business cycles in emerging markets may no longer be synchronized with those in the OECD. As such, despite being integrated with the rest of the world via trade and financial flows, it was felt that slowdown in the world economy would not bring growth to a grinding halt in these economies, as it had done in USA and Europe. For the domestic market had the potential to drive demand led growth in these populous developing nations, given that they practiced sound macroeconomic policies and kept a check on the pace of financial deregulation and capital account liberalization. Yet, it did not seem likely that the domestic market in these economies would be sufficient to *lead* recovery in the world economy (Nayyar, 2011). However, as the global recession deepened, increasingly the 'de-coupling' hypotheses seemed to lose empirical support, especially with slowdown of growth in China, it was argued that in a globalized world it was virtually impossible for countries to remain insulated from the effects of an economic crisis of this magnitude (see e.g., Akyuz, 2013a and b;).

So what explains the initial growth recovery and subsequent slowdown in the developing world in the post-recession phase? The explanation is closely linked to the counter cyclical Keynesian policy response in developing and developed countries and to the unique position of the Chinese economy in the developing world. In what follows we first outline the impact of the trade channel and thereafter the impact of capital flows in transmitting effects of the recession to developing countries that have been identified in the literature.

By the time the recession came, the global value chain had become highly developed with concomitant growth in cross-border trade in manufactures. As such, as growth slowed down in the US and Europe and demand for manufactures fell, the impact became manifested in a dramatic fall in trade flows (Eichengreen, 2009). The collapse of trade flows had adverse implications for developing economies like China and other Asian economies that relied on export led growth, based on export of manufactures to OECD markets.

On the positive side, these economies had accumulated huge foreign exchange reserves, which was an important factor supporting the counter cyclical policies they put in place with emphasis on domestic demand led expansion, as the global slowdown manifested itself. The expansionary policy response from developing country governments, in conjunction with firm commitment to monetary easing by the Fed, no doubt, were important reasons for the initial recovery (Rakshit, 2012). On the flip side there had to be a departure from the export led growth strategy as demand slowed down first in the US and then in Europe.

The resultant change in pattern of growth was most evident in the Chinese economy, which accelerated capital formation, switching from export-led to investment led growth. It has been argued that expansion in China was a critical factor shaping the impact of the recession on developing nations, both because it revived exports especially in the Asian region and also because it led to a surge in commodity prices providing critical balance of payments support to primary product exporters (Akyuz, 2013b). However, the import content of domestic consumption in China is lower than import content of Chinese exports setting limits to whether domestic demand led Chinese expansion could revive exports of manufactures. No doubt, after the initial downturn in Japan due to the Fukushima disaster in 2011, the subsequent rebuilding programme and the expansionary stimulus from policies of Abenomics in Japan also played a positive role in reviving growth in developing country exports. However, growth recovery is still slow in the US and especially Europe, while the investment led stimulus seems to have run out of steam with factory output slowing down in China by the end of 2013, evident in sluggish commodity prices in world markets. The resulting growth slowdown in the developing world seems to have no immediate chance of a turnaround within sight. The distribution of income in the developed world had worsened in the post-recession phase with widening income inequality manifested in falling wage shares, a factor that would surely tend to arrest buoyancy in aggregate demand looking ahead in the near future.

The impact of the recession on India was by and large comparable to that of other developing countries, especially insofar as the trade channel was concerned. India experienced dramatic growth in GDP of almost 9 percent witnessed between 2003 and 2008, largely driven by favourable external factors that spurred unprecedented export growth during this period. As the crisis set in, initially there was a shallow recession followed by a strong growth recovery, which was shaped by revival of international trade together with an expansionary policy response. However, India could not sustain economic growth at high rates witnessed in the pre-recession phase and prospects of recovery from its current slump appear bleak. A unique feature of India's growth experience has been the sterling performance of service exports. A substantial literature has examined various aspects of India's services exports and even termed India's growth story as one of 'service-led' growth (see for instance, Dasgupta and Singh, 2005 a &b; Eichengreen and Gupta, 2010; Gordon and Gupta, 2004 and Singh, 2006). It is possible that the impact of the global recession on a service exporter is different in magnitude and in qualitative aspects from that on exporters of manufactured goods. However, the literature does not have any clear cut answers in this regard and this is a lacuna that can be addressed by future research in this area.

The impact of the recession was also manifested via a collapse in capital flows, especially from the Eurozone from where much of the flows originated. In the pre-recession phase massive capital inflows into the emerging market economies had led to burgeoning foreign exchange reserves, which in turn lowered their costs of credit. However, this did not always result in an investment boom (*inter alia,* often due to the returns on investment projects being limited by infrastructural constraints). Rather, it contributed to falling cost of borrowing and rise in bank credit to the private sector creating a consumption-led boom in case of countries like India (Nagaraj, 2013). The collapse of capital flows also led to a consequent downturn in borrowing led private consumption. Perhaps the greatest casualty of the global recession has been the resultant uncertainty in the business climate that in turn had a negative effect on real investments, which arrested the flow of foreign capital into the real sector in emerging markets. There has been steady revival in portfolio flows of FIIs into emerging economy stock markets; however, the volatility of such flows has only been on the rise. For instance, with news like that of "QE tapering" (gradual reversal of monetary easing by the US central bank), slowdown in growth in Chinese factory output and so on, stock markets across Asia take a plunge and the resultant uncertainty does little to revive business climate within the domestic economy.

Analytical Framework

With globalization domestic and international markets become intertwined in complex ways. The analysis below attempts to capture the ways in which an external crisis is likely to impact aggregate demand in the context of large economies like India and China where the domestic market is likely to be an important driver of growth.

In what follows we outline the ways in which a developing country may be integrated with the world economy through the channels of trade and capital flows and how each of these dimensions is likely to affect aggregate demand in case there is an external crisis.

We first examine the role of trade in goods and services that affect a country's current account. Thereafter, we examine the impact of capital flows that enter the capital account of balance of payments. In this context we also discuss the various ways in which financial integration is likely to affect the asset and real estate markets, tending to create bubbles, bursting of which can affect the health of the financial sector in general and the banking sector in particular.

International Trade Flows and the Current Account Balance

International trade is one of the most important channels through which the impact of an external shock is likely to be felt at the national level. Developed countries markets, especially the US and Europe are the most important destination for exports from developing countries. As such any growth slowdown in the US and Eurozone is bound to affect developing country exports. Yet with reduction of trade barriers across the developing world, developing countries have formed a substantial network of trade linkages among themselves; with enhanced prosperity in the developing world this might even act as a safety net, mitigating , or partially absorbing the impact of shocks in external demand arising in the developed world.

It is clear that an external crisis originating in a country's export markets is likely to be manifested in reduced export earnings. Ultimately the income and price elasticities of demand for exports would determine whether the contraction is led by falling quantum of exports or, prices or, some combination of the two. The commodity composition of exports could play a key role in shaping the way the trade channel transmits the effects of an external shock. For instance, the existing literature draws attention to differences in growth experience of primary goods exporters vis a vis exporters of manufacturing goods (see McMillan and Rodrik, (2011) and Palma (2006) for a discussion on the contrasting economic performances of exporters in Latin America and Africa and exporters of manufactures in Asia). Also world commodity prices are known to display far greater volatility than prices of manufactures, another factor likely to create a differential impact on countries specializing in production and export of these different categories of goods. The import content of domestic absorption tends to rise with trade liberalization. As such trade and current account deficits are likely to widen following an external shock, for while exports fall, imports may be slow to adjust, especially if domestic demand remains buoyant.

Critical support to developing countries' current accounts comes from remittance inflows from workers employed abroad. However, with economic recession in industrialized countries a slowdown in remittances is very likely, with adverse impacts on developing countries' current accounts. In an environment of economic uncertainty, migrants may not be in a position to support families in their countries of origin. For economies (especially those where GNI exceeds GDP by a large margin) with a significant share of households dependent on migrants' remittances this may lead to a slowdown in consumption demand and in this way, serve as an important channel through which an external crisis is transmitted to the domestic economy.

All these factors point to inevitable widening of current account deficits in the wake of a recession in the OECD, with associated implications for financing the deficit that affects the capital account and overall balance of payments position.

Capital Flows and Their Implications

Globalization has led to large scale financial liberalization across developed and developing countries leading to a large degree of integration of financial markets in developed and emerging market economies. Financial centres in the developed world play a critical role by influencing the quantum and direction of cross-border capital flows across the world economy and it is likely that impact of a crisis in the developed world will be felt as much in terms of capital flows as in terms of slowdown in trade flows.

Our discussion in the previous section clearly brings out the genesis of the global crisis was in the financial sector of the US economy. Given the inter-linked nature of financial markets, to analyse the implications of the crisis for developing economies it is important to first understand how the upheaval in the US financial sector affected international capital flows and hence stock markets and the banking sector in emerging market economies.

The role of foreign capital in emerging economies has been very well researched, especially in context of the literature that examines the causes of different crisis episodes in developing economies, viz., the Latin American debt crisis of the 1980s; repeated currency crises in Latin American countries like Mexico, Argentina; the Asian crisis of 1997 and so on. This literature highlights the potentially de-stabilising role of international capital flows, especially in economies with fixed exchange rate regimes. Buoyant capital flows into emerging market economies can lead to burgeoning foreign exchange reserves, which in turn lowers the costs of credit and raises aggregate demand, paving the way for rising inflation. Capital inflows can also lead to strengthening of the domestic currency, which along with inflationary pressures might lead to substantial real appreciation of the currency which can have a negative impact on exports.

On the other hand, advocates of capital account convertibility, dwell on the positive effects of capital flows especially when it takes the form of non-debt creating FDI. It is very well established, especially based on the experience of the Asian economies that FDI in the tradable sector can lead the process of industrialization and growth of a country based on its success in tapping external markets. FDI can bring in know-how and efficient production techniques, enhancing competitiveness of manufactured goods for exports, and thereby helping to overcome constraints on industrialization imposed by limited size of the domestic market. However, in case of economies with large domestic markets, unless there is regulation to prevent it, FDI might well be domestic market seeking, in which case the welfare effects would be determined by the linkage effects established with the rest of economy.

On balance we may conclude that inflow of foreign capital may not always result in an investment boom (*inter alia,* often due to the returns on investment projects being limited by infrastructural constraints); rather, it might lead to rise in bank credit to the private sector creating a consumption-led boom. Thus capital flows from the developed world might fuel demand-led growth in developing countries; in case inflation is fueled by growth in aggregate demand, this can erode competitiveness of exports. While, to the extent domestic demand spills over to the external sector, this would also widen trade and current account deficits.

Thus in some cases demand led growth in developing countries is itself fueled by capital flows from the developing world. This gives rise to at least *two possible scenarios* in case of an external shock.

One possibility is a sharp contraction of international capital flows into the developing world following the financial crisis in the developed world, which could initiate a collapse of the consumption led boom and consequently usher in a slowdown in the rate of growth. An economy's ability to weather an external shock is essentially a function of underlying macroeconomic fundamentals (see e.g., Krugman, 2008; Obstfeld and Taylor, 2004; Reinhart, and Rogoff, 2009 etc.). In case easy availability of international finance led to over-leveraging by the private and public sectors, a sudden stop in flow of such funds could set in motion a downward spiral that might even culminate in an external crisis.

A sudden, sharp reduction in inflow could bring about a demand contraction, as it would necessitate spending cuts by the public sector, shelving of investment projects by private firms and reduction in debt financed consumption spending by the household sector. In some situations, especially in countries with fixed exchange rate regimes, fall in capital inflows arrest growth in foreign exchange reserves, which might even create expectations of an impending currency crisis. Once in place, such expectations fuel capital outflows, leading to loss of foreign exchange reserves, undermining a country's ability to defend a fixed parity and ultimately leading to a massive devaluation and abandonment of fixed exchange rates. This would be a case of self-fulfilling expectations, culminating in a full blown currency crisis.

An external crisis originating in the developed world may create a situation where international capital continues to flow from these countries to the developing nations. This may be the case when domestic markets and / or financial markets offer higher rates of return on capital in developing countries than in the developed world. In this case poorer nations would continue to grow despite crisis in the richer countries. However, how long such a situation persists would depend, *inter alia*, upon at least two sets of forces. The positive effect of domestic demand on growth vis a vis the negative effect of a slowdown in export growth that would inevitably follow in case the rich nations provided the primary export markets of the poorer countries.

In general, it is expected that portfolio flows are relatively more footloose as compared to FDI flows and hence the former are more likely to flow out following a crisis than the latter. On the other hand, given that FDI flows have a longer 'lock-in' period as compared to portfolio flows, there may be a sharp drop in FDI from the developed world in an era of economic uncertainty, when capital may prefer to stay footloose, so as to retain a quick exit option in case of contagion. The net effect of these flows would depend on a number of factors, including investor sentiments and perception regarding future growth prospects of the recipient countries.

In what follows, we present findings from a data analysis that tries to capture critical dimensions of these two nations' engagement with the world economy. Thereafter we present some preliminary findings from a simple demand side growth decomposition exercise for China and India aimed at gauging the relative impacts of external vis a vis domestic components of aggregate demand on output growth in the aftermath of the global crisis.

INDIA AND CHINA: DIMENSIONS OF ENGAGEMENT WITH THE WORLD ECONOMY

The period 2003 to 2007 had witnessed sustained growth of world trade and output and China and India were no exceptions to this pattern, with real output growing at over 11 percent per annum in China and nearly 9 percent per annum in India. The growth rate dipped sharply in 2008 in both economies (Figure 1). This was when collapse of Lehman Brothers in September, 2008 had thrown the world financial sector in turmoil. Yet recovery was relatively fast, especially in India where growth rate was over 8 percent in 2009 and by 2010, it seemed well under way in both economies. The recovery, though small, came even as the US recession deepened; for unemployment in the US peaked at 10 percent in 2009 as the economy reached the trough of its business cycle.

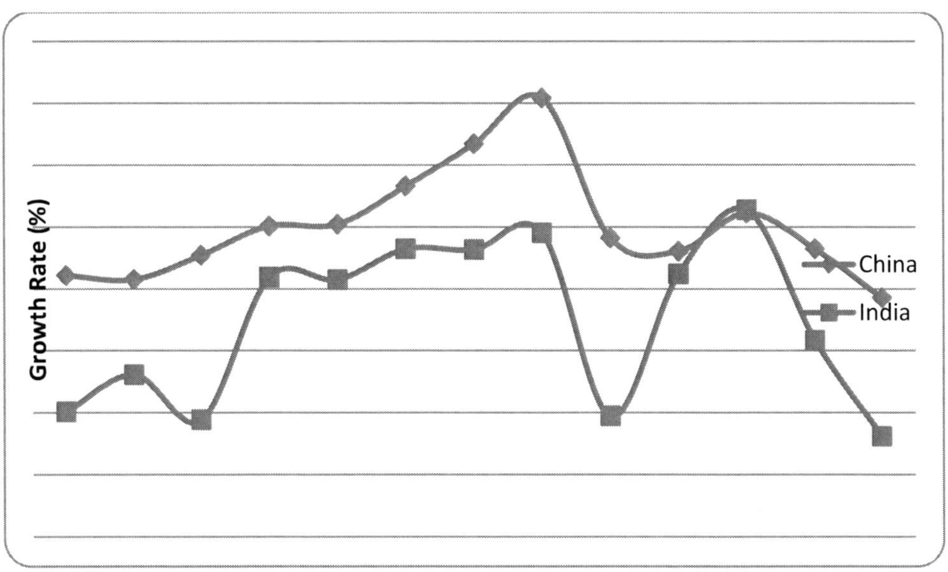

Source: Author's calculations based on United Nations National Accounts Statistics (http://unstats.un.org/unsd/snaama)

Figure 1. GDP Growth: 2000 to 2012 (percentage).

However growth recovery was short-lived in both China and India; since 2011 a prolonged slowdown is evident in both economies that continued through 2012, a period which saw the Eurozone economic crisis mature and deepen. By the end of 2013 signs of recovery in the Eurozone were signaling the worst seemed over and US recovery seemed on its way, yet growth in both China and India was not restored to pre-2007 levels, with no immediate prospects of a turnaround apparent.

The importance of the external sector in the growth experience of both economies is evident in the current account and in performance of exports. In 2008 a sharp rise in the current account deficit for India and a shrinking of China's substantial surplus current account balance heralded the trend that was to follow (Figure 2). India's deficit widened steadily, touching almost 5 percent of GDP, triggering worries with respect to financing of the deficit and even possibility of an external crisis with sliding value of the currency. In case of China the trade impact of the crisis was manifested in a steadily falling current account surplus, which peaked in 2007 and has been on a slide since, for the first time since 2000.

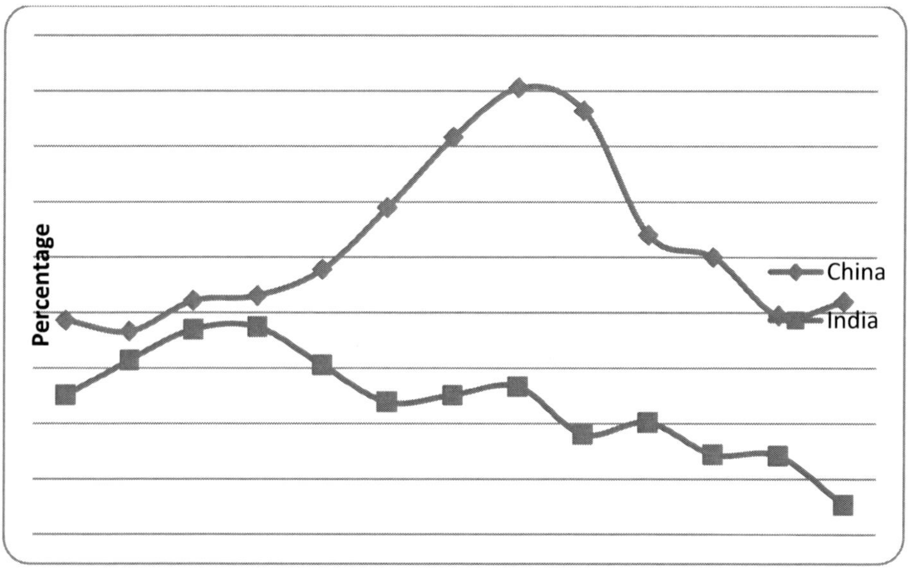

Source: UNCTAD Statistical Database (http://unctadstat.unctad.org/ReportFolders/reportFolders.aspx)

Figure 2. Current Account Deficit (% GDP): 2000 to 2012.

A comparison of the balance of goods and services trade for China and India reveal two things; differences in the composition of the trade basket in terms of goods and services and the channel through which the slowdown in trade actually occurred in each country. For China, the size of the surplus balance in goods trade fell sharply since 2008, showing signs of recovery only in 2012 (Figure 3). India had a deficit in goods trade which had widened during its growth phase of 2003 to 2007; however since 2008 the trade balance deteriorated sharply and steadily, crossing the $100 billion mark in 2011. Figures 3 and 4 clearly demonstrate China's export success in goods and that of India's in services. However, the size of India's positive trade balance on services was far smaller than the deficit on goods trade, while China's deficit on account of services was small compared to its positive trade balance in goods, reflecting the relatively stronger position of China with respect to international trade. China's services trade balance deteriorated sharply from 2010 onwards mainly owing to a sharp rise in import demand; while for India there was a pick up in the size of the surplus on services trade mainly owing to revival in export demand. In case of India therefore while services exports revived providing support to the current account, goods exports were more of less stagnant, in contrast to China, which experienced mild pick up in goods exports by 2012.

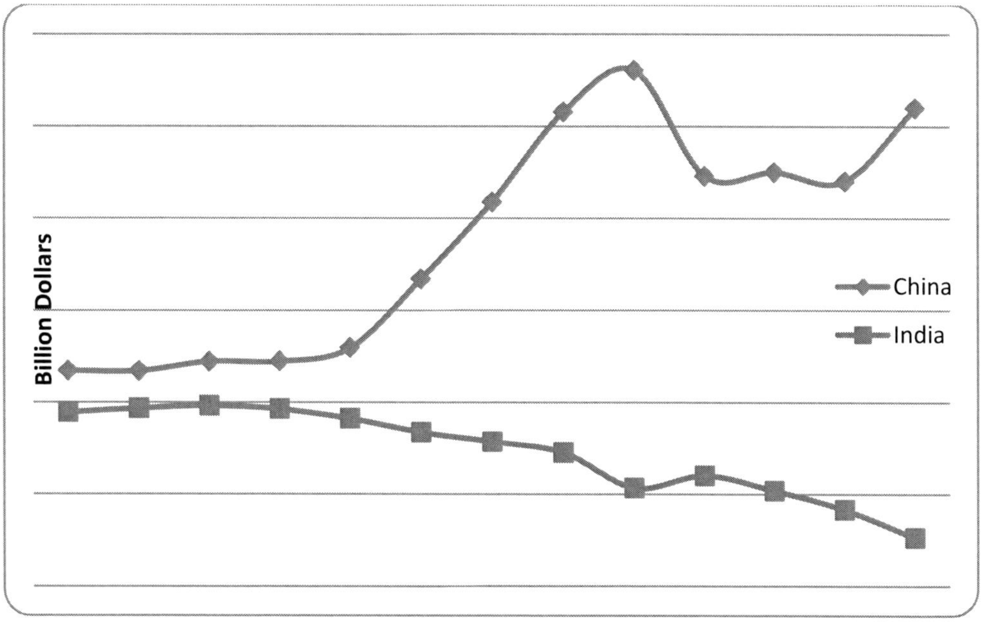

Source: Authors calculations based on UNCTAD Statistical Database (http://unctadstat.unctad.org/ReportFolders/reportFolders.aspx)

Figure 3. Balance of Goods Trade: 2000 to 2012 (billion dollars).

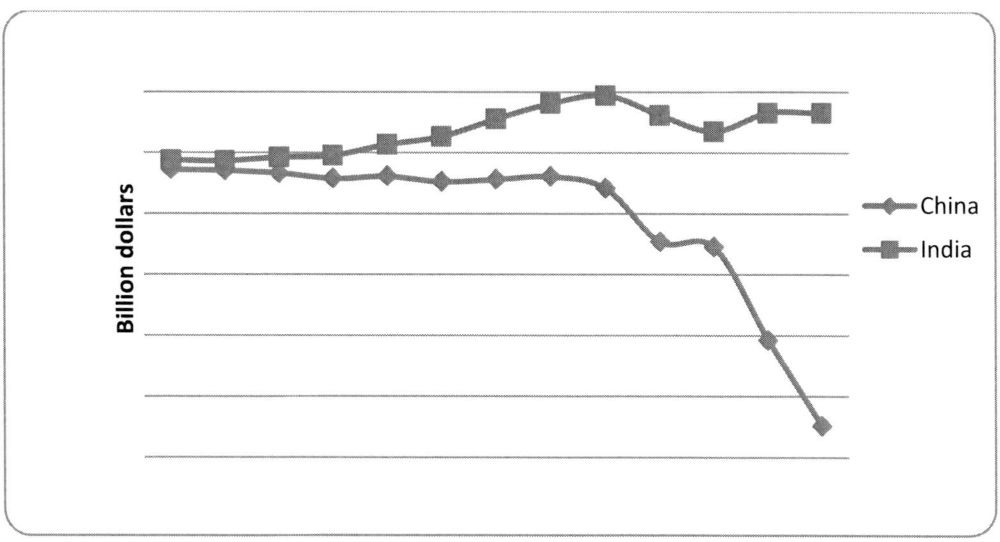

Source: Authors calculations based on UNCTAD Statistical Database (http://unctadstat.unctad.org/ReportFolders/reportFolders.aspx)

Figure 4. Balance of Services Trade: 2000 to 2012 (billion dollars).

Remittance inflows also provided critical support to the current account in both China and India; except for a small dip in 2009, these flows remained buoyant in both countries (Figure 5).

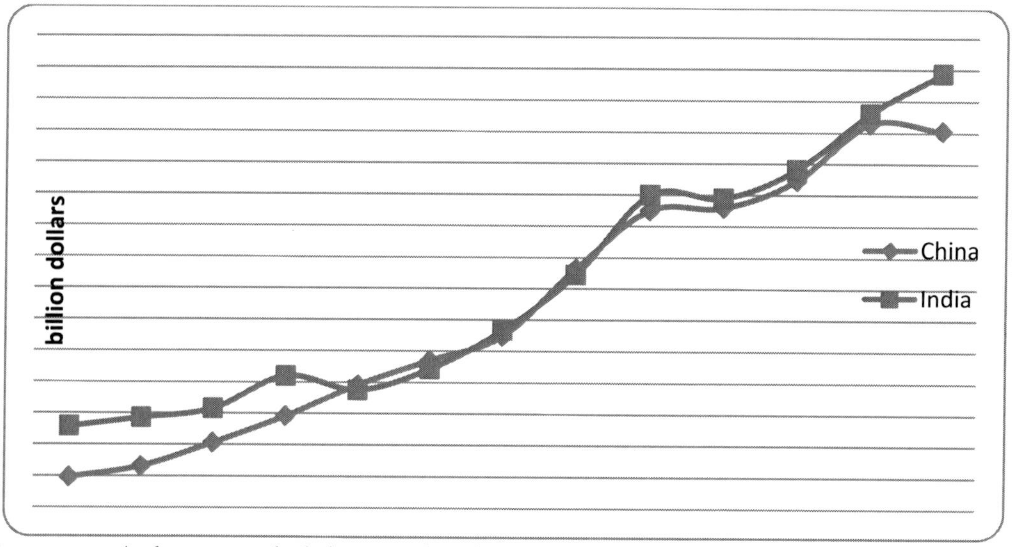

Source: Authors calculations based on UNCTAD Statistical Database (http://unctadstat.unctad.org/ReportFolders/reportFolders.aspx)

Figure 5. Remittance Inflows: 2000 to 2012 (billion dollars).

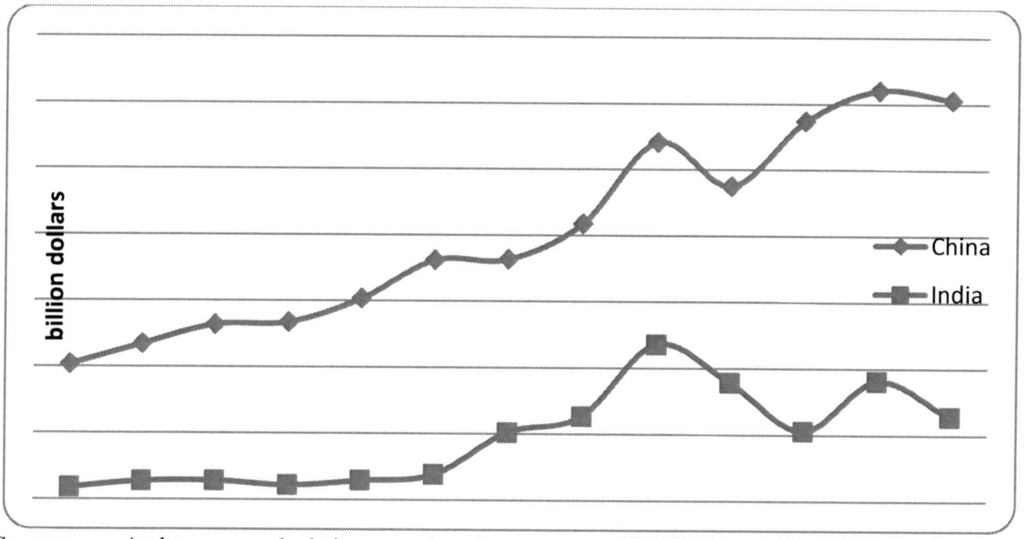

Source: Authors calculations based on UNCTAD Statistical Database (http://unctadstat.unctad.org/ReportFolders/reportFolders.aspx)

Figure 6. FDI Inflows: 2000 to 2012 (billion dollars).

So far as capital flows are concerned, non-debt creating inflows of Foreign Direct Investment (FDI) were important in both economies, though scale of such flows was much larger for the Chinese as compared to the Indian economy (Figure 6). In 2012, the inward FDI *stock* amounted to about 10.3 percent of GDP, while between 2007 and 2012 average annual *inflows* were about 5 percent of investment (gross fixed capital formation) and 6.4 percent of total merchandise and services trade for China; the corresponding figures for India were 12.2 percent, 7 percent and 10 percent respectively. Analysis of FDI inflows shows a sharp fall in the inflows in 2009 in both economies. Thereafter inflows picked up for China in 2010, but the earlier trend of steady growth in FDI inflows was not observed, with signs of a slowdown, even slight fall apparent by 2012. For India FDI inflows witnessed a small recovery in 2011, but remained well below the peak observed in 2008.

An important distinction between China and India with respect to FDI relates to its role within the economy. While it's well known that FDI played an important supportive, even causal role in China's performance in manufactured exports and the economy's integration with the global value chain, the Indian story has been different (Chandrasekhar, 1997). For India no doubt FDI flows bolstered the balance of payments and contributed to foreign exchange reserves; however it has been argued that much of these flows have entered the equity market (the definition of FDI being investment in equity amounting to more that 10 percent). In the Indian context, the role of FDI in promoting exports is unclear and there is evidence to indicate that India has attracted domestic-market seeking rather than export-oriented FDI (Aggarwal, 2002; Joseph and Reddy, 2009; Sharma, 2000).

The above analysis of change in external factors indicates these factors contributed to the growth performance in the period prior to the crisis that was characterized by rising exports and capital flows in both India and China. India's growth was relatively more import intensive as evident from its small current account deficit prior to 2008 and services exports was an important factor driving this growth. China's experience was in contrast fueled by an impressive performance with respect to goods exports. However, in the aftermath of the crisis, to begin with the external factors turned adverse, both with respect to trade and capital flows; a mild recovery followed, especially with respect to services exports for India and with respect to capital flows in China, but the magnitude of these factors could not possibly explain the growth revival that followed in these two economies. This indicates the importance of domestic demand and the expansionary policy response adopted in the two nations. We briefly analyse this data before reporting results from a more detailed growth accounting exercise.

The importance and steady increase in external demand for domestic goods in both India and China in the first half of the 2000s decade is evident from the rising share of exports in GDP in both economies (Figure 7).

In both economies external demand showed a sharp decline in 2009 in the aftermath of the crisis, followed by a weak revival. There was a corresponding rise in the share of domestic demand for domestic goods (gross domestic absorption (comprising consumption by private and government and investment demand) less imports), which increased sharply in the post-recession phase in both economies and thereafter stabilized in India and showed a small upward trend in China in 2012 (Figure 8).

Analysing the composition of gross domestic absorption for the Chinese and Indian economies (Figures 9 and 10) reveals several similarities and differences between the two economies in terms of composition of aggregate demand and the process of adjustment in the aftermath of the crisis. To begin with, the share of aggregate consumption in gross domestic absorption is much higher in the Indian economy as compared to in China. However, in the post crisis period while there was a further compression of consumption at the cost of investment in China, in case of India, initially the share of consumption picked up in 2008 and except for a slight dip in 2010 when there was a growth recovery, remained more or less stable.

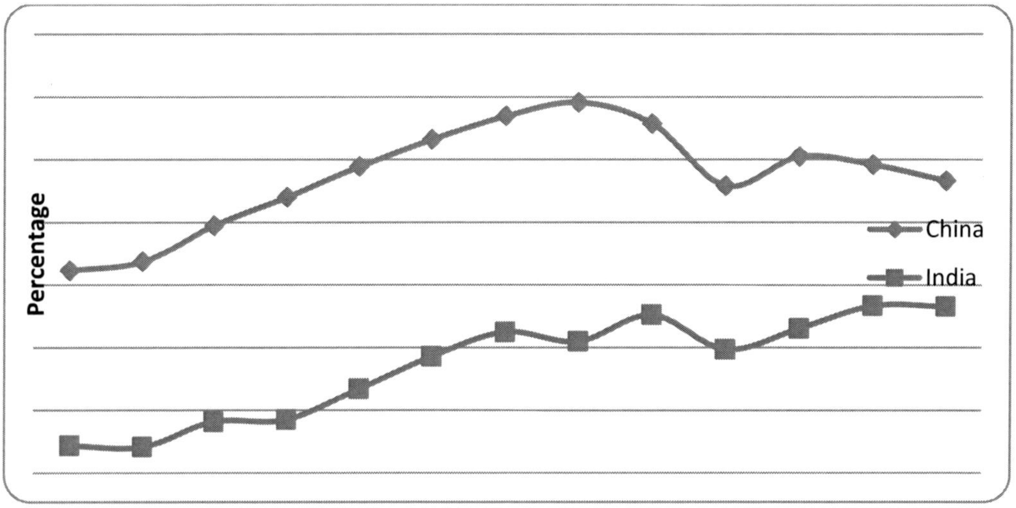

Source: Author's calculations based on United Nations National Accounts Statistics (http://unstats.un.org/unsd/snaama)

Figure 7. Export Demand: 2000 to 2012 (% GDP).

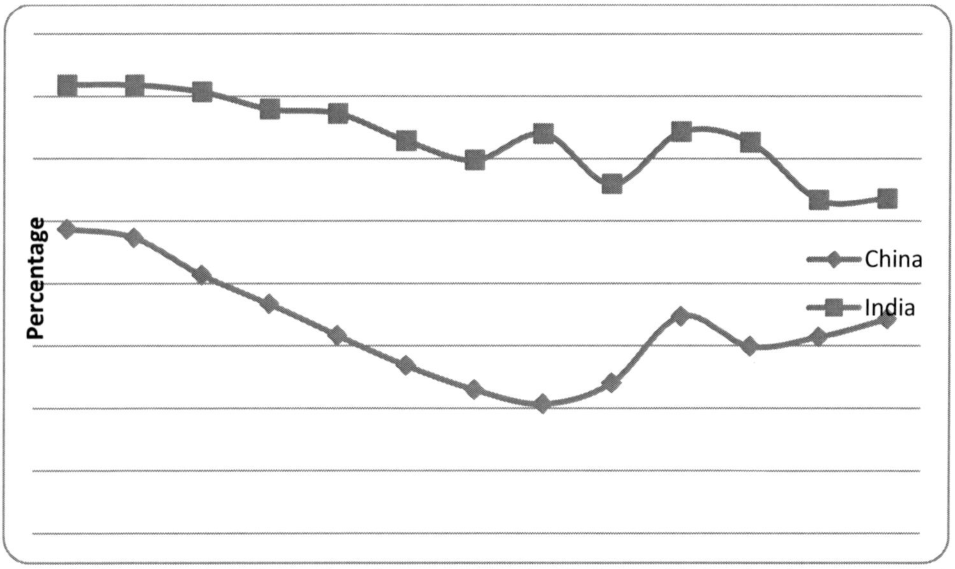

Source: Author's calculations based on United Nations National Accounts Statistics (http://unstats.un.org/unsd/snaama)

Figure 8. Domestic Demand for Domestic Goods (C+I+G - M): 2000 to 2012 (% GDP).

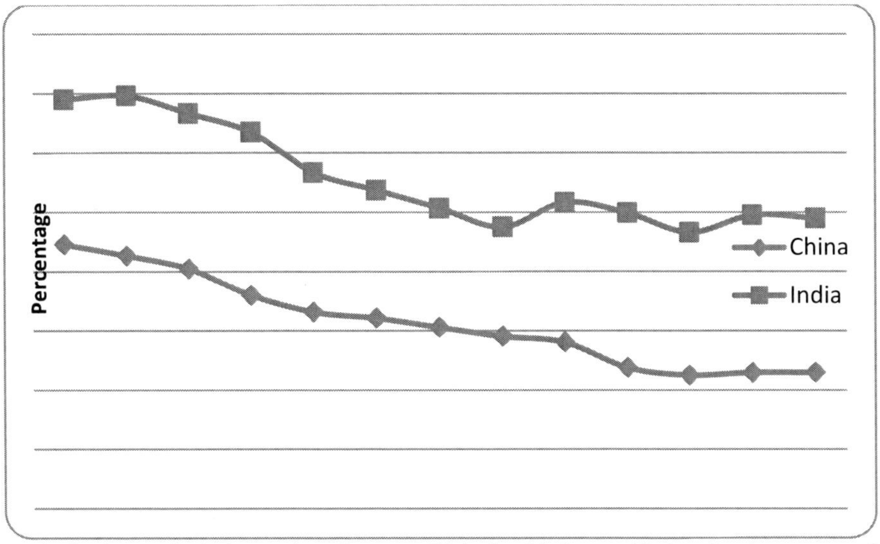

Source: Author's calculations based on United Nations National Accounts Statistics (http://unstats.un.org/unsd/snaama)

Figure 9. Aggregate Final Consumption (Private and Govt) : 2000 to 2012 (% of Gross Domestic Absorption (C+I+G).

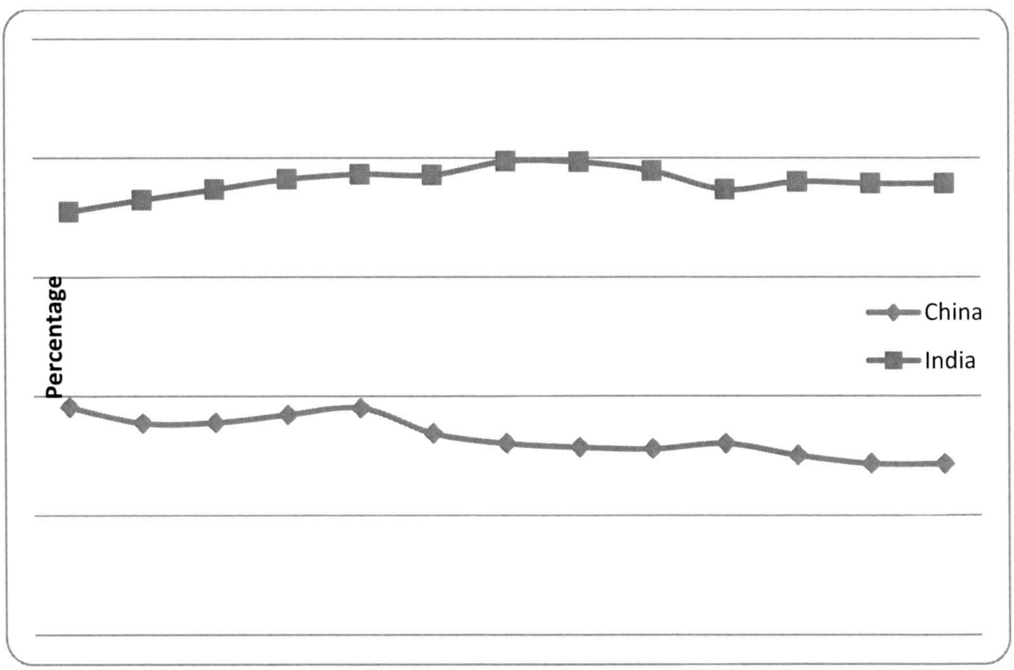

Source: Author's calculations based on United Nations National Accounts Statistics (http://unstats.un.org/unsd/snaama)

Figure 10. Household Consumption: 2000 to 2012 (% Share in Aggregate Final Consumption)

Share of household consumption accounted for a higher share of aggregate consumption in India as compared to China, while the reverse was true in case of government consumption (Figures 10 and 11). In India the share of household consumption fell slightly in 2009 and stabilized thereafter. The downward trend in share of household consumption in China was maintained even after 2008. In China the trend of gradual rise in the share of government consumption expenditure observed since 2005 was maintained in the post-crisis phase as well. In India, share of government consumption, which had been on a slight downward trend since 2003, rose in 2009 and remained more or less stable thereafter. This indicates government consumption was relatively more important in the growth recovery observed in 2010 in both economies.

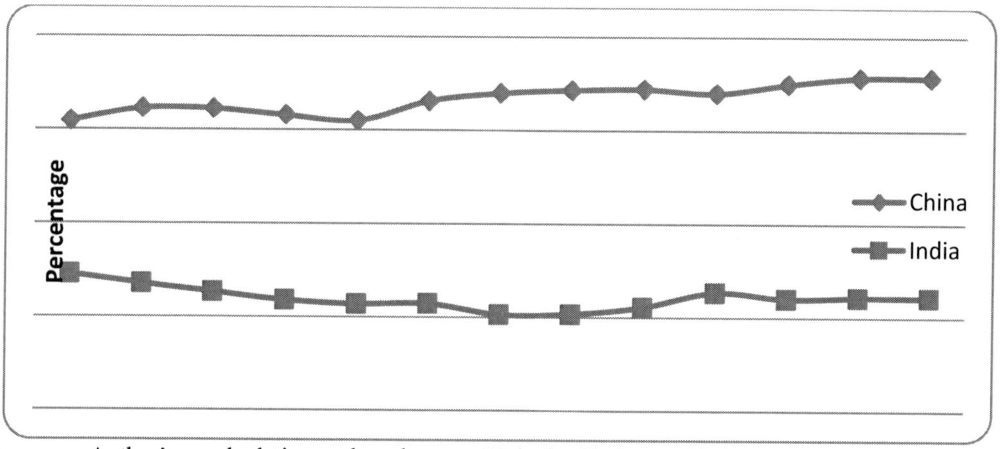

Source: Author's calculations based on United Nations National Accounts Statistics (http://unstats.un.org/unsd/snaama)

Figure 11. Govt . Consumption : 2000 to 2012 (% Share in Aggregate Final Consumption).

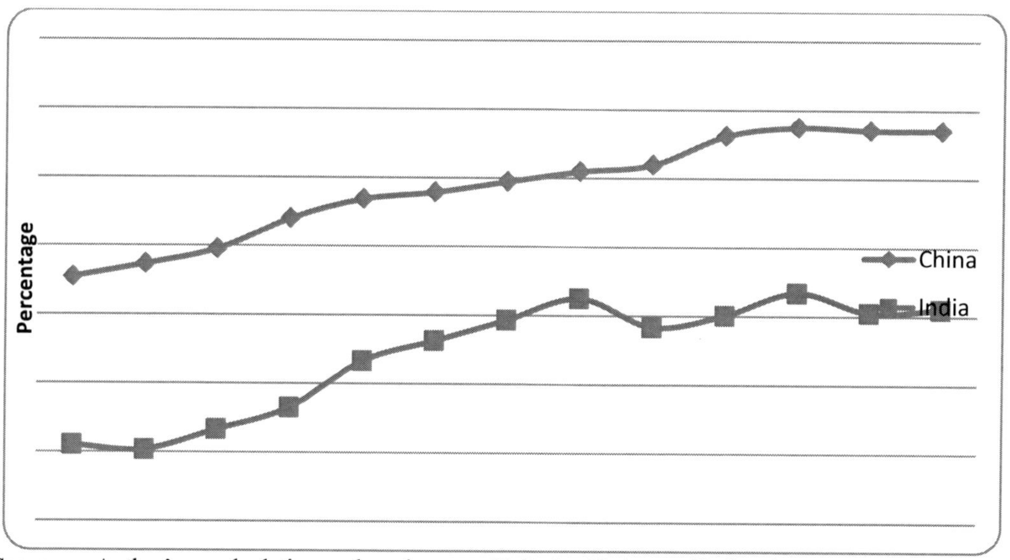

Source: Author's calculations based on United Nations National Accounts Statistics (http://unstats.un.org/unsd/snaama)

Figure 12. Gross Capital Formation : 2000 to 2012 (% of Gross Domestic Absorption (C+I+G).

Domestic investments played an important role in the Indian and Chinese economies in the post-recession phase, with share of gross capital formation in aggregate domestic absorption rising sharply between 2008 and 2010 in both economies. Thereafter in both economies this share was more or less constant. The growth slowdown after 2010 indicates this investment stimulus was an important factor in the growth recovery in 2010.

The growth decomposition exercise provides further insights into the factors that contributed to the change in economic growth in these two economies, especially in the period following the global crisis.

INDIA AND CHINA : FINDINGS FROM A GROWTH DECOMPOSITION EXERCISE

In what follows we decompose GDP growth from the expenditure side as we try to see the effect of the global slowdown on the different components of aggregate demand for the Chinese and Indian economies. In particular our objective is to identify the relative importance of external and domestic demand for these two economies and especially analyse their relative roles in the growth revival and subsequent slowdown in the post-crisis period. Insofar as we use aggregate data for our exercise, without a break up of aggregate imports into imports of intermediates and final consumption, our exercise may be somewhat inaccurate. However, it does give some idea regarding the direction and magnitude of the changes involved.

Out analysis is based on the national income identity. In what follows we decompose GDP growth from the expenditure side as we try to see the effect of the global slowdown on the different components of aggregate demand (following Mukhopadhyay, 1998; Kranendonk and Verbruggen, 2008). For each final expenditure category, we show by how much GDP would have changed if other GDP components remained unchanged. The percentage contributions of expenditure categories are obtained by expressing the year-to-year change in a component of GDP (e.g., Investment or government consumption) as a percentage of GDP in the previous year. The calculations are reported in Table 1 below. This particular methodology seems appropriate as in this paper we are essentially focusing on short run demand adjustments in an economy in response to an external shock. Therefore we do not adopt the production function based growth accounting techniques that are typically employed to estimate the relative contributions of factor accumulation and productivity growth to the long run rate of growth in an economy.

Analysis of demand side factors in the two countries growth experiences in the pre-crisis period, 2003 to 2007, demonstrates the importance of external demand, especially for China. In each of these years export growth accounted for about half the total GDP growth witnessed in China during this period. The pattern of import growth in China demonstrated the import intensity of Chinese exports, with import growth collapsing and picking up in tandem with growth in exports. After 2008, the recovery in Chinese growth was primarily investment led. In 2009 especially practically all of the observed growth was due to the investment stimulus which helped the nation grow despite a slowdown in external demand. Consumption demand was stable, but clearly not enough to prevent a slowdown that seemed apparent with the growth slowdown in 2012 which followed the reduction in the investment-GDP ratio. In fact with this ratio touching 45 percent of GDP (Table 2), China may not be far from reaching the limits to factor accumulation, putting a question mark on the success of this strategy in the future.

The pattern of growth experienced by India from 2003 to 2007 shows the growing importance of exports, but our analysis indicates it was not entirely export led. Rather, growth in private consumption and in the rate of investment played a very important role in the growth performance during this period. One of the main transformations observed in the Indian economy during the pre-recession growth phase (2003 to 2007) was the investment-GDP ratio crossing the 30 percent mark (Table 2), inching closer to the levels achieved in the East Asian economies. A fallout of this growth in domestic demand in an open economy was growth in imports at a faster pace than exports that led to a current account deficit well before the sub-prime crisis had started taking shape. Import growth remained high in 2010 and 2011 when household consumption grew steadily, only to decline with a weakening of demand, indicating relatively high import content of domestic consumption.

Table 1. Percentage Contribution of Aggregate Expenditure Categories to GDP Growth

Years	Private Consumption	Government Consumption	Investment	Exports	Imports	External Sector	GDP growth
				CHINA			
2000	3.7	1.9	3.6	5.0	4.2	0.8	8.4
2001	2.7	1.5	3.2	2.9	3.0	-0.1	8.3
2002	3.0	1.1	4.6	5.6	5.1	0.5	9.1
2003	2.9	0.8	6.0	5.5	5.5	-0.1	10.0
2004	3.2	0.9	4.7	5.9	5.5	0.4	10.1
2005	2.7	1.8	4.7	6.3	4.1	2.2	11.3
2006	3.6	1.6	5.0	6.8	5.0	1.8	12.7
2007	4.1	1.6	5.3	6.7	4.4	2.3	14.2
2008	3.1	1.2	3.7	2.0	1.2	0.7	9.6
2009	3.5	1.2	8.9	-1.9	1.3	-3.2	9.2
2010	3.1	1.5	5.0	6.0	5.8	0.2	10.4
2011	3.6	1.6	4.3	2.6	3.0	-0.4	9.3
2012	3.0	1.2	3.9	1.3	1.5	-0.2	7.7
				INDIA			
2000	2.1	0.1	-0.1	1.9	0.7	1.3	4.0
2001	3.7	0.3	1.7	0.5	0.4	0.1	5.2
2002	1.8	0.0	1.6	2.5	1.7	0.8	3.8
2003	3.7	0.3	3.7	1.3	2.1	-0.8	8.4
2004	3.1	0.4	5.4	3.9	3.6	0.3	8.3
2005	5.1	1.0	4.6	4.4	5.9	-1.6	9.3
2006	4.9	0.4	4.3	3.9	4.7	-0.8	9.3
2007	5.4	1.0	5.2	1.3	2.5	-1.2	9.8
2008	4.2	1.1	1.5	3.0	5.6	-2.6	3.9
2009	4.4	1.5	3.3	-1.1	-0.6	-0.4	8.5
2010	5.0	0.7	5.3	3.9	4.1	-0.2	10.5
2011	4.6	0.9	1.6	3.3	5.9	-2.6	6.3
2012	2.3	0.4	0.3	0.7	2.1	-1.4	3.2

Source: United Nations National Accounts Statistics (http://unstats.un.org/unsd/snaama).

The relative importance of investment in the growth experience is evident from the growth collapse in 2008 that occurred despite a revival of export growth and despite growth in private consumption, as investment fell sharply during this period. Thereafter, despite poor growth in exports, the overall rate of growth picked up with revival in investment. Once again in 2012, domestic demand, especially investment contributed very little to the rate of growth, consumption was also sluggish and with poor showing with respect to exports, a slowdown was clearly evident.

Findings from this exercise demonstrate the importance of international trade for the Chinese economy; in the absence of revival in export demand a slowdown seems inevitable, especially as the economy has already attained a very high investment-GDP ratio. In case of India, while exports did have a positive contribution, the impact of the uncertain investment climate seems to be taking a toll on growth by affecting the rate of capital formation. It is well known that uncertainty created especially by volatility in capital flows tend to have a negative impact on investments. It may be argued that the disruption of long term capital flows or FDI and the enhanced volatility of portfolio flows, owing to the ongoing crisis is taking a toll on capital formation and hence growth by having a negative impact on an important component of domestic demand, viz., investments.

Table 2. Share of Final Expenditure Categories in GDP

Years	Private Consumption	Government Consumption	Investment	Exports	Imports
		CHINA			
2000	44.5	15.2	35.1	26.1	21.5
2001	43.6	15.4	35.3	26.8	22.6
2002	42.8	15.1	36.6	29.7	25.4
2003	41.5	14.4	38.7	32.0	28.1
2004	40.6	13.9	39.4	34.4	30.6
2005	38.9	14.1	39.6	36.6	31.1
2006	37.7	14.0	39.6	38.5	32.1
2007	36.7	13.7	39.3	39.6	32.0
2008	36.3	13.6	39.3	37.9	30.3
2009	36.5	13.5	44.1	32.9	28.9
2010	35.8	13.6	44.5	35.2	31.4
2011	36.1	13.9	44.6	34.6	31.5
2012	36.3	14.0	45.1	33.3	30.6
		INDIA			
2000	61.9	12.9	24.3	12.2	14.5
2001	62.3	12.6	24.7	12.1	14.2
2002	61.8	12.1	25.3	14.1	15.3
2003	60.4	11.4	26.8	14.2	16.1
2004	58.6	10.9	29.8	16.7	18.2
2005	58.3	10.9	31.5	19.3	22.0
2006	57.9	10.3	32.8	21.2	24.5
2007	57.6	10.3	34.5	20.5	24.6
2008	59.5	10.9	34.7	22.6	29.0
2009	58.9	11.5	35.0	19.9	26.2
2010	57.8	11.0	36.4	21.5	27.4
2011	58.7	11.2	35.8	23.3	31.3
2012	59.1	11.3	35.0	23.3	32.4

Source: United Nations National Accounts Statistics (http://unstats.un.org/unsd/snaama)

Conclusion

In this paper we tried to capture the extent of integration of the Indian and Chinese economies with the world market, as we tried to analyse these economies experience in the post-recession period given the large size of their domestic markets. Our analysis indicates that while external causes linked to trade and capital flows were the most important channels transmitting the effect of the global recession to these economies, factors affecting investor confidence and the investment-GDP ratio may hold the key to growth performance in these economies. In fact, the atmosphere of economic uncertainty at the current conjuncture, most apparent in volatility of international capital flows, is perhaps one of the most important factors affecting investment climate in developing economies.

The importance of high and growing investment ratios has been demonstrated time and again, especially in the East Asian economies. Clearly, this is the key area that policy makers must address as they try to dispel the gloom cast by prospects of the current growth slowdown in two of the largest economies in the developing world.

It has been suggested in the literature that developing countries should adopt a more graded approach towards globalization and liberalization policies in the wake of the crisis. However, this may not be a feasible approach in a world where globalization has progressed so far and spread across a wide spectrum of countries. Rather countries must adopt a more guarded approach towards capital account convertibility. In this era of near perfect capital mobility, it is next to impossible to arrest international capital's natural urge to maximize profits through arbitrage. Even international coordination to regulate capital flows is unlikely to succeed, as, the payoffs from deviation from any coordinated agreement is likely to be too high to make any such arrangement feasible. So countries must adopt a cautious approach towards capital account convertibility and keep capital controls in place in order to minimize damage owing to sudden capital surges or outflows that can inflict serious damage to otherwise stable policy atmosphere within nations.

A floodgate of research areas have opened up in the wake of the global crisis. One such area that may be taken up is to construct an index of external vulnerability which would give policy makers some prior idea regarding the magnitude of the impact of an external shock. To do this first one has to identify variables that capture the extent of integration of the domestic with the world economy. Thereafter the index would be constructed by applying a suitable weighting structure, based on the variables most likely to be affected by an external shock and their relative importance at the aggregate level.

Further, on a related though somewhat different point, a detailed empirical study may be undertaken for a select group of developing countries, to examine the relative importance of intra-developing country vis a vis developed-developing country trade shares and relating this to growth performance during the global downturn.

References

Aggarwal, A., (2002). Liberalisation, Multinational Enterprises and Export Performance: Evidence from Indian manufacturing. *Journal of Development Studies, 38*,119-13.

Akyuz, Y.,(2013a).Waving or Drowning: Developing Countries after the Financial Crisis. *South Centre Research Paper* No. 48, June, website *http://www.southcentre.int/research-paper-48-june-2013/*

Akyuz, Y., (2013b). Waving or Drowning: Developing Countries after the Financial Crisis. *Economic and Political* Weekly, *48*, 38-48.

Aloui, R., Aissa, M.S.B. & Nguyen, D.K. (2011). Global Financial Crisis, Extreme Interdependences and Contagion Effects : The Role of Economic Structure. *Journal of Banking and Finance 35*, 130-141.

Bernanke, B. (2010). Causes of the Recent Financial and Economic Crisis. website *http://www.federalreserve.gov/newsevents/testimony/bernanke20100902a.htm.*

Chandrasekhar, C.P. (1997). The Trade-Investment Nexus and Industrialization: An Assessment Based on the Asian Experience. In Nayyar, D. (Ed.), *Trade and Industrialization*. New Delhi: Oxford University Press.

Dasgupta, S. & Singh, A. (2005a). *Will Services be the New Engine of Economic Growth in India?* Centre for Business Research, University of Cambridge Working Paper No. 310, September.

Dasgupta, S. & Singh, A. (2005b). *Manufacturing, Services and Premature Deindustrialization in Developing countries: a Kaldorian Empirical Analysis*. Paper presented at WIDER Jubilee Conference in Helsinki.

Eichengreen, B. (2009). Comments in Collapse in World Trade : A Symposium of Views. *The International Economy,* Spring.

Eichengreen, B. & Gupta, P. (2010). *The Service Sector as India's Road to Economic Growth.* Working Paper No. 249, New Delhi : ICRIER.

Ghosh, J. & Chandrasekhar, C.P. (2009). The Costs of 'Coupling' : The Global Crisis and the Indian Economy. *Cambridge Journal of Economics, 33*, 725-739.

Gordon, J. & Gupta, P. (2004). Understanding India's Services Revolution. *IMF Working Paper, 04/171*, September.

Gorton, G. & Metrick, A. (2012). Getting up to Speed on the Financial Crisis : A One-Weekend-Reader's Guide. *Journal of Economic Literature, 50*, 128-150.

Joseph, T. & Reddy. V. N. (2009). FDI Spillovers and Export Performance of Indian Manufacturing Firms after Liberalisation. *Economic and Political Weekly, 64,* 97-105.

Keynes, J.M. (1936). The General Theory of Employment, *Interest and Money*. London : Macmillan.

Kim, I.J. (2012). The Global Financial Crisis and the Challenges of the Korean Economy. *Seoul Journal of Economics, 25*, 339-366.

Kranendonk, H. & Verbruggen, J. (2008). Decomposition of GDP-growth in some European Countries and the United States. *De Economist* 157.

Krugman, P. (2008). *The Return of Depression Economics and the Crisis of 2008*. London : Penguin Books.

Lo, A. (2012). Reading about the Financial Crisis : A Twenty-One-Book Review. *Journal of Economic Literature, 50*, 151-178.

Massa, I., Keane, J. & Kennan, J. (2012). *The Euro Zone Crisis and Developing Countries.* Working Paper 345, London : Overseas Development Institute.

McMillan, M., & Rodrik, D. (2011*). Globalization, structural change, and productivity growth;* NBER working paper 17143. Cambridge : NBER.

McNally, C. (2008). China and the Global Financial Crisis. *Asia Pacific Bulletin,26,* December,12.website *http://www.eastwestcenter.org/publications/china-and-global-financial-crisis.*

Mukhopadhyay, H. (1998). Structural Adjustment Programs:Some New Findings. *Review of Development Economics, 2,* 191-210.

Nagaraj, R. (2013). India's Dream Run, 2003-08:Understanding the Boom and its Aftermath. *Economic and Political Weekly, 48*, 39-51.

Nayyar, D. (2011). The Financial Crisis, the Great Recession and the Developing World. *Global Policy, 2,* 20-32.

Obstfeld, M. (1998). The Global Capital Market : Benefactor or Menace ? *Journal of Economic Perspectives 12 (4)*, 9-30.

Obstfeld, M. & Taylor, A. (2004). *Global Capital Flows:Integration, Crisis and Growth.* Cambridge : Cambridge University Press.

Palma J. (2006). Growth after Globalisation: A 'Structuralist-Kaldorian' Game of Musical Chairs ? Background paper for World Economic and Social Survey 2006. website *www.un.org/esa/policy/backgroundpapers/palma_final_paper.pdf*

Park, Y.C. (2011). The Global Financial Crisis : Decoupling of East Asia – Myth or Reality. ADBI Working Series Paper No. 289. Tokyo : Asian Development Bank Institute. website*http://www.adbi.org/workingpaper/2011/06/22/4615.gfc.decoupling*

Ram Mohan, T. (2009). The Impact of the Crisis on the Indian Economy. *Economic and Political Weekly, 44,* 107-114.

Rakshit, M. (2012). Keynes and the Contemporary Economic Crisis. *Money & Finance,* ICRA Bulletin, September, 43-87.

Reinhart, C.M. and Rogoff, K.S. (2009). *This Time is Different.* Princeton and Oxford : Princeton University Press.

Singh, N. (2006). Services-Led Industrialization in India: Assessment and Lessons. MPRA Paper No.1446. website *http://mpra.ub.uni-muenchen.de/1446/*

Sharma, K. (2000). *Export Growth in India: Has FDI Played a Role?* Discussion Paper 816, Yale University : Economic Growth Centre.

UNCTAD (2009). *Global Economic Crisis: Implications for Trade and Development.* Geneva : Report by UNCTAD secretariat.

Whalley, J., Agarwal, M., Cai, Y., Dong, Y., Tian, H. & L. Wang, (2009). China and the Financial Crisis. *Report of Task Force* (chaired by John Whalley) under the Chinese Academy of Social Sciences/ CIGI Young Scholars Network for Chinese Public Policy. website *http://dspace.cigilibrary.org/jspui/handle/123456789/25133.*

In: Current Issues in International Trade
Editor: Gouranga G. Das
ISBN: 978-1-63321-405-7

Chapter 2

DEVELOPMENT OF ASIA'S INDUSTRIAL NETWORK AND CROSS-PACIFIC TRADE

Hongyul Han [•]
Department of Economics, Hanyang University,
Ansan (Eirca Campus),
South Korea

ABSTRACT

The rise of Chinese economy seems to disrupt the long-established flying geese model of industrialization in Asia. As China becomes the center of regional trade and investment, other developing countries find it hard to move up the ladder of industrial development. Examination of cross pacific trade shows fast upgrading of a China's export structure.

In contrast, ASEAN countries are not successful enough to follow the paths of Korea and Taiwan. The production network is dispersed throughout the world, which brings attention to trade values in the global economy. The global imbalance as represented by China's surplus accompanies increase in both China's valued added in U.S. exports and US value added in China's exports.

The production network is increasingly interlinked among China, Korea and ASEAN countries. Bilateral flows of value added among these countries have significantly increased. As China is shifting away from a downstream position of the supply chain, their exports of intermediate products in the high technology sector are increasingly contributing to advanced countries' high technology exports.

Keywords: Globalization, Flying Geese, Value-added, Comparative Advantage, TiVA Database

[•] E-mail: hyhan@hanyang.ac.kr.

INTRODUCTION: CHINA IN THE SEQUENTIAL INDUSTRIALIZATION OF ASIA

The rise of Chinese economy reshapes the world economy in various ways. The global imbalance had long concerned Japan over decades, but it is now mostly attributable to the imbalance between China and the U.S. The global imbalance continues to be a cross-pacific issue as the U.S. deficit accounts for about two third of the world's current account deficits, and East Asian countries take almost half of the world's current account surplus (see Figure 1). It implies that the East Asian region provides most of the net global savings in the world capital market. In particular, China's huge surplus often poses potential threats to international financial markets and sustainability of US budget deficit. Also, with its huge expansion of domestic market and export performance, China is frequently practicing administrative protections such as antidumping measures.[1] However, proliferation of the administrative protection has been effectively kept under control by WTO, through which the world trade environment seems to be sufficiently free from protectionism. Finally, Chinese expansion is shaking the regional production network, which has been established for a long time in East Asia. The emergence of China is about to end almost a half-century-long chain of industrialization of the flying geese model in East Asia. China continues to grow fast to encompass the ASEAN region into its production network.

At the beginning of 2000, China continued to accelerate its exports, particularly to the U.S., leading to the U.S.'s huge trade deficit with China. The U.S. trade deficit recorded over 270 billion US dollars in 2010 from 80 billion in 2000. China is responsible for over 40% of total US trade deficit. However, it does not necessarily indicate a lack of U.S.'s competitiveness in manufacturing. It simply shows that the U.S. spends more than it saves. In addition, it does not necessarily mean that the U.S. and China are competing in manufacturing exports, because their unit values of the same product categories are significantly different: China sells low unit value products to the U.S. whereas the U.S. sells high unit value products throughout the world (Bailey, 2011).

Goods Balance Current Account Balance

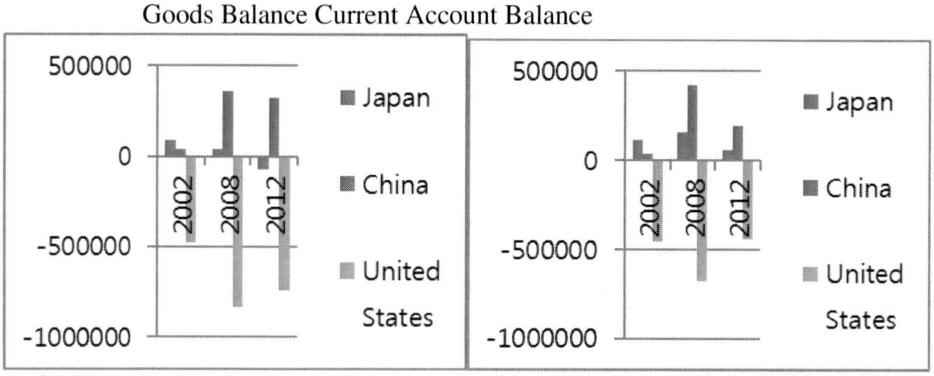

Source: OECD STAN Database.

Figure 1. External Balances: U.S. China, Japan.

[1] According to the WTO, as of 2012, China was reported to have administered 200 anti-dumping measures, mostly on imports from U.S., Japan and Korea.

In fact, the new cross-pacific imbalance originates from changes in a regional export structure among Asian countries. Most Asian countries, including Japan, Korea and other NICs experienced significant reduction of trade surpluses with the U.S. during this period.

The U.S. has often criticized China's foreign exchange rate policy aimed to keep its export price competitiveness. But the increasing substitution of Asian countries' exports by China is mainly caused by the shift of global imbalance, The global imbalance has remained unchanged since 1970 in terms of trade relations between the U.S. and Asia. The real change took place when the cross-pacific trade has started changing in nature along with China's export structure.

During the course of competing with regional advanced countries and capturing a significant market share in the U.S., China seems to have surpassed ASEAN countries in the flying geese model. Moreover, the change in the order of line-up demonstrates a completely different development prospective for other developing countries, particularly ASEAN countries.

The cross-pacific trade flows may reflect structural transformation in the region with regard to countries' relative position in the ladder of industrial development. The major economic powers of East Asia, Japan, Korea and China, are creating a new pattern of industrial relationship.

Korea has almost completed the catch-up process as early as 2000 after several decades of industrialization. It now competes with Japan in world export markets of technology-intensive products as well as heavy and chemical industry products. While China is believed to be lagging behind those two countries in many aspects, China is deemed to be able to catch up with the other two countries in most manufacturing industries of standard technologies within a short period of time. The catch-up process of the flying geese model describes sequential upgrades of countries' industrial structures along different stages of industrialization. Korea, Taiwan, and China have sequentially upgraded their industry structures for the past half-century. Also the Chinese development model has the same key characteristics of the East Asian development model. It includes credit rationing by state, direct support for both private and state-owned enterprises, and an active trade policy for export promotion and import substitution. However, the complex economic relationship has developed, as China not only fast upgrades its industrial structure but also expands its production network with neighboring countries. The change is characterized by many expressions such as bamboo capitalism or water lily capitalism, depending on the nature of division of labor or agglomeration pattern of industrial activities, specifically in the East Asian region including Southeast Asia. (Park, 2005) This relatively recent development has significant impacts on both intra-regional trade and cross-pacific trade because it reflects deeper globalization of the production process.

Figure 2 describes the progress of industrial development in the Asian region over the past half a century. In earlier stages, the flying geese model of regional industrialization included relocation of industries based on regional structure of comparative advantage. The regional division of labor was easily established due to the difference in factor abundance among the neighboring countries. In East Asia, for instance, with the hike of wages, declining industries of Japan such as textile and footwear industries were taken over from Korea and Taiwan from the early 1970s. Kojima (1978) argued that the Japanese FDI within the framework of the flying geese model was intrinsically different from FDI of other developed countries.

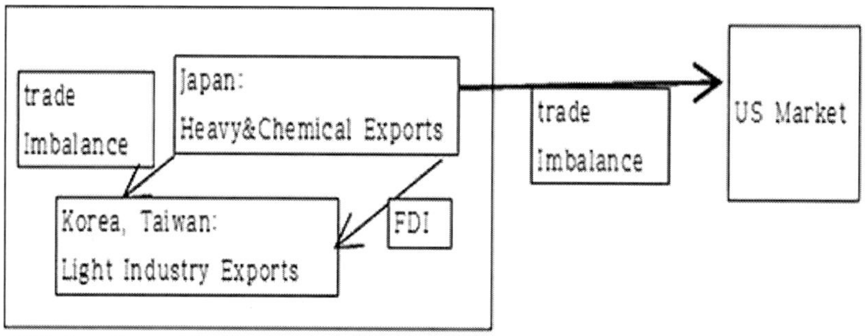

First Phase of Flying Geese Model: 1970s.

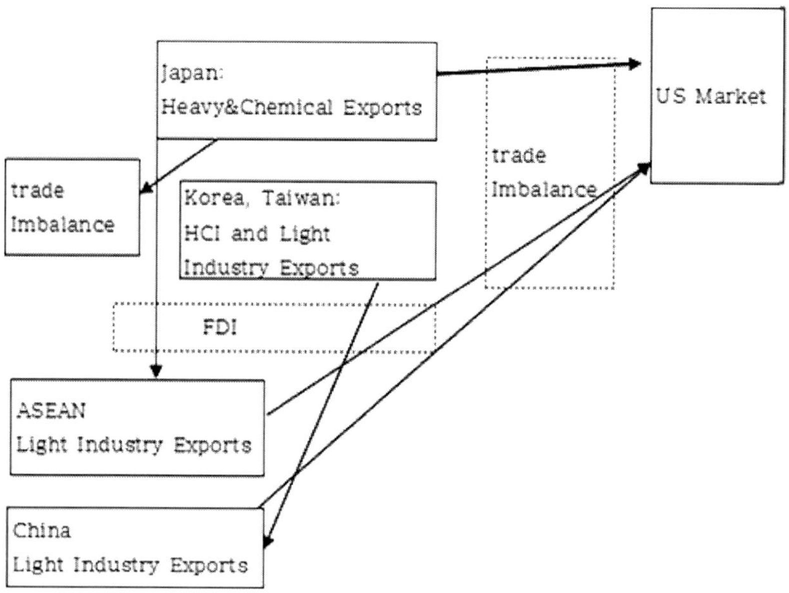

Second Phase of Frying Geese Model:1980s.

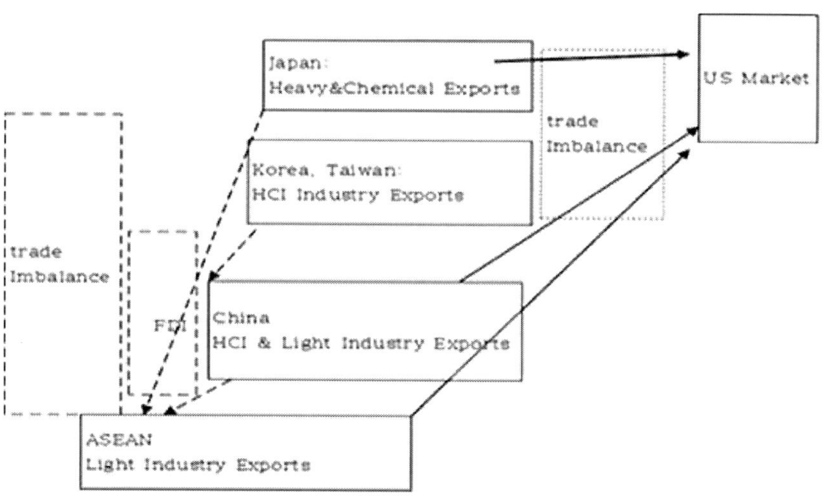

Disruption of the Flying Geese Model.

Figure 2. Phases of Asian Sequential Industrial Development.

While FDI is usually motivated by utilization of host countries' domestic markets, Japanese FDI contributed to the industrialization of host countries by transferring Japanese production capacity due to weakening of its price competitiveness in the international markets. (Park, ibid). This pattern of FDI was followed by Korea (the second stage in Figure 2). Korea established a heavy and chemical industry by late 1980s, initiated by the massive industrial policy in the early 1970s. As Korea started to lose price competitiveness of exports to ASEAN countries, it started to relocate many light industries including textile, clothing and footwear to ASEAN countries. After China started carrying out policy reforms in 1990s, Korean firms invested in China. However, the change of host countries did not change the main characteristics. Most FDI were made to take advantage of low labor costs of China. Lately, growth of China appears to disrupt the flying geese model, overturning the order of industrialization in the East Asia. The regional production networks thereafter showed dramatic development. There are a growing number of predictions that China would break the long-standing chain of regional industrial development in the Asian region with the expansion of its own production network and clustering of economic activities in the Southeast Asian region. By 2005, the center of the network had fast shifted to China. China became the largest destination of intermediate and capital goods. Supply chains towards China are characterized by a high degree of fragmentation and sophistication, incorporating a substantial amount of value-added from each country involved. (WTO-JETRO, 2011)

Development of Regional Production Network and Trade Pattern

Changes in the U.S. Import Market Structure

The world has witnessed a big-bang growth of China's production and export capacity in the last decade. But it is not fully agreed whether or not the change truly accompanies a substantial degree of qualitative transformation of regional production network. It is argued that China's export performance is still based on a low end of value chain in the region. On one hand, the new global imbalance has concurred with China's fast upgrading of its export structure to higher technology-intensive sectors. The exports of labor-intensive manufactures have shown a decreasing trend in Chinese economy (Yoshida and Ito, 2007). On the other hand, some argue that more than half of the total export accounts for processed exports by foreign enterprises investing in China, which leaves only a small fraction of value added to the domestic economy (Kim et al., 2012). Massive Chinese export is based on intraregional interdependence characterized by the triangular trading pattern among the major East Asian economies, Japan, Korea and Taiwan. MNEs operating in ASEAN countries produce sophisticated technology-intensive parts and capital goods, which are then shipped to China to be assembled with low labor costs. The final products are then exported to the world market. Unlike trade patterns in other parts of the world, East Asia shows increasingly deepening interdependence through vertical intra-industry trade. Vertical integration and fragmentation of production processes among these countries are based on comparative advantages (Das and Han, 2013).

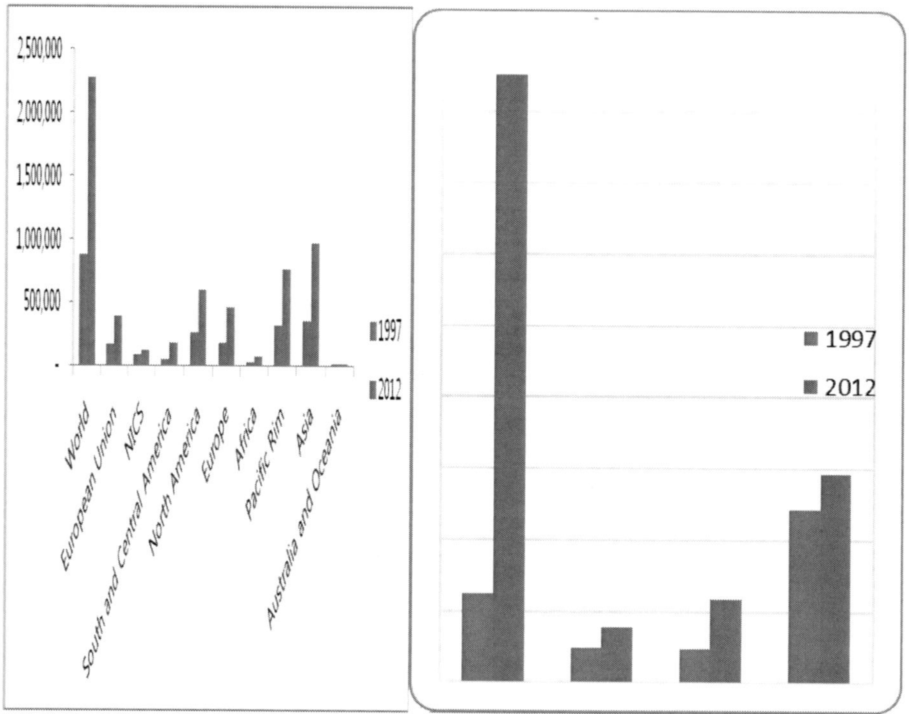

Source: Based on Data from US Bureau of Census website: www.doc.gov.

Figure 3. Geographical Export Structure: World and US.

How has the development of production network in East Asia translated itself into reality of trade flows, particularly between Asia and the U.S.? Figure 3 shows changes in a geographical import structure between the U.S. and the world during the period of 1997-2012. According to the US Bureau of Census, U.S.'s main import partners are: China (18 percent of total imports), European Union (16 percent), Canada (14 percent), Mexico (12 percent) and Japan (6 percent).

The US import market grew from 900 billion USD to over 2 trillion USD. During this period, Korea, China and Japan showed a remarkably distinctive performance in the US market,. China's export grew from 65 billion USD to 417 billion USD. Korea had shown the second largest export growth, from 23 to 58 billion USD. However, Japanese export recorded only a slight increase from 124 to 132 billion USD in 2011. Actually, Japanese export to the US market has declined since 2006 in which it reached 152 billion USD. In sum, China's exports doubled the growth of US import market, while Korea managed to maintain high growth rates and Japan lost market share substantially.

Obviously, the cross-pacific trade is complementary. Japan, Korea and China led the world economy through merchandise trade while the U.S. showed relatively bigger share of service trade. Exports of manufacturing goods of China take over 90% of its total export and Japan and Korea's merchandise exports are over 80%. The U.S's. service export reached almost 30% of total export. Korea and China clearly show export competitiveness in medium and low technology-intensive products, while Japan has advantage in medium to high technology export.

Also, the cross traffic is strongly related with related-party trade (intra-firm trade), which includes trade by the U.S. companies with their subsidiaries abroad as well as trade by U.S.

subsidiaries of foreign companies with their parent companies (US Bureau of Census, 2013). The related-party trade accounted for 41.7 percent ($1,582.3 billion) of total goods trade ($3,797.5 billion) in 2012. The growth rate of related-party trade almost doubles the overall trade growth rate, 6.6% and 3.5% respectively. The related-party trade in consumption goods exceeded non-related party trade. This suggests that cross-pacific trade flows may involve complex exchange of value added between trading partners.

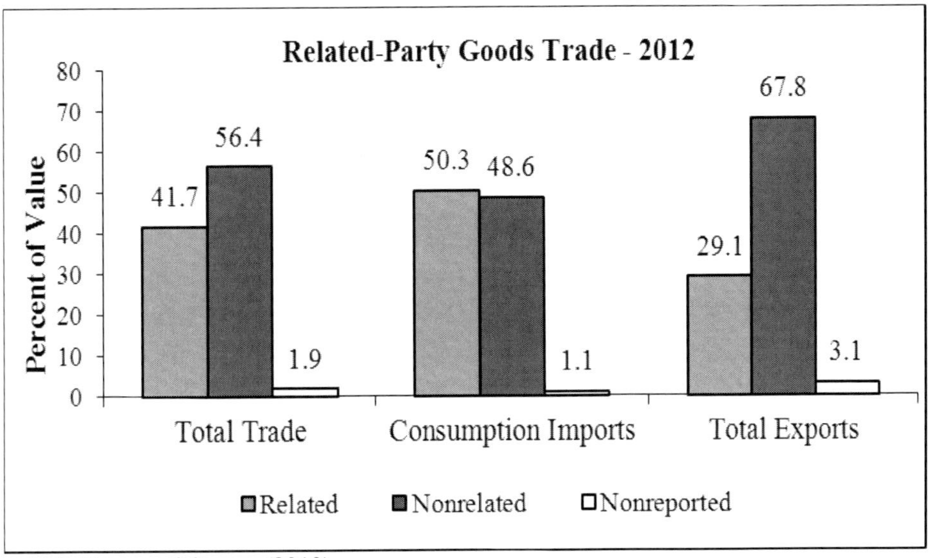

Source: U.S. Bureau of Census (2013).

Figure 4. US Intra- Firm Trade.

Table 1. Changes in US Import Structure by Use-Category and Technology Level

	1990	1995	2000	2005	2007	2009	2011
Total Imports	534,153	780,944	1,285,841	1,732,320	2,017,120	1,601,895	2,262,585
By Use							
Intermediate goods	51.90	50.00	48.70	50.50	51.10	48.80	53.40
Household consumption	20.40	19.90	19.30	19.80	19.80	21.20	18.20
Capital goods	11.30	12.20	12.30	11.30	11.60	11.60	11.20
Mixed end-use	13.30	14.80	15.80	15.20	14.30	14.60	14.40
By Technology Level							
High Tech	0.18	0.24	0.24	0.21	0.20	0.24	0.21
Medium high Tech	0.29	0.31	0.29	0.28	0.28	0.25	0.27
Medium low Tech	0.13	0.11	0.11	0.13	0.14	0.13	0.14
Low tech	0.21	0.21	0.19	0.19	0.18	0.19	0.17
ICT	0.13	0.19	0.19	0.15	0.14	0.16	0.14

Source: OECD STAN Database.

Table 1 shows US imports by use-category for the last two decades based on the OECD STAN database. Apparently, a US import structure by use-category has not changed significantly. The U.S.'s main imports are industrial supplies (32 percent of total imports) of which crude oil alone accounts for half. Others include: Capital Goods (14 percent); Automotive vehicles, parts, and engines (13 percent); Consumer Goods (12 percent) and Foods, Feeds, and Beverages (5 percent). Imports by technology level also show no significant shifts.

There was moderate increase in imports of high technology from 18% in 1990 to 21% in 2011. However, the level of imports of high and medium technology products show some fluctuations. The shares increased to 55% from 53% between 1995 and 2000, but it returned to the level of 1990 at 48% in 2011. At the same time, imports of lower-technology products had decreased continuously from 21% to 14% in 2011. Imports of ICT products hiked in 2000 and returned to the level of 1990 in 2011. IT booms in 1990s must have been conducive to this fluctuation.

Table 2 describes the US import structure by a product group at HS 2 digit level based on the trade statistics of the International Trade Center. Basically, the import structure by a product group has not changed significantly. During the period of 2001 - 2011, imports have almost doubled, from 1.18 trillion USD to 2.33 trillion USD. The most notable change is imports of energy such as mineral fuels and oils (HS 27). It became the leading group of import products in the beginning of 2004. The next top three categories of imports at a HS 2 digit level include machinery (HS 84), electrical and electronic equipment (HS 85) and vehicles (HS 87). Top three importing products, besides energy imports, take about 40% of total merchandise imports. Except for vehicle imports, top import product groups kept up with the average growth rate. While the leading import sector remains fundamentally unchanged, a number of other sectors have shown faster increase in growth rate than the growth of overall imports. They include imports of pharmaceutical products (HS 30), which increased four folds during the period 2001-2012. Imports of pearls and precious stones metals, coins (HS 71), plastics and articles thereof (HS39) iron or steel and articles thereof (HS 73,72) increased higher than the average import growth during the same period. Imports of consumption goods showed slower growth, including those of the textile and apparel sectors. Also, automobile imports grew slower than the average even though it still remained on the top list of imports.

Asia's Adjustment to the US Market

How are Asian countries adapting to the change (or lack of) in US import market? The answer to this question would provide a different perspective to understand the new pattern of industrial relationship in Asia after the almost half-a-century-long flying geese model of industrial development.

Developed East Asian countries export a large amount of technology-intensive capital and intermediate goods, while relatively less developed countries in the region largely export lower skill-intensive consumer goods. Thus, in essence, there is a complementary relationship between China and less developed Asian countries on one hand, and between China and regional developed countries on the other. Table 3 shows how China has kept up with the US import market structure during the last decade.

Table 2. Changes in US Top 15 Imports by Product Group
Unit. 1,000 USD

HS	Product	2001	2004	2007	2011	2012
Rank in 2012	All products	1,180,073,832	1,525,268,509	2,017,120,776	1,966,496,750	2,333,805,233
'27	Mineral fuels, oils, distillation products, etc.	129,143,808	216,439,075	372,341,595	362,726,741	433,361,870
'84	Machinery, nuclear reactors, boilers, etc.	164,880,754	205,770,722	256,322,763	255,284,603	314,553,543
'85	Electrical, electronic equipment	157,373,654	188,873,940	253,600,325	262,979,583	296,396,935
'87	Vehicles other than railway, tramway	161,908,066	194,484,325	218,153,543	186,117,555	244,200,232
'90	Optical, photo, technical, medical, apparatus	35,395,290	45,261,285	54,743,106	59,808,389	69,797,763
'99	Commodities not elsewhere specified	49,104,104	50,515,896	61,218,527	56,013,619	66,376,094
'30	Pharmaceutica l products	16,045,880	31,555,746	49,205,767	62,074,558	64,390,139
'71	Pearls, precious stones, metals	26,177,046	33,348,928	47,582,536	52,297,727	62,920,085
'29	Organic chemicals	32,420,319	38,998,873	46,143,289	48,903,519	54,595,483
'94	Furniture, lighting, signs, prefabricated buildings	25,184,994	37,274,757	44,882,684	41,279,536	47,854,476
'39	Plastics and articles thereof	20,159,196	28,288,581	36,459,734	36,906,967	44,245,005
'61	Articles of apparel, accessories, knit or crochet	27,909,631	33,035,984	39,650,951	39,952,651	42,597,282
'73	Articles of iron or steel	14,820,381	21,206,177	33,716,364	28,263,261	39,745,003
'62	Articles of apparel, accessories, not knit	32,910,820	36,926,880	39,269,256	35,694,143	
'72	Iron and steel	11,362,159	24,008,932	27,078,829	22,517,939	30,449,773

Source: International Trade Center Database.

Table 3. Changes in US Imports and Asian Exports (2001 and 2012)

2001 Top US Imports		C	J	K	2012 Top US Imports		C	J	K
'27	Mineral fuels, oils, distillation products, etc.	'85	87	85	'84	Machinery, nuclear reactors, boilers, etc.	'84	87	87
'84	Machinery, nuclear reactors, boilers, etc.	'84	84	87	'87	Vehicles other than railway, tramway	'85	84	85
'85	Electrical, electronic equipment	'64	85	84	'85	Electrical, electronic equipment	'94	85	84
'87	Vehicles other than railway, tramway	'95	90	62	'27	Mineral fuels, oils, distillation products, etc.	'61	90	27
'90	Optical, photo, technical, medical, etc. apparatus	'94	99	61	'99	Commodities not elsewhere specified	'64	99	73
'99	Commodities not elsewhere specified	'39	29	73	'90	Optical, photo, technical, medical, etc. apparatus	'62	88	40
'30	Pharmaceutical products	'62	88	27	'62	Articles of apparel, accessories, not knit or crochet	'95	29	89
'71	Pearls, precious stones, metals, coins, etc.	'42	73	72	'29	Organic chemicals	'39	73	72
'29	Organic chemicals	'90	39	90	'61	Articles of apparel, accessories, knit or crochet	'87	40	39
'94	Furniture, lighting, signs, prefabricated buildings	'73	40	39	'71	Pearls, precious stones, metals, coins, etc.	'73	39	29
'39	Plastics and articles thereof	'87	30	40	'94	Furniture, lighting, signs, prefabricated buildings	'90	72	90
'61	Articles of apparel, accessories, knit or crochet	'29	95	71	'95	Toys, games, sports requisites	'42	38	88
'73	Articles of iron or steel	'63	37	29	'88		'63	71	48
'62	Articles of apparel, accessories, not knit or crochet	'82	38	48	'39	Plastics and articles thereof	'29	82	82
'72	Iron and steel	'67	72	54	'30		'40	37	74

Source: International Trade Center Database.

Besides the US imports of mineral fuels (HS 27), which topped in 2001, China's exports were included as seven product groups at a 2 digit HS level in the list of the U.S. top 10 import product groups. Only four product groups were included in 2001 from which China was fast expanding its overall exports to the US market. In the case of Japan, the number of export groups, in fact, decreased from eight to six. Korea experienced the same decrease in the top ten matching product groups with Japan at six. China's world market share on intermediate products increased from 4.4% in 2003 to 9.8% in 2012. Market share of capital good increased from 8.7% to 24.3% during the same period. China is in the second position in the intermediate product export after Germany.

With regard to the export performance of major Asian countries, it would be interesting to quote Kwan (2002), "Based on a comparison of the trade structures among Asian nations, we find that they are broadly in line with their respective levels of economic development. In short, there is no evidence showing that the flying-geese formation has been disrupted by the emergence of China. Even in China's fast-growing IT-product sector, the country's export competitiveness still lags far behind not only Japan, but also other Asian countries. There is a clear division of labor between Japan and China, with the former specializing in high-value-added products and the latter in low-value-added products. There is little overlap, especially in the high-value-added categories". However, the table seems to suggest otherwise because China's industrial development is presented by a new reality of cross-pacific trade flows. Chinese commodity trade is different from the characteristics of a typical developing country in 1980s.

Even though China's exports to the U.S. market mostly consist of manufacturing products of intermediate level of technology, they appear to shift toward high-tech manufactures. ASEAN's export structure in Table 4 demonstrates a clear difference. Top ASEAN exports show lower growth rates than the average. Exports of electrical and electronic equipment (HS 85) increased only by 30% during the period. More strikingly, exports of machinery (HS 84) have decreased significantly. On the other hand, the traditional exports of developing countries such as textile and textile products (HS 61, HS62) have increased faster than the average.

Also, the export performance of ASEAN is in a stark comparison with China's export performance of overall technological upgrade in the U.S. market. "*China's massive export boom in computers and electronics derives from the fact that it is a very good place to assemble electronic products that clearly benefit U.S. companies' profits.*"(Bailey, Ibid) It raises the question of whether China's expansion is 'a threat' to or 'an opportunity' for its neighboring developing countries. The U.S. import doubled during the last decade. But ASEAN exports to the U.S. market increased by 50% during the same period. The export performance by product group is even more striking. Leading export products of ASEAN countries such as electrical equipment (HS 84) and machinery (HS 85) showed slower growth than the average. ASEAN appears to be moving back to lower value added exports. Though one may question China's success in moving up the ladder of technology levels, it seems clear enough to conclude that China is passing ASEAN countries in the ladder of industrial development. As China's manufacturing sector moves forward, it surely created strong competitive pressures on other producers along production chains within the region. China's productivity improvement ahead of wage increase seems to push ASEAN competitors back in markets for labor-intensive and the low-skilled end of the market. Huang(2012) argues, for example, that, " *Malaysia is a classic example, where failure in up-skilling the manufacturing workforce and ill-judged industrial policies have raised the specter of being caught in the so-called 'middle income trap'.*

Table 4. Change of ASEAN Exports to the U.S.

	Product label	Import from ASEAN		Total Import	
		Value in 2001	Value in 2012	Value in 2001	Value in 2012
	All products	79665803	127192288	1180073832	2333805200
'85	Electrical electronic equipment	23100621	29951311	157373654	296396935
'84	Machinery nuclear reactors, boilers, etc.	21916637	17572375	164880754	314553543
'61	Articles of apparel, accessories, knit or crochet	4094391	10817701	27909631	42597282
'62	Articles of apparel, accessories, not knit or crochet	4969983	7134136	32910820	38091467
'40	Rubber and articles thereof	1710187	7084253	9904637	29861021
'29	Organic chemicals	1004667	5414355	32420319	54595483
'90	Optical, photo, technical, medical, etc. apparatus	1779224	4976171	53395290	69797763
'94	Furniture, lighting, signs,prefabricated buildings	1836921	4792042	25184994	47854476
'99	Commodities not elsewhere	2150738	4586474	49104104	66376094
'64	Footwear, gaiters and the like parrs thereof	1267820	3655964	16009440	24861687
'03	Fish, crustanceans, molluscs, aquatic invertebratesnes	1778178	3100145	8329576	13347119
'15	Animal, vegetable fats and oils, cleavage product, etc	325869	2159421	1265473	6222873
'16	Meat, fish and seafood preparations nes	1110493	2142080	2421469	4664547
'71	Pearls, precious stones, metals, coins, etc	1010280	1878818	26177046	62920085
'27	Mineral fuels, oils, distillations products, etc	1793984	1837348	129143808	433361870

Source: same as above.

The challenge is not the specter of Chinese competition, which provides the opportunity to lift manufacturing productivity, upgrade trade and industrial structure, and lift national incomes: the challenge is national failure in investment and reform to achieve that outcome. Many in Indonesia also worry about how to find a way in international markets for manufactures around the juggernaut of growing Chinese competitiveness; the more Indonesia closes off competition and back-tracks on openness and reform the more likely Indonesia's respectable growth and industrial transformation are likely to splutter to a halt."

A study by the KIET (2010) provides a useful accounting in this context. It compares how manufacturing sectors contributed to the trade balance of major economies by a measure of changes in comparative advantage by a technology level. The indices for cross-pacific trade tell us that the ICT was the leading sector for Asian economies in terms of contribution to trade balances. As of 2009, the ICT sector took a total of 4% of regional trade surplus while high tech and medium tech manufacturing sectors were responsible for trade deficits as much as 3.2% and 4.3% respectively. The indices for Asian economies were dominated by Chinese performance, particularly for lower technology sectors. Korea showed stronger advantage in the ICT industry in trade with the U.S. According to the study, during the period 2000~2008, China showed an upgrade of its structure of comparative advantage; the disadvantage in ICT in 2000 turned into comparative advantages by. 2008, while its comparative advantage in lower technology-intensive products weakened significantly.

DEVELOPMENT OF PRODUCTION NETWORK AND TRADE IN VALUES

China in the Chain of Asian Countries' Industrialization Link

The last half century of Asia's flying geese model of industrial development can be divided into 3 periods (Figure 1), in which leading Northeast Asian countries were growth champions in each period (Nüble 2011). In the core of this process was a massive industrial policy to promote heavy and chemical industries (Park, 2004). In 1970s, after a couple of failed attempts to establish heavy and chemical industries (HCI) in 1960s, Korea followed the policy of Japan in 1950s, adopting almost the same menu of industry and trade policy options. Korea's catch up strategy brought about an overlapping structure of East Asia's industrialization. First, Japan's FDI of domestically declining labor-intensive industries to other part of Asia contributed to the early industrialization of the second-tier countries. Second, however, the Japanese investment targeted the Southeast Asian countries in order to establish production network of domestic firms as well as to exploit local markets. The investment focused on automobile and electronics industries. As a result of Korea's establishment of HCI industries, Korea and Japan entered a direct competition with Japanese exports.

The flying geese model expanded geographically as the Korean and Taiwanese firms started to relocate declining domestic industries of textile and footwear in Southeast Asian countries. However as we see now, the host countries in ASEAN region are not successful enough to follow the paths of Korea and Taiwan. The tail group of flying geese hasn't moved up to join the upper income group. There seems to be a couple of explanations. First, the Japanese investment by leading firms of target industries accompanied Japanese key part suppliers. This strategy led the Southeast Asian countries to remain mostly at export processing industries. This is particularly different from industrialization of Korea and Taiwan, which aggressively applied export promotion and import substitution measures in order to replace foreign capital and part supplies with domestic products. Second, unlike Korea which relied on both foreign and domestic savings instead of FDI in the process of capital accumulation, Southeast Asian countries chose to invite FDI, particularly from Japan. It resulted in huge difference in establishing and upgrading a domestic industrial structure in a longer term. Korea and Taiwan have caught up with Japan in many advanced manufacturing industries while Southeast Asian countries still remain at the tail group of flying geese model. Vertical division of labor characterizes the industrial relationship between Japan and Southeast Asian countries while horizontal integration is prevalent between Japan, Korea and Taiwan.

From a macroeconomic point of view, the sequential industrial development in the region of Asia is characterized by massive capital formation since 1960s. The industrial policy is per se a public policy to expand the country's supply capacity in the strategically chosen sectors. Extensive and hybrid policy measures are utilized; fiscal and monetary policy, trade policy, science and technology policy and education policy. However, it is worth to note that fortified supply capacity is sustainable only if sufficient demand supports the increased supply capacity. In other words, an industrial policy serves at best a necessary condition for a country to establish a desired industrial structure.[2]. Hence, an industrial policy usually accompanies import substitution. Even most export-oriented industrialization called for import substitution of intermediate and capital goods in the earlier stages. In the industrialization process of the Korean economy, the import substitution policy played a crucial role, particularly in 1970s. Even when overall contribution of import substitution may appear to be small for overall manufactures, disaggregated manufacturing data reveals that it helped growing target industries (Kim 2012). Also, as far as Korea is concerned, import substitution successfully transformed the targeted industries into the export-oriented industries.

When the emergence of Chinese economy disrupts the flying geese model, the Southeast Asian countries are facing completely different domestic and international economic environments for effective implementation of industrial policy measures. Therefore, for Southeast Asian countries, it is a legitimate concern that their exports are squeezed out by the emergence of the Chinese export, and their attempts to achieve an advanced industry structure faces serious challenges. For instance, even though the MFA (Multi-Fiber Arrangement), implemented to restrict trades in textile and apparel sectors, was abolished 10 years after the completion of the Uruguay Round, it is believed that China benefited most from the textile agreement. Originally, MFA abolition was adopted as a key negotiation agenda representing developing countries' interests to participate in the Uruguay Round and was supposed to assist exports of less developed countries. For Asian countries, the U.S. import market has

[2] For instance, the Korean War of 1950-1953 provided a substantial demand enough to support the Japanese industrial supply capacity. For Korea, massive investments in HCI struggled from the low capacity utilization because of insufficient market demand for almost 10 years until mid-80s when the world economy rebounded. As economies of scale characterize heavy and chemical industries, those industries needed massive export demand to be sustainable. However, Korea's industrial policy was hit by sluggish world demand due to first and second oil shocks. Korean economy could establish the current structure of industry partly thanks to the recovery of world economy after the Plaza Accord in 1985 which provided a hugely favorable macroeconomic environment for Korean exports.

always served as the most important demand for their exports. So the rapid growth of China abruptly intensified competition in the US. It has deprived Southeast Asian countries of opportunities and time to upgrade their industry structures. In addition to the fact that these countries were subject to chronic deficit with Japan due to their vertical integration with the Japanese economy, expansion of trade with China could pose potential threats to the industrialization process.

Also as seen in Table 5, a tripartite trade structure has evolved quite rapidly among China, Korea and Japan, which further deteriorated export demand for the ASEAN countries. In the beginning, China started to replace ASEAN countries by explosively expanding the production capacity and exporting processed products. Holst and Weiss (2005) showed systematically that ASEAN and China experienced "*intensified export competition in prominent third markets such as Japan and the US. More extensive trade flow analysis reveals, however, that in the long run globalization can accommodate export growth by all the economies of East Asia, if aggregate growth can be sustained to facilitate the structural adjustments necessary for an optimal regional division of labour Furthermore, this loss tends to be greatest in the export activities in which ASEAN economies are most specialized, findings that confirm and sharpen current thinking on short-run loss of competitiveness to China.*" In fact, it appears that this effect was more intense over the ASEAN-4 economies but much less so on Japan and the NIEs. Also, crowding out is happening in FDI. While China's host of FDI steadily and continuously increased, Southeast Asian countries were not restoring the pre-Asian financial crisis level.

China's Catch-Up and Value Added Embedded in Cross-Pacific Trade

Apparently, the emergence of China seems to have asymmetric implication on the East Asian economies. It brought about both expansion of intraregional trade and trade with the rest of world and the re-organization of production network in East Asia. Northeast Asian economies that are higher on the economic value chain have benefited greatly from China's low-end-manufacturing strengths. Table 5 in the previous section supports that China has become a major partner in the development of East Asian production networks, and hence its trade performance has also become highly dependent on the investment from Korea, Japan and Taiwan. They have contributed both to the accelerated increase of China's exports and to their rapid technological upgrading over the last ten years.

They have managed to strengthen their position at the high end of the consumer electronics and IT products. Meanwhile, production patterns in the region are affecting investment and labor markets in Southeast Asia. Recently, China has been increasing final consumption goods to Southeast Asia, which will likely weaken the production bases in these countries. Actually, Southeast countries showed poorer export performance in 2013. If this trend continues, it would "*complicate the sub-region's efforts to moderate widening income disparities, increase productivity and escape the middle-income trap. Southeast Asian economies that are more like China in terms of their labor endowments and skills structure are less well positioned to cope with the new competition*" (Huang 2013).

China has continued to upgrade its technological capacity partly in response to the rising costs of production. China has been successful enough in this regard to take a bigger market share than Korea in major export markets around 2000.

Table 5. Comparison of export Structure between Korea and Japan to China

		Primary products	Semi-processed		Parts	Capital Goods	Consumer Goods
Korea	2000	0.2	14.0		6.8	4.7	9.6
	2008	0.3	12.3		9.1	10.5	6.1
Japan	2000	1.2	14.8		16.5	16.0	11.6
	2008	1.3	15.1		12.2	12.8	14.4
		High Technology	ICT	Medium-High Technology	Medium-Law Technology	Law Technology	Total Manufactures
Korea	2000	1.5	6.1	14.1	10.8	16.2	10.6
	2008	8.7	26.9	25.4	11.3	20.8	21.8
Japan	2000	1.7	5.6	5.4	7.6	26.3	6.3
	2008	4.4	21.6	13.0	15.6	34.0	15.5

Source: Korea Institute for Economics and Technology (2010).

China's world market share of key 47 industries (defined at HS 4 digit product group) started to exceed that of Korea in 2001(KIET 2013). Also, the same trend is observed in overall exports. In 2001, Korea out-numbered China by 41 to 5. In 2011, China exceeded Korea by 31 to 5. During the same period, Korea also caught up with Japanese export. As a result, Japan, Korea and China are in direct export competition. It appears that China needs more time to catch up technologically with Korea in terms of patent registration (ibid) as the gap between Korea and China is still significantly large. However, China's patent registration trend shows that it started to accelerate in around 2010.

Until China dominated world export market, ASEAN countries and China had competed in major export markets. Although those economies adopted similar growth strategy of hosting massive FDI, the balance between two economies had moved in favor of China. Now, there is growing evidence that China and ASEAN are experiencing a new form of production sharing. Thanks to the fast growth of Chinese economy, ASEAN has expanded their exports to China. In spite of China's huge trade surplus, it has relied on imports of parts and capital goods from Japan and Korea, China's import of intermediate goods from these countries has been decreasing gradually. At the same time, China has recently carried out rapid increase in exports to most of the ASEAN countries, and it dramatically turned around its trade deficit with ASEAN countries into surplus in 2011. Major exports of ASEAN countries include primary products. Some regional advanced countries like Malaysia and Thailand export medium quality semiconductors and parts to China. However, it is expected that China's import demand for these products would diminish as it keeps increasing domestic production and its economic growth slows down.

The fast globalization process for the past several decades calls for careful analysis on trade flows. Globalization of production processes implies increasing frequency of intra-firm trade, which makes ordinary trade statistics involve the problem of double counting of value added in trades. In order to accurately measure true benefits or value added to the exporting countries, it is necessary to examine trade flows of value added embedded in exports and imports.[3] Not surprisingly, a significant part of the values embodied in Chinese exports is increasingly originating from other countries.

If evaluated in terms of value added by exporting countries, Chinese export and trade surplus could be found to be overestimated. If supply chains producing for the US market relocates to China, the trade flow of value added embedded in exports need to be reevaluated. The WTO-JETRO (2011) illustrated that " *China's presence has dramatically increased over the last two decades, while the influence of the United States and Japan shows a sharp decline*" Though assessment of value trade enables us to avoid overestimation of China's export, China's share of value trade in exports of its trading partners has still been showing an increasing trend. The OECD provides a good source of data in this regard. The OECD's 'The Trade in Value Added (TiVA) database' is derived the OECD Input Output Tables linked together using the Bilateral Trade Database in goods by industry and end-use.

Table 6 describes a detailed change in China's exports in terms of value added embedded in exports, by source country and by major export products. Domestic value added embedded in China's export decreased significantly from 81% to 67% between 2000 and 2009, which reflects China's increased foreign sourcing or FDI. Obviously in the Chinese case, the most significant change in geographical value added can be found in increase of inputs from ASEAN countries followed by Korea. In contrast, the U.S has augmented its' share only modestly, reflecting US's continued pattern of investment in China to process and import final goods. However, Japan increased its share only marginally. The most notable change is observed in sourcing from the ASEAN region. Value added embedded in China's export increased from 1.4% to 3.4%. Especially, China has dramatically increased machinery inputs 6 times those of ASEAN during the same period. It is interesting that domestically embedded value added has not changed very much in machinery. The origins of embedded value added for the product group have changed from the U.S. and Japan to ASEAN and Korea. Considering machinery is among the most important export products, it implies that China still remains mostly at the level of processing and assembling of imported materials and parts.

Table 7 shows quite a contrasting case of Malaysia from China. During the same period, Malaysia's domestic value added embedded in exports has increased from 0.491 to 0.526. The change came from dramatic diversion of sourcing origins. First, value added of Malaysia's export embedded from China tripled (from 0.01 to 0.032). Also, ASEAN increased its share of domestic value moderately. On the other hand, roles of Japan and the US had decreased significantly from 0.126 and 0.106 to 0.066 and 0.075, respectively. This has been driven mainly by the change in machinery exports. That is, value added from China grew by 4 times while Japan and the US experienced a substantial loss of their share of value added in machinery exports. Similar pattern is observed in the exports of electrical and electronic equipment, and to a lesser extent, in chemical, products, non-metallic products and base metals. Particularly, the Japanese value added embedded in Malaysia's exports has decreased across the board. Considering the geographical nature of cross-pacific imbalance, this trend implies that production activities are turning away from ASEAN to China.

[3] A famous case by Dedrick et.al. (2010) was presented using the value chain of i-phone production. It was shown that The study showed that of the $144 (Chinese) factory-gate price of an iPod, less than 10% contributed to Chinese value added, with the bulk of the components (about $100) being imported from Japan, with much of the rest coming from the US and Korea.

Table 6. Value added embodied in gross exports: China

China	2000	Japan	Korea	US	China	ASEAN	2009	Japan	Korea	US	China	ASEAN
TOTAL	1	0.040	0.018	0.025	0.812	0.014	1	0.044	0.029	0.036	0.674	0.034
Food products	0.118	0.002	0.003	0.001	0.107	0.000	0.069	0.001	0.001	0.000	0.064	0.001
Wood, paper	0.126	0.005	0.003	0.003	0.101	0.002	0.106	0.006	0.004	0.006	0.071	0.004
Chemicals	0.062	0.005	0.001	0.002	0.046	0.000	0.073	0.005	0.002	0.002	0.052	0.001
Machinery	0.135	0.009	0.005	0.007	0.102	0.002	0.151	0.007	0.010	0.006	0.099	0.012
Construction	0.118	0.004	0.001	0.002	0.101	0.001	0.103	0.004	0.002	0.002	0.076	0.003

Source: OECD STAN The Trade in Value Added (TiVA) database.

Table 7. Value added embodied in gross exports: Malaysia

Malaysia	Total 2000	Japan	Korea	US	China	Malaysia	ASEAN	Total 2009	Japan	Korea	US	China	Malaysia	ASEAN
	1.000	0.126	0.021	0.106	0.010	0.491	0.536	1.000	0.066	0.020	0.075	0.032	0.526	0.589
Chem.	0.034	0.006	0.002	0.004	0.001	0.007	0.011	0.038	0.003	0.001	0.003	0.003	0.011	0.017
metals	0.088	0.026	0.005	0.009	0.002	0.004	0.010	0.082	0.015	0.005	0.007	0.007	0.007	0.015
Mach.	0.055	0.011	0.002	0.018	0.000	0.001	0.006	0.054	0.005	0.001	0.013	0.004	0.002	0.009
Elec	0.045	0.007	0.004	0.016	0.001	0.001	0.007	0.037	0.004	0.002	0.010	0.004	0.001	0.010
Trans	0.434	0.028	0.002	0.005	0.001	0.380	0.385	0.410	0.012	0.003	0.005	0.002	0.370	0.377
Dist.	0.097	0.012	0.002	0.006	0.001	0.054	0.058	0.117	0.006	0.001	0.004	0.003	0.077	0.083
Bus.	0.083	0.009	0.001	0.030	0.000	0.005	0.008	0.070	0.005	0.002	0.020	0.001	0.008	0.010

Source: Same as above.

Table 8. Value added embodied in gross exports: Korea

Korea	Total	Japan	Korea	US	China	ASEAN	Total	Japan	Korea	EU	China	ASEAN
TOTAL:	1.000	0.067	0.671	0.064	0.018	0.026	1.000	0.051	0.594	0.046	0.048	0.038
Mining	0.077	0.000	0.002	0.001	0.002	0.010	0.119	0.000	0.002	0.001	0.003	0.012
Chemicals Metallic	0.125	0.010	0.087	0.008	0.002	0.003	0.106	0.009	0.063	0.006	0.005	0.004
Basic metals	0.074	0.010	0.047	0.004	0.002	0.001	0.082	0.010	0.049	0.003	0.007	0.001
Machinery	0.032	0.003	0.023	0.003	0.000	0.000	0.039	0.002	0.029	0.002	0.001	0.000
Electrical	0.172	0.013	0.131	0.013	0.003	0.003	0.130	0.004	0.093	0.003	0.010	0.009
Transportation equipment	0.049	0.001	0.045	0.001	0.000	0.000	0.066	0.002	0.060	0.001	0.001	0.000
Electricity, gas,	0.021	0.002	0.014	0.001	0.001	0.000	0.020	0.002	0.013	0.000	0.001	0.000
Financial Service	0.043	0.003	0.031	0.003	0.001	0.001	0.041	0.003	0.026	0.003	0.002	0.001
Business Service	0.089	0.007	0.053	0.014	0.001	0.001	0.116	0.005	0.073	0.012	0.002	0.002

Source: Same as above

Table 9. Value added embodied in gross exports: Japan

Japan	2000	Japan	Korea	US	China	ASEAN	2009	Japan	Korea	US	China	ASEAN
Total	1.000	0.901	0.006	0.025	0.007	0.012	1.000	0.852	0.006	0.022	0.017	0.017
Chemicals	0.084	0.076	0.001	0.001	0.001	0.001	0.090	0.078	0.001	0.002	0.002	0.002
Basic metals	0.077	0.069	0.001	0.001	0.001	0.001	0.088	0.078	0.001	0.001	0.002	0.001
Machinery	0.068	0.066	0.000	0.001	0.000	0.000	0.056	0.054	0.000	0.000	0.001	0.000
Electrical	0.199	0.180	0.001	0.010	0.001	0.002	0.127	0.109	0.001	0.006	0.004	0.003
Transportation equipment	0.099	0.096	0.000	0.001	0.000	0.000	0.102	0.098	0.000	0.001	0.001	0.000
Mfg. Nec	0.026	0.024	0.000	0.001	0.000	0.000	0.025	0.023	0.000	0.000	0.001	0.000
Wholesale Service	0.119	0.105	0.001	0.003	0.001	0.002	0.118	0.102	0.001	0.002	0.002	0.003
Business Service.	0.089	0.079	0.001	0.003	0.000	0.000	0.093	0.080	0.001	0.004	0.001	0.001

Source: Same as above

Table 10. Value added embodied in gross exports: US

US	2000	Japan	Korea	U S	China	ASEAN	EU	2009	JPN	Kor	US	China	ASEAN	Eu
TOTAL	1.000	0.014	0.004	0.911	0.003	0.005	0.028	1.000	0.009	0.003	0.887	0.009	0.006	0.032
Chemicals	0.078	0.001	0.000	0.068	0.000	0.001	0.004	0.112	0.001	0.000	0.100	0.001	0.001	0.005
Basic metals	0.062	0.001	0.000	0.052	0.000	0.000	0.003	0.053	0.001	0.000	0.043	0.001	0.000	0.003
Machinery	0.044	0.000	0.000	0.042	0.000	0.000	0.001	0.037	0.000	0.000	0.035	0.000	0.000	0.001
Electrical	0.205	0.004	0.001	0.192	0.001	0.002	0.002	0.096	0.002	0.001	0.084	0.002	0.002	0.002
Transportation Equipment	0.051	0.002	0.000	0.044	0.000	0.000	0.002	0.047	0.001	0.000	0.043	0.000	0.000	0.001
Wholesale	0.106	0.001	0.000	0.098	0.000	0.000	0.002	0.100	0.001	0.000	0.092	0.001	0.001	0.002
Transportation Service	0.088	0.001	0.000	0.082	0.000	0.000	0.002	0.085	0.001	0.000	0.079	0.000	0.000	0.002
Financial Service	0.052	0.001	0.000	0.048	0.000	0.000	0.001	0.075	0.000	0.000	0.068	0.000	0.000	0.003
Business Service	0.158	0.001	0.000	0.150	0.000	0.000	0.004	0.208	0.001	0.000	0.195	0.000	0.000	0.007

Source: Same as above

Korea's data shows similar pattern with Malaysia except for domestic sourcing. That is, Korea's exports increased value added embedded from China and ASEAN. They increased from 0.018 and 0.026 in 2000 to 0.048 and 0.038, respectively. It's different from Malaysia as its domestically added value has substantially decreased. This change is most apparent in electrical equipment, in which Korea has reduced both domestic value added and those from Japan and the U.S. Value added embedded from China and ASEAN in exports of electrical equipment had increased from 0.003 to 0.01 and 0.009, respectively. The pattern is exactly the same in the case of Japanese export of electrical equipment. Also, Chinese value added embedded in Japanese overall exports reached to the level of ASEAN's in 2009. In the case of the U.S. exports, China's value added had increased substantially from 0.003 to 0.009. In other words, the U.S. is experiencing a significant increase of FDI from China.

The examination of trade in value added embedded in exports of major Asian economies provides a picture of development of regional production network. The following <Figure 5> summarizes the observations. First, the global imbalance as represented by China's surplus also accompanies increase in China's valued added in U.S. exports and only modest increase in US value added in China's export. Interestingly, the Japanese valued added in China's export increased only marginally. Second, closer production network seems to be developing among China, Korea and ASEAN countries. Bilateral flows of value added among these countries have significantly increased. China's position in the supply chain is moving away from downstream. China's exports of intermediate products in the high technology sector are increasingly contributing to advanced countries' high technology exports.

CONCLUSION

The high share of intraregional trade reflects intensive trade in parts and vertical integration in Asia. The trend has been strengthened through FDI in the region by Japan and other advanced East Asian countries. Recently, the agglomeration of production activities in China and neighboring Southeast Asian countries is creating a new dimension of regional production network, particularly in the high-technology industries. It was possible by China's improvement of transportation, distribution and logistics service as well as the regulatory reform after joining the WTO. Advance in China's regional integration with neighbors is reflected by increases in value added embedded in intra-regional and cross-pacific trade. More than a third of intra-regional FDI is undertaken by China, while regional advanced countries are keeping a high level of FDI in China.

Obviously, the rise of Chinese economy disrupted the long-established flying geese model of industrialization in Asia. As China becomes the center of regional trade and investment, other developing countries find it hard to move up the ladder of industrial development. Examination of cross-pacific trade shows fast upgrading of China's export structure. In contrast, ASEAN countries have not been successful enough to follow the paths of Korea and Taiwan. It seems to justify the hypothesis of China 'fear' to these regional countries. While it is true that China's expansion is increasingly providing trade opportunities for ASEAN countries, it appears that most of the countries in the region find it difficult to get out of the middle-income trap.

Dispersed production network worldwide makes it important to look more closely at the trade of values embedded in order to assess production activities in practice more accurately. The OECD's TiVA database allows us to trace the change in production network. The global imbalance as represented by China's surplus also accompanies increase in China's valued added in U.S. exports and decrease in US value added in China's export. The same pattern is observed between China and Japan. Bilateral flows of value added among China and regional developed Northeast Asian countries have significantly increased. Also, China's position in the supply chain is moving away from downstream and China's exports of intermediate products in the high technology sector are increasingly contributing to advanced countries' high technology exports.

REFERENCES

Chi Hung KWAN, 2002, The Rise of China and Asia's Flying-Geese Pattern of Economic Development: An Empirical Analysis Based on US Import Statistics, *RIETI Discussion Paper Series*, 02-E-009.

David Roland Holstl and John Weiss, 2004, ASEAN and China: Export Rivalsor Partners in Regional Growth?, Blackwell Publishing Ltd.

Guranga Das and Hongyul Han, 2013,"Trade in Middle Products between South Korea and China: A Survey on the Extent of Offshore Production Sharing" in The Oxford Handbook of Offshoring and Global Employment , Ashok Bardhan, Dwight M. Jaffee, and Cynthia A. Kroll (eds.) Forthcoming in December, 201.

Hang Young Lee and Joonkoo Lee, 2012, China's Post-WTO Export Growth and the Restructuring of Asian Production Network:A Global Value Chain Approach(in Korean), in *The Korean Society,* Volume 13-1.

Insoo Han, Keunyeob Oh, YooJinman, 2012, Changes in Competitiveness of LCD Industry of East Asia: from Bamboo Capitalism to Water Lily(in Korean), *Journal of International Telecommunications Policy Review,* Vol.19 No.1 (2012. 3) pp.15-41.

IMF, 2011, Changing Patterns of Global Trade, mimeo, Prepared by the Strategy, Policy Department.

Irmgard Nübler, 2011, Industrial policies and capabilities for catching up Frameworks and paradigms, Employment Working Paper No. 77, ILO.

KIET, 2010, Analysis of the International Division of Labor among Korea, China, and Japan, and Promotion of its Cooperation, (in Korean*) KIET Policy Analysis,* 2010-583, pp 66.

Kim, Chuk-Kyo, 2012, Korea's Economic Development,(in Korean) Pakyoungsa, Seoul Korea.

Kim, Yongyul and Yoon Woojin, 2013, Evaluation of Manufacturing Industries from the perspective of Catch-Up process,(in Korean) Issue Paper 2013-304, Korea Institute for Economics and Technology, pp 25-34.

Kozo Kiyota†, Yoko Sazanami‡ and Yu Ching Wong, Intra-regional Trade in Asia: Dynamics of Production Sharing, Working Paper, Yokohama National University.

Park, Bunsoon, 2005, The rise of the Chinese Economy and changes in Regional Economic Development Model(in Korean), Issue Paper, Samsung Economic Research Institute.

Prema-Chandra Athukorala, 2010, Production Networks and Trade Patterns in East Asia: Regionalization or Globalization?, ADB Working Paper Series on Regional Economic Integration No. 56.

Sarah Y. Tong and Lim Tin Seng, 2009, Sino-ASEAN Economic Integration And its Impact on Intra ASEAN Trade, EAI Working Paper No. 144, National University of Singapore.

Timothy J. Sturgeon and Richard K. Lester, The New Global Supply-Base: New Challenges for Local Suppliers in East Asia IPC Working Paper Series MIT-IPC-03-006, Industrial Performance Center, Massachusetts Institute of Technology.

WTO-JETRO, 2011, Trade patterns and global value chains in East Asia: From trade in goods to trade in task.

Yukon Huang, 2012, China's economic rise: opportunity or threat for East Asia? East Asia Forum, Carnegie Endowment.

Yunhua Liu, 2007, ASEAN and China: Managing Competition and Exploring Complementarities, Paper for 2007 International Conference "FTA, Regional Integration and Development" Busan, Korea, December 18~19, 2007.

Appendix: Value Added Embodied in Exports

China	2000	Japan	Korea	US	China	ASEAN	2009	Japan	Korea	US	China	ASEAN
TOTAL	1	0.040	0.018	0.025	0.812	0.014	1	0.044	0.029	0.036	0.674	0.034
Primary	0.077	0.000	0.000	0.001	0.072	0.001	0.064	0.000	0.000	0.002	0.055	0.002
Mining	0.065	0.000	0.000	0.000	0.048	0.002	0.080	0.000	0.000	0.001	0.028	0.004
Food products	0.025	0.000	0.000	0.000	0.023	0.000	0.018	0.000	0.000	0.000	0.016	0.001
Textiles	0.118	0.002	0.003	0.001	0.107	0.000	0.069	0.001	0.001	0.000	0.064	0.001
Wood, paper	0.024	0.001	0.001	0.001	0.017	0.001	0.027	0.001	0.000	0.001	0.019	0.001
Chemicals	0.126	0.005	0.003	0.003	0.101	0.002	0.106	0.006	0.004	0.006	0.071	0.004
Basic metals	0.062	0.005	0.001	0.002	0.046	0.000	0.073	0.005	0.002	0.002	0.052	0.001
Machinery	0.023	0.002	0.000	0.001	0.017	0.000	0.040	0.002	0.001	0.001	0.030	0.000
Electrical, optical	0.135	0.009	0.005	0.007	0.102	0.002	0.151	0.007	0.010	0.006	0.099	0.012
Transport equip	0.016	0.000	0.000	0.000	0.015	0.000	0.021	0.002	0.001	0.001	0.016	0.000
Mfg.nec;	0.017	0.001	0.000	0.000	0.015	0.000	0.033	0.002	0.000	0.001	0.027	0.000
Electricity, gas	0.037	0.001	0.000	0.000	0.032	0.000	0.023	0.001	0.001	0.000	0.017	0.000
Construction	0.002	0.000	0.000	0.000	0.001	0.000	0.003	0.000	0.000	0.000	0.001	0.000
Wholesale retail	0.118	0.004	0.001	0.002	0.101	0.001	0.103	0.004	0.002	0.002	0.076	0.003
Transport storage	0.062	0.002	0.001	0.002	0.050	0.001	0.047	0.004	0.002	0.002	0.025	0.002
Financial	0.045	0.002	0.001	0.002	0.033	0.001	0.044	0.002	0.001	0.002	0.033	0.001
Business services	0.042	0.003	0.001	0.003	0.026	0.000	0.078	0.004	0.004	0.008	0.032	0.002
Other services	0.006	0.001	0.000	0.000	0.003	0.000	0.020	0.001	0.000	0.001	0.014	0.000

Korea	Total	Japan	Korea	US	China	ASEAN	Total	Japan	Korea	US	China	ASEAN
TOTAL: TOTAL	1.000	0.067	0.671	0.064	0.018	0.026	1.000	0.051	0.594	0.046	0.048	0.038
Primary(Agri.)	0.018	0.000	0.011	0.001	0.001	0.001	0.012	0.000	0.005	0.001	0.002	0.001
Mining	0.077	0.000	0.002	0.001	0.002	0.010	0.119	0.000	0.002	0.001	0.003	0.012
Food products	0.009	0.000	0.006	0.001	0.000	0.000	0.006	0.000	0.004	0.000	0.001	0.000
Textiles	0.053	0.001	0.047	0.001	0.001	0.001	0.016	0.000	0.014	0.000	0.001	0.000
Wood, paper	0.020	0.002	0.013	0.002	0.000	0.001	0.018	0.001	0.011	0.001	0.001	0.001
Chemicals	0.125	0.010	0.087	0.008	0.002	0.003	0.106	0.009	0.063	0.006	0.005	0.004
Basic metals	0.074	0.010	0.047	0.004	0.002	0.001	0.082	0.010	0.049	0.003	0.007	0.001
Machinery	0.032	0.003	0.023	0.003	0.000	0.000	0.039	0.002	0.029	0.002	0.001	0.000
Electrical equip	0.172	0.013	0.131	0.013	0.003	0.003	0.130	0.004	0.093	0.003	0.010	0.009
Transport equip	0.049	0.001	0.045	0.001	0.000	0.000	0.066	0.002	0.060	0.001	0.001	0.000
Electricity, gas	0.021	0.002	0.014	0.001	0.001	0.000	0.020	0.002	0.013	0.000	0.001	0.000
Construction	0.004	0.001	0.002	0.000	0.000	0.000	0.004	0.001	0.002	0.000	0.000	0.000
Wholesale retail	0.105	0.006	0.081	0.004	0.002	0.002	0.099	0.006	0.064	0.004	0.005	0.003
Transport, storage	0.090	0.006	0.064	0.007	0.001	0.001	0.103	0.006	0.072	0.005	0.002	0.002
Financial	0.043	0.003	0.031	0.003	0.001	0.001	0.041	0.003	0.026	0.003	0.002	0.001
Business	0.089	0.007	0.053	0.014	0.001	0.001	0.116	0.005	0.073	0.012	0.002	0.002

Appendix. (Continued)

Japan	2000	Japan	Korea	US	China	ASEAN	EU	2009	Japan	Korea	US	China	ASEAN	EU
Total	1.000	0.901	0.006	0.025	0.007	0.012	0.020	1.000	0.852	0.006	0.022	0.017	0.017	0.028
Agriculture	0.006	0.004	0.000	0.000	0.000	0.000	0.000	0.006	0.004	0.000	0.000	0.001	0.000	0.000
Mining	0.017	0.001	0.000	0.000	0.001	0.003	0.001	0.046	0.001	0.000	0.000	0.001	0.006	0.002
Food	0.006	0.006	0.000	0.000	0.000	0.000	0.000	0.007	0.007	0.000	0.000	0.000	0.000	0.000
Textiles	0.009	0.007	0.000	0.000	0.000	0.000	0.000	0.006	0.005	0.000	0.000	0.001	0.000	0.000
Wood, paper	0.024	0.021	0.000	0.001	0.000	0.000	0.001	0.021	0.018	0.000	0.001	0.000	0.000	0.001
Chemicals	0.084	0.076	0.001	0.001	0.001	0.001	0.002	0.090	0.078	0.001	0.002	0.002	0.002	0.004
Basic metals	0.077	0.069	0.001	0.001	0.001	0.001	0.002	0.088	0.078	0.001	0.001	0.002	0.001	0.003
Machinery	0.068	0.066	0.000	0.001	0.000	0.000	0.001	0.056	0.054	0.000	0.000	0.001	0.000	0.001
Electrical	0.199	0.180	0.001	0.010	0.001	0.002	0.002	0.127	0.109	0.001	0.006	0.004	0.003	0.002
Tran.eqip.	0.099	0.096	0.000	0.001	0.000	0.000	0.001	0.102	0.098	0.000	0.001	0.001	0.000	0.001
Mfg. Nec	0.026	0.024	0.000	0.001	0.000	0.000	0.000	0.025	0.023	0.000	0.000	0.001	0.000	0.000
Electricity, gas	0.027	0.025	0.000	0.000	0.000	0.000	0.000	0.024	0.022	0.000	0.000	0.000	0.000	0.001
Construction	0.009	0.008	0.000	0.000	0.000	0.000	0.000	0.007	0.007	0.000	0.000	0.000	0.000	0.000
Wholesale	0.119	0.105	0.001	0.003	0.001	0.002	0.004	0.118	0.102	0.001	0.002	0.002	0.003	0.004
Transport	0.074	0.067	0.000	0.001	0.000	0.001	0.002	0.118	0.111	0.000	0.001	0.001	0.001	0.002
Financial	0.048	0.045	0.000	0.001	0.000	0.000	0.001	0.048	0.043	0.000	0.001	0.001	0.001	0.001
Business svc.	0.089	0.079	0.001	0.003	0.000	0.000	0.003	0.093	0.080	0.001	0.004	0.001	0.001	0.005

Other svc	0.020	0.019	0.000	0.000	0.000	0.000	0.000	0.017	0.015	0.000	0.000	0.000	0.000	0.001
US	2000	*Japan*	*Korea*	*U S*	*China*	*ASEAN*	*UEu*	*2009*	*Japan*	*Korea*	*U S*	*China*	*ASEAN*	*Japan*
TOTAL	1.000	0.014	0.004	0.911	0.003	0.005	0.028	1.000	0.009	0.003	0.887	0.009	0.006	0.032
Agriculture	0.018	0.000	0.000	0.016	0.000	0.000	0.000	0.024	0.000	0.000	0.022	0.000	0.000	0.000
Mining	0.019	0.000	0.000	0.008	0.000	0.000	0.002	0.050	0.000	0.000	0.021	0.000	0.001	0.002
Food	0.013	0.000	0.000	0.012	0.000	0.000	0.000	0.018	0.000	0.000	0.017	0.000	0.000	0.000
Textiles	0.017	0.000	0.000	0.016	0.000	0.000	0.000	0.006	0.000	0.000	0.005	0.000	0.000	0.000
Wood, paper	0.037	0.000	0.000	0.034	0.000	0.000	0.001	0.035	0.000	0.000	0.033	0.000	0.000	0.001
Chemicals	0.078	0.001	0.000	0.068	0.000	0.001	0.004	0.112	0.001	0.000	0.100	0.001	0.001	0.005
Basic metals	0.062	0.001	0.000	0.052	0.000	0.000	0.003	0.053	0.001	0.000	0.043	0.001	0.000	0.003
Machinery	0.044	0.000	0.000	0.042	0.000	0.000	0.001	0.037	0.000	0.000	0.035	0.000	0.000	0.001
Electrical	0.205	0.004	0.001	0.192	0.001	0.002	0.002	0.096	0.002	0.001	0.084	0.002	0.002	0.002
Transportation. Equipment	0.051	0.002	0.000	0.044	0.000	0.000	0.002	0.047	0.001	0.000	0.043	0.000	0.000	0.001
Mfg.nec	0.012	0.000	0.000	0.012	0.000	0.000	0.000	0.016	0.000	0.000	0.015	0.000	0.000	0.000
Elec.& gas	0.015	0.000	0.000	0.013	0.000	0.000	0.001	0.010	0.000	0.000	0.008	0.000	0.000	0.001
Construction	0.004	0.000	0.000	0.003	0.000	0.000	0.000	0.005	0.000	0.000	0.005	0.000	0.000	0.000
Wholesale,	0.106	0.001	0.000	0.098	0.000	0.000	0.002	0.100	0.001	0.000	0.092	0.001	0.001	0.002
Transport	0.088	0.001	0.000	0.082	0.000	0.000	0.002	0.085	0.001	0.000	0.079	0.000	0.000	0.002
Financial	0.052	0.001	0.000	0.048	0.000	0.000	0.001	0.075	0.000	0.000	0.068	0.000	0.000	0.003
Business service	0.158	0.001	0.000	0.150	0.000	0.000	0.004	0.208	0.001	0.000	0.195	0.000	0.000	0.007
Other service	0.022	0.000	0.000	0.020	0.000	0.000	0.001	0.023	0.000	0.000	0.021	0.000	0.000	0.001

Appendix. (Continued)

Malaysia	*2000*	*Japan*	*Korea*	*US*	*China*	*Malaysia*	*ASEAN*		*2009*	*Japan*	*Korea*	*US*	*China*	*Malaysia*	*ASEAN*
	1.000	0.126	0.021	0.106	0.010	0.491	0.536		1.000	0.066	0.020	0.075	0.032	0.526	0.589
Mining	0.022	0.000	0.000	0.000	0.001	0.003	0.005		0.049	0.000	0.000	0.001	0.002	0.006	0.012
Textiles	0.004	0.000	0.000	0.000	0.000	0.002	0.002		0.004	0.000	0.000	0.000	0.001	0.002	0.003
Wood, paper	0.011	0.002	0.000	0.002	0.000	0.002	0.003		0.010	0.001	0.000	0.001	0.001	0.003	0.004
Chemicals	0.034	0.006	0.002	0.004	0.001	0.007	0.011		0.038	0.003	0.001	0.003	0.003	0.011	0.017
Basic metals	0.088	0.026	0.005	0.009	0.002	0.004	0.010		0.082	0.015	0.005	0.007	0.007	0.007	0.015
Machinery and equipment	0.055	0.011	0.002	0.018	0.000	0.001	0.006		0.054	0.005	0.001	0.013	0.004	0.002	0.009
Electrical and optical	0.045	0.007	0.004	0.016	0.001	0.001	0.007		0.037	0.004	0.002	0.010	0.004	0.001	0.010
Transport equipment	0.434	0.028	0.002	0.005	0.001	0.380	0.385		0.410	0.012	0.003	0.005	0.002	0.370	0.377
Electricity, gas	0.022	0.004	0.001	0.001	0.001	0.009	0.010		0.016	0.002	0.001	0.001	0.001	0.007	0.008
Construction	0.005	0.001	0.000	0.000	0.000	0.002	0.002		0.007	0.001	0.000	0.000	0.000	0.003	0.004
Wholesale and retail	0.097	0.012	0.002	0.006	0.001	0.054	0.058		0.117	0.006	0.001	0.004	0.003	0.077	0.083
Transport and storage	0.050	0.007	0.001	0.008	0.001	0.006	0.011		0.049	0.007	0.002	0.005	0.001	0.008	0.014
Financial intermediation	0.034	0.006	0.001	0.004	0.000	0.012	0.014		0.035	0.003	0.001	0.004	0.001	0.016	0.017
Business service	0.083	0.009	0.001	0.030	0.000	0.005	0.008		0.070	0.005	0.002	0.020	0.001	0.008	0.010

In: Current Issues in International Trade
Editor: Gouranga G. Das

ISBN: 978-1-63321-405-7

Chapter 3

CHINA-AFRICA'S TRADE PATTERNS AND POTENTIALS FOR TECHNOLOGY UPGRADING IN AFRICA

Jean-Claude Maswana*
Tsukuba University

ABSTRACT

The chapter examines the changing patterns of Africa's exports to China and their implications for technology upgrading in Africa. To detect shifting patterns of China-Africa's trade from 2000 to 2010, the analysis resorts to two alternative trade analytical tools—namely factor intensity analysis and recycled comparative advantage—and confront the detected patterns to some theoretical and empirical benchmarks. The dataset is constructed from the UN-COMTRADE Statistics. The results suggest that, contrary to numerous claims elsewhere, the sectoral composition of African exports has remained largely intact. Even worrisome, African economies are further specializing in export sectors with diminishing returns and poor technological progress; meaning that the expected technological upgrading, induced from trading with China, is not (yet) occurring in Africa.

Keywords: Trade Patterns, Technology Upgrading, Factor Intensity of Trade, China, Africa

INTRODUCTION

A substantial body of literature in development economics suggests that for countries whose growth is led by export, changes in trade patterns condition growth sustainability (Ocampo, Rada, and Taylor 2009). That is, in the long-term economic growth depends in no small measure on the composition of a nation's export bundle (Caves, Frankel, and Jones

* Graduate School of Business Sciences, MBA-IB,3-29-1 Otsuka, Bunkyo-ku, Tokyo 112-0012, Japan; Email: maswana@mbaib.gsbs.tsukuba.ac.jp

1996). Also, development theories and history have shown that sustained economic growth and acceleration of industrial upgrading entail shifting away from specialization in sectors with diminishing returns and poor technological progress, such as primary and extractive sectors and related exports, to sectors with increasing returns, generally technology-intensive manufacturing and related exports (Chenery and Syrquin 1975; Kuznets 1967). Such was the case in East Asia as South Korea, Taiwan, and Hong Kong moved quickly out of resource-based exports and into labor-intensive manufacture. In these East Asian economies, the sustained rise in exports and economic growth would not have been possible had they stuck with their initial comparative advantages for a longer period of time (UNTCAD 1996). In fact, new export patterns emerge continually as a result of industrial upgrading[1] via either "flying geese" type foreign direct investment (Akamatsu 1962; UNTCAD 1996) or various forms of technology imitation (Posner 1961). Such new and higher forms of technological capability enhance productivity gains and bring about further upgrading in technology-intensive industries (Stehrer and Worz 2003; Worz 2004).

In addition to enhancing technology and productivity gains, changes in trade patterns and the potential for industrial upgrading through exports also vary, depending on destination-specific factors (Amurgo-Pacheco and Pierola 2008; Grossman and Helpman 1994; Romalis, 2004), the argument being that trading with larger and rapidly growing markets implies a higher probability of demand for more and new products and thus the exportation of more of such product varieties. This increasing demand may provide sources of technology upgrading that contribute to a rise in productivity, and therefore to an increase in the industrial strengths of exporting firms, in a developing country. Taken together, changes in export patterns and destination effects can provide early indications of the occurrence of industrial upgrading and sustainability of economic growth in the long run. Naturally, this idea sounds appealing to African[2] countries engaged in trade with rapidly growing China.

Nonetheless, despite the phenomenal growth of African exports to China—an average of 33% annually between 2000 and 2010—little attention is paid to whether trade patterns of African exports corroborate the above theoretical predictions and empirical facts. At the risk of stating the obvious, when policy makers ignore the distinction between export expansion and composition shift, they tend to assume that all exports are proof of comparative advantage and imply sustained growth and long-run economic gains. Relatedly, there are serious concerns that point to Africa running a greater risk of falling into the trap of resource dependence (Golstein et al. 2007), which is unlikely to ignite industrial upgrading and thus drivers of long-run economic growth.

With the above motivation in mind, the main aim of this study was twofold. The first goal was to explore evidence of the changing patterns of Africa's exports to China in terms of technology intensity, because such changes are linked to a higher potential for economic growth through industrial upgrading. The analytical framework incorporates the factor intensity analysis used by Krause (1987) and the "flying geese" hypothesis (a measure of transferred comparative advantage between interdependent economies) proposed by Akamatsu (1962) and UNTCAD (1996). With respect to analytical benchmark, the shifting patterns of African exports (to China, to the world as a whole, and to the EU) were compared

[1] Following Gereffi (2005), industrial upgrading is defined as the process by which a country moves from low-value to relatively high-value exports.

[2] Unless otherwise specified, Africa here refers mainly to Sub-Saharan Africa (SSA).

to the corresponding categories of exports from Southeast Asia (Cambodia, Indonesia, Malaysia, Vietnam, and Thailand) to China.

The key conclusion of the study suggests that, contrary to numerous claims elsewhere and despite the rapid growth of trade between Africa and China, the sectoral composition of African exports has remained largely intact. Apparently, the expected technological upgrading is not (yet) occurring. This conclusion, albeit a simple reconfirmation of a known fact, has important implications. In particular, it suggests that simply increasing the volume of exports to China may have been a necessary igniter of growth thus far, but it may not be a sufficient driver of long-run economic growth, as African economies are further specializing in export sectors with diminishing returns and poor technological progress.

The rest of the paper is organized as follows: The second section examines Africa's exports to China in terms of factor intensity content as well as in terms of a recycled comparative advantage of the "flying-geese" type. The third section takes the effects reported in the two previous sections and empirically tests them on aggregate growth models for individual African countries. Finally, the last section discusses the implications for upgrading of manufacturing and economic growth.

China-Africa's Trade: Descriptive and Data

Factors Intensity Analysis

By grouping exports on the basis of factor intensity, our objective is to identify a set of industries that are technologically simple/complex and hence offer less/more scope for learning-by-doing as predicted by the endogenous growth literature. In addition, according to Dosi, Pavitt, and Soete (1990), an economy's pattern of growth is related to its pattern of technological upgrading, which suggests that, all else being equal, changes in the share of technology intensive exports may well indicate the growth potentials from trade. Following Hinloopen and van Marrewijk (2006), we use the factor intensity classification that distinguishes between five broad factor-intensity categories (SITC Rev. 2 at the 2 or 3-digit level[3]):

A Primary products, e.g., meat, dairy, cereals, fruit, coffee, minerals, and oil.
B Natural resource intensive products, e.g., leather, wood, pig iron, and copper.
C Unskilled labor intensive products, e.g., textiles, clothing, ships, and footwear.
D Human capital intensive products, e.g., perfumes, cosmetics, cars, and watches.

[3] In the classification of industries into technology intensive groups, it should be noted that the available data do not allow us to capture all aspects of technological differences. What is available to us, as noted above, is the trade data at two to three-digit level of SITC Rev 2. The data at this level, although reasonably disaggregated, combine activities at different levels of technological complexity under the same category. For instance, the office computing/accounting machinery group includes the simple calculator and computers (Parameswaran 2006). Yet, as the exports of most African countries are unsophisticated, any further disaggregation will provide no additional insights. Additionally, it should be noted that the indices of technology-intensive exports presented here should be taken as a proxy of export "sophistication level" rather than that of technology in the strictest sense. This is so because the technology level reflects the intensity of the research and development in the given field, which need not be (and often is not) located where plants are producing (for further discussion, see Gertler 2006).

E Technology intensive products, e.g., chemicals, electronics, tools, and electric items.

Table 1. Africa, Africa-China, and China-Asia3's Trade Pattern Based on Factor Intensities. (Exports and imports in % of total)

		Trade in 2000						Trade in 2009					
		Africa		Africa-EU		Africa2-EU		Africa		Africa-EU		Africa2-EU	
		Exports	Imports	Exports	Imports	Exports	Imports	Export	Imports	Exports	Imports	Exports	Imports
Primary products (excl. petroleum oil)		**11.08**	**11.61**	**11.61**	**10.40**	**28.75**	**18.47**	**13.38**	**14.10**	**14.03**	**12.86**	**32.19**	**15.05**
Primary products (incl. 33.3 - 33.4 petroleum oil)		19.12	19.74	45.26	27.38	62.91	21.65	22.73	24.95	35.69	23.64	68.78	19.43
Resource intensive		**4.13**	**4.30**	**4.25**	**4.28**	**16.41**	**2.93**	**3.87**	**3.77**	**11.05**	**9.84**	**9.16**	**4.21**
Unskilled labor intensive		**9.54**	**9.60**	**9.63**	**7.95**	**5.33**	**3.87**	**8.75**	**8.02**	**29.08**	**18.58**	**4.88**	**2.84**
Human capital intensive		**19.38**	**19.23**	**21.64**	**24.48**	**1.18**	**21.98**	**17.77**	**17.27**	**21.19**	**23.66**	**1.42**	**21.86**
53	Dyeing, tanning and coloring materials	0.52	0.51	0.58	0.76	0.01	0.77	0.44	0.40	1.53	1.89	0.01	0.52
55	Oils and perfume materials	0.69	0.64	0.86	1.11	0.08	1.16	0.88	0.80	3.32	4.28	0.10	1.14
62	Rubber manufactures	0.68	0.69	0.82	0.87	0.01	1.09	0.73	0.73	2.81	2.78	0.02	1.08
64	Paper	1.59	1.57	2.00	2.36	0.15	2.43	1.24	1.18	5.13	5.96	0.27	1.47
67.2 - 67.9	Iron and steel	2.03	2.07	2.37	2.75	0.02	2.67	2.27	2.23	7.41	8.42	0.05	2.18
69	manufactures & metals	1.88	1.95	2.23	2.30	0.14	2.68	2.07	1.99	7.38	7.41	0.20	3.41
76.1- 76.3	Monitor, sound recording	1.17	1.17	1.06	0.59	0.00	0.25	1.17	1.30	4.23	2.62	0.01	0.37
78	Road vehicles	8.56	8.41	9.56	11.36	0.25	8.42	6.47	6.34	25.45	28.68	0.36	9.83
79.1	Railway vehicles	0.13	0.12	0.13	0.16	0.00	0.23	0.17	0.16	0.66	0.86	0.00	0.05
88.5	Watches and clocks	0.30	0.28	0.20	0.07	0.06	0.03	0.24	0.22	0.53	0.19	0.02	0.03
89.2, 89.6 - 89.9	Other manufactured items	1.85	1.83	1.84	2.15	0.46	2.25	2.09	1.90	6.19	5.94	0.39	1.77
Technology intensive		**40.52**	**40.33**	**39.22**	**41.48**	**0.91**	**40.67**	**39.23**	**39.20**	**36.68**	**41.73**	**2.36**	**41.64**
51	Organic chemicals	2.07	2.25	2.25	3.38	0.02	1.36	2.27	2.46	7.35	9.34	0.17	0.82
52	Inorganic chemicals	0.52	0.60	0.47	0.63	0.08	1.15	0.58	0.68	1.63	2.03	0.02	0.65
54	Medicinal, pharmaceutical items	1.68	1.70	2.26	3.08	0.02	4.00	3.62	3.44	16.38	18.98	0.15	3.93
56	Fertilizers	0.19	0.27	0.16	0.20	0.01	0.88	0.30	0.34	0.52	0.67	0.04	0.98
57	Plastic in primary forms	0.02	0.02	0.02	0.01	0.00	0.08	0.02	0.02	0.05	0.05	0.00	0.045
58	Plastic in non-primary forms	1.93	1.98	2.24	2.67	0.01	2.32	2.10	2.08	6.75	7.82	0.02	1.85
59	Chemical materials	0.97	0.95	1.11	1.35	0.01	2.11	1.17	1.09	4.08	4.58	0.10	1.87
71	Power-generating machinery	2.47	2.44	2.39	2.71	0.07	3.42	2.32	2.37	6.97	9.20	0.17	3.81
72	Machinery for particular industries	2.69	2.43	2.37	3.34	0.10	5.71	2.50	2.19	5.50	8.76	0.28	6.25
73	Metal working machinery	0.62	0.60	0.61	0.65	0.01	0.28	0.46	0.44	1.19	1.80	0.01	0.29
74	General industry machinery	3.34	3.28	3.69	4.45	0.05	4.99	3.80	3.54	11.27	14.92	0.08	6.71
75	Office machines	5.47	5.75	5.68	4.00	0.02	1.75	4.05	3.95	10.76	6.12	0.05	1.74
76.4	Telecommunication equipment	3.43	3.31	3.23	3.12	0.03	2.94	3.16	3.21	6.68	5.02	0.10	3.36
77	Electrical machinery	9.49	9.60	7.04	6.32	0.04	4.69	7.71	8.23	17.00	15.73	0.14	4.65
79.2	Aircraft	1.57	1.24	1.66	1.52	0.06	0.99	1.07	1.25	3.48	4.79	0.63	0.95
87	Professional, scientific & controlling instruments	1.80	1.75	1.74	1.72	0.09	1.16	2.25	2.12	5.89	5.67	0.13	1.37
88.1 - 88.4	Photographic, cinematographic goods	0.93	0.83	0.78	0.74	0.02	0.45	0.55	0.51	1.43	1.25	0.01	0.32
89.2 - 89.3	Other manufactured	1.32	1.33	1.53	1.60	0.26	2.39	1.30	1.28	4.98	5.02	0.24	2.03
SITC not specified		7.31	6.79	7.71	8.29	13.27	8.91	7.66	6.80	23.94	24.26	13.40	10.02
Total		100	100	100	100	100	100	100	100	100	100	100	100

Notes: Classification of products according to factor intensity is based on Hinloopen and Marrewijk (2004).
a) Primary products include: SITC 0, 1, 2, 3 (excl. 33.3, 33.4), and 4.
b) Resource intensive products include: SITC 61, 63, 66.1, 66.2, 66.3, 66.7, 67.1, and 68.
c) Unskilled labor intensive products include: SITC 65, 66.4, 66.5, 66.6, 79.3, 81, 82, 83, 84, 85, 89.4, and 89.5.
d) Not specified SITC sub - sectors include SITC 29, 59, 66, 69, 79.
e) EU consists of 27 member countries, as of January 1st, 2007.
Source: Author's compilation and calculations, Data source: UN COMTRADE 2010

Table 2. Africa2, Africa2-China, and China-Southeast Asia's External Trade Patterns Based on Factor Intensities (Exports and imports in % of total)

		Trade in 2000						Trade in 2009					
		Africa2		Africa2-China		China-Southeast Asia5		Africa2		Africa2-China		China-Southeast Asia5	
		Exports	Imports	Exports	Imports	Exports	Imports	Export	Imports	Exports	Imports	Exports	Imports
Primary products (excl. petroleum oil)		**21.33**	**18.65**	**20.91**	**13.96**	**17.09**	**33.27**	**23.78**	**15.62**	**12.95**	**3.34**	**10.30**	**30.19**
Primary products (incl. 33.3– -33.4 petroleum oil)		76.79	31.61	96.32	15.47	22.86	45.08	79.74	24.26	90.86	3.40	13.99	36.58
Resource intensive		**7.87**	**3.38**	**1.42**	**1.53**	**2.96**	**5.07**	**6.85**	**3.81**	**6.07**	**4.52**	**2.96**	**1.60**
Unskilled labor intensive		**4.26**	**6.78**	**0.23**	**27.67**	**11.53**	**2.86**	**2.75**	**4.38**	**0.35**	**11.22**	**17.37**	**1.93**
Human capital intensive		**2.61**	**21.42**	**1.53**	**20.00**	**19.71**	**5.67**	**2.30**	**25.79**	**0.77**	**28.52**	**12.80**	**4.50**
53	Dyeing, tanning and coloring materials	0.06	0.62	0.00	0.68	0.89	0.16	0.04	0.43	0.00	0.31	0.58	0.16
55	Oils and perfume materials	0.59	1.12	0.02	0.39	0.33	0.12	0.44	1.20	0.02	1.63	0.31	0.21
62	Rubber manufactures	0.04	1.21	0.02	2.46	0.63	0.31	0.02	1.38	0.00	2.78	0.49	2.42
64	Paper	0.21	2.07	0.02	0.82	0.56	3.39	0.20	1.45	0.00	1.00	0.63	0.37
67.2 - 67.9	Iron and steel	0.22	3.08	1.22	1.25	3.74	1.13	0.21	3.70	0.00	3.04	3.15	0.13
69	manufactures & metals	0.37	2.53	0.19	5.94	2.35	0.26	0.31	4.10	0.45	6.70	2.80	0.26
76.1- 76.3	Monitor, sound recording	0.08	0.53	0.01	2.06	2.55	0.03	0.01	0.83	0.00	3.13	0.79	0.54
78	Road vehicles	0.40	8.23	0.03	3.70	7.26	0.12	0.41	11.38	0.29	8.03	2.44	0.17
79.1	Railway vehicles	0.01	0.14	N.A	0.02	0.03	0.00	0.00	0.07	0.00	0.11	0.05	0.00
88.5	Watches and clocks	0.03	0.06	0.00	0.32	0.47	0.04	0.02	0.03	0.00	0.06	0.07	0.07
89.2, 89.6 - 89.9	Other manufactured items	0.60	1.82	0.02	2.36	0.89	0.11	0.63	1.22	0.00	1.72	1.51	0.19
Technology intensive		**1.96**	**28.60**	**0.19**	**25.17**	**36.82**	**39.54**	**3.26**	**32.61**	**0.81**	**40.21**	**45.64**	**53.81**
51	Organic chemicals	0.03	0.92	0.02	1.69	1.51	3.08	0.10	0.95	0.01	1.74	1.91	3.02
52	Inorganic chemicals	0.28	0.83	0.00	1.02	2.64	0.10	0.28	0.82	0.04	1.14	1.41	0.08
54	Medicinal, pharmaceutical items	0.09	2.24	0.00	1.44	0.73	0.01	0.10	2.20	0.00	0.70	0.67	0.01
56	Fertilizers	0.08	1.34	N.A	0.23	1.55	0.00	0.08	1.31	N.A	0.31	1.11	0.00
57	Plastic in primary forms	0.00	0.07	N.A	0.14	0.03	N.A	0.01	0.09	N.A	0.03	0.06	0.00
58	Plastic in nonprimary forms	0.08	2.15	0.00	1.14	0.46	6.22	0.22	2.78	0.22	1.70	1.02	3.63
59	Chemical materials	0.08	1.38	0.01	0.82	1.14	0.80	0.11	1.30	0.00	1.05	1.18	0.81
71	Power-generating machinery	0.06	1.93	0.00	1.68	2.01	0.81	0.15	2.32	0.00	2.86	3.34	0.48
72	Machinery for particular industries	0.20	3.85	0.12	3.98	2.33	0.32	0.53	4.84	0.05	5.49	2.76	0.19
73	Metal working machinery	0.01	0.20	0.01	0.52	0.47	0.13	0.02	0.35	0.01	0.83	0.60	0.04
74	General industry machinery	0.12	3.55	0.00	2.07	2.86	1.19	0.14	4.85	0.02	6.21	5.22	0.93
75	Office machines	0.02	1.20	0.00	0.66	4.97	9.07	0.03	1.20	0.01	1.16	7.17	13.25
76.4	Telecommunication equipment	0.03	1.85	0.00	0.95	6.55	2.55	0.09	2.57	0.12	7.09	6.21	3.10
77	Electrical machinery	0.15	3.40	0.01	5.17	7.54	14.50	0.25	3.93	0.32	6.80	8.39	27.24
79.2	Aircraft	0.04	0.65	0.00	1.08	0.58	0.00	0.25	0.37	0.00	0.04	0.01	0.00
87	Professional, scientific & controlling instruments	0.06	0.74	0.01	1.15	0.46	0.18	0.07	0.90	0.00	1.18	3.20	0.66
88.1 - 88.4	Photographic, cinematographic goods	0.02	0.31	0.00	0.15	0.49	0.39	0.01	0.31	0.00	0.33	0.58	0.23
89.2 - 89.3	Other manufactured items	0.60	2.00	0.00	1.28	0.49	0.18	0.80	1.50	0.01	1.53	0.83	0.14
SITC not specified		6.52	8.21	0.31	10.16	6.13	1.77	5.09	9.14	1.13	12.12	7.24	1.57
Total		100	100	100	100	100	100	100	100	100	100	100	100

Notes: The classification of products according to factor intensity is based on Hinloopen and van Marrewijk (2004). SITC 33.3 and 33.4
a) Primary products include SITC 0, 1, 2, 3 (excl. 33.3, 33.4), and 4.
b) Resource intensive products include SITC 61, 63, 66.1, 66.2, 66.3, 66.7, 67.1, and 68.
c) Unskilled labor intensive products include SITC 65, 66.4, 66.5, 66.6, 79.3, 81, 82, 83, 84, 85, 89.4, and 89.5.
d) Nonspecified SITC subsectors include SITC 29, 59, 66, 69, and 79.
e) Africa2 denotes all sub-Saharan African countries excluding South Africa; Southeast Asia5 comprises Cambodia, Indonesia, Malaysia, Viet Nam, and Thailand.
Source: Author's compilation and calculations; data from the UN Comtrade database, 2010

The classification of industries into factor intensive groups is based on their capital-labor ratio (capital intensity) as in Hinloopen and van Marrewijk (2006) and Lall (2000a). This classification takes into account the mix of different skill, technology, capital, and scale requirements at the final product stage: Unskilled labor intensive products are those products with the lowest value-added per worker. Technology intensive products are those goods with the highest ratios of research and development expenditures to value-added. Human capital intensive products are those with relatively lower ratios of R&D to value-added than technology intensive products (for further discussion, see Amighini 2005; Krause 1987; Neven 1995).

Tables 1, 2 and A1 illustrate the factor intensity breakdown of overall African trade in 2000 and 2009, as well as that of Africa-China, China-Asia, Africa-EU, and China-Developing Asia[4] trade in those years. Table 1 highlights the obvious: in contrast to China's trade dynamics, African trade has undergone no structural change from labor intensive to human capital intensive or technology driven industrial production. There has, however, been a fundamental shift in the share of China's technology intensive exports to East Asia, from 31% in 2000 to 54% in 2009.

Comparing the share of Africa's total trade (exports and imports) in technology intensive goods with the world to that with China also shows that Africa's share of trade with the world in this category remained virtually unchanged in 2009 relative to 2000, while Africa experienced significant growth in the share of technology intensive imports from China (from 34% to 49%). The share of African primary commodity products exported to China during that period increased from 16% to 23%. Another significant factor in the overall trade growth in this category is a rapid increase in trade in oil and copper.

It is also interesting to note that even though the share of China's labor intensive exports to East Asia declined significantly (from 33% in 2000 to 18% in 2009), the share of Africa's exports to China in this category also fell from 10% to 3% during the same period. The significance of this shift is demonstrated by the export/import ratio for African trade with China in labor intensive products, which was 1/3 in 2000 but declined to 1/7 in 2009. As both Africa and China are labor abundant, based on a simple Heckscher-Ohlin theory, this shrinking labor intensive share could mean a missed opportunity for trade to enhance employment in Africa.

Table 1 also shows that the patterns and magnitudes of China–East Asia trade between 2000 and 2009 are different from those for China–Africa trade, although compared to Japan and South Korea, both Africa and China are abundantly endowed with labor and natural resources. Net trade data indicate, however, that China, despite being a net importer of primary commodities from Africa, has a large trade surplus with Africa in nondurable consumer goods. At the same time, it also has large trade deficits with Japan and other East Asian economies in basic manufactured intermediate goods, machinery, and transportation equipment. This observation suggests that the China and East Asian economies have enabled African economies to further integrate the rising epicenter of global growth. Ultimately, with respect to Africa, a trade surplus with Japan and deficits with Africa in primary commodities

[4] China's (and by extension East Asia's) changing export pattern matters insofar as it indirectly reflects the direction of technological change at the world economy level and how developing regions are reaping the globally available trade and technology potentials. Hence, comparison of the shifting patterns of African exports (to China, the world and EU) is enabled by comparison with the corresponding categories for Southeast Asia (Cambodia, Indonesia, Malaysia, Viet Nam and Thailand) and China.

are the basic features of China's current foreign trade. Moreover, although the share of human capital intensive goods exported from Africa2 (Africa minus south Africa) to China changed slightly over the 2000–2009 period, the share of goods in this category exported from China to Southeast Asia dropped from 19.7% to 12.8% (Table 2). The share of primary products (excluding oil) exported from Africa to China over this period, on the other hand, rose from 11.2% to 18.7% (Table 1), although when oil is included, these figures are 16.5% and 23.8%, respectively.

The differences between patterns in China's trade with Africa, and with Southeast Asia5 (Cambodia, Indonesia, Malaysia, Viet Nam and Thailand)[5] are even more revealing. China's share of technology intensive products exported to Asia increased from 36% in 2000 to 45% in 2009, but its share of products in this category imported from Southeast Asia5 increased from 39.5% to 53%. The trade data for Africa2, reported in Table 2, are even more revealing. The most dramatic change resulting from the exclusion of the South African data manifests in the technology intensive trade category. Here, the share of exports from the rest of Africa, although twice as large in 2009 as in 2000 (in exports to both the world and China), is insignificant, especially in comparison to the share of exports to China from Southeast Asia5. Other evidence of such trade pattern differences is that the category "primary products and petroleum oil" accounts for nearly all of Africa's exports to China (96.32% in 2000 and 90.86% in 2009). In its total exports to the world, Africa2 is also specializing in primary commodity exports (76.79% in 2000 to 79.74% in 2009), although its trade with China reflects a reverse trend (from 96.32% in 2000 to 90.86% in 2009).

Interestingly, Table 1 plainly shows that the growth of China's exports in the technology intensive category took place simultaneously with that of its imports in the same category. For example, while its 2000 share of technology intensive exports to East Asia3 represented 31% of total exports (against 60% of its import share from that region), in 2009, its share of exports reached 54% (against 68% of import share). The African import share in the category, in contrast, remained insignificant and below unity even though Africa2's technology intensive exports rose substantially from 25% to 40 over the period (see Table 3). Meanwhile, Southeast Asia5's share of technology intensive exports to China rose from 39% in 2000 to 53% in 2009 (Table 2), a 14 percentage point increase, while its import share from China (i.e., China's exports to the region) in this category rose 9 percentage points over the period under study. Africa's export patterns relative to China's or even relative to Africa's traditional trade partners in the EU, however, is different from that of either China or East Asia5. It is apparent that from 2000 to 2009, Africa's comparative advantage relative to the EU shifted strongly toward labor intensive exports. This trend is in contrast to that recorded by Africa in both its overall trade and that with China. In addition, the share of primary products (including oil) in total African exports to the EU declined significantly, from 45% in 2000 to 35% in 2009, a decline that contrasts with the increases in the shares of total African exports in this category to the world (from 19% to 22%) and to China (16% to 23%) (see Table 1). At the same time, the shares of resource intensive and human capital intensive products exported from Africa to China and the EU remained virtually unchanged. Moreover, the share of technology intensive goods exported from Africa to China was higher than the corresponding

[5] Most of these are developing countries in the process of reversing many factors underlying Africa's generally poor performance on export diversification. In this respect, assessing their trade patterns provides a valuable benchmark for comparison.

share to the world and remained so over the period in question (52.5% and 40.5% in 2000 for exports to China and the world, respectively, and 53% and 39.2% in 2009).

Second, the share of products in the primary commodity category exported from sub-Saharan Africa minus South Africa (SSA2) to the EU over the same period jumped from 63% to 68% (Table 4), while the corresponding share in this category to China dropped from 96% to 90% (Table 3). One explanation for this difference lies in the characteristics of Chinese investment in Africa, which is heavily concentrated in the mining industry. Chinese enterprises have thus become an important force propelling African commodity exports. Third, it should be noted that in the resource intensive category, the share of exports from SSA2 to China increased over the period (from 1.42% to 6.07%), while the corresponding share from SSA2 to the EU declined (16.42% to 9.16%). In part, this difference may reflect the changing distribution of global production. As China becomes the "world's factory," it diverts trade that previously followed the S–N pattern; that is, it draws in more primary exports from SSA. As a result, SSA's exports of non-oil primary commodities to the EU decline (as a share of the total) because it is now exporting them to the EU "through" China (in the form of basic manufactured products) rather than directly. The trend in the human capital intensive category also indicates a decline in exports to China and a rise in imports from China, while the share of exports from SSA2 to the EU remained virtually unchanged.

These trade patterns may also reflect the persistent technology gaps between African countries and their trading partners. This hypothetical interpretation can be indirectly verified by reorganizing the data in terms of easily imitable technology intensive[6] exports to China (as a share of total exports to China). Using the SITC Rev. 3 classification, Table 3 shows that SSA's share in each of the major items in this category has barely changed over the period. Admittedly, the share of inorganic chemical has doubled, but it still remains insignificant, and shares of office machines and organic chemicals have both declined from 3.4% and 5.7% in 2000, respectively, to 3.2% and 5.3% in 2009. In Southeast Asia5, in contrast, the share of office machines rose from 8.6% to 13.3%. This snapshot, although it by no means illustrates the overall trend, still provides substantial evidence that learning by exporting is not happening. Rather, trade tends to induce more imitation in a developing country by giving its producers several types of incentives to quickly learn trading partners' technology. Table 3 also suggests that imitation in categories in which China is gradually importing from other developing economies (e.g., office machines) increases the probability that imitation in a typical African firm is likely to succeed because market uncertainty (generally associated with innovation) and costs will be low.

The overall evidence drawn from the analysis of factor intensity is threefold. First, the relative importance of primary products did not decline: these products still play a significant role in Africa's exports. Second, exports of manufactures and technology intensive products from Africa2 to China are still insignificant. Third, using the pattern of trade with East Asia as a reference, empirical evidence from China–Southeast Asia5 (Table 3) lends credence to the idea that if trade intensity changes rapidly, the process of industrialization in general—and of export-led industrial growth in particular—is driven not by resource endowment but by the knowledge and skills needed for the production of technology intensive goods. As pointed out in Section 2, these skills are acquired mainly through imitation (Prosner, 1965) or technology transfer via FDI. Hence, with respect to the former channel, whether African countries are

[6] SITC Rev. 3: 51, 52, 54.1, 58, 59, and 75 (for further information, see Yilmaz 2002).

able to capture any positive effects can only be empirically determined indirectly in a growth empiric's framework. As for the latter channel, as reviewed in Section 2, the question of interest is consistent with the recycled comparative advantage reality of international trade, which is factually described below.

Table 3. SSA and Southeast Asia5: Easily Imitable Technology Intensive Exports (to China)

		SSA to China	Southeast Asia5 to China
Code	Commodity Description	% of total exports	% of total exports
2000			
S3-51	Organic chemicals	3.4	4.1
S3-52	Inorganic chemicals	0.3	0.1
S3-541	Medicines, etc., exc. Grp 542	0.2	0.0
S3-58	Plastic, nonprimary form	5.4	6.2
S3-59	Chemical materials, n.e.s.	1.1	0.8
S3-75	Office machines, adp mach.	5.9	8.6
		16.3	19.2
2009			
S3-51	Organic chemicals	3.2	4.5
S3-52	Inorganic chemicals	0.6	0.1
S3-541	Medicines, etc., exc. grp542	0.2	0.0
S3-58	Plastic, non-primary form	4.3	3.7
S3-59	Chemical materials, n.e.s.	1.0	1.3
S3-75	Office machines, adp mach.	5.3	13.3
		14.6	22.9

Source: Author's calculations; data from UN Comtrade database, 2010.

Recycled Comparative Advantage Analysis

In accordance to Ozawa (2010), the essence of growth lies in a process of climbing the ladder of comparative advantage from labor-intensive to gradually and increasingly more technology intensive industries on the part of catching-up countries (Ozawa 2010). By grouping market share of certain export items of China and Africa, our goal is to build an index that can provide a preliminary description of the above process of recycled comparative advantage, better known as the "flying geese pattern of trade substitution". As is evident, the recycled comparative advantage analysis is based in two postulates in the context of this paper. First, it assumes that for China, trade with Africa in new activities—such as when a stage of production can be detached and relocated—can be unskilled labor intensive relative to China's own endowments but skilled labor intensive relative to Africa's endowments. Second, as noted in the literature review, the flying geese paradigm assign an important role to outward FDI by relatively advanced countries, applicable in the present context of China as a way of "recycling comparative advantage" (UNCTAD 1996) to relatively less developed countries in Africa.

Admittedly, China has been able to strengthen its position in more skill and technology intensive production lines even though its competitive advantages in more labor intensive products like footwear have declined with recent wage escalation. In a few cases, production has even moved to countries where costs are lower (Huang 2012), particularly developing economies. The question therefore arises of whether there is any indication that African economies have been upgrading their exports through the flying geese path? The likelihood that China will relocate its labor intensive factories to Africa flying geese style is questioned in a recent paper by Ozawa and Bellak (2010). In attempting to answer this question, low-wage and recently emerged Asian economies such as Cambodia, Indonesia, Malaysia, Thailand, and Viet Nam can provide useful examples of how this transition has been and is still being accomplished.

To evaluate the role played by China in the dynamic process of shifting comparative advantage for African economies, we relate each product's export share in China's total exports (rather than world trade as in Balassa's RCA) by comparing shifts in the market share of declining sectors in China to those for the corresponding sectors in Africa and East Asia. In particular, we compute the market shares of exports from China for the period 1995–2010 at the 3-digit SITC level. From those results, we identify the 16 products with the largest declines in export share and obtain their market shares. Finally, using these 16 commodities as proxies, we construct aggregate market shares for exports from SSA and Southeast Asia5 to China, and from SSA and China to the entire world[7], all of which are shown in Figure 1.

As the figure illustrates, Southeast Asia5 is increasing its share of exports to China in commodities in which China is experiencing a market share decline (as shown by the rise in its composite index). SSA, however, is seeing a reduction in its composite index. Evidently, the flying geese pattern of integration is not yet occurring between China and Africa. The data also suggest that similar declining trend in African composite index relative to the world. China's share of exports in the 16 commodities selected has fallen steadily since 1995; Africa's share, which fell quite a bit through much of the 1990s, has remained small and fallen only a little over the past decade. Again, we see strong signs that the share of exports from Southeast Asia5 to China has soared, while the shares of exports from Africa and China have stagnated or even declined.

Understandably, it is clear that the shifts in the composite index of individual African countries (similar to the one depicted in Figure 1) are not exactly the same. Recalling that the flying geese hypothesis emphasizes an emerging pattern of trade specialization in lagging economies, the effects of regional specialization in Africa caused by China's recycled comparative advantage can be alternatively gauged by simply plugging the constructed composite indices for individual African countries into the growth regression. Although extremely simple, this measure provides a useful starting point for investigating potential specialization effects on growth. The intuition here is that an increase in this composite index, however, can be expected to contribute positively to African growth; a prediction that can be empirically tested in future investigations.

[7] Note that recent versions of the flying geese model predict that the lead economy sets in motion new industries in the follower country via delocation and trade and later serves as a market for exports of the same industries. For this reason, index for Africa (SSA) include two alternative destination: the one consistent with the original FG model (with China as destination) and the modified version (with the World as destination).

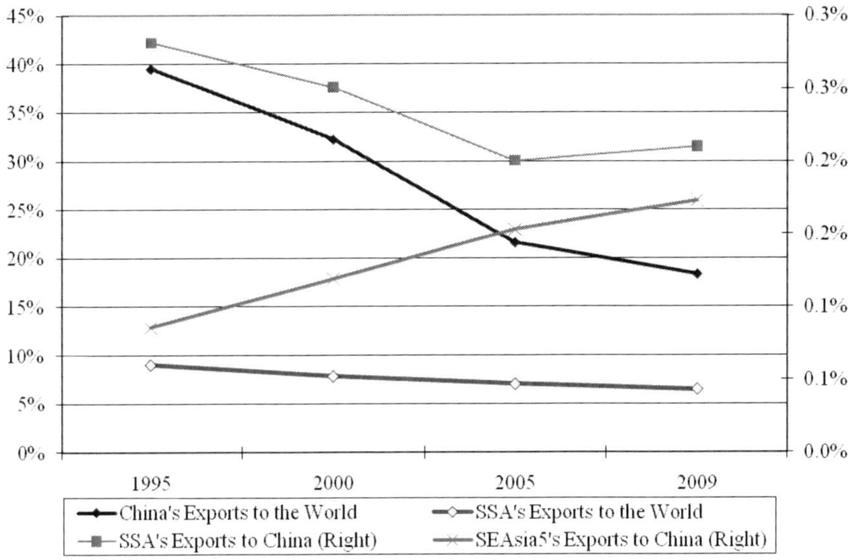

Notes: Composite commodities include S3-651, textile yarn; S3-652, cotton fabrics, woven; S3-653, fabrics, man-made fibers; S3-658, textile articles n.e.s.; S3-671, pig iron; S3-762, radio-broadcast receivers; S3-831, trunks, suitcases, bags, etc.; S3-841, men's, boys' clothing; S3-842, women's, girls' clothing; S3-845, other textile apparel, n.e.s.; S3-848, clothing, nontextile; and headgear; S3-851, footwear; S3-885, watches and clocks; S3-893, articles, n.e.s., of plastics; S3-894, baby carriages, toys, games; and S3-899, misc. manufactured goods. The calculation excludes petroleum oils and crude.

SSA = all sub-Saharan African countries; SEAsia5 = Cambodia, Indonesia, Malaysia, Thailand, and Vietnam.

Source: UN Comtrade database, 2011.

Figure 1. Composite Index of Market Share of the Top 16 Declining Commodities, 1995–2009.

CONCLUSION

This paper set out to determine whether shares of trade have expanded or contracted in sectors with greater potential for technological progress as a result of the explosion in China–Africa trade; with the expectation that such changes in trade patterns to reflect ongoing industrial upgrading. By use of two different measures of trade patterns (factor intensity analysis and recycled comparative advantage analysis), the overall results indicate that despite the rapid growth in China–Africa trade, the sectoral composition of African exports to China have worsened—toward greater specialization into non-processed primary commodities—during the period 2000–2009. Furthermore, when the data for South Africa were included, it was found that African trade with China had meager expansionary effects on the shares of growth-generating sectors such as technology-intensive exports. Excluding the data for South Africa, however, revealed that the patterns of African trade with China were virtually unchanged over the study period. The absence of structural change is quite revealing when comparing patterns displayed by Africa with those by Southeast Asia. In the latter region, significant expansion in technology-intensive exports, which encompass most manufactured exports, occurred over the aforementioned period. Above all, simply increasing the volume of exports to China may have been a necessary igniter of growth thus far, but it may not be a sufficient driver of long-run economic growth, as most African economies are further specializing in export sectors with diminishing returns and poor technological progress.

Along with technological transfer through the recycled comparative advantage framework, our conclusion is that Chinese firms operating in Africa do not take advantage of their competitive advantage in technical know-how, and hence do not play the role of "leader geese" in competitively exporting new products to the Chinese markets. In general, therefore, it seems that despite the effects of scale on economic growth, the growing presence of China in Africa has not (yet) opened up new possibilities for industrialization on the continent.

Overall, the present study contributes to the nascent empirical literature assessing the impact of China's rising presence in Africa by highlighting the disturbing evidence of the absence of industrial upgrading. Evidently, in the absence of industrial upgrading, the sustainability of the growth in exports recorded by African countries remains questionable. Ultimately, an increase in African exports to China will not act as a catalyst for technological upgrading or an engine of economic growth unless African countries acquire new sets of skills that build competitive advantages in technology-intensive sectors, especially in easily imitable industries. Assuming that such evolution is possible, how can the existing globally available technological knowledge enhance specialization through easy imitation? It is precisely in this direction that many of the most interesting insights can be drawn, offering provocative avenues for future study.

References

Akamatsu, K. (1962). A historical pattern of economic growth in developing countries. *The Developing Economies Preliminary Issue 1,* 3–25.

Amighini, A. (2005). China in the international fragmentation of production: Evidence from ICT industry. *The European Journal of Comparative Economics 2 (2)*, 203–219.

Amurgo-Pacheco, A., & M.D. Pierola. (2008). Patterns of export diversification in developing countries: Intensive and extensive margins. *World Bank Policy Research Working Paper No. 4473.*

Caves, R. E., J. A. Frankel, & R. W. Jones. (1996). *World trade and payments. 7th edition*, Harper Collins.

Chenery, H. B., & M. Syrquin. (1975). *Patterns of development, 1950-1970.* London: Oxford University Press.

Dosi, G., K. Pavitt, & L. Soete. (1990). *The economics of technical change and international trade*. New York: Harvester Wheatsheaf.

Feenstra, R.C., & G. Hanson. (1996). Foreign investment, outsourcing, and relative wages. In *Political economy of trade policy*, eds. R.C. Feenstra, G.M. Grossman, and D.A. Irwin. MIT Press: Cambridge.

Gereffi, G. (2005). The global economy: Organization, governance, and development. In *The Handbook of Economic Sociology, second edition*, eds. N.J. Smelser, and R. Swedberg, 160–182. Princeton: Princeton University Press and Russell Sage Foundation.

Hinloopen, J. & C. van Marrewijk. (2004). Dynamics of Chinese comparative advantage. *Tinbergen Institute Discussion Paper* TI2004-034/2.

Huang, Y. (2012). *In the middle kingdom's shadow*. Wall Street Journal on March 27.

Jones, R. W., & H. Kierzkowski. (1990). The role of services in production and international trade: A theoretical framework. In *The political economy of international trade: Essays in honor of Robert E. Baldwin*, eds. R. Jones, and A. Krueger, 31–48. Cambridge: Blackwell.

Jones, R. W., & H. Kierzkowski. (2001). A framework for fragmentation. In *Fragmentation: New production patterns in the world economy*, eds. S. Arndt, and H. Kierzkowski, 17–34. New York: Oxford University Press.

Krause, L.B. (1987). The structure of trade in manufactured goods in the East and Southeast Asian region. In *Trade and structural change in Pacific Asia*, eds. C. I. Bradford, and W.H. Branson, NBER conference report.

Kuznets, S. (1967). Quantitative aspects of the economic growth of nations: X. level and structure of foreign trade: Long-term trends. *Economic Development and Cultural Change 15 (2),* 2, 1–140.

Lall, S. (2000a). *Export performance, technological upgrading and FDI strategies in the Asian newly industrializing economies.* UN, CEPAL-Serie Desarrollo productivo No 88, Santiago.

Lall, S. (2000b). Skills, competitiveness and policy in developing countries. *QEH Working Paper Series QEHWPS46.*

Neven, D. (1995). Trade liberalisation with Eastern nations: Some distribution issues. *European Economic Review 39*, 622–632.

Ocampo, J. A., C. Rada, & L. Taylor. (2009). *Growth and policy in developing countries: A structuralist approach.* New York: Columbia University Press.

Ozawa, T. (2010). The (Japan-born) "flying geese" theory of economic development revisited and reformulated from a structuralist perspective. *Center on Japanese Economy and Business, Columbia Business School Working Paper Series 291.*

Ozawa, T., & C. Bellak. (2010). *Will China relocate its labor-intensive factories to Africa, flying-geese style?* Columbia FDI Perspectives No. 28.

Parameswaran, M. (2006). *Trade induced structural change and its implications for technological progress: Evidence from Indian manufacturing industry.* Mimeo, Centre for Development Studies, Kerala.

Posner, M.V. (1961). International trade and technical change. *Oxford Economic Papers 13* (3), 323–341.

Romalis, J. (2004). Factor proportions and the structure of commodity trade. *American Economic Review 94*, 67–97.

Stehrer, R., & J. Worz. (2003). Industrial diversity, trade patterns and productivity convergence. *WIIW Working Paper no. 23.*

United Nations (UN) Comtrade Database. (2011). United Nations Statistical Division; Data retrieved January 20, 2011, from *http://comtrade.un.org/*

UNCTAD. (1996). *Trade and Development Report.* Geneva: United Nations.

Worz, J. (2004). Skill intensity in foreign trade and economic growth. *Tinbergen Institute Discussion Paper TI 2004-059/2.*

Yilmaz, B. (2002). The role of trade strategies for economic development: A comparison of foreign trade between Turkey and South Korea. *Russian and East European Finance and Trade 38* (2), 59–78.

APPENDIX

Table A1. Africa-EU's trade pattern according to factor intensities. (Exports and imports in % of total)

		Trade in 2000						Trade in 2009					
		Africa		Africa-EU		Africa2-EU		Africa		Africa-EU		Africa2-EU	
		Exports	Imports	Exports	Imports	Exports	Imports	Export	Imports	Exports	Imports	Exports	Imports
Primary products (excl. petroleum oil)		**11.08**	**11.61**	**11.61**	**10.40**	**28.75**	**18.47**	**13.38**	**14.10**	**14.03**	**12.86**	**32.19**	**15.05**
Primary products (incl. 33.3 - 33.4 petroleum oil)		19.12	19.74	45.26	27.38	62.91	21.65	22.73	24.95	35.69	23.64	68.78	19.43
Resource intensive		**4.13**	**4.30**	**4.25**	**4.28**	**16.41**	**2.93**	**3.87**	**3.77**	**11.05**	**9.84**	**9.16**	**4.21**
Unskilled labor intensive		**9.54**	**9.60**	**9.63**	**7.95**	**5.33**	**3.87**	**8.75**	**8.02**	**29.08**	**18.58**	**4.88**	**2.84**
Human capital intensive		**19.38**	**19.23**	**21.64**	**24.48**	**1.18**	**21.98**	**17.77**	**17.27**	**21.19**	**23.66**	**1.42**	**21.86**
53	Dyeing, tanning and coloring materials	0.52	0.51	0.58	0.76	0.01	0.77	0.44	0.40	1.53	1.89	0.01	0.52
55	Oils and perfume materials	0.69	0.64	0.86	1.11	0.08	1.16	0.88	0.80	3.32	4.28	0.10	1.14
62	Rubber manufactures	0.68	0.69	0.82	0.87	0.01	1.09	0.73	0.73	2.81	2.78	0.02	1.08
64	Paper	1.59	1.57	2.00	2.36	0.15	2.43	1.24	1.18	5.13	5.96	0.27	1.47
67.2 - 67.9	Iron and steel	2.03	2.07	2.37	2.75	0.02	2.67	2.27	2.23	7.41	8.42	0.05	2.18
69	manufactures & metals	1.88	1.95	2.23	2.30	0.14	2.68	2.07	1.99	7.38	7.41	0.20	3.41
76.1- 76.3	Monitor, sound recording	1.17	1.17	1.06	0.59	0.00	0.25	1.17	1.30	4.23	2.62	0.01	0.37
78	Road vehicles	8.56	8.41	9.56	11.36	0.25	8.42	6.47	6.34	25.45	28.68	0.36	9.83
79.1	Railway vehicles	0.13	0.12	0.13	0.16	0.00	0.23	0.17	0.16	0.66	0.86	0.00	0.05
88.5	Watches and clocks	0.30	0.28	0.20	0.07	0.06	0.03	0.24	0.22	0.53	0.19	0.02	0.03
89.2, 89.6 - 89.9	Other manufactured items	1.85	1.83	1.84	2.15	0.46	2.25	2.09	1.90	6.19	5.94	0.39	1.77
Technology intensive		**40.52**	**40.33**	**39.22**	**41.48**	**0.91**	**40.67**	**39.23**	**39.20**	**36.68**	**41.73**	**2.36**	**41.64**
51	Organic chemicals	2.07	2.25	2.25	3.38	0.02	1.36	2.27	2.46	7.35	9.34	0.17	0.82
52	Inorganic chemicals	0.52	0.60	0.47	0.63	0.08	1.15	0.58	0.68	1.63	2.03	0.02	0.65
54	Medicinal, pharmaceutical items	1.68	1.70	2.26	3.08	0.02	4.00	3.62	3.44	16.38	18.98	0.15	3.93
56	Fertilizers	0.19	0.27	0.16	0.20	0.01	0.88	0.30	0.34	0.52	0.67	0.04	0.98
57	Plastic in primary forms	0.02	0.02	0.02	0.01	0.00	0.08	0.02	0.02	0.05	0.05	0.00	0.045
58	Plastic in non-primary forms	1.93	1.98	2.24	2.67	0.01	2.32	2.10	2.08	6.75	7.82	0.02	1.85
59	Chemical materials	0.97	0.95	1.11	1.35	0.01	2.11	1.17	1.09	4.08	4.58	0.10	1.87
71	Power-generating machinery	2.47	2.44	2.39	2.71	0.07	3.42	2.32	2.37	6.97	9.20	0.17	3.81
72	Machinery for particular industries	2.69	2.43	2.37	3.34	0.10	5.71	2.50	2.19	5.50	8.76	0.28	6.25
73	Metal working machinery	0.62	0.60	0.61	0.65	0.01	0.28	0.46	0.44	1.19	1.80	0.01	0.29
74	General industry machinery	3.34	3.28	3.69	4.45	0.05	4.99	3.80	3.54	11.27	14.92	0.08	6.71
75	Office machines	5.47	5.75	5.68	4.00	0.02	1.75	4.05	3.95	10.76	6.12	0.05	1.74
76.4	Telecommunication equipment	3.43	3.31	3.23	3.12	0.03	2.94	3.16	3.21	6.68	5.02	0.10	3.36
77	Electrical machinery	9.49	9.60	7.04	6.32	0.04	4.69	7.71	8.23	17.00	15.73	0.14	4.65
79.2	Aircraft	1.57	1.24	1.66	1.52	0.06	0.99	1.07	1.25	3.48	4.79	0.63	0.95
87	Professional, scientific & controlling instruments	1.80	1.75	1.74	1.72	0.09	1.16	2.25	2.12	5.89	5.67	0.13	1.37
88.1 - 88.4	Photographic, cinematographic goods	0.93	0.83	0.78	0.74	0.02	0.45	0.55	0.51	1.43	1.25	0.01	0.32
89.2 - 89.3	Other manufactured	1.32	1.33	1.53	1.60	0.26	2.39	1.30	1.28	4.98	5.02	0.24	2.03
SITC not specified		7.31	6.79	7.71	8.29	13.27	8.91	7.66	6.80	23.94	24.26	13.40	10.02
Total		100	100	100	100	100	100	100	100	100	100	100	100

Notes: Classification of products according to factor intensity is based on Hinloopen and Marrewijk (2004).
a) Primary products include: SITC 0, 1, 2, 3 (excl. 33.3, 33.4), and 4.
b) Resource intensive products include: SITC 61, 63, 66.1, 66.2, 66.3, 66.7, 67.1, and 68.
c) Unskilled labor intensive products include: SITC 65, 66.4, 66.5, 66.6, 79.3, 81, 82, 83, 84, 85, 89.4, and 89.5.
d) Not specified SITC sub - sectors include SITC 29, 59, 66, 69, 79.
e) EU consists of 27 member countries, as of January 1st, 2007.
Source: Author's compilation and calculations, Data source: UN COMTRADE 2010

INDEX TERMS

1 Factor intensities: the relative proportions of various factors of production used in producing goods and services. The factor-intensity of the techniques of production used by a cost-minimizing firm depends on the relative prices of different factors of production. For any given set of relative factor prices, some goods are produced using a lot of labor and little capital: such goods are labor-intensive. Others are produced using a lot of capital and very little labor: such goods are capital-intensive.

2 "flying geese" hypothesis: A pattern of industrialization that depicts changing patterns of comparative advantage and trade as developing countries follow more advanced countries from which they acquire technologies through trade and investment. The name derives from a graph by the Japanese economist Kaname Akamatsu (1932, 1961), in which a pattern of import-production-export process of trade specialization is described. The process starts with imports setting in motion a sequence of adaptive innovation through imitation and adaptation, then upgrading effort unfolds and later export follows.

3 Industrial upgrading: Industrial upgrading is an economic process of transformation from low value-added industries (e.g., light industries) to higher value-added industries (e.g., heavy and higher-tech industries) or a change from endowed assets (i.e., natural resources and unskilled labor) to created assets (physical capital, skilled labor, social capital).

4 Recycled comparative advantage: the change in the geography of comparative advantages in various industries.

5 SITC: Standard International Trade Classification is a standard numerical code used by the United Nations to classify commodities used in international trade.

In: Current Issues in International Trade
Editor: Gouranga G. Das
ISBN: 978-1-63321-405-7

Chapter 4

STRUCTURAL BREAKS AND THE EFFECT OF EXCHANGE RATE ON INDIA'S EXPORTS

Ranajoy Bhattacharyya [*] ***and Jaydeep Mukherjee***
Indian Institute of Foreign Trade, Kolkata Campus,
Salt lake, Kolkata, India

ABSTRACT

It is shown that the 36 country real effective exchange rate of India, which is I(1), becomes stationary once a single exogenous shock (corresponding to the implementation of the liberalization policy by the government of India) is separated from its stochastic component and modeled as a break in the deterministic trend. The implication of this for the export supply function is enormous. While without the break, real export has had a long run relationship with a real effective exchange rate and gross domestic product, and the break the relationship no longer exists.

JEL Code: F 31

Keywords: Real Exports, Real Effective Exchange Rate, Structural Breaks, Unit Root, Cointegration

INTRODUCTION AND OVERVIEW

It is well known that structural breaks can alter the level of integration of time series (see Perron (1989)). In this paper we investigate whether such a thing has happened for India. The past two decades have been decades of extensive policy reforms in India. These reforms were gradually implemented since 1991 at the behest of the International Monetary Fund and touched upon almost every aspect of India's economy. One of the primary areas targeted by the reforms was the foreign exchange market. Another prime target was India's international

[*] Corresponding Author: Ranajoy Bhattacharyya, Email: ranajoy@iift.ac.in.

trade[1]. With such momentous changes happening in both these sectors, it is to be expected that the reforms will cast their spell on the variables associated with these sectors and on any interrelationship that may exist between them.

One aspect of this interrelationship is the relationship between export and its relative price in terms of the foreign currency represented by the real exchange rate[2]. Empirical studies across the globe have yielded mixed results for the exchange rate variable both in export demand and export supply equations. The results are sensitive to the choices of sample period, model specification and countries considered[3]. The primary reason for this is that relative price is one of a long list of factors that potentially affects export. In the Indian context, studies conducted over different periods of time and over several categories of models (with different sets of co-independent variables) have reported both presence and absence of possible links between exchange rates and exports. For instance, using the data for the period 1962-87, Joshi and little (1994) have found the price elasticity of demand for exports to be about 1.1 in the short run and about 3 in the long-run. Their study has also shown higher export growth during 1970s and from the mid-1980s when the real devaluation of the rupee was maintained, and a lull in export growth during the real appreciation of the rupee in the early 1960s and the first half of 1980s. Using a non-structural eclectic model for the period 1963-94, Srinivasan (1998) have also reported relative prices as a significant export determinant in India. Veeramani (2008), using a longer time period from 1960-2007, have found that the appreciation of the REER leads to a fall in the dollar value of India's merchandise exports. However, the degree of such negative association between exports and the REER has declined since 2002; while the role of the rate of growth of India's real GDP and that of the world exports have assumed greater importance. His analysis also suggested that the strong growth of India's merchandise exports during 2002-07 is likely to continue for at least five years after the period considered by him (2008-12). However, Nayyar (1988), Ghosh (1990), Sarkar (1994), and Sinha Roy (2001) have taken the opposite stand on whether relative prices are significant as a determinant in explaining export performance and argue for instance, that Indian exports are not necessarily price responsive as turning points in India's export performance were not often led by the movements in exchange rate.

None of these papers however consider the regime shift due to the implementation of the liberalization policies explicitly in their data analysis. As we will see below, a mere visual examination of a plot of (at least some of) the relevant series clearly reveal breaks in the trend curve around the time the liberalization policies were implemented. Our main focus in this paper is to determine the influence of these breaks on the outcome of the unit root as well as cointegration tests involving the series.

Even disregarding the issue of structural breaks due to liberalization, it is hard to form an a priori hypothesis about the export-exchange rate link. As several authors have argued, India's imports are expected to be less responsive than India's exports to changes in relative price. This is because a large part of India's imports (especially oil) are necessities with low

---

[1] India was traditionally one of the least open economies of the world (For example, if we consider the beginning of the decade data for PENN's (PWT 6.2) 'openness in constant prices' variable, the best rank India ever had in terms of openness during this period was in 1970 when it was ranked 9th among the least open economies). In the trade sector, reforms mostly consisted of dismantling restrictions to import. However several export incentives were also conceived and implemented in this period.

[2] The Reserve Bank of India defines the nominal and real effective exchange rates (NEER and REER) in terms of rupees (see below).

[3] See, for example, Wilson and Tat (2001) and Bahmani-Oskooee and Kara (2003) for two recent studies.

elasticity of demand. On the other hand, India's major exports have traditionally been less sophisticated unskilled labour or resource intensive goods which many other countries produce. Thus the exporters have an option of turning to other markets if the international prices of Indian goods rise. Pitted against this is the fact that most Indian exporters quote the price of their products in terms of local currencies (mostly Dollars or Euros). This raises the possibility of zero pass-through of exchange rates to export prices. In fact, it has been found that the pass-through of exchange rates to goods imported by the US priced in terms of dollars is only about 25% as against 95% for goods priced in non-dollars (see Gopinath et al., 2010). If this is true for Indian exporters then the effect of exchange rate is expected to be low for them. What this means is that since the possibility of losing international markets to competitors looms large for Indian exporters, they may be more willing to absorb price fluctuations to keep their markets intact. In these situations the relationship between exports and exchange rates is likely to break down. Finally the post reform period for India coincided with the period of globalization the world over with trade flows reaching unprecedented heights. This 'world trade effect' reached India's shores as well raising the possibility of washing away any negative effects that exchange rates might have created[4]. Logically therefore the conclusion is far from being foregone – an ideal situation for the issue to be settled empirically.

DATA AND METHODOLOGY

The Exchange Rate Series

Figure 1 plots the nominal and real effective exchange rate (NEER and REER) for India between 1970 and 2007[5] where the two exchange rates are defined as:

$$NEER = \prod_{i=1}^{n}\left(\frac{e}{e_i}\right)^{w_i} \text{ and}$$

$$REER = \prod_{i=1}^{n}\left[\left(\frac{e}{e_i}\right)\left(\frac{P}{P_i}\right)\right]^{w_i}$$

where e: Exchange rate of Indian Rupee against Special Drawing Rights (SDRs) (SDR per rupee); e_i: Exchange rate of the i-th country's currency against SDRs (SDR per i^{th} currency); w_i: $\frac{X_i + M_i}{\sum(X_i + M_i)}$ (trade based weights) such that $\prod_{i=1}^{n} w_i = 1$, where X_i is export and M_i is import from the ith country; P: India's wholesale price index; P_i: CPI of the ith country; n: 36

---

[4] A decomposition of India's growth rate of exports show that 'world trade effect' usually dominates other effects (see Veeramani, 2007).

[5] All the data used in this paper has been compiled from Handbook of Statistics on Indian Economy (2008-09), published by Reserve Bank of India. All the variables are expressed in natural logarithms and are calculated at constant prices.

(Number of countries involved in constructing the index). The indices are expressed per unit of rupee so that a rise implies appreciation of the rupee (see, RBI, 2005 p 1063).

NEER shows a sharp fall over the period with an almost horizontal portion from 1999-2000. REER (dotted line) on the other hand shows a sharp fall until 1993-94 and rising trend thereafter[6]. Taking REER alone there are two opposing phases in its evolution over time (this, cannot be said of the NEER):

- A depreciating part (up to 1993-94)
- An appreciating part (after 1993-94)

These segments of the REER curve are drawn separately in Figures 2 and 3. It can be seen from the diagrams that for the downward sloping phase the coefficient of the time trend is -0.03, whereas that of for the upward rising phase it is 0.01. Comparing the movement of the nominal rupee dollar exchange rate (not reported here) with those of NEER and REER we find that it behaves almost exactly as NEER and unlike REER with a clear depreciation up to 2000-01 and a slight appreciation thereafter[7]. To the extent that India's economic reforms were initiated in 1991 and trade and current account convertibility of the rupee was initiated in 1993 and 1994, visual observations are strongly suggestive of an indelible effect of policy reforms on all the three exchange rates. A visual examination of the (log values) of real export and real GDP series (to be plotted below in section 3 figures 5 and 6), reveal an upward trend for the period 1970-71 to 2006-07[8].

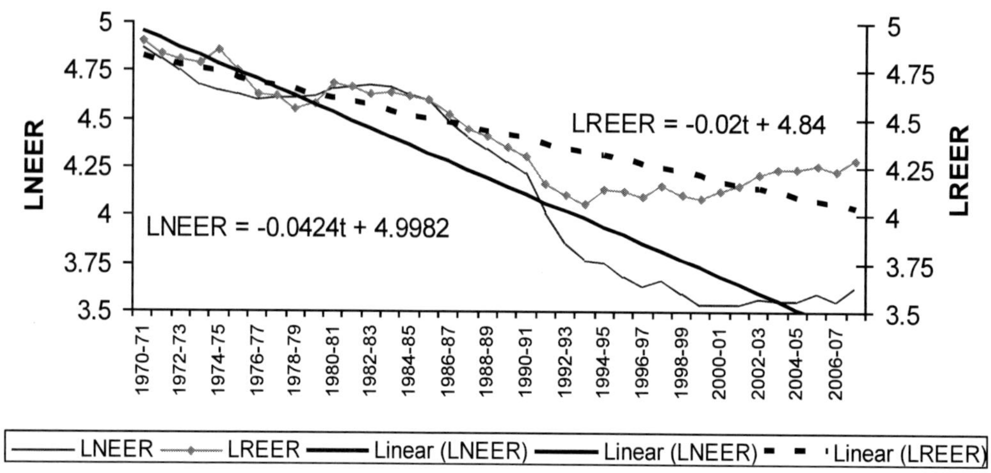

Figure 1. Annual Trend in LREER & LNEER.

---

[6] Interestingly NEER depreciated at a higher rate than REER for the whole period under consideration. After 1993-94 REER started rising (appreciated). However NEER continued to fall (depreciate) till 2000-01. There is thus a degree of asymmetry in their behavior during the period after 1993-94 implying a higher inflation rate for India compared to its major trading partners.

[7] In fact the correlation of the dollar rupee exchange rate with NEER is 0.94, and that with REER is 0.82.

[8] The presence of structural breaks, though not so momentous, is noticeable around the period of India's policy reforms for these two variables as well (see below).

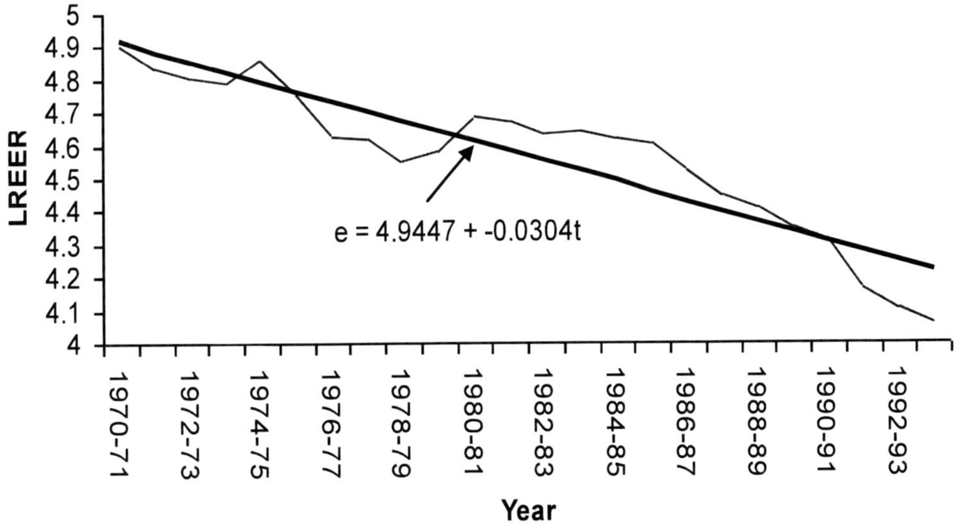

Figure 2. Phase I; LREER (1970-71 – 1993-94).

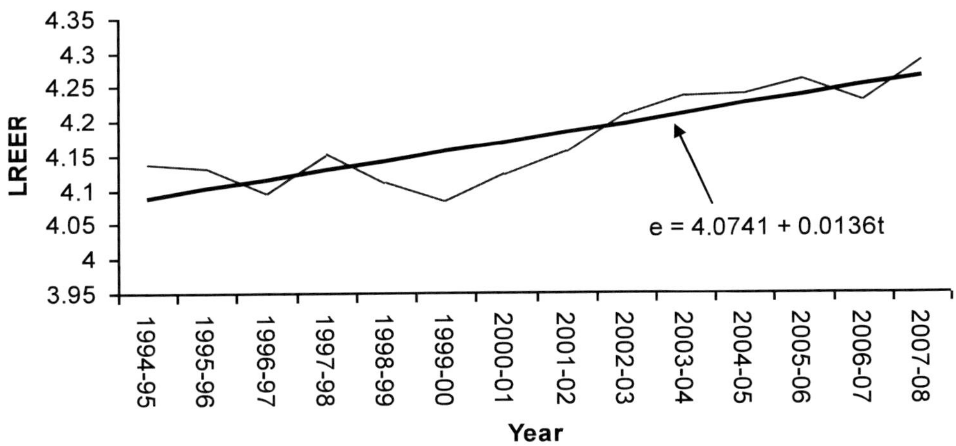

Figure 3. Phase II; (1994-95 – 2006-07).

Exchange Rates and Exports: The Casual Link

Before turning to the relationship between the exchange rate and exports formally let us take a quick look at the kind of problem that we are likely to face while trying to explain India's export with the exchange rate disregarding the role of economic reforms. The plot of the two series reveal that the significant change in trend of the REER series has not been observed for exports (trend is positive throughout). We can thus immediately identify two eras in the relationship between the variables. In the first era lasting up to 1993-94, the relationship between the two is exactly what the textbook argues: exchange rate depreciation having a positive effect on exports. In the second era starting from 1993-94 the expected relationship between REER and exports has however reversed. The dichotomy is revealed in terms of correlations in Table 1. Even though magnitudes of correlations for two variables over time are meaningless as they are always expected to be high, the signs are still meaningful. It can be seen in the last row of the Table 1, the sign of the correlation coefficient between export and exchange rate has reversed in the 1994-95 to 2007-08 periods. This is true both for levels and growth rates (first difference of logs of the variables) as far as REER is concerned and only for growth rates for NEER. A cursory look at the data is thus strongly suggestive of a break in the *relationship* (in contrast to the variables themselves) between the variables. Does the overall relationship in the entire period survive this break? This is the question that we turn to now.

Table 1. Correlation Coefficients between Export and Exchange Rate

Year	Export & REER	Export & NEER
	Level (1st Diff)	Level (1st Diff)
70-71 to 07-08	-0.86 (-0.36)	-0.95 (-0.21)
70-71 to 93-94	-0.97 (-0.62)	-0.92 (-0.40)
94-95 to 07-08	+0.89 (+0.07)	-0.42 (+0.15)

Source: DGCI&S and Reserve Bank of India.

METHODOLOGY

There are a plethora of unit root tests with varied properties to choose from. Unit root test against a single-break stationary alternative was proposed by Perron (1989) and Zivot and Andrews (1992). It was extended to a two-break stationary alternative by Lumsdaine and Papell (1997) and up to five-break alternative, with an a priori unknown number of breaks, by Kapetianos (2005). However, as pointed out by Bec and Bassil (2009), these tests maintain the linearity assumption under the unit root null hypothesis. If a break exists under the null of unit root, they will exhibit size distortions (over rejection of the null) as well as the wrong estimation of the break point (see also Nunes, Newbold and Kuan, 1997, Altinay, 2005, Kim and Perron, 2009). To overcome this problem, Lee and Strazicich (2003, 2004) have developed an alternative (at most two) endogenous break unit root test that uses the Lagrange Multiplier (LM) test statistics, and allows for breaks both under the null and the alternative hypothesis. Thus, any conclusion on the rejection of unit root null based on this LM test provides quite strong evidence of stationarity. We thus choose Lee and Strazicich (2003, 2004) over other tests, though we consider a single break in the series. The strategy of cointegration will be specified after the results for the unit root tests are presented.

ANALYSIS OF RESULTS

A fundamental decision that has to be taken before we proceed with determining the order of integration of the variables is the number of breaks/kinks we intend to internalize. Most data series experience multiple changes in slope and intercept over a period of time like for instance the LREER series plotted in the previous section, all of which can be reported as breaks (either in intercept or slope or both) on the basis of statistical tests. On the other hand, during a regime shift we should expect multiple changes in polices as markets are gradually deregulated. All of these policy changes do not amount to breaks in the series. Thus choosing the number of breaks for the data analysis is ultimately subjective. Domain knowledge dictates that there was *one* regime shift for India (implementation of liberalization), that it started informally from the mid-1980s and formally from 1991 and that the regime shift was ushered in by a series of policy changes all of which can be interpreted as small steps in a single direction. Take the example of the nominal exchange rate. Policy changes began with the rupee being devalued by 8 % in July 1, 1991 and by 11% in July 3, 1991. It was made partially convertible on March 1992 in the trade account with the introduction of the (dual) liberalized Exchange Rate Management System (LERMS). The dual exchange rate system of March 1992 was unified and the rupee was made fully convertible on the trade account on February 1993. And finally the rupee was made fully convertible in the current account in August 1994 thus achieving the Article VIII status of IMF. In spite of multiple policy changes as we have shown in the previous section, the data for nominal and real exchange rates show just one regime shift in the period after 1991. Further though there are multiple kink points, the kink points do not necessarily coincide with the dates of the policy changes. We therefore conclude that in spite of the multiple policy changes as well as multiple kinks, it is appropriate to interpret domain knowledge to be supportive of a single break for the real exchange rate corresponding to the implementation of the liberalization policies. For analogous reasons we allow for single breaks for the gross domestic product and the real export series as well.

Tables 2 - 5 estimates the following export supply function for the Indian economy between 1970 and 2007:

$$LREX_t = \alpha + \beta_0 LREER_t + \beta_1 LY_t + u_t$$

where LREX is India's real value of export, LREER is India's real effective exchange rate and LY is India's Gross Domestic Product (GDP) all in their natural logs. Tables 2 and 3 confirm the existence of one structural break for all the three series. As expected the break date for LREER coincides with the policy of devaluation. Interestingly the breaks in LREX and LY are *before* the formal implementation of the liberalization polices.

After accounting for one break in the deterministic trend the outcome of the unit root test shows that while LREER is I(0), LREX and LY are both I(1). Clearly therefore standard methods of cointegration of I (1) variables are not applicable in this case. The strategy that we use is (a) to reduce all the variables to I (0) by a single differencing of LREX and LY and run OLS and (b) to use the ARDL method on the level variables. The corresponding equations for the two cases are:

(a) $\Delta LREX_t = \alpha_0 + \phi_0 t + (\alpha_{1+i} - \alpha_0) D_{1985+i} + (\phi_{1+i} - \phi_0) D_{1985+i} t + \beta_0 LREER_t + \beta_1 \Delta LY_t + u_t$

(b) $$\Delta LREX_t = \alpha_0 + \phi_0 t + (\alpha_{1+i} - \alpha_0) D_{1985+i} + (\phi_{1+i} - \phi_0) D_{1985+i} t + \sum_{k=1}^{p} \beta_k \Delta LREX_{t-k} + \sum_{l=1}^{p} \chi_l \Delta LREER_{t-l} + \sum_{m=1}^{p} \delta_m \Delta LY_{t-m} + \lambda_1 LREX_{t-1} + \lambda_2 LREER_{t-1} + \lambda_3 LY_{t-1} + u_t$$

for each i=0…10,

where Δ is the first difference operator[9] and the optimal lag length for the ARDL method turns out to be (1,0,0,0)[10]. We assume that the break in the relationship between the variables could have occurred at a maximum of ten lags from the date of informal implementation of the liberalization policies in 1985. Thus D_{1985+i} (i=0…10) is defined as follows:

$D_{1985+i}=0$ for $t<1985+i$ $=1$ for $t\geq 1985+i$

Table 2. Unit Root Tests with One Structural Break (at Level)[1]

Series	Model	Break Point	Optimal Lags	T-Statistic	Critical Values at 1%	Critical Values at 5%	Result
LREX	Break (Intercept & Trend)	1990	7	-0.80	(-5.05 to -5.11)	(-4.45 to -4.51)	Unit Root
LREER	Break (Intercept & Trend)	1991	5	-5.06	(-5.05 to -5.11)	(-4.45 to -4.51)	I(0)
LY	Break (Intercept & Trend)	1989	3	-3.14	(-5.05 to -5.11)	(-4.45 to -4.51)	Unit Root

Note: 1. Method applied is Lee and Strazicich's (2004).

Table 3. Unit Root Tests with One Structural Break (at First Difference)[1]

Series	Model	Break Point	Optimal Lags	T-statistic	Critical Values at 1%	Critical Values at 5%	Result
LREX	Break (Intercept & Trend)	2001	2	-5.06	(-5.05 to -5.11)	(-4.45 to -4.51)	I(1)
LY	Break (Intercept & Trend)	1990	0	-8.31	(-5.05 to -5.11)	(-4.45 to -4.51)	I(1)

Note: 1. Method applied is Lee and Strazicich's (2004).

The crash (break only in intercept) and growth (break only in slope) models in the second equations were estimated separately so that there are (10 +20=) 30 equations to estimate in (a) and (b). The equations in (b) show the relationship between LREER and LREX at the level

[9] The rest of the Greek letters in the equations being the coefficients to be estimated.

[10] The Schwarz Bayesian Criterion (SBC) was used for determining the lag lengths.

while those in equations in (a) show the relationship between LREER and the one period relative growth rate of LREX[11].

The results for the equations in (a) and (b) are reported in Tables 4 and 5. It is clear from the tables that LREER does not have any statistically significant relationship either with LREX or its one period relative growth rate. However, there is a statistically significant cointegrating relationship with LREER without structural break (see the appendix[12]).

Table 4. OLS Regression with I(0) variables

	t_{1985}[3]	t_{1986}	t_{1987}	t_{1988}	t_{1989}	t_{1990}	t_{1991}	t_{1992}	t_{1993}	t_{1994}	t_{1995}
Constant	-1.05	-1.84*	-1.71***	-0.76	-0.18	0.63	0.84	0.18	0.04	0.61	0.88
LREER	1.30	2.06*	1.87***	0.86	0.25	-0.58	-0.79	-0.12	0.01	-0.56	-0.84
DLY	0.35	0.13	-0.03	-0.02	0.26	0.18	0.17	0.20	0.17	0.25	0.26
Trend	-2.27*	-1.90***	-0.97	-0.42	-0.41	-0.70	-0.89	-0.46	-0.37	-0.64	-0.74
D	-1.39	-0.30	0.19	-0.30	-0.68	-1.39	-1.45	-0.66	-0.40	-1.16	-1.66***
DT	3.21*	2.79*	1.75***	1.22	1.18	1.59	1.63	0.94	0.71	1.31	1.72***

Notes: 1. Dependent variable DLREX. 2. The figures in the table indicate the estimated t-statistic.3. t-statistic. (*) and (***) indicate statistical significance at 1% and 10% levels respectively. 4. Residuals are stationary at 5% level.

Table 5. ARDL Cointegration with Level Variables

Year	Type of Break	F-Statistic	W-Statistic	Year	Type of Break	F-Statistic	W-Statistic
1985	Intercept	2.4	9.62	1991	Intercept	2	8
	Trend	3.57	14.29		Trend	1.55	6.2
1986	Intercept	2.7	10.81	1992	Intercept	2.34	9.36
	Trend	3.12	12.47		Trend	1.76	7.06
1987	Intercept	1.8	7.2	1993	Intercept	1.57	6.28
	Trend	1.72	6.86		Trend	1.37	5.5
1988	Intercept	1.54	6.15	1994	Intercept	1.4	5.62
	Trend	1.37	5.49		Trend	1.44	5.78
1989	Intercept	1.41	5.65	1995	Intercept	1.64	6.59
	Trend	1.43	5.74		Trend	2.06	6.01
1990	Intercept	1.45	5.81				
	Trend	1.37	5.49				

Notes: 1. Dependant variable LREX. 2. Critical value bounds for the F-Statistic at 5% are (3.54, 4.82) for intercept and (4.51, 5.78) for trend and for the W-statistics at 5% are (14.16, 19.28) for the intercept and (18.06, 23.12) for trend (see Pesaran and Shin (1999)).

Statistically, the difference in the result is due to the incorrect determination of the order of integration of the LREER series. As it turns out, LREER falls within a class of variables

[11] Thus, say, $\hat{x}_{it} = \frac{dx}{x}$ in this discrete case has been written as $\Delta \ln x_t$ ($\ln x_t - \ln x_{t-1}$).

[12] Veeramani (2008) conducts a similar exercise (as in the appendix) for the period 1960-2007 and arrive at the similar conclusions. Working with several forms of quarterly REER (including the 5-country trade weighted version and the ones where the wholesale price index for India is replaced by the consumer price index) between 1993 1nd 2001 Kohli (2002) finds that REER is mostly stationary. None of these papers consider structural breaks.

first analyzed by Perron (1989)[13]. Using the argument in that paper we can argue that with an obvious regime shift for LREER resulting in a significant shift of intercept as well as the slope of the trend function (see figure 4), the ADF test is no more consistent and the unit root hypothesis has been accepted by the test for the level variable even though it is not true. The magnitude of the shift (at the break point) is strong enough for the ADF test to give erroneous results.

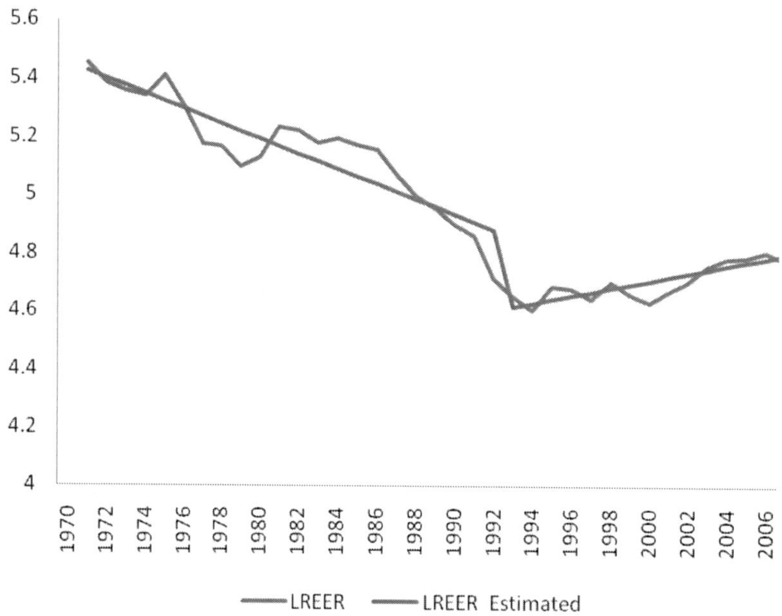

Note: The broken trend line is a fitted trend by (OLS) of the form $\hat{y}_t = \hat{\mu} + \hat{\gamma}_1 DU_t + \hat{\beta} t + \hat{\gamma}_2 DT_t$, where $DU_t = DT_t = 0$ if $t <= 1991$ and $DU_t = 1$, $DT_t = t$ if $t > 1991$.

Figure 4. Regime Shift in the (log) value of "REX".

On the other hand, Figures 5 and 6 clearly show that nothing so momentous happened with LREX and LY. Their trends are smooth compared to LREER. Logically the low variability of the LREX series is due to the fact that the main impact of reform in the trade sector in India was in imports rather than exports. Imports were considerably more regulated than exports so that there was much more for the government to do with imports compared to exports. Also, the relatively minor changes that were undertaken for exports were introduced over a long period of time resulting in a relatively smoother transition. Thus although there were continuous changes in export mix and also the destination, the acceleration in growth was broad-based, with a double-digit growth rate registered across all the commodity groups and service sectors. Export performance improved after reforms at a comparatively greater pace. For the period 1970 to 1990 total merchandise exports grew at 37.49 per cent while for the period 1990 to 2008 the growth rate increased to 48.33 per cent[14]. The case of GDP is

[13] Perron (1989) showed that a large number of variables found to be I (1) by Nelson and Plosser (1982) without break become I (0) after internalizing the break. Many subsequent papers (in fact almost all papers on structural break have raised and discussed these issues).

[14] Source: WITS

different, with export accounting for a small part of GDP it had its own story to tell independently of exchange rates. The decade of eighties was marked by the emergence of the Indian economy out of the low growth syndrome of the previous three decades; the pick-up benefitted from the initiation of some reform measures since mid-eighties aimed at increasing domestic competitiveness.

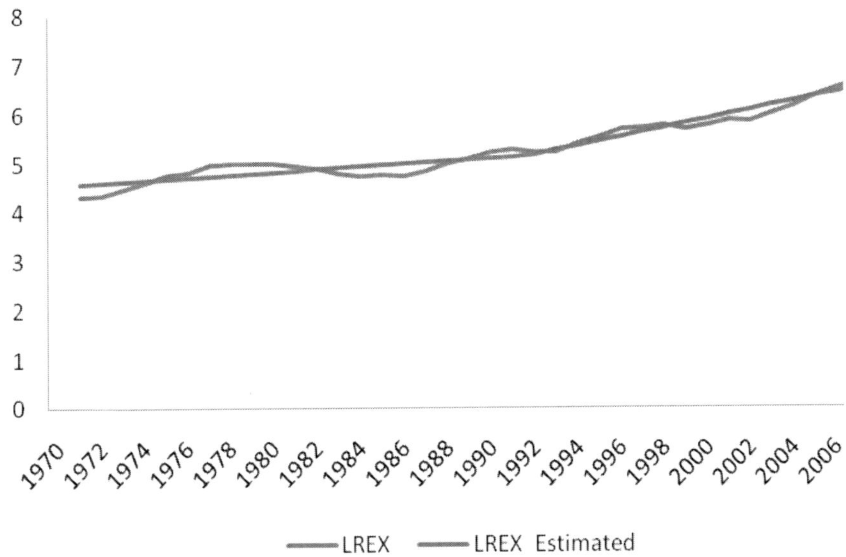

Note: The broken trend line is a fitted trend by (OLS) of the form $\hat{y}_t = \hat{\mu} + \hat{\gamma}_1 DU_t + \hat{\beta} t + \hat{\gamma}_2 DT_t$, where $DU_t = DT_t = 0$ if $t <= 1990$ and $DU_t = 1$, $DT_t = t$ if $t > 1990$

Figure 5. Regime Shift in the (log) value of "REX".

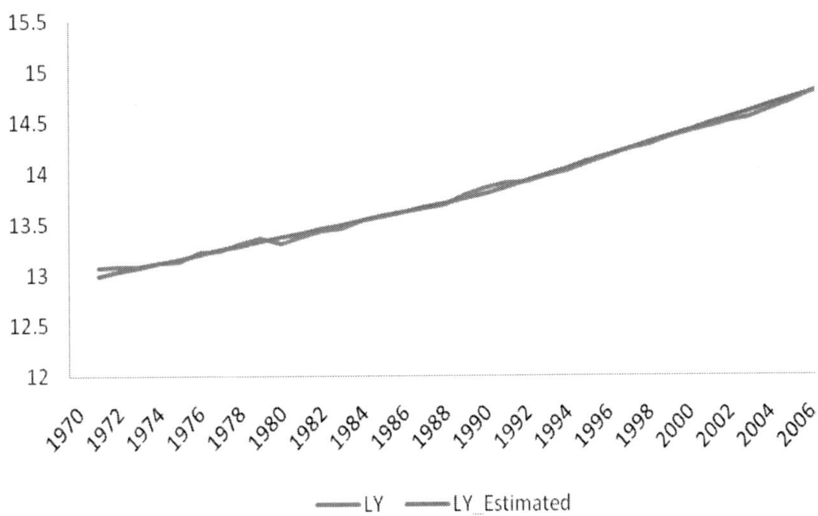

Note: The broken trend line is a fitted trend by (OLS) of the form $\hat{y}_t = \hat{\mu} + \hat{\gamma}_1 DU_t + \hat{\beta} t + \hat{\gamma}_2 DT_t$, where $DU_t = DT_t = 0$ if $t <= 1989$ and $DU_t = 1$, $DT_t = t$ if $t > 1989$.

Figure 6. Regime Shift in the (log) value of "Y".

The political instability and the Gulf war coupled with rising current account deficits, and dwindling foreign exchange reserves, resulted in a dip in the average of the annual growth rate of GDP dipped during the three year period of fiscal contraction from 1990-91 to 1992-93[15]. Thereafter, the growth impulses gathered the necessary momentum and exhibit a near upward trend.

CONCLUSION

The government of India's New Economic Policy of 1991 had two parts. The main aim was to change the structure of the economy from a government oriented one to a market oriented one. This was the long term objective which was expected to be implemented in phases over a period of ten or twenty years. The other objective was to stabilize the economy while the policies are being implemented. These policies mostly consisted of monetary and fiscal policies and were clearly short term in nature implemented from time to time and adjusted or withdrawn according to the prevailing situation at any point of time.

The journey from a mixed economy with socialistic objectives towards a free market economy with competitive objectives has to be an extremely tedious one anywhere in the world. For a country as massive and as complex and chaotic as India it is natural to expect the journey to be next to impossible. However they did not have a choice as they were made to follow a liberalization package of the IMF.

The IMF's liberalization package touched upon every aspect of the economy. Since simultaneous implementation of all of them was not feasible a question of sequentiality in the policies came to the fore and was much discussed by economists in the early 1990s. One of the first policies to be implemented was the exchange rate policy. It should be understood that before the decade of the 1990s India's exchange rate was more or less fixed. Between 1947 and 1975 the rupee was pegged to the pound sterling after which it was pegged to a basket of currencies[16]. The Reserve bank of India announced the exchange rates on the basis of the daily exchange rate movements of a select number of currencies (of India's major trading partners). The fluctuations were intended mainly to keep the real exchange rate constant.

From this system of fixed (or "implicitly adjustable peg") exchange rates the Indian government shifted to a flexible exchange rate system (in the current account) by 1992-93. The shift was achieved by devaluations as well as removal of regulations. The devaluation of the currency created a break in the exchange rate series and the removal of regulations affected its over-time movements. However exports, which did not face such drastic policy changes and was riding the crest of booming world trade due to liberalization performed relatively steadily over time. Thus the two variables became delineated after the post reform period, exports continuously rising at a time when the rupee was actually appreciating in terms of the real effective exchange rate. This weakened the impact of the real effective exchange rate on exports to insignificant levels. Exports in India are mostly caused by other factors, not by the real effective exchange rate.

---

[15] It is not surprising therefore that Lee and Strazicich's (2004) break-point for LY has been estimated at 1989-90.

[16] There was a period in 1971 when the rupee was pegged to the dollar rather than the sterling at Rs 7.5 to the dollar. The sterling peg returned from January 1972 and continued till September 1975. In June 1972 the sterling started to float so that the peg implied that the value of the rupee had to be kept stable with respect to the (floating) sterling.

APPENDIX: ANALYSIS WITHOUT STRUCTURAL BREAKS

(Note since all the variables are I (1) without structural break we have used the two step Granger procedure for cointegration)

Table A1. Unit Root Tests

Variables	ADF[1]		PP[2]		Conclusion
	Level	First Difference	Level	First Difference	
LREX	-1.09	-3.23***	-0.70	-3.20***	I(1)
LREER	-0.49	-4.75*	-0.75	-4.76*	I(1)
LY	-1.27	-7.55*	-1.27	-8.77*	I(1)

Note: 1. Augmented Dickey-Fuller test. 2. Philips-Perron test. 3. Asterisks (*), (**) and (***) denote statistically significant at 1%, 5% and 10% levels respectively. 4. Results reported are those with drift and trend.

Table A2. Cointegration

	(2)
LREER	.40** (1.95)
LY	1.25* (13.05)
Constant	-14.09* (-6.22)

Note: 1. Asterisks (*) and (**) denote statistically significant at 1% and 5% levels respectively. 2. t-statistic in parentheses. 3. Dependent variable log of India's real exports. 4. Error is white noise (ADF statistic: -3.01).

ACKNOWLEDGMENTS

This paper is based on Bhattacharyya and Mukherjee (2012). We are indebted to Vijaya Katti, T P Ghosh, Jayesh Sen and Pradyut Pyne. Errors are ours.

REFERENCES

Bahmani-Oskooee, Mohsen, and Orhan Kara, 2003. "Relative responsiveness of trade flows to a change in prices and exchange rate", *International Review of Applied Economics*, 17:293-308

Bhattacharyya, R. and Mukherjee, J. 2012. "Do Exchange Rates Affect Exports in India", Working Paper no. 314, Forum for Research in Empirical International Trade.

Christiano, Lawrence J., 1992. "Searching for a Break in GNP", *Journal of Business and Economic Statistics,* 10: 237-250.

Dickey, D.A. and W.A. Fuller, 1979. "Distribution of the Estimators for Autoregressive Time series with a Unit Root", *Journal of American Statistical Association*, 74: 427-31.

Ghosh, 1990. "Exchange Rates and Trade Balance Some Aspects of Recent Indian Experience", *Economic and Political Weekly,* 441-445, March.

Gopinath, G., Itskhoki, O and Rigobon, R (2010), Currency Choice and Exchange Rate Pass-through, Harvard University, Mimeo.

Gregory, A. and B. Hansen, 1996. "Residual-Based Tests for Cointegration in Models with Regime Shifts", *Journal of Econometrics*, 70: 99–126.

Herzer, D. and Nowak-Lehmann D., 2006. "Is there a long-run relationship between exports and imports in Chile?", *Applied Economics Letters*, 13: 981–986.

Joshi, V. and I.M.D. Little, 1994. *India: Macroeconomics and Political Economy, 1964-1991*, Delhi: Oxford University Press.

Kim, D. and P Perron (2009) "Unit Root Tests Allowing For A Break in the Trend Function at an Unknown Time Under Both the Null and Alternative Hypotheses", *Journal of Econometrics*, 148: 1-13.

Kohli, R. (2002), Real Exchange Rate Stationarity in Managed Floats, *Economic and Political Weekly*, February 2, 2002, p 475- 482.

Kunitomo, N., 1996. "Tests of Unit Roots and Cointegration Hypotheses in Econometric Models", *Japanese Economic Review*, 47: 79-109.

Leybourne, S. J. and P. Newbold, 2003. "Spurious rejections by cointegration tests induced by structural breaks", *Applied Economics*, 35: 1117-1121.

Nelson, C. R., And C. I. Plosser (1982): 'Trends and Random Walks in Macroeconomic Time Series," Journal of Monetary Economics, 10, 139-162.

Nayyar, D., 1988. 'India's Export Performance: Underlying Factors and Constraints', in R.E.B. Lucas and G.F. Papanek (eds.), *The Indian Economy: Recent Development and Future Prospects*, Delhi: Oxford University Press.

Perron, P., 1989. "The Great Crash, the Oil Price Shock, and the Unit Root Hypothesis", *Econometrica*, 57: 1361-1401.

Pesaran MH and Shin Y. 1999. An autoregressive distributed lag modelling approach to cointegration analysis. Chapter 11 in *Econometrics and Economic Theory in the 20th Century: The Ragnar Frisch Centennial Symposium*, Strom S (ed.). Cambridge University Press: Cambridge.

Phillips, R. C. B. and P Perron, 1988. 'Testing for a Unit Root in Time Series Regression', *Biometrika,* 335-346.

Reserve Bank of India (2005), *Reserve Bank of India Bulletin*, December, 2005.

Sarkar, P., 1994. 'India's Balance of Payment and Exchange Rae Behaviour since 1971: A New Approach', *Economic and Political Weekly,* 29: 43-48.

Sinha Roy, S., 2001. 'Post-reforms Exports Growth in India: An Exploratory Analysis', *RIS Discussion Paper # 13*, New Delhi: Research and Information System for the Non-aligned and Other Developing Countries.

Srinivasan, T.N., 1998. 'India's Export Performance: A Comparative Analysis' in I.J. Ahluwalia and I.M.D. Little (eds.), *India's Economic Reforms and Development: Essays for Manmohan Singh*, Delhi: Oxford University Press.

____ (2007). 'Sources of India's Export Growth in Pre and Post Reform Periods', *Economic and Political weekly*, June 23, 2007 p 2419-2427.

Veeramani, C., 2008. 'Impact of Exchange Rate Appreciation on India's Exports', *Economic and Political Weekly,* 22: 10-15.

Wilson, John F, and Wendy E. Takacs, 1979, "Differential responses to price and exchange rate influences in the foreign trade of selected industrial countries", *Review of Economics and Statistics*, 61:267-79.

Zivot, E. and D. Andrews, 1992. "Further Evidence on the Great Crash, the Oil Price Shock and the Unit Root Hypothesis", *Journal of Business and Economic Statistics* 10: 251-270.

In: Current Issues in International Trade
Editor: Gouranga G. Das

ISBN: 978-1-63321-405-7

Chapter 5

COMPLEMENTARITIES OF INDIA–RUSSIA ECONOMIC RELATIONS: PRESENT STATUS AND FUTURE PROSPECTS

Sanjib Pohit*

Professor AcSIR and Senior Principal Scientist,
CSIR-National Institute of Science, Technology and Development Studies,
Pusa Gate Dr. K.S. Krishnan Marg, New Delhi

ABSTRACT

This chapter examines complementarities and potentialities in merchandise trade in general and high-technology trade in particular between India and Russia. The analysis shows that bilateral trade flow is small even though trade complementarities in the segment of high technology as well as in merchandise trade in general exist. Inefficient trade logistics networks, absence of mutual recognition of standard, lack of bilateral technology and skill transfer, and low level of connectivity between private sectors of either country are some of the factors responsible for not realizing the potentials of trade. The economic cooperation between the two would diminish further in the coming years if we take into account the move by India to enter into Free Trade Agreement (FTA) with major trading partners such as European Union and Japan. The private sector of OECD countries has closer link with Indian private sector, the principal engine of economic and trade growth. In this context, the governments of Russia and India need to play a proactive role to raise the level of economic engagement.

Keywords; India, Russia, High Technology, CGE model, Trade

INTRODUCTION

Since independence and until the late 1960s, India was a champion of the nonalignment movement, without aligning herself with either the Eastern bloc or the Western bloc.

* Email: spohit@gmail.com; spohit@nistads.res.in

However, foreign exchange constraints of the independent India in the 1960s and the introduction of rupee trade for importing capital goods from the Eastern bloc intensified the economic relationship between India and the same. The 1971 India–Pakistan war further cemented the economic relationship between India and Russia when the latter took the Indian side by giving diplomatic and military support for the Bangladesh liberation war. Since then, Russia has been one of the principal suppliers of armament, which continued until now. However, the economic ties diminished greatly with the collapse of the Soviet Union in 1991. For most of the post-Soviet era, annual bilateral trade between the two countries has hovered around US $2–3 billion a year. It increased to US $8 billion in 2009 and further to US $11.04 billion in 2012. Since the signing of the "Declaration on the India Russia Strategic Partnership" in October 2000 during the visit of the then president Vladimir Putin to India, there has been a qualitative strengthening of the relationship. During the visit of President Dmitry Medvedev to India in December 2010, it was mutually decided to elevate the bilateral relationship to the level of a "Special and Privileged Strategic Partnership."

India has always viewed Russia as a time-tested, trustworthy, and reliable strategic partner. However, economic ties are at a low level between the two, compared with a country like China, with whom India has a border dispute since the India–China war. Currently, trade between India and China has risen to US $66 billion in 2012 and the plan is to augment it to US $100 billion by 2015. In a recent visit to India, the Chinese premier Li Keqiang has proposed closer economic relations between China and India and possibly a China–India free trade agreement (FTA). The sheer economic size of an FTA between the two has special significance both bilaterally and for the global trading system.[1] However, India has yet to opt for the same because of huge trade deficit amounting to US $26 billion in 2012 that India has with China. There has been a substantial change in India's trade policy in recent years, and this has included increased emphasis on forming regional trade and economic alliances and signing FTAs and preferential trade agreements (PTAs) with other countries and trade groups for market access and greater economic clout (see Table 1). In addition to the agreement already concluded, India is party to 14 regional frameworks agreements with important trading partners including the EU, the negotiation of which is at an advanced stage.

In this context, the prospect for the vibrant growth of Indian-Russian economic ties barring defense is bleak unless complementarities in trade exist between the two. Against this background, this chapter examines the complementarities and potentials of trade between India and Russia in the light of the realignment of India trading relations. Our purview of analysis includes scope of technology and skill transfer between the two countries, how it stands against India's other trading partners, and quantification of possible gains from closed economic relationship between the two. The structure of the rest of the chapter is as follows. Following the introduction, section 2 analyzes the complementarities of technology trade between India and Russia and how it compares in relation to India's other trading partners. Section 3 analyzes the complementarities in technology and skill between India and Russia. In section 4, we quantify the complementarities and potentials of merchandise trade in general between India and Russia and gains that can accrue to both countries from a closed economic relationship. Finally, section 5 provides some concluding remarks.

[1] There are also other attractions of an FTA between these two economies. It is hoped that the mutual benefits from an FTA would make it easier to settle the border issue between the two countries. Also, there seems to be a convergence of interest in the Doha Round of multilateral trade negotiations.

Table 1. India RTAs in Force

RTA Name	Coverage	Type	Date of notification	Notification	Date of entry into force	Status
ASEAN–India	Goods	FTA	August 19, 2010	Enabling Clause	January 1, 2010	In Force
Chile–India	Goods	PSA	January 13, 2009	Enabling Clause	August 17, 2007	In Force
India–Afghanistan	Goods	PSA	March 8, 2010	Enabling Clause	May 13, 2003	In Force
India–Bhutan	Goods	FTA	June 30, 2008	Enabling Clause	July 29, 2006	In Force
India–Japan	Goods & Services	FTA & EIA	September 14, 2011	GATT Art. XXIV & GATS Art. V	August 1, 2011	In Force
India–Malaysia	Goods & Services	FTA & EIA	September 6, 2011	Enabling Clause & GATS Art. V	July 1, 2011	In Force
India–Nepal	Goods	PSA	August 2, 2010	Enabling Clause	October 27, 2009	In Force
India–Singapore	Goods & Services	FTA & EIA	May 3, 2007	GATT Art. XXIV & GATS Art. V	August 1, 2005	In Force
India–Sri Lanka	Goods	FTA	June 17, 2002	Enabling Clause	December 15, 2001	In Force
Korea, Republic of India	Goods & Services	FTA & EIA	June 23, 2010	GATT Art. XXIV & GATS Art. V	June 1, 2010	In Force
MERCOSUR*–India	Goods	PSA	February 23, 2010	Enabling Clause	June 1, 2009	In Force

Source: www.wto.org, Note: i) SAFTA is not shown here, ii) MERCOSUR comprises Argentina, Brazil, Paraguay, and Uruguay.

Complementarities of Economic Relationship between India and Russia

The two countries closely cooperate in diverse spheres, including defense, civil nuclear energy, space, science and technology, hydrocarbons, trade and investment, cultural and humanitarian fields, etc. In the coming years, the role of technology would be an important factor in respect of India's trade with any trading partners in general and with Russia in particular. This is because the president of India has declared the present decade as the decade of innovation and the prime minister has called upon the country's scientists to unleash the best innovative potential in the innovation decade. Even though India is yet to formally adopt a national innovation policy, the different ministries and departments associated with various sectors have articulated and budgeted for three main innovation policy challenges: enhancing innovation potential in new technologies, building technological capabilities and competitiveness in the manufacturing and service sector, and reconfiguring the formal and informal sectors.

How deepening is the role of technology in trade between India and Russia? To examine the same, we analyze the trend of trade in high-technology (HT) items between India and Russia. We focus on trade of non-defense items within the segment of HT trade since data of same are available for all countries. Moreover, with the Westerns countries, including USA, lifting of the sanction of exports of defense items to India, India has now a wider choice of sourcing of defense imports. Thus, defense ties may not be the stimulus for India–Russia economic ties in the coming years.

To start with, we specify the different HT components of manufacturing products. The product approach is most commonly used to identify technology-intensive industries and products. The classification was made by the OECD Secretariat in collaboration with Eurostat; the objective is to finalize the approach by sector and to provide a more appropriate instrument for analyzing international trade. The list proposed by the OECD Secretariat in 1994 represented an important first step in this new field and served as the basis for subsequent work (OECD, 2008). Since 1994, the five-digit foreign trade classification SITC Rev. 3 has been replaced by the six-digit Harmonized System classification (252 HS 6-digit codes are currently allocated as HT products). Generally, these codes correspond to items of following broad groups: (a) aerospace items; (b) computers-office machines; (c) electronics-telecommunications items; (d) pharmacy products; (e) scientific instruments; (f) electrical machineries; (g) nonelectrical machineries; and (h) chemicals. The source of our data is the World Bank's online WITS database. In what follows, we analyze the performance of India and Russia's trade in respect to HT products in recent years, focusing particularly on bilateral HT flows.

Aggregate Trend Analysis

Currently, the HT export market in the world is dominated by China.[2] Previously, it was dominated by the United States. In 2000, the export of HT products from China was US $22.3 billion, which increased to more than 11 times to US $260.3 billion in 2011. The growth rate is as high as 25.03%. This is clearly showing how aggressively China is trying to control the HT export in the world. In the case of United States, the export of HT products was US $128.1 billion in 2000, which fell sharply to US $115.6 billion in 2011. European Union is also dominating the world HT export market recently. In 2000, the export from European Union was US $106.9 billion, which almost doubled in 2011, reaching US $212.2 billion in that year. It is also interesting to note that the value of HT export from China alone is much more than the value of HT export from European Union.

Table 2 shows the share of top 10 exporters of HT products in the world market. China is dominating with more than one-fifth of the total world HT export share. After China, Germany and United States have the largest shares. Note that the share of China in the world market has been growing rapidly over the past decade. It was 3.55% in 2000, which rose to 20.18% in 2011.

In the case of United States, however, we observe a sharp decline in the share in world HT market. Together, these top 10 countries in 2011 dominated 74.79% of the world's export of HT products, which was 67.8% in 2000.

[2] Author's estimate based on WITS database.

Table 2. Share of Top 10 Countries in the World's Export of HT Products (%)

	2000	2005	2006	2007	2008	2009	2010	2011
China	3.55	11.68	12.67	14.99	15.72	16.68	18.83	20.18
Germany	8.49	9.64	9.54	8.99	8.73	9.54	9.30	10.03
US	20.40	14.78	14.91	16.15	15.29	10.31	9.57	8.96
Hong Kong	4.02	5.57	5.36	5.69	5.67	5.97	6.77	7.15
France	6.35	5.47	5.51	5.60	6.12	6.65	6.97	6.71
Korea, Rep.	3.61	4.35	4.43	5.62	5.70	6.68	6.67	5.89
Japan	9.65	6.53	5.80	5.04	4.81	4.63	5.02	4.90
UK	6.12	6.20	8.17	4.16	3.82	4.27	3.97	4.32
Switzerland	1.96	2.56	2.42	2.76	3.11	3.50	3.21	3.47
Singapore	3.66	4.27	4.39	3.08	3.76	3.15	3.50	3.17

Source: Author's estimate based on WITS Database.

It is evident from Table 2 that Russia does not figure in the list of top 10 countries specializing in HT exports in the world. Incidentally, many of the countries figuring in this list are OECD countries, with whom India shares a vibrant trade relationship.

Table 3 shows additional summary statistics in respect of HT trade of India, Russia, USA, EU, and China. As this table shows, India's overall HT exports has risen from US $2.06 billion in 2000 to US $4.1 billion in 2005 and further to US $12.8 billion in 2011. During the same time frame, Russia's HT export has increased from US$ 3.9 billion in 2000 to US $5.4 billion in 2011. By contrast, China's HT exports rose from US $41.7 billion in 2000 to US $457 billion in 2011. The dismal performance of India and Russia is also reflected in other summary indicators, such as the share of HT trade in the respective country's GNP, or in manufactured exports, or in the share of country's HT trade in world HT trade. This compares poorly with China's (EU's) share of about 20.2 (38.4) percentage point of HT exports in world's HT exports. Thus, it seems that there exist limited complementarities in technology trade between India and Russia. In fact, it is better to foster closer link with China or EU or the OECD countries in general if India intends to upgrade technology via import route. To some extent, India has taken it forward by launching FTA negotiation with EU. Negotiation is in the advanced stage and is expected to be signed soon.

Trade Engagement in HT Products between India and Russia

We have seen that India and Russia are small players in the global space of HT exports. Given the close relationship between the governments over several years, one would expect synergies in trade in general and HT in particular to exist between them.

The data on economic engagement in the realm of HT trade are shown in Tables 4 and 5. As Table 4 shows, Russia's share in India's HT exports in most of the product category is 1% or below, except in pharmacy products where the share is 3%. Moreover, we find that Russia's position as trading partner has continuously declined over the years.

Table 3. Aggregate Exports /Imports of HT products by India, Russia, China, and USA

Item	Year	India		Russia		China		USA		EU	
		Export	Import	Export	Import	Export	Import	Export	Import	Export	Import
Absolute (US $ Million)	2000	2062	4259	3908	38464	41736	58641	197466	268346	390587	
	2005	4139	19867	3820	13386	215928	247258	190737	267176	552675	
	2009	10728	27916	4527	19140	309601	25968.5*	132407	265470.3*	511823	
	2011	12871		5444		457107		145273		623105	
Share of Manufactured Exports (%)	2000	6.3		16.1		18.9		33.8		21.2	
	2005	5.8		8.4		30.8		29.9		18.2	
	2009	9.1		9.2		27.5		21.5		15.3	
	2011	6.7		7.8		25.8		18.1		15.5	
Share of World Trade (%)	2000	0.24		0.4		3.55		20.40		40.35	
	2005	0.33	1.16	0.3	0.95	11.68	15.44	14.78	15.40	42.83	
	2009	0.94	1.49	0.24	1.25	16.68	13.44	10.31	13.54	27.20	
	2011	0.96		0.34		20.18		8.96		38.43	
Share of GNP (%)	2000	0.1		0.4		1.4		2.0		3.7	
	2005	0.2		0.2		4.1		1.5		4.2	
	2009	0.3		0.2		3.4		1.0		3.3	
	2011	0.3		0.2		4.0		1.0		3.8	

* Corresponds to 2008 data, Source: Author's estimate from www.wits.worldbank.org.

Table 4. Product-wise India's HT exports

Products	India's HT Exports					
	2000		2005		2009	
	Total	Share of Russia	Total	Share of Russia	Total	Share of Russia
	(1000 US $)	%	(1000 US $)	%	(1000 US $)	%
Aerospace	3166	2%	11658	0%	237958	0%
Computers office machines	166010	1%	282679	0%	411334	0%
Electronics-telecommunication	473966	1%	589000	1%	4828792	0%
Pharmacy	465060	5%	970665	5%	2204013	3%
Scientific Instruments	166349	6%	440824	0%	827558	0%
Electrical Machinery	6014	1%	35767	8%	100725	0%
Chemicals	278161	1%	966967	1%	2246943	1%
Nonelectrical Machinery	8316	0%	83906	0%	313447	0%

Source: Author's estimate from www.wits.worldbank.org.

Table 5. Product-wise Russia's HT Exports

Products	Russia's HT Exports					
	2000		2005		2009	
	Total	Share of India	Total	Share of India	Total	Share of India
	(1000 US $)	%	(1000 US $)	%	(1000 US $)	%
Aerospace	819305	9%	1647624	8%	1119096	40%
Computers office machines	49931	8%	60887	38%	177594	42%
Electronics-telecommunication	459361	12%	606963	23%	793332	27%
Pharmacy	51582	4%	69254	0%	104344	1%
Scientific Instruments	496499	5%	429263	3%	593968	18%
Electrical Machinery	42338	3%	121796	19%	105293	30%
Chemicals	1465746	0%	351751	0%	432949	8%
Nonelectrical Machinery	529371	0%	807890	0%	1389235	9%

Source: Author's estimate from www.wits.worldbank.org.

By contrast, India seems to be an important trading partner of Russia (Table 5), with the share ranging 30–40% in three product categories. Furthermore, we find that India's position as a trading partner of Russia has improved between the years 2000 and 2009. The three product categories in which Russia dominates are aerospace items, computer office machines, and electrical machinery and electronic telecommunication items.

How does Russia fare in relation to India's top 10 destinations of HT exports? As Figure 1 indicates, the top 10 destinations for India's exports are United States, United Arab Emirates, the Netherlands, China, Nigeria, Germany, Italy, Russian Federation, Indonesia, and Brazil.

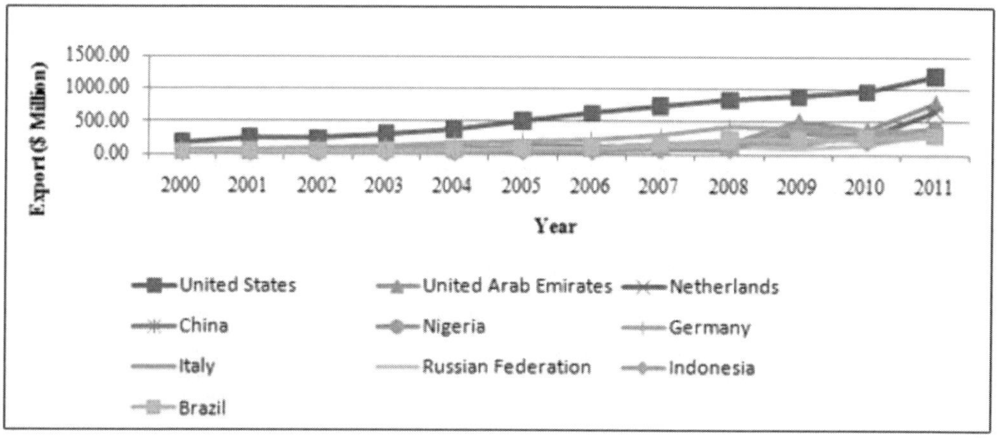

Source: WITS Database.

Figure 1. Top 10 Exporting Destinations of India.

Table 6. Share of Top 10 Countries in the India's Export of HT Products (%)

	2000	2005	2006	2007	2008	2009	2010	2011
United States	11.34	16.56	17.34	16.06	13.18	9.24	11.36	10.29
United Arab Emirates	2.15	3.20	2.81	3.03	2.60	5.34	4.43	6.76
The Netherlands	4.50	3.25	2.43	2.78	2.20	2.00	3.25	5.60
China	2.42	3.61	3.36	3.12	2.82	3.49	3.43	3.52
Nigeria	1.70	1.97	2.40	2.01	1.99	3.98	2.48	3.40
Germany	4.79	6.48	6.08	6.39	6.88	4.19	4.34	3.13
Italy	3.08	2.01	2.24	2.50	2.39	1.53	3.82	3.01
Russian Federation	1.54	2.06	2.34	2.27	1.80	0.94	1.61	2.94
Indonesia	0.96	1.21	1.04	1.29	1.16	4.45	2.28	2.55
Brazil	2.27	3.03	2.88	3.51	3.55	2.43	2.93	2.46

Source: Author's estimates based on WITS.

Currently, the share of the top 10 exporting destinations of India's HT export is 43.68%, which was 34.75% in 2000. This clearly indicates that India, over the time, has been concentrating majorly on her top 10 exporting destinations. With regard to Russia, it seems to be on the rise in recent years. But, the share is still less than 3%. This is much less than India's shares of exports to countries like Italy, UAE, etc.

To explore the reason behind the low level of economic engagement between Indian and Russia, we analyze the HT products at 4/5 digit level of disaggregation that these two countries export to the rest of the world (ROW). The relevant statistics are collated in Table 7. As this table shows, out of the HT items under aerospace product category that India exports to the ROW, India was able to export only 43% of the same to Russia in 2009. Except for pharmacy category, we find that India is able to export only 50% or less of products to Russia that she exports to the ROW! Even in pharmacy, in which it is widely recognized that India has a comparative advantage due to low production cost of generic drugs, not all products that India exports to the ROW are being exported to Russia. The picture is better on the other side (Russia to India). Under three categories, the value of the percentage is more than 80%. In one category (computer office machines), Russia is able to export to India all of the products that she exports to the ROW.

Table 7. Percentage of Exportable Products in Total that are Bilaterally Traded in 2009

Product Type	Percentage of number of exportable products at SITC 4/5 digit level in total that are exported from	
	India to Russia	Russia to India
Aerospace	43%	36%
Computers office machines	44%	100%
Electronics-telecommunication	40%	89%
Pharmacy	75%	14%
Scientific Instruments	51%	71%
Electrical Machinery	30%	80%
Chemicals	54%	38%
Nonelectrical Machinery	16%	36%

Source: Author's estimate from www.wits.worldbank.org.

Table 8. Number of HT Products being Exported

Country	2000	2011
Brazil	211	197
India	224	226
China	229	217
South Africa	227	211
Russia	232	187
USA	248	233
Germany	238	224
Japan	232	217
Korea	222	224
World	248	244

Source: Author's estimate based on WITS database.

It must be mentioned that India has a wider spectrum of HT products that is exported to the ROW relative to Russia. Out of 244 HT products that are listed in 2010, India exports 221 products, whereas Russia exports 185 products (Table 8). As Table 8 indicates, China or the OECD countries are better placed to meet India's demand of HT products for technology upgradation.

Since the major trading partners of exportable HT products of India are mainly developed economies such as USA, EU, Japan, and China, it appears that inferior variety of products may not be the sole reason for the low level of trade. Does low level of trade occur due to mismatch in demand and supply of products? In other words, perhaps the principal HT products that India exports to the ROW do not figure among the major items of Russia's import from the ROW and vice versa. In that case, a low level of trade between the two countries is expected. Since the top three items of HT exports (imports) in any category constitute more than 50% of India's HT exports (imports) under the same category, we have matched the top three items of HT exports of either country with the top three items of imports of partner countries. If there is a perfect match (100%), then the top three items of India's HT exports should be same as the top three items of Russia's HT imports and vice versa.

The matching indicator (in percent) is shown in Table 9. As Table 9 indicates, the value of matching indicator is generally less than 50%. In the case of chemicals, there is zero matching among the top three items of exports (imports) of India and Russia. This probably suggests that the low level of engagement in bilateral trade in the category of HT, to some extent, occurs due to low of level of complementarily in HT trade between these two countries.

Of course, HT trade flow, like any other commodity, is influenced by duties and nontariff barriers (NTBs). If barriers are high, trade would be low. Both countries are governed by the WTO rules and have accorded MFN status to each other. In an earlier study, Pohit (2012) has suggested that tariff is not a barrier for India's HT exports, but the NTBs are a factor responsible for the low level of export. However, the absence of mutual recognition of standard and conformity assessment procedures is a barrier for export in the case of trade with Russia. This is particularly true in case of pharmacy exports (see Sen, 2011).

Table 9. Matching of Top 3 products of Bilateral Trade

Product Type	Matching in Percent
Aerospace	17%
Computers office machines	33%
Electronics-telecommunication	33%
Pharmacy	17%
Scientific Instruments	50%
Electrical Machinery	33%
Chemicals	0
Nonelectrical Machinery	33%

Source: Author's estimate from www.wits.worldbank.org. The year for which the analysis is done is 2009.

FDI CHANNEL OF TRADE

Presently, trade between multinational affiliates located in different countries is a significant factor for growth of technology trade between countries. If FDI flows between India and Russia are small, low level of trade under this channel is expected. An analysis of sources of FDI inflows in India indicates that Russia does not figure as an important source of FDI inflows (Table 10). As this table shows, OECD countries are the main sources of FDI flows in India. Mauritius also figures in the list, because of the FDI flows from many OECD countries are routed through Mauritius to take advantage of their existing tax regime existing.

Table 10. India's Inward FDI Flows by Source Countries (%)

	2000–03	2004–08
Developed countries	52	34
Developing Countries	48	66
Mauritius	41	49.5
USA	13	7.6
U.K.	8	7.1
Singapore	2	9.9
The Netherlands	7	4.7
Japan	9	2.4
Germany	4	2.8
France	3	1.4
Korea	1	0.6
Switzerland	2	1

Source: DIPP, Government of India.

Table 11. India's Outward FDI Stocks: Geographical Structure (%)

	Outward FDI Stocks of 2006
Developed Countries	32.2
Developing Countries	67.8
Asia	19.9
Africa	20.4
EU	12.7
CIS	17.3
Other Europe	0.9
Latin American & Caribbean	10.4
Oceania	3
North America	15.4

Source: OECD, Investment Policy Review, India, 2009.

Table 12. Russia's FDI: Geographical Structure, 2007 (%)

	FDI Inward Stock	FDI Outward Stock
Cyprus	34.4	13.5
The Netherlands	34.2	51.9
Luxembourg	0.7	
UK	3.3	4.7
Germany	4.4	1.9
USA	3.5	8.1
Ireland	0.4	
France	1.5	
Switzerland	1.6	0.6
Virgin Island	2.8	0.3
Ukraine		0.9
Belarus		4.7
Others	13.2	13.4

Table 13. FDI flows in Billion US $ at current price

Outward FDI flows	2000	2001	2002	2003	2004	2005	2006	2007	2008	2009	2010	2011	2012
India	1	1	2	2	2	3	14	17	21	16	16	12	9
Russian Federation	3	3	4	10	14	18	30	46	56	43	53	67	51

Source: Estimated from http://unctadstat.unctad.org/TableViewer/tableView.aspx.

By contrast, CIS countries figure as a chosen destination of outward FDI stocks by Indian firms (Table 11). Among the CIS countries, Russia is an important destination.

An analysis of the principal sources of FDI inward stock in Russia or the destination of outward FDI stock from Russia does not identify India as an important partner (see Table 12).

It must be mentioned that that outward FDI flows by India or Russia are no more insignificant (Table 13). It is just that Russian MNCs or Indian MNCs do not consider the partner country as a prospective destination for investment. For long, the relationship between the two has flourished due to official leverage, and public sector companies in either country took the lead for economic tie-ups. With public sector in either country taking a back seat in the post-reform period as the engine of growth, economic relationship has also declined. In today's world, the private sector is the driver of growth in any country. So unless they increase their presence in the partner country, trade through FDI route cannot expand. The government in either country needs to take proactive stand such that private sector in either country engages with each other. Nowadays, the OECD countries are sources as well as destinations of FDI inflows to India and FDI outflows from India, respectively, because the Indian private sector has developed close business links with the OECD countries since independence. The same does not hold in case of private sectors of India and Russia due to the dominant role played by the public sector of either country in the pre-reform era. Hence, a proactive stand by both the governments is required to nurture this source of trade.

State of Logistics Networks

Another problem resulting in the low level of trade is inefficient logistics networks for trade between the two. In the past decades, trade between the two has been managed by government agencies.

The aspect of efficient logistics network was not a factor governing trade, but strategic relationship between the two was the guiding motive behind trade. Of late, the size of government-controlled trade has declined. By contrast, the private sectors are currently the major engine of growth/trade in either country. Profit is the principal motive of their trade. If logistics networks for trade are not efficient, the private sector would avoid trading with each other. They would look elsewhere for a market. This has been happening for trade in general and HT products in particular. Trade from the OECD countries benefits because of an efficient logistics channel. Its absence is also a contributing factor for the low level of India's trade with the neighboring South Asian countries, or even in African countries. Since India has a close tie-up with South East countries, the logistics network in that route is well developed, and China has basically explored this route for expanding trade with India, or other developed economies.

Of course, China has also invested heavily on improving the logistic network for their trade all around the globe. It is not a coincident that China has emerged as a major partner country of trade for both India and Russia.

Complementarities in Technology and Skills between India and Russia

Often frontier technology comes bundled with FDI inflows. Such technology spillovers of foreign capital lead to gains in host countries. For generation as well as diffusion of technology, skilled manpower is essential. We have seen that FDI flow is minimal between India and Russia. It may be possible that low-level FDI flow is due to the absence of technology generation between them or due to absence of complementarities in technology and skills.

Table 14 indicates that government expenditure on R&D as percent of GDP was only 0.88% in India in 2007 and 1.05% in Russia in 2011, significantly lower than technology-driven countries such as USA, Japan, or even lower than that of China. Furthermore, we see technicians in R&D per million people in India is significantly lower than in Russia, even though Russian's numbers are almost half that of a technology-rich country like Germany (Table 15).

Table 14. Government's Expenditure on R& D as % of GDP

Year	USA	Japan	EU27	China	India*	Russia
2000	2.74	3.04	1.74	0.90	0.78	1.05
2001	2.76	3.12	1.76	0.95	0.76	1.18
2002	2.66	3.17	1.77	1.07	0.75	1.25
2003	2.66	3.20	1.76	1.13	0.74	1.29
2004	2.55	3.13	1.73	1.24	0.78	1.15
2005	2.59	3.31	1.74	1.32	0.88	1.07
2006	2.65	3.41	1.76	1.39	0.87	1.07
2007	2.72	3.46	1.77	1.40	0.88	1.12
2008	2.86	3.47	1.84	1.47		1.04
2009	2.91	3.36	1.92	1.70		1.25
2010	2.83	3.26	1.91	1.76		1.16
2011	2.77	..	1.94	1.84		1.05

Source: www.OECD- ilibrary.org and www.data.worldbank.org, *Refers to India's financial year/.

Table 15. Technicians in R&D per million people

Country Name	1996	2005
India	112	94
Russian Federation	654	519
Germany	1346	1148

Source: www.data.worldbank.org.

Table 16. Technology Generation Capability of Selected Countries

	Foreign Ownership of Domestic Inventions					% of Patents owned by Foreign Residents			
Country	Total Patents	Total co-operation with abroad	Japan	United States	European Union (27)	Total co-operation with abroad	Japan	United States	European Union
	YEAR 2009								
India	1051	392		175	121	37.3		16.7	11.5
Russia	557	142	5	47	61	25.5	0.9	8.4	11.0
China	7572	1095	50	375	482	14.5	0.7	5.0	6.4
USA	30089	3471	310		1858	11.5	1.0		6.2
Japan	17567	549		240	209	3.1		1.4	1.2
EU-27	32123	4109	204	2156	3650	12.8	0.6	6.7	11.4
	YEAR 2000								
India	329	125	1	66	47	38.0	0.3	20.1	14.3
Russia	680	242	5	88	79	35.6	0.7	12.9	11.6
China	1673	251	14	147	57	15.0	0.8	8.8	3.4
USA	42863	4326	381		2623	10.1	0.9		6.1
Japan	11186	934		562	274	8.3		5.0	2.4
EU-27	38972	4892	165	3132	3727	12.6	0.4	8.0	9.6

Source: www.statistics.oecd.org.

In sum, there is a lack of enabling environment for closer India–Russia cooperation in the technical field. During the years 2003–2009, about 900 foreign firms invested in R&D sector in India (see Mrinalini, 2013). Most of them are OECD countries, namely USA, UK, Germany, France, and Japan. Again, Russian MNCs are absent in this kind of ventures.

We also find from the patent generation data in Table 16 that technology-generation capability of both India and Russia has increased between 2000 and 2009. As this table indicates, technology generation by these two countries is significantly lower than that of China and, of course, technology-rich countries such as USA and Japan. It is also evident that collaborating partners of inventions are not in either country but are in countries like Japan, USA, and EU. It appears that there is little exchange of skills with regard to technology generation between India and Russia. Furthermore, emigration data of (skilled) labor of India and Russia indicate that neither India nor Russia is their favorite chosen country for emigration.[1] In addition, language is a barrier for India–Russian cooperation and emigration, unlike for OECD countries. Thus, it appears that both the governments need to take proactive action to develop complementarities in technology and skills to further bilateral trade between themselves.

Complementarities and Potentials in Merchandise Trade and Economic Benefits

In the earlier section, we have seen that economic engagement in the realm of technology trade is low between India and Russia. To what extent does economic engagement exist in the case of merchandise trade? Does trade potential exist between the two? This section analyzes these issues. The data for this analysis are based on Global Trade Analysis Project (GTAP) data base, version 8, which provides consistent comprehensive bilateral trade flows at broad sectoral level. The relevant statistics are shown in Table 17.[2] As this table shows, OECD countries, namely Japan, NAFTA, and EU, have emerged as most important partners for both India and Russia. China is also an important partner of Russia. As the share of total trade, exports to Russia from India and vice versa seems to be negligible.

We have seen that the present economic engagement is low between India and Russia. Naturally, a question arises whether trade complementarities exists between the two that may lead to gains in economic welfare in both countries. To do ex-ante analysis, we have used the well-known GTAP (Global Trade Analysis Project) modeling framework, which is documented in detail in Hertel (1997). The GTAP model is a multiregion, multisector, static computable general equilibrium model (CGE) based on the neoclassical macroeconomic theory.[3] Thus, markets are perfectly competitive and profit-maximizing producers use the technology that exhibits constant returns to scale. Like any other general equilibrium model, GTAP provides detailed bilateral trade, transport, and protection data with the vertical and horizontal linkages between all product markets, both within the model's chosen countries and regions and between the countries and regions via bilateral trade flows.

[1] See www.worldbank.org/prospects/migrationandremittances.
[2] We have aggregated the data obtained from GTAP using the aggregation concordance map given in Table 12.
[3] A brief description of the model is given in Annex 1.

Table 17. Major Export Partners of India and Russia, year 2007

Product Category	India's Exports Share to					Russia's Exports Share to				
	Russia	China	Japan	NAFTA	EU	India	China	Japan	NAFTA	EU
Grains and Crops	2%	11%	1%	8%	16%	8%	1%	0%	0%	10%
Forestry and Fishery	0%	0%	1%	4%	7%	1%	9%	1%	9%	31%
Mining	1%	1%	4%	23%	30%	0%	56%	15%	0%	21%
Livestock and Meat Products	0%	77%	5%	1%	6%	0%	5%	3%	4%	61%
Processed Food	2%	5%	8%	13%	19%	0%	18%	9%	7%	14%
Textiles and Wearing Apparels	1%	1%	1%	28%	39%	1%	2%	0%	2%	28%
Leather products	1%	6%	1%	12%	64%	0%	3%	0%	1%	67%
Light Manufactures	0%	2%	2%	30%	20%	2%	8%	3%	4%	31%
Petroleum and Coal products	0%	0%	5%	7%	18%	0%	3%	1%	16%	58%
Chemicals, Rubber, and Plastic products	2%	7%	2%	17%	21%	2%	10%	0%	9%	37%
Heavy manufacture	1%	6%	2%	15%	21%	2%	3%	6%	10%	30%
Transport Equipment	1%	0%	1%	14%	29%	1%	1%	0%	4%	15%
Electronic Equipment	1%	6%	1%	18%	30%	4%	6%	0%	4%	33%

Source: Author's estimate from GTAP database.

For the purpose of this study, we have used the standard GTAP model (version 6.2) consisting of 9 regions and 16 sectors (see Table 18 for sectoral description). The aggregation of sectors and regions has been carried out keeping in view the important trading partners of India and Russia.

The policy inputs to the model are various kinds of tariff and NTBs, subsidy parameter, Hicks-neutral productivity parameters, etc. (see Hertel, 1997, for full list policy shocks parameters). When a policy shock is given to the model, resources are allocated along the line of comparative advantage, which results in change in welfare through channels such as terms of trade effects and efficiency gains from trade. It should be noted that the model simulates only static gains based on a single set of equilibrium conditions rather than relationships that vary over time. Moreover, the present version of the model used in the study does not allow for very long-run adjustments that could occur through capital accumulation, population growth, and technological change. To find out the trade potential between India and Russia, we have undertaken three illustrative simulations as given below:

Simulation 1: India and Russia abolish completely bilateral tariffs and NTB on trade on commodities. In other words, India and Russia sign a free trade agreement on goods.

Table 18. Sectors and Regions of the CGE Model used for the present study

Regions		Sectors	
1	China	1	Grains and Crops (Rice, Wheat, Cereal Grains, Oilseeds, Vegetables, Fruits and nuts, Sugar cane, Sugar beet, Plant-based fibers, Crops nec)
2	Japan	2	Livestock and Meat Products (Cattle, Sheep, Goat, Horses, Animal products nec, Wool, Silk-worm, cocoons, Meat & Meat products)
3	India	3	Forestry and Fishery
4	Russia	4	Mining (Coal, Oil, Gas, Minerals nec)
5	South Africa	5	Processed Food (Processed rice, Food products nec, Beverages &Tobacco products Vegetable oil and fats, Sugar, Dairy products)
6	NAFTA (USA, Canada, Mexico)	6	Textiles and Wearing Apparels
7	Brazil	7	Leather products
8	European Union (27 member countries)	8	Light Manufactures (Wood products, Paper products publishing, Metal products, Manufacture nec)
9	Rest of World	9	Petroleum and Coal products
		10	Chemicals, Rubber &Plastic products
		11	Heavy manufacture (Mineral products, Ferrous Metal, Metals nec, Machinery and Equipments nec)
		12	Transport Equipments (Motor Vehicles, Transport Equipments & parts)
		13	Electronic Equipments
		14	Utilities (Electricity, Water supply, Gas distribution, Construction)
		15	Transport and communication (Trade, Transport nec, Sea Transport, Air transport, Communication)
		16	Other Services

Note: nec - Not elsewhere classified.

Simulation 2: Simulation 1 + 10% improvement in trade facilitation parameters. This simulation would capture the gains in trade if the trade logistics network, which is poorly developed in case of bilateral trade between India and Russia, is improved.

Simulation 3: Simulation 2 + India signs FTA with EU and Japan.

India has already signed FTA with Japan and EU, the negotiations are at an advanced stage. This simulation would highlight the impact on India–Russia economic ties in view of India's proactiveness with FTAs.

The results of the simulations are shown in Table 19. As Table 19 indicates, India's income rises by US $ 232 million when India and Russia abolish completely the bilateral barriers on trade in goods. Under this simulation, Russia's income rises by US $ 124 million. Note that the principal source of welfare gain in case of India is allocative efficiency effects, while the same in case of Russia is gains from terms of trade effects. In simulation 2, which incorporates simulation 1 plus productivity improvement in trade facilitation measures, we find that there are further gains, albeit small, in both countries. As this table shows, real returns to factors gain in both countries in both these simulations. Thus, this is a win–win situation in both counties.

It is evident that economic complementarities exist between India and Russia, only the government as well as private corporate sectors of either country need to be proactive in exploiting the benefits.

Table 19. Welfare effects of Economic Integration between India and Russia

Indicator	Simulation 1		Simulation 2		Simulation 3	
	India	Russia	India	Russia	India	Russia
Equivalent Variation (US $ Mill.)	232.55	124.39	309.6	142.34	3280.28	-237.96
Allocative Efficiency Effects	244.62	-94.82	286.98	-108.85	4244.13	-253.1
Terms of Trade Effects	0.3	271.03	3.35	297.17	-536.28	17.52
Real Return to Unskilled Labor (% Change)	0.03	0.06	0.04	0.07	0.57	0.06
Real Return to Skilled Labor (% Change)	0.02	0.05	0.03	0.05	0.42	0.04
Real Return to Capital (% Change)	0.02	0.02	0.03	0.02	0.34	-0.01
Simulation 1: Complete Removal of tariffs on goods between India and Russia						
Simulation 2: Simulation 1 + 20% improvement in trade facilitation parameters Simulation 3: Simulation 2 + India has FTA with Japan, EU						

Note: Author's estimate. The figure in parenthesis indicates percent of GNP.

India's proactiveness toward signing FTA with major trading partners does not augur well for Russia. When India enters into FTA with EU or Japan as in simulation 3, India gains to the tune of US $ 3.3 billion.

The principal source is allocative efficiency effect. In this case, Russia's welfare declines by US $ 237 million. Under this simulation, welfare of Japan and EU increases by US $ 1.1 billion and US $ 5.1 billion, respectively.[4] The returns to factors are positive for India. Clearly, it indicates that Russia and India's economic ties would further diminish in the coming years unless an enabling environment is created by the governments of both countries for fostering private sector participation.

Table 20 indicates the sectors that gain in exports under simulation 2 and simulation 3. It must be noted that the percentage change are of a large magnitude in several sectors due to a low level of trade in the base year.

As this table shows, exports from either country to the partners increase significantly for mining and manufacturing sector under simulation 2. HT products are embedded in several sectors of this model economy, particularly nonfood manufacturing sectors. Growth in exports in these sectors implies existence of significant trade potentiality including that in HT products. What is probably needed is the environment, improved trade logistics networks, and corporate-to-corporate networks.

However, the export picture changes somewhat under simulation 3. In the entire manufacturing sector, Russia's exports to India decline relative to simulation 2. These are basically sourced from EU and Japan. India's export to Russia changes only marginally. India's export to EU and Japan rises significantly.

In sum, India–Russia trade would probably go down in the aftermath of India signing FTA with EU and Japan.

[4] Author's estimate based on model run (not shown in Table).

Table 20. Export Growth (Percentage Change)

Goods Sector Only	Simulation 2				Simulation 3					
	India's export to			Russia's Export to India	India's export to			Russia's Export to India	EU's Export to India	Japan's Export to India
	Russia	EU	Japan		Russia	EU	Japan			
Grains and Crops	8.15	-0.13	-0.13	7	7.6	-0.24	-0.57	7.87	-0.40	-0.29
Livestock and Meat Products	0.99	-0.25	-0.22	5.81	-0.39	-0.74	-1.35	7.01	0.11	0.33
Forestry and Fishery	5.32	-0.11	-0.07	9.5	4.98	-0.03	-0.31	9.6	-0.48	-0.32
Mining	93.76	-0.02	-0.19	120.96	92.97	-0.44	-1.06	108.8	138.96	121.45
Processed Food	67.72	-0.07	-0.06	208.47	67.9	33.24	10.73	202.09	201.80	126.92
Textiles and Wearing Apparels	105.15	-0.06	-0.06	106.11	106.25	54.02	38.64	101.64	95.78	92.24
Leather products	67.95	-0.16	-0.17	96.52	69.18	20.93	103.74	81.93	82.24	85.31
Light Manufactures	85.66	0.09	0.1	98.16	89.08	6.43	4.67	83.88	72.44	74.37
Petroleum and Coal products	20.92	0.24	0.19	58.33	24.46	3.63	4.91	55.33	50.93	51.72
Chemicals, Rubber, and Plastic products	59.34	0.19	0.18	82.01	63.61	7.88	5.22	69.32	70.54	69.20
Heavy manufacture	53.01	0.15	0.16	119.62	57.96	7.42	10.25	95.28	72.91	77.35
Transport Equipments	38.84	0.07	0.07	83.66	42.6	18.68	3.94	63.98	42.09	123.47
Electronic Equipments	24	0.13	0.14	38.32	29.2	10.35	5.1	34.06	19.10	30.79

Note: Author's estimate.

Concluding Remarks

This chapter makes an attempt to understand the complementarities between the economic ties of India and Russia. The analysis shows that bilateral trade flow is minimal, even though trade complementarities between the two countries exist. Both the countries seem to trade more with OECD countries or China. In the realm of HT trade, and FDI flows, OECD countries seem to be their natural partners. Weak business links of the private sector of the two countries along with inefficiency in logistic trade networks are the bottlenecks for trade between them. We find that significant potential exists for growth in bilateral trade, whether in the realms of HT trade or in general merchandise trade if bilateral barriers in trade are abolished and governments of both countries create an enabling environment for close business cooperation. In view of India's stand toward FTAs, it could be a reality that India/Russia economic ties would further decline in the coming years.

Annex 1. GTAP Model

In the GTAP model, the firm's production structure is characterized by constant elasticity of substitution functional forms to combine intermediate inputs and primary factors of production such as land, natural resources, skilled and unskilled labor, and capital. Intermediate inputs are composites of foreign and domestically produced components. In our model run, we have considered only three factors of production, namely unskilled labor, skilled labor, and capital. International trade is characterized by Armington specification (Armington, 1969) such that foreign components of intermediate goods are differentiated by region of origin. Thus, firms can decide the sources of their imports, and based on the composite import price they decide on the optimal mix of the domestic and imported inputs. On factor market, full employment is assumed with labor and capital being mobile within the countries but immobile internationally. On the demand side of the GTAP model, each region is composed of a representative household who disposes of the entire regional income according to a Cobb–Douglas utility function specified over three forms of final demand, such as private household expenditure, government expenditure, and savings. Now, private household expenditure is defined over a constant difference of elasticity (CDE) demand system that permits different price and income responsiveness across countries (MacDougall, 2003).

Moreover, there is an explicit treatment for international trade and transport margins and a global banking sector intermediates between global savings and consumption. The model determines trade balance in each region endogenously, and hence foreign capital inflow may supplement regional domestic savings.

The closure of the model is of general neoclassical general equilibrium type with saving investment equality and clearance of the factor markets. It ensures endogenous wages and full employment of all the resources. Each of the economic relationships described in the model is based on literature reviews and econometric estimates.

References

Badri Narayanan G. and Terrie L. Walmsley, (Ed). Global Trade, Assistance, and Production: The GTAP 7 Data Base, Center for Global Trade Analysis, Purdue University. 2008.

Balassa, B. 1965. "Trade Liberalisation and Revealed Comparative Advantage." *The Manchester School,* 33, 99–123.

Hertel. T. W. (Ed). Global Trade Analysis: Modelling and Applications. Cambridge University Press. 1997.

Hatzichronoglou, Thomas. "Revisions of the High Technology Sector and Product Classification," OECD/GD(97)216, Paris, OECD, 1997.

Mani, Sunil. 2004. "Exports of High Technology Products from Developing Countries: Are the figures real or are they statistical artefacts," in Mani, Sunil and Henny Romijn (ed.) Innovation, Learning and Technological Dynamism of Developing Countries, Tokyo: United Nations University Press, pp. 12-47.

Mani, Sunil. 2010. "India," in UNESCO Science Report, pp. 363-377, UNESCO Publishing Paris.

Meri, Thomas. 2008. "Trade in High Tech Products: Statistics in focus," Science and Technology, July.

Mrinalini, N. 2013. "Foreign R&D centres in India: Is there any positive impact?", Current Science, Vol. 105, No. 6, 25 September

OECD. 2008. Working Party on International Trade in Goods and Trade in Services Statistics, STD/SES/WPTGS(2008)10.

OECD. 2008. Investment Policy Reviews: Russian Federation.

OECD. 2009. Investment Policy Reviews: India.

Pohit, Sanjib. 2009. "Trends in High-Technology Trade," in Banerjee, P. (ed.) India Science & Technology 2009, published by NISTADS (CSIR), pp. 131-134.

Pohit, Sanjib. 2011a. "High Technology Merchandise Trade: Where do India Stands?" NISTADS, unpublished mimeo.

Pohit, Sanjib and S. Basu. 2012. "High Technology Merchandise Exports: Where does India Stand?" South Asia Economic Journal, Vol. 13, September, No. 2, pp. 183–206.

Pohit, Sanjib 2011b. "Complementarities and Potentials of High Technology Trade, Technology and Skill Transfers between India-Russia," presented in International Conference on Social-economic and technological innovations in the globalising world (economy) (STIGE-2011): Mechanism and Institutions, organised by CSIR-NISTADS, November 2-5, New Delhi, India.

Sinha Roy, Saikat. 2004. "Complementarities and Potentials of Intra-regional Transfers of Investments, Technology and Skills in Asia." RIS Discussion Paper, No. 79/2004.

Sen, Amit. 2011. *Economic Times*, 15-16 June.

WTO. 1996. Trade and Foreign Direct Investment. www.wto.org/english/news_e/pres96_e/pr057_e.htm.

PART II: ANALYTICAL FRAMEWORKS TO MODEL SELECTIVE ISSUES

In: Current Issues in International Trade
Editor: Gouranga G. Das

ISBN: 978-1-63321-405-7

Chapter 6

INTERNATIONAL TRADE, GRAVITY EQUATIONS AND TOURISM: AN APPLICATION FOR INTRA-LATIN AMERICAN TRADE FLOWS*

Maria Santana-Gallego*, Francisco J. Ledesma-Rodríguez and Jorge V. Pérez-Rodríguez

[1]Universidad de La Laguna
Departamento de Economía Aplicada
Facultad de Economía y Empresa
Universidad de Las Islas Baleares
[2]Universidad de La Laguna
Departamento de Análisis Económico
Facultad de Ciencias Económicas y Empresariales
Universidad de La Laguna
[3]Universidad de Las Palmas
Dpto. de Métodos Cuantitativos en Economía y Gestión.
Facultad de Ciencias Económicas y Empresariales.
Universidad de Las Palmas de Gran Canaria. Las Palmas.

ABSTRACT

The main objective of the present chapter is to revisit the traditional estimates from the trade gravity equation in two ways. First, by recognizing the presence of "zero" trade flows between countries by following the methodology proposed by Helpman, Melitz and Rubinstein (2008), thereafter HMR. Disregarding countries that do not trade with each other implies that important information is not being considered and hence estimates could be biased. Second, the potential omission of a relevant variable that may lead to biased estimates is addressed. In particular, tourist arrivals is introduced as a potential

---

* We thank the Spanish Ministry of Economy and Competitiveness for financial support (ECO2011-23189). Also we want to thank the United Nations World Tourism Organisation for kindly providing tourism data.

* Tel: 971171383, E-mail: maria.santana@uib.es.

omitted factor in traditional trade gravity specifications since international visits could reduce both, fixed and variable costs of exporting. In that sense, the framework proposed by HMR is modified to theoretically justify the inclusion of tourism as an explanatory variable for explaining international trade. Finally, an empirical exercise is carried out to describe intra-Latin American trade flows for the period 1995-2010. Results suggest that not considering "zero" trade flows and the omission of tourism may contribute to explain the presence of an upward bias in the estimation of the effect of key variables of gravity equations.

JEL Code: F10
Keywords: Currency unions, international trade, tourism, gravity equations

INTRODUCTION

In the last two decades a growing literature in international trade focuses on the empirical determinants of the volume of international trade based on the estimation of gravity equations. The standard gravity model recognizes that international tourism is increasing in GDP and decreasing in the distance between countries. Extended versions of the model introduce demographical, historical, cultural and economic factors affecting trade costs. Gravity equation has become a major tool for the empirics of international trade. Indeed this model has been used to find answers to relevant issues of the International Economics, such as the relationship between borders and trade and the impact of free trade agreements and currency unions on this flow.[1].

A traditional critique to gravity equation is about the lack of theoretical underpinnings of the estimated gravity equations. However nowadays international economists recognize that the gravity specification can be supported by Heckscher-Ohlin models, models based in differences in technology across countries, and the new models that introduce increasing returns and product differentiation (Deardoff, 1998). Moreover, Anderson and Van Wincoop (2003) developed a method that consistently and efficiently estimates a theoretical gravity equation by considering multilateral and bilateral trade resistances. Rose and Van Wincoop (2001) proposed the inclusion of country fixed effects as a way to approximate the multilateral resistances.

In the present paper, the traditional estimates from the trade gravity equation are revisited in two ways. First, the new methodology proposed by Helpman, Melitz and Rubistein (2008) is carried out. This approach presents a theoretical framework to study bilateral trade flows across countries. According to these authors, not all firms in the country have a productivity level high enough to generate profits to cover fixed costs of exporting. In that sense, if fixed costs are high enough, no firms in a country may find it profitable to export and hence "zeros" naturally arise in trade data. This is known as country selection bias. The HMR approach holds that by disregarding countries that do not trade with each other, important information is not being considered and hence estimates could be biased.

Second, the potential omission of a relevant variable in trade gravity equations is addressed. In this research the omission of international tourism is proposed as a suitable candidate to explain the possible overvalued estimate of the impact of a common currency on

[1] See for instance Rose (2000), Persson (2001), Glick and Rose (2002) and Anderson and Van Wincoop (2003).

trade. Moreover, tourism is introduced in the well-founded HMR model by recognizing that tourism could reduce fixed and variable costs of exporting. If so, tourism arrivals arise as an explanatory variable in the probit equation for firm selection and in the gravity equation.

We deal with both proposes, i.e., the HMR approach and the introduction of tourism as an additional regressor of gravity equations, for the case study of intra-Latin American trade. There are few papers that explore the Latin American trade by using a gravity model. However, during the last years, some scholars have asked if integration agreements have been important for the Latin America regionalisation process. For instance, Carrillo-Tudela and Li (2004) and Agudelo, Benitez, and Davidson (2006) apply a gravity model to examine the effects of the Andean Community and Mercosur on both intra-regional and intra-industrial trade in Latin American countries. Martinez-Zarzoso and Nowak-Lehmann (2003) studied Mercosur-European Union trade while Cortes (2007) explores the composition of trade between Australia and Latin America. Thus further analysis revisiting traditional estimates from trade gravity equation, is required, since this is going to provide a deeper understanding of Latin American trade flows.

The paper is organized as follows. In the following section, the HMR approach is presented in detail, while in the following one, the HMR model is modified to introduce tourism. Then, an empirical analysis is carried out where the modified model is estimated for the case of intra-Latin American trade flows and in the last section some conclusions are drawn.

THE HMR APPROACH

Gravity model is a workhorse in a number of empirical issues addressed by the International Economics. This model is used to estimate the effects of economic and non-economic events and factors on international flows of goods, migrants, investment and tourists. Indeed the evaluations of free trade agreements, international borders and currency unions are the main fields of application of gravity equations.

HMR presents a theoretical framework to study bilateral trade flows across countries. The model presents three features that make it suitable to describe empirical patterns of bilateral trade flows. First, the model can yield asymmetric trade flows between country pairs depending on the direction of export flows (from i to j versus from j to i).

Second, it can generate zero trade flows in both directions between some countries, as well as zero exports from one country, say j, to a second country i, together with positive exports from country i to country j.

Third, a well-founded empirical framework for estimating the gravity equation for trade flows is developed. Therefore, the HMR model has the potential to explain prevalent regularities in trade data reflected in the sample: the asymmetry in bilateral trade flows between country pairs and the high presence of zeroes.

The HMR approach generalizes the Anderson and VanWincoop (2003) model in two ways. First, it accounts for firm heterogeneity and fixed trade costs and second, deals with asymmetries in the volume of exports between two countries. HMR use their theoretical model to develop a two-stage estimation procedure. In the first stage, a probit equation is estimated for the probability that country j exports to country i while in the second stage predicted components of probit are used to estimate the gravity equation for positive exports flows.

In this section the HMR proposal is presented in detail as a suitable framework to revisit Rose's empirical findings. In their model, a utility function *à la* Dixit-Stiglitz is assumed to allow for product differentiation. Producers face both variable and fixed costs of exporting to each destination country by recognizing that profitability of exports to a particular destination depends on both a genuine transport cost and a fixed cost of serving that particular country. The monopolistic competition equilibrium yields a gravity equation as well as a firm selection equation.

Consumption

Let a world with J countries, indexed by j=1, 2,..., J, where a set of goods B_j is available for consumption in country j. Consumers of country j maximize a CES utility function given by

$$u_j = \left[\int_{l \in B_j} x_j(l)^{\varepsilon - 1/\varepsilon} dl\right]^{\varepsilon/\varepsilon - 1}, \varepsilon > 1$$

where $x_j(l)$ is the country j's consumption of product l and ε is the elasticity of substitution across products.

Solving the first-order conditions of the consumer problem yields the country j's demand for product l

$$x_j(l) = \frac{\breve{p}_j(l)^{-\varepsilon} Y_j}{P_j^{1-\varepsilon}} \tag{1}$$

where Y_j is the income of country j, $\breve{p}_j(l)$ is the price of product l in country j and P_j is the country j's dual price index given by

$$P_j = \left[\int_{l \in B_j} \breve{p}_j(l)^{1-\varepsilon} dl\right]^{1/(1-\varepsilon)} \tag{2}$$

Taking into account that

$$\frac{\partial P_j}{\partial \breve{p}_j(l)} = P_j^{\varepsilon} \breve{p}_j^{-\varepsilon} \tag{3}$$

Price demand elasticity for the good l produced in country j is

$$\frac{\partial x_j(l)}{\partial \breve{p}_j(l)}\frac{\breve{p}_j(l)}{x_j(l)} = -\varepsilon - (1-\varepsilon)\frac{\breve{p}_j(l)^{1-\varepsilon}}{P_j^{1-\varepsilon}} \tag{4}$$

The "large group" assumption assures that the second term in the right hand side is near zero, and as a result elasticity is approximated to $-\varepsilon$.

Production

Each firm of each country produces a distinct good and this may be supported by the presence of scale economies.

The number of bundles used by a firm to produce one unit of output is a being c_j the (country-specific) cost of a bundle supported by a firm country *j*. As a result, $c_j a$ is the minimum cost of a firm of country *j* producing one unit of output. Moreover, a cumulative distribution function $G(a)$ with support $\lfloor a_{L,} a_H \rfloor$ describes the distribution of *a* across firms, where $a_H > a_L > 0$ and this distribution function is assumed to describe the same in all countries.

A producer only supports a production cost when selling in the home market. However a producer of country *j* faces two types of additional costs of selling in country *i*: a transport variable cost τ_{ij} and a fixed cost $c_j f_{ij}$ of serving other market. τ_{ij} represents an iceberg transport cost so that only arrive to destination $1/\tau_{ij}$ units when one unit of product is shipped from *j* to *i*. Therefore, for domestic trade f_{jj} equals zero and τ_{jj} equals one while for international trade $f_{ij} > 0$ while $\tau_{jj} > 1$.

Profit maximization is carried out to find the price of a good *l* produced in country *j* that is sold in country *i*. The profit equation is

$$\Pi_{ij} = \breve{p}_j(l)x_j(l) - c_j a\tau_{ij}x_j(l) - c_j f_{ij} \tag{5}$$

where the second term in the right hand side recognizes that $\tau_{ij}x_j(l)$ units of a good are shipped in order to sell $x_j(l)$ units in country *i*.

The first-order condition for a firm producing a good *l* in country *j* to be sold in country *i* is given by

$$\frac{\partial \Pi_{ij}}{\partial \breve{p}_j(l)} = \left(\breve{p}_j(l) - c_j a\tau_{ij}\right)\frac{\partial x_j(l)}{\partial \breve{p}_j(l)} + x_j(l) = 0 \tag{6}$$

Taking into account equations (3) and (4), the first-order condition (6) provides the price of a good *l* produced in country *j* that is sold in country *i*

$$\breve{p}_j(l) = \frac{\varepsilon}{\varepsilon - 1} c_j a \tau_{ij} \tag{6}$$

By substituting (6’) in (5), the maximized operating profits for a firm producing a good l in country j to be sold in country i are

$$\Pi^*_{ij}(a) = \frac{1}{\varepsilon}\left[\frac{\varepsilon \tau_{ij} c_j a}{(\varepsilon - 1)P_i}\right]^{1-\varepsilon} Y_i - c_j f_{ij} \tag{7}$$

Sales in country $i \neq j$ are profitable if profits in equation (7) are non-negative. This is the case when $a \leq a_{ij}$, since a is an inverse measure of productivity and a_{ij} is the threshold for a making operating profits equal to zero, so that

$$\frac{1}{\varepsilon}\left[\frac{\varepsilon \tau_{ij} c_j a_{ij}}{(\varepsilon - 1)P_i}\right]^{1-\varepsilon} Y_i = c_j f_{ij} \tag{8}$$

Only a fraction $G(a_{ij})$ of the N_j firms of country j has non-negative profits, so they will export to country i. Note that if $a_{ij} \leq a_L$, no firm in country j finds profitable to export to country i. Precisely, this may explain zero trade data for a number of country pairs. On the contrary, when $a_{ij} \geq a_H$ all firms from country j would export to country i.

International Trade

Turning to bilateral trade, by combining (1) and (6’), and by aggregating across firms, the value of country i’s imports from j is

$$M_{ij} = \left(\frac{\varepsilon c_j \tau_{ij}}{(\varepsilon - 1)P_i}\right)^{1-\varepsilon} Y_i \int_{a_L}^{a_{ij}} a^{1-\varepsilon} dG(a) N_j \tag{9}$$

Let

$$V_{ij} = \begin{cases} \int_{a_L}^{a_{ij}} a^{1-\varepsilon} dG(a) & \text{for } a_{ij} \geq a_L \\ \text{and zero otherwise} \end{cases} \tag{10}$$

Therefore, equation (9) may be rewritten as

$$M_{ij} = \left(\frac{\varepsilon c_j \tau_{ij}}{(\varepsilon - 1)P_i}\right)^{1-\varepsilon} Y_i V_{ij} N_j \tag{9’}$$

Which reflects the positive influence of multilateral resistance P_j to bilateral trade and the negative effect of bilateral resistance τ_{ij}. Again bilateral trade is zero if $a_{ij} \leq a_L$.

Finally, using equations (2), (6') and (10), the price index of country i can be written as

$$P_i^{1-\varepsilon} = \sum_{j=1}^{J} \left(\frac{\varepsilon c_j \tau_{ij}}{(\varepsilon - 1)} \right)^{1-\varepsilon} N_j V_{ij} \tag{11}$$

In order to obtain the empirical equations to be estimated, HMR approach assumes a truncated Pareto distribution for productivity *1/a* across firms, so that

$$G(a) = \frac{(a^k - a_L^k)}{(a_H^k - a_L^k)} \tag{12}$$

and, as a consequence,

$$dG(a) = \frac{ka^{k-1}}{(a_H^k - a_L^k)} da \tag{13}$$

where $k > \varepsilon - 1$ determines the shape of the distribution. Now by substituting (13) in (10), V_{ij} can be expressed as

$$V_{ij} = \int_{a_L}^{a_{ij}} a^{1-\varepsilon} \frac{ka^{k-1}}{(a_H^k - a_L^k)} da \tag{14}$$

after some algebra as

$$V_{ij} = \frac{ka_L^{k-\varepsilon+1}}{(k-\varepsilon+1)(a_H^k - a_L^k)_{ij}} \left[\left(\frac{a_{ij}}{a_L} \right)^{k-\varepsilon+1} - 1 \right] \tag{14}$$

where the term in brackets is denoted by W_{ij} by Helpman et al. (2008) and it is restricted to be non-negative. As a consequence, the expression for W_{ij} can be expressed as

$$W_{ij} = \max \left[\left(\frac{a_{ij}}{a_L} \right)^{k-\varepsilon+1} - 1, 0 \right] \tag{15}$$

Note that V_{ij} increases monotonically with a_{ij} and therefore with the share $G(a_{ij})$ of firms exporting from country j to country i. As a consequence, from equation (9') a growth in the number of firms exporting from country j to country i increases the value of country i's imports from j.

Taking logarithms in (9')

$$m_{ij} = (\varepsilon - 1)\ln((\varepsilon - 1)/\varepsilon) - (\varepsilon - 1)\ln c_j + n_j + (\varepsilon - 1)p_i + y_i + (1 - \varepsilon)\ln \tau_{ij} + v_{ij} \quad (16)$$

where lowercase variables denote logarithms of uppercase variables. HMR approach assumes that the transport cost is given by

$$\tau_{ij} = \left[D_{ij}^{\gamma} e^{-u_{ij}}\right]^{1/\varepsilon-1}$$

where u_{ij} are i.i.d. unmeasured trade frictions and D_{ij} is the distance between countries i and j. Taking logarithms in the expression of the transport cost and in (14), and substituting in (16), the gravity equation to be estimated can be expressed as

$$m_{ij} = \beta_0 + \lambda_j + \chi_i - \gamma d_{ij} + w_{ij} + u_{ij} \quad (16')$$

where

$\beta_0 = (\varepsilon - 1)\ln \alpha + \ln\left[\frac{k a_L^{k-\varepsilon+1}}{\left(a_H^k - a_L^k\right)\left(k - \varepsilon + 1\right)}\right]$ is the constant term

$\chi_i = (\varepsilon - 1)p_i + y_i$ is a fixed effect of the importing country

$\lambda_j = (1 - \varepsilon)\ln c_j + n_j$ is a fixed effect of the exporting country

Following HMR, their approach incorporates two main differences with respect to previous work. First, w_{ij} is included in equation (16'). This additional variable depends on a_{ij} which is determined by variables in equation (8), namely income and multilateral resistance of the destination country, as well as fixed and variable costs of serving market i from country j. Second, HMR approach considers zero trade data.

Firm Selection into the Export Market

The selection of firms into export markets, represented by the variable W_{ij} is determined by the cut-off value of a_{ij}, which is implicitly defined by the zero profit condition. In that sense, HMR approach proposes a latent variable from the operating profits in equation (8) so that

$$Z_{ij} = \frac{\frac{1}{\varepsilon}\left[\frac{\varepsilon \tau_{ij} c_j a_L}{(\varepsilon - 1)P_i}\right]^{1-\varepsilon} Y_i}{c_j f_{ij}} \quad (17)$$

Z_{in} represents the ratio of operating variable profits for the firm with the highest level of productivity, as measured by $1/a_L$ to the fixed costs of serving country i from country j. Z_{ij} lower than one suggests that the most productive firm of j cannot find profitable the export to i. In that case zero trade between the pair of countries is observed. On the contrary, Z_{ij} higher than one implies positive exports from j to i.

Precisely, when Z_{ij} is higher than one, W_{ij} is increasing in Z_{ij}. In other words, the variable that controls for the fraction of firms that export from j to i is increasing in the new latent variable Z_{ij}.

This relationship can be examined from (8) by calculating the ratio

$$\frac{a_{ij}}{a_L} = \left(\frac{\varepsilon c_j f_{ij}}{Y_i}\right)^{1/1-\varepsilon} \frac{P_i(\varepsilon - 1)}{\varepsilon \tau_{ij} c_j a_L} \tag{18}$$

As can be easily proved from equation (17), this ratio equals $Z_{ij}^{1/(\varepsilon-1)}$, and equation (15) can be rewritten as

$$W_{ij} = Z_{ij}^{(k-\varepsilon+1)/(\varepsilon-1)} - 1 \tag{19}$$

Taking logarithms in (17) and by substituting the expression of the logs of transport costs

$$\begin{aligned} z_{ij} = \ln\left(\frac{1}{\varepsilon}\right) + (\varepsilon - 1)\ln\left(\frac{\varepsilon - 1}{\varepsilon}\right) + (1-\varepsilon)\ln a_L - \varepsilon \ln c_j + (\varepsilon - 1)p_i + y_i \\ +(1-\varepsilon)\ln \tau_{ij} - \ln f_{ij} + u_{ij} \end{aligned} \tag{20}$$

where lowercase variables denote logarithms of uppercase variables. A positive value of the new latent variable z_{ij} indicates that country j exports to country i.

Let define the term of fixed costs as

$$f_{ij} = \exp(\phi_{ex,j} + \phi_{im,i} + \kappa\phi_{ij} - v_{ij}) \tag{21}$$

where $\phi_{ex,j}$, $\phi_{im,i}$ and ϕ_{ij} measure trade fixed costs for the export country, the import country and the pair of countries, respectively. v_{ij} are unmeasured trade frictions making trade fixed costs stochastic. By applying logarithms to (21) and substituting in (20), the latent variable can be expressed as

$$z_{ij} = \gamma_0 + \xi_j + \zeta_i + \gamma d_{ij} - \kappa\phi_{ij} + \eta_{ij} \tag{20'}$$

where

$\gamma_0 = \ln(1/\varepsilon) + (\varepsilon - 1)\ln((\varepsilon - 1/\varepsilon) + (1-\varepsilon)\ln a_L$ is a constant term

$\xi_j = -\varepsilon \ln c_j - \phi_{ex,j}$ which is an exporter fixed effect

$\zeta_i = y_i + (\varepsilon - 1)p_i - \phi_{im,i}$ which is an importer fixed effect

$\eta_{ij} = u_{ij} + v_{ij} \sim N(0, \delta_u^2 + \delta_v^2)$ is the error term correlated with the error term u_{ij} in the gravity equation (16').

Using equation (20'), an indicator variable T_{ij} can be defined so that it equals 1 if country j exports to country i. Therefore the probability that country j exports to country i can be expressed using the following probit equation[2]

$$\rho_{ij} = \Pr(T_{ij} = 1 | \text{observed variables}) = \Phi(\gamma_0 + \xi_j + \zeta_i - \gamma d_{ij} - \kappa\phi_{ij}) \tag{22}$$

where $\Phi(.)$ is the accumulative standard normal distribution function. HMR approach consists in the estimation of the probit equation (22) in a first stage and the gravity equation (16') in a second stage.

ADDING TOURISM TO THE HMR APPROACH

As presented in the introduction of this chapter, one of the contributions of the present analysis is the consideration of tourism as a potential omitted factor to explain trade flows. In this section tourism is included in the HMR model.

A simple way to introduce tourism in HMR framework is by recognizing that bilateral tourism can reduce both trade variable costs and trade fixed costs associated with exports. For instance, tourism may improve the knowledge about foreign culture and, as a consequence, about business habits and practices in other countries. Furthermore, tourism facilitates and stimulates to learn other languages, making bilateral trade easier. In addition, international tourism needs good basic facilities, services, and infrastructure such as transportation and communication systems that are also necessary for trade activity to function.

Tourist arrivals may result in the promotion of trade in terms of both, the existence of bilateral trade and its volume. Therefore, the promotional effect of trade through tourism may be interpreted as the consequence of a reduction of both trade fixed costs, as measured by f_{ij}, and trade variable costs, as measured by τ_{ij}. In this research the equations for variable and fixed trade costs of serving a market are rewritten respectively as

[2] Since $\delta_\eta^2 = \delta_u^2 + \delta_v^2 = 1$ is not imposed, (20') is divided by the standard deviation δ_η^2 to specify the probit equation [22].

$$\tau_{ij} = \left[D_{ij}^{\gamma} Tou_{ij}^{-\psi} e^{-u_{ij}}\right]^{1/\varepsilon - 1}$$

and

$$f_{ij} = Tou_{ij}^{-\beta} \exp(\phi_{ex,j} + \phi_{im,i} + \kappa\phi_{ij} - v_{ij})$$

where Tou_{ij} represents tourist arrivals to country j from country i and parameters β and ψ are positive.

By substituting these two expressions in (16') and (22), the gravity equation and the probit equation can be expressed respectively as

$$m_{ij} = \beta_0 + \lambda_j + \chi_i - \gamma d_{ij} + \psi Tou_{ij} + w_{ij} + u_{ij} \tag{23}$$

and

$$\begin{aligned} \rho_{ij} &= \Pr(T_{ij} = 1 | \text{observed variables}) = \Phi(\gamma_0 + \xi_j + \zeta_i \\ &+ (\beta + \psi) \ln Tou_{ij} - \gamma dij - \kappa\phi_{ij}) \end{aligned} \tag{24}$$

A look at equations (23) and (24) shows that tourism promotes both, the probability that j exports to i and the magnitude of this export, *via* a reduction of variable and fixed trade costs.

An Empirical Analysis

The empirical analysis of this section is supported by the HMR theoretical framework. This methodology accounts for zero trade flows between pair of countries. The first stage of the model involves the estimate of a probit model for the probability that country j exports to country i. To that end, a dataset containing enough zero trade flows between country pairs is necessary. Therefore, a panel dataset which considers 30 Latin American countries for the period 1995 to 2010 is used[3]. For a total of 11,203 observations, 8,377 positive exports, which suppose a 75% of the sample (hence, zero trade flows represent a 25% of the sample).

The dependent variable, export flows from country j to country i, comes from the *Direction of Trade* dataset published by the *International Monetary Fund*. The data comprises bilateral merchandise trade and requires to be converted into real terms by using US GDP deflator, obtained from the *World Development Indicators* (2006) and the *UNCTAD Handbook of Statistics* (2008).

Tourism data, tourist arrivals to country j from country i, is obtained from the *United Nations World Tourism Organisation (UNWTO)* and includes annual international arrivals by country of origin. The distance variable and dummy variables for common language (*Lang)*, common border (*Border)*, colonial ties (*Colony)* and number of landlocked countries in the

[3] The list of countries used in the analysis and their share of trade and tourism movements are presented in Table A.1.

pair (*Landl*) are collected from the *Centre d'Etudes Prospectives et d'Informations Internationales (CEPII)* dataset while number of islands in the pair (*Island*), and Free Trade Agreements (*FTA*) were obtained from Andrew K. Rose's website and the *CIA Factbook*.

HMR follows a two-stage estimation procedure. In the first stage a Probit, equation (24), is estimated by maximum likelihood and two controls are generated. In the second stage, the gravity equation (23) is consistently estimated by adding the two control variables saved from the first stage. Let $\hat{z}_{ij} = \Phi^{-1}(\hat{p}_{ij})$ be the predicted value of the latent variable. The first control is for country selection into trading, captured by the inverse Mills ratio defined by $\hat{\bar{\eta}}_{ij} = \phi(\hat{z}_{ij})/\Phi(\hat{z}_{ij})$, where $\phi(.)$ is the standard normal density function. The second control is the endogenous number of exporters defined by $\hat{\bar{w}}_{ij} \equiv \ln(\exp[\delta(\hat{z}_{ij} + \hat{\bar{\eta}}_{ij})] - 1)$ with $\hat{\bar{z}}_{ij} = \hat{z}_{ij} + \hat{\bar{\eta}}_{ij}$. Therefore, equation (23) can be estimated using the transformation:

$$m_{ij} = \beta_0 + \lambda_j + \chi_i - \gamma d_{ij} + \psi Tou_{ij} + \vartheta \hat{\bar{\eta}}_{ij} + \ln(\exp[\delta(\hat{z}_{ij} + \hat{\bar{\eta}}_{ij})] - 1) + u_{ij} \tag{23'}$$

As previously mentioned, the main objective of our research is to analyse whether tourism has been a traditionally omitted factor in gravity equations for trade. Hence, all the equations are estimated twice, without tourism and with tourism. The results of the HMR approach appear in Table 1.

The estimates for the Probit regression without including and including tourism are presented in column 1a and 1b of Table 1, respectively. These results suggest that variables commonly considered in gravity equation also affect the probability that two countries trade which each others. Particularly, countries that are closer are more likely to trade. Moreover, sharing a common border, a common language, a common colonizer and belonging to the same regional free trade agreement (FTA) increase the probability to trade while the number of islands and the number of landlocked countries in the pair reduce this probability[4]. Regarding the variable of interest, tourism appears as positive and significant in the probit regression. As presented in section 3, tourist arrivals may increase the probability of trading between countries since tourism flows reduce trade fixed-costs. Estimates from the first stage are used to construct $\hat{\bar{\eta}}_{ij}$ and $\hat{\bar{w}}_{ij}$.[5] In the second stage, both the non-linear coefficient δ and the linear coefficient for $\hat{\bar{\eta}}_{ij}$ are estimated. Columns 2a and 2b of Table 1 present the results for the benchmark gravity equation estimated by ordinary least squares (OLS) without these controls while columns 3a and 3b present the estimate of the maximum likelihood (ML) by not including and including tourism, respectively.

[4] For identification reasons, one variable from the first stage requires to be excluded in the second stage. According to Gil-Pareja et al., (2009) this could be a variable that affects the probability of exporting to a country but not the volume. Alternatively, a variable which affects both decisions in opposite directions would also work. Similarly to Helpman et al., (2008) and Gil-Pareja et al., (2009), common language is excluded in the second stage.

[5] Following HMR (2008), there are country pairs whose characteristics are such that their probability of trade is indistinguishable from 1. Therefore, the same $\hat{z}_{ij}$ is assigned to country pairs with an estimated $\rho_{ij} > 0.9999999$.

Table 1. Intra-Latin American trade

	1st Stage				2nd Stage											
	Probit				Benchmark-Model (OLS-FE)				Non-Linear Model (Max Likelihood)				Polynomial Model (OLS-FE)			
variables	(1a)		(1b)		(2a)		(2b)		(3a)		(3b)		(4a)		(4b)	
Constant	8.050		7.644	***	7.586	***	6.710	***	11.777	***	11.331	***	3.335	***	3.009	***
	0.56	***	0.59		0.39		0.41		0.72		0.73		0.77		0.76	
Tourism			0.024	*			0.050	***			0.035	***			0.020	**
			0.01				0.01				0.01				0.01	
Dist	-0.801	***	-0.764	***	-1.359	***	-1.246	***	-1.016	***	-0.967	***	-1.030	***	-0.992	***
	0.07		0.07		0.03		0.04		0.06		0.06		0.06		0.06	
ComCol	0.957	***	0.915	***	2.933	***	2.702	***	2.010	***	1.930	***	1.937	***	1.883	***
	0.15		0.15		0.10		0.11		0.17		0.17		0.18		0.18	
Smctry	0.445		0.414		0.313	***	0.304	***	0.088		0.095		0.100	*	0.112	**
	0.31		0.31		0.06		0.06		0.06		0.06		0.06		0.06	
Lang	1.078	***	1.031	***												
	0.10		0.11													
Border	0.772	***	0.707	**	0.572	***	0.485	***	0.168	***	0.135	**	0.298	***	0.274	***
	0.30		0.30		0.05		0.06		0.07		0.06		0.07		0.07	
RTA	0.500	***	0.493	***	1.388	***	1.351	***	1.116	***	1.111	***	1.124	***	1.116	***
	0.07		0.07		0.05		0.05		0.05		0.05		0.06		0.05	
Island	-0.713	***	-0.710	***	1.238	***	1.029	***	-2.162	***	-2.154	***	0.143	***	0.133	***
	0.20		0.20		0.12		0.12		0.14		0.14		0.21		0.22	
Landl	-2.083	***	-1.986	***	-3.934	***	-3.839	***	-5.960	***	-5.857	***	-5.459		-5.431	
	0.18		0.19		0.40		0.40		0.22		0.22		0.46		0.45	
$\hat{\bar{Z}}_{ij}$													2.535	***	2.557	***
													0.28		0.28	
$\hat{\bar{Z}}^2_{ij}$													-0.396	***	-0.410	***
													0.06		0.06	
$\hat{\bar{Z}}^3_{ij}$													0.022	***	0.024	***
													0.00		0.00	
$\hat{\bar{\eta}}_{ij}$									0.943	***	0.965	***	1.415	***	1.425	***
									0.10		0.09		0.14		0.14	
σ									1.882	***	1.880	***				
									0.02		0.02					
Obs	11203		11203		8377		8377		8377		8377		8377		8377	
R2	0.5249		0.5252		0.8015		0.8024						0.8106		0.811	

Notes: exporter, importer and year fixed effect are not reported.
Standard errors (SE) robust to heteroskedasticity are computed by using Huber-White estimator.
Robust SE appears within parentheses. t-statistics available upon request.
Significance at one (***), at five (**) and at ten per cent (*).

As found in Helpman et al., (2008), the heterogeneity bias in the estimated effects of trade barriers is important. In general, the estimates of the effects of trade frictions in the benchmark gravity equation are biased upward.

Focusing on the estimates of the ML presented in columns 3a and 3b, the significance and sign of the variables are as expected. Results suggest that exports decrease in distance and increase in tourist arrivals to country j from country i. According to the extended theoretical model that incorporates tourism, both distance and tourist arrivals affect transport costs, the former increasing them while the later decreasing costs. Sharing a common border, common colonizer and belonging to the same FTA affects positively the volume of exports while landlocked countries and islands in the pair reduce trade.

The comparison of estimates presented in Table 1 suggests that the upward bias in the regressors of the gravity equations is due to both, the inappropriate procedure of estimation to address the non-zero trade problem and the omission of international tourism as a relevant variable affecting international trade via trade costs.

Finally, following HMR (2008), the parameterization assumptions that determine the functional forms are progressively relaxed. In this sense, the Pareto distribution assumption for the inverse of productivity a is relaxed, allowing for a general specification of V_{ij}. Hence, the control function $\hat{\bar{w}}_{ij}$ is approximated by a polynomial in $\hat{\bar{z}}_{ij}, v(\hat{\bar{z}}_{ij})$. As the nonlinearity is eliminated, this second stage can be easily estimated by OLS.

As in the seminal paper, the $v(\hat{\bar{z}}_{ij})$ is expanded until a cubic polynomial[6] and the results are very similar to the ML estimates. Again, the inclusion of tourism in the model generally reduces the magnitude of the estimates for the traditional regressors of the gravity equation[7]. This confirms the main finding from the two stage procedure, i.e., the traditional estimates from gravity equations may be biases due to omitted factors and the way to deal with zero trade data.

CONCLUSION

Gravity equations are commonly estimated in order to shed light on main issues of International Economics. Often the results from gravity models have motivated intense debates related to the sign and magnitude of these estimates. In this paper, two contributions to this debate are made. First, the recent method proposed by Helpman, Melitz and Rubinstein (2008) is used, and second, tourism is introduced as an explanatory variable in the trade equation. It is recognised that tourism may reduce fixed and variable trade costs, and hence affecting extensive and intensive margin of trade.

Two main results are reached. First, tourism affects positively both, the probability of exporting and the volume of exports between two countries. Thus, the results suggest that tourist arrivals are a relevant factor explaining trade flows. Second, the estimates seem to be upward biased. As a consequence, the omission of this relevant variable and the no consideration of zero trade data may contribute to explain the presence of an upward bias in the estimation of the effect of the traditional regressors of gravity equations on international trade.

---

[6] In practice, the polynomial is expanded until a tenth power although not noticeable changes for expanding $v(\hat{\bar{z}}_{ij})$ beyond a cubic polynomial are found.

[7] This reduction of the coefficients of interest differs from the one obtained from NLS estimation and must be taken with caution. Although polynomial approximation allows for more statistical flexibility, ML estimation deals with the well-founded HMR model presented in sections 2 and 3.

APPENDIX

Table A1. Intra-Latin American trade and tourism flows (average 1995-2010)

Country	% share tourist arrivals	% share of exports
Antigua and Barbuda	0.08	0.00
Argentina	18.03	19.43
Barbados	0.44	0.13
Belize	0.14	0.04
Bolivia	0.97	1.74
Brazil	16.40	27.73
Chile	11.11	7.82
Colombia	3.01	6.96
Costa Rica	4.18	1.77
Cuba	1.98	0.32
Dominica	0.09	0.04
Dominican Republic	1.16	0.52
Ecuador	2.99	3.46
El Salvador	4.20	1.31
Grenada	0.08	0.02
Guatemala	5.10	2.19
Guyana	0.03	0.12
Haiti	0.06	0.03
Honduras	2.28	0.57
Jamaica	0.22	0.08
Mexico	1.45	11.10
Nicaragua	2.73	0.40
Panama	2.67	0.29
Paraguay	2.37	1.48
Peru	4.68	3.26
Saint Kitts and Nevis	0.02	0.00
Saint Lucia	0.19	0.02
Suriname	0.03	0.04
Uruguay	12.09	1.96
Venezuela, RB	1.21	7.13

REFERENCES

Agudelo, D., G.J. Benítez and L. Davidson (2006): "A South American Perspective: Regional versus Global Trade Patterns". Working Papers, 2006 (16), Indiana University. Kelley School of Business.

Anderson, J. E. and E. Van Wincoop (2003): "Gravity with Gravitas: A Solution to the Border Puzzle". *American Economic Review* 93, No. 1, pp. 170-192.

Bergstrand, J. H. (1989): "The Generalized Gravity Equation, Monopolistic Competition, and the Factor-Proportions Theory in International Trade". *Review of Economics and Statistics* 71(1): 143-153.

Carrillo-Tudela, C. and C. A Li (2004): "Trade Blocks and the Gravity Model: Evidence from Latin American Countries". *Journal of Economic Integration*, 19, pp. 667-689.

Cortes, M. (2007): "Composition of Trade between Australia and Latin America: Gravity Model" Working Paper 2007 (19), Department of Economics, University of Wollongong.

Deardoff, A. V. (1998): "Determinants of bilateral trade: Does gravity work in a Neoclassical World?", in J. Frankel (ed.), The regionalization of the world economy, pp. 7-22. University of Chicago Press.

Gil-Pareja, S., R. Llorca-Vivero and J.A. Martínez Serrano (2009): "Continental bias in trade". *Documentos de Trabajo FUNCAS*, Nº. 440, 2009.

Glick, R. and A.K. Rose (2002): "Does a currency union affect trade? The time-series evidence". *European Economic Review* 46, pp. 1125-1151.

Helpman, E., Melitz, M. and Y. Rubinstein (2008): "Estimating trade flows: trading partners and trading volumes". *Quarterly Journal of Economics* 123 (2): 441-487.

Martinez-Zarzoso, I., and F. Nowak-Lehmann (2003): "Augmented gravity model: An empirical application to Mercosur-European Union trade flows". *Journal of Applied Economics,* (6)2, pp. 291-316

Rose, A.K. (2000): "One money, one market: Estimating the effect of common currencies on trade". *Economic Policy* 20, pp. 9-45.

Rose, A.K. and T.D. Stanley (2005): "A meta-analysis of the effect of common currencies on international trade". *Journal of Economic Surveys* 19 (3), pp. 347-365.

Rose A.K. and E. Van Wincoop (2001): "National money as a barrier to trade". *American Economic Review* 91, No. 2, pp. 386-390.

Thom, R. and B. Walsh (2002): "The effect of a common currency on trade: Ireland before and after the sterling link". *European Economic Review* 46, pp. 1111-1123.

In: Current Issues in International Trade
Editor: Gouranga G. Das

ISBN: 978-1-63321-405-7

Chapter 7

A Factor Endowment Explanation for China's Emergence As an International Trading Power: Calibrating the Dornbusch-Fischer-Samuelson Model for China's Trade, 1968-2008

Roger White*
Whittier College, CA, US

Abstract

Much has been made of the rise of China's economy and its emergence as a global trading power. Standard trade theory holds that comparative advantage is the basis for mutually beneficial exchange and, as such, it is the basis for international trade. In this chapter, we examine changes in labor supplies, capital stocks, and technology as possible explanations for the rise of China as an international trading power. Calibration of the Dornbusch-Fisher-Samuelson model suggests that China has gained comparative advantage relative to the US and to the cohort of high income countries considered in this study. Even though US production has increased since 1968 at both the extensive margin and at the intensive margin, China's emergence as a trading power may have adversely affected US labor. To discern the extent of labor market effects that may be attributable to increased trade, and particularly the effects of increased trade with China, we conduct a regression analysis using data for the years 1972-2007 to explore trade-induced changes in industry-level employment and average wages for both production workers and non-production workers in the US manufacturing sector. Among other findings, greater import penetration from China has negatively affected employment of both production workers and non-production workers, and increased exports to China have had a limited positive effect on the average wages of non-production workers.

Keywords: China, Comparative advantage, Exports, Imports, Manufacturing

---

* Whittier College, Department of Economics. 13406 E. Philadelphia Street, Whittier, CA 90608 USA. Email: rwhite1@whittier.edu.

INTRODUCTION

In December 1978, China embarked on a series of transformative economic reforms that emphasized the adoption of capitalist market principles. The reforms and associated open-door policies led China's economy to become integrated into the global economy by way of increased international trade and investment flows. China's trade volume (i.e., the sum of its exports and imports) ranked 29th in the world in 1978 at $64.5 billion; however, by 2011, its trade volume had increased, in real terms, to $2.72 trillion, second only to the United States as the world's top trading country [18]. Thus, during this period, China's trade volume increased at an average annual rate of 12 percent. This growth in trade volume coincided with a period during which China's real Gross Domestic Product (GDP) grew at a robust average annual rate of nearly 10 percent.

The importance of trade as a determinant of economic growth is established in Frankel and Romer [7]. Rather than focusing on the relationship between China's increased trade volume and its economic growth, in this chapter we explore changes in relative factor endowments (i.e., capital, labor, and technology) as the underlying basis for China's emergence as an international trading power. Specifically, we apply data for China and 97 countries for which complete data are available during the period from 1960 through 2008 to the Dornbusch-Fisher-Samuelson (DFS) model of comparative advantage [2]. We calibrate the DFS model to consider changes in China's factor endowments relative to i) the full cohort of 97 trading partners, ii) the United States, and iii-vii) cohorts of trading partners that are categorized by World Bank income classifications (i.e., high, middle, upper middle, lower middle, and low income countries). The calibration exercises provide insights/expectations regarding shifts in China's comparative advantage.

The DFS model extends the factor endowments approach to comparative advantage determination introduced by Ricardo [16] and extended by Heckscher [9] and Ohlin [15]. Emphasizing the contribution of Dornbusch, Fisher and Samuelson, Krugman [13] described the model as "160 years of international economics in one paper." Heuristically, the model permits consideration of the impacts of changes in relative labor supplies, advances in technology, and changes in capital stocks, either in isolation or collectively, on comparative advantage. We rely on the most basic version of the DFS model as it is sufficient for the purpose of motivating an empirical examination of the potential influences of trade on industry-level employment and average wages in the US manufacturing sector.

Between 1968 and 2008, the rest of the world (i.e., the 97 trading partners in our dataset), realized growth in its collective labor force and capital stock and it experienced technology gains. China, however, experienced even larger increases in the size of its labor force, its capital stock, and the level of technology embodied in its output. The more rapid growth in factor endowments for China has implications for factor productivity and factor prices which, in turn, affects product prices and the range of products for which China and the rest of the world hold comparative advantage in the production of. Because changes in factor endowments have implications for production, it follows that they also affect the pattern of international trade.

David Ricardo formalized the concept of comparative advantage as the basis for mutually-beneficial exchange. All trading partners hold a comparative advantage in the production of at least one good or service (i.e., each trading partner can produce at a lower opportunity cost than another producer). In Ricardo's example, Britain ultimately produces and exports cloth to Portugal in exchange for port wine. The result is that, in aggregate, consumers in both Britain and Portugal are able to consume more cloth and more port wine than if the countries remained in isolation. Both countries benefit in a macro sense from the voluntary exchange; however, wine producers in Britain and cloth producers in Portugal, driven out of business by more efficiently-produced imports, are worse off as a result of the exchange, and cloth consumers in Britain and wine consumers in Portugal are worse off due to higher product prices. In other words, standard trade theory predicts that specialization and trade in accordance with comparative advantage will produce "winners" and "losers" on a micro level. The net benefits, however, are expected to be positive – again, in a macro sense – as the gains received by the winners exceed the losses incurred by the losers.

Our econometric analysis examines the effects of increased trade, particularly increased trade with China, on workers in the US manufacturing sector. Specifically, we examine data for 75 3-digit Census of Population Industrial Classification (CIC) industries in the US manufacturing sector during the period from 1972 through 2007 to determine the extent to which increased trade flows affect industry-level employment and average annual wages for production and non-production workers. Effectively, calibration of the DFS model allows for examination of the underlying basis for observed increases in trade, and our econometric analysis considers the potential effects of this trade on US workers.

We proceed as follows. We next introduce the DFS model and then glean predicted shifts in comparative advantage by calibrating the model. This is followed by a presentation of the findings from our econometric analysis. We end with final thoughts and conclusions.

A Dornbusch-Fisher-Samuelson Model Primer

Establishing an Initial Equilibrium

Considering all countries other than China as "foreign", and identifying these countries by "*", we begin by assuming that both China and foreign are able to produce and consume large numbers of goods. Denoting these goods with the lowercase letter 'z', we order all z goods along a continuum that ranges in value from zero to one to produce an index of goods identified as Z. We next define $a(z)$ and $a^*(z)$ as the unit labor requirements for the zth good in China and foreign, respectively. Combining the unit labor requirements as $\frac{a^*(z)}{a(z)}$ results in a measure of China's productivity to foreign's productivity in terms of the zth good. Using this ratio, we rank all goods along the (0, 1) continuum in descending order of China's comparative advantage. Graphically, we plot the resulting $A(z)$ schedule, $A(Z) = \frac{a^*(z)}{a(z)}$, against our index of goods, Z, in Figure 1.

To determine which goods will be produced in China and which will be produced in foreign, we must consider the ratio of nominal wages in China to nominal wages in foreign: $\frac{w}{w^*} = \Theta$. This ratio is measured on the y axis in Figure 1. Because the DFS model is a long-run model, full-employment and perfect competition are assumed. Perfectly competitive markets imply that the cost of producing a given good *z* in China is *p(z) = wa(z)*. Likewise, the cost of producing the same good in foreign is *p*(z) = w*a*(z)*. The good, *z*, will be cheaper to produce in China if *wa(z) < w*a*(z)*, or, equivalently, if $\Theta < A(z)$. Thus, as noted in Figure 1, for a given *A(z)* schedule, the ratio of China-to-foreign nominal wage rates establishes the pattern of comparative advantage and, hence, the pattern of international specialization.

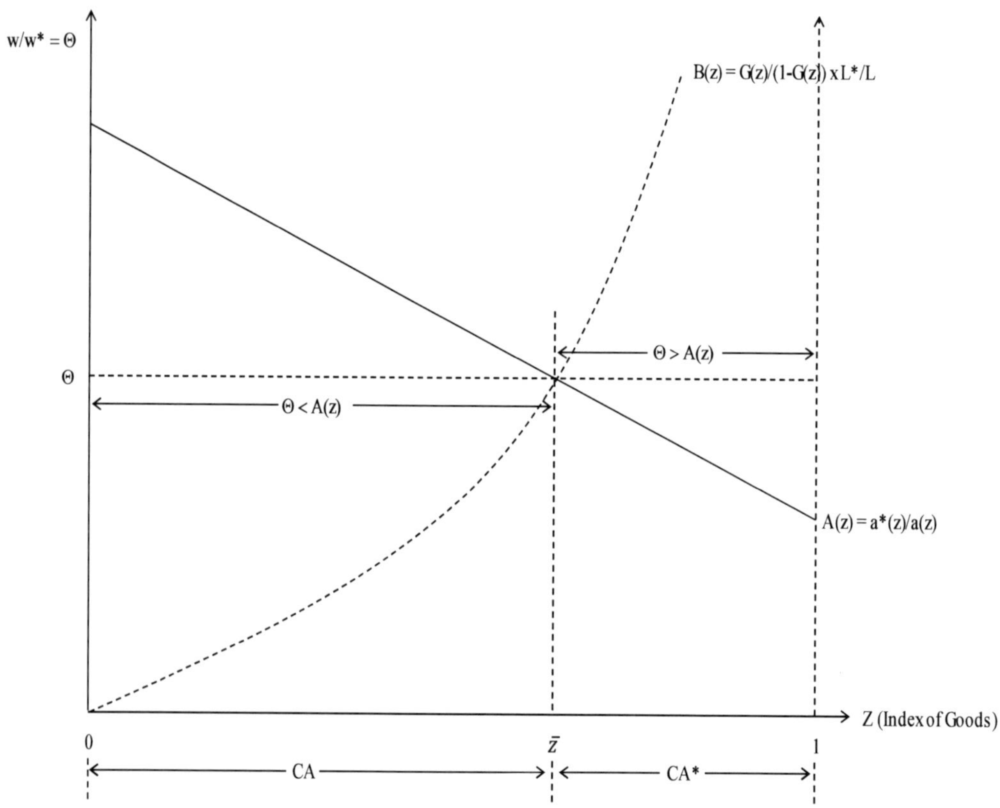

Figure 1. Initial Equilibrium in the DFS Framework.

In Figure 1, $\bar{z}$ represents the marginal good that both countries produce (i.e., the good for which $\Theta = A(z)$). All goods to the left of $\bar{z}$ along the continuum will be produced in China since $\Theta < A(z)$, and all goods to the right of $\bar{z}$ will be produced at foreign because $\Theta > A(z)$. This means that the range of the continuum for which China holds comparative advantage (CA) is given as $0 \rightarrow \bar{z}$, and the range of the continuum for which foreign holds comparative advantage in production (CA*) is given as $\bar{z} \rightarrow 1$.

To establish a value for Θ, we must add the *B(z)* schedule to Figure 1. This requires invoking a simplifying assumption that all consumers spend a constant fraction of their income on each *z* good. This restricts movement of the *B(z)* schedule to represent only changes in relative labor supplies. We define *G(z)* to be the fraction of world income spent on China-produced goods, and we assume that these expenditure shares remain constant. The total value of spending on China's production is given by the product of the nominal wage rate, w, and the labor supply, L, or the product of $G(z)$ and world income. Since world income is the sum of China's income and foreign's income, we have that $wL = G(z)(wL+w^*L^*)$. Solving for $\frac{w}{w^*}$ (i.e., Θ) results in $\frac{w}{w^*} = \frac{G(z)}{1-G(z)} x \frac{L^*}{L} = \Theta$. Thus, our expression for the $B(z)$ schedule, illustrated in Figure 1, is given as $B(z) = \frac{G(z)}{1-G(z)} x \frac{L^*}{L}$.

Examples of Comparative Statics Using the DFS Model

In Panel A of Figure 2, we illustrate a hypothetical increase in L relative to L^* which, all else equal, causes the $B(z)$ schedule to pivot down. This pivot moves us to a new equilibrium where the $B(z)'$ schedule intersects the $A(z)$ schedule and Θ decreases to Θ'. The resulting gain in comparative advantage for China (i.e., the loss of comparative advantage by foreign) is illustrated by the movement along the x axis from $\bar{z}$ to $\hat{z}$. The basis for the change in comparative advantage is intuitive. To ensure full-employment, the increase in L relative to L^* produces a decrease in w relative to w^*, and as Θ decreases we see that $p(z)$ decreases relative to $p^*(z)$.

Similar to the example of an increase in L relative to L*, we can trace the comparative statics associated with changes in relative capital stocks (K and K^*) or technology levels (T and T^*) to determine corresponding changes in comparative advantage. Increases in K^* or T^* lower the foreign unit labor requirement ($a^*(z)$). Likewise, an increase in either K or T would lower China's unit labor requirement ($a(z)$). The effects of changes in capital stocks and technology levels are analogous in terms of shifting the $A(z)$ schedule and, thus, in affecting price levels ($p(z)$ and/or $p^*(z)$) and in the determination of comparative advantage.

Assuming that the foreign capital stock, K^*, increases relative to China's capital stock, K, we have that $a^*(z)$ decreases relative to $a(z)$ and, as a result, the $A(z)$ schedule shifts down to $A(z)'$ and a new equilibrium is established at the intersection of the $A(z)'$ schedule and the $B(z)$ schedule. This is illustrated above in Panel B of Figure 2. As a result of the increased productivity of foreign labor, Θ decreases to Θ' and foreign gains comparative advantage. This is illustrated by the movement along the x axis from $\bar{z}$ to $\tilde{z}$. The basis for these dynamics is as follows. This increase in the productivity of foreign workers increases w^* relative to w; however, the proportional decrease in Θ is less than the proportional decrease in the $A(z)$ schedule (as indicated by the vertical distances between Θ and Θ' and between the $A(z)$ and $A(z)'$ schedules). Thus, $p^*(z)$ falls to $p^*(z)'$. Since both changes in relative capital stocks and technology levels produce analogous shifts in the $A(z)$ schedule, identical comparative statics apply in the case where T^* increases relative to T.

Panel A: An Increase in L Relative to L*

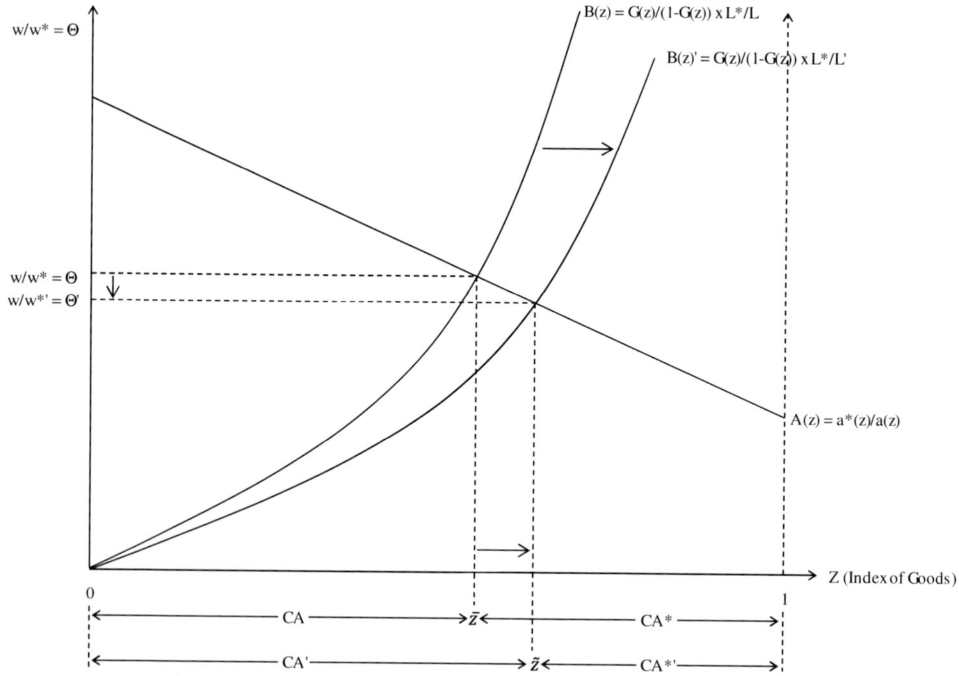

Panel B: An Increase in K* and/or A* Relative to K and A

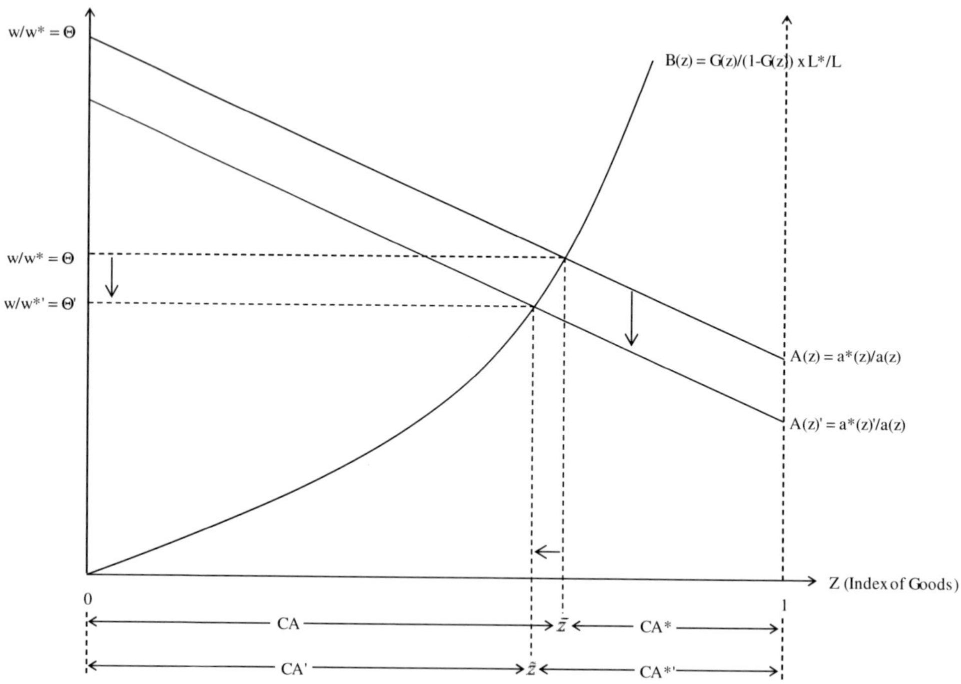

Figure 2. Examples of Comparative Statics in the DFS Framework.

Table 1. Possible DFS Outcomes

Panel A: Home gains / Foreign loses Comparative Advantage

Outcome	Δ Θ	Δ A(z)	Δ B(z)
1	+	+	No Δ
2	+	+	-
3	-	No Δ	-
4	-	+	-
5	No Δ	+	-

Panel B: Foreign gains / Home loses Comparative Advantage

Outcome	Δ Θ	Δ A(z)	Δ B(z)
6	+	No Δ	+
7	+	-	+
8	-	-	.
9	-	-	+
10	No Δ	-	+

Panel C: No change or indeterminable change in Comparative Advantage

Outcome	Δ Θ	Δ A(z)	Δ B(z)
11	+[a]	+[a]	+[a]
12	-[a]	-[a]	-[a]
13	No Δ	No Δ	No Δ

[a] The outcome, with respect to comparative advantage, is dependent on the relative magnitudes of the shifts in the A(z) and B(z) schedules.

Panel D: Outcomes that are not consistent with the DFS Model

Outcome	Δ Θ	Δ A(z)	Δ B(z)
i	+	No Δ	No Δ
ii	+	No Δ	-
iii	+	-	No Δ
iv	+	-	-
v	-	+	No Δ
vi	-	+	+
vii	-	No Δ	No Δ
viii	-	No Δ	+
ix	No Δ	+	No Δ
x	No Δ	+	+
xi	No Δ	-	-
xii	No Δ	-	No Δ
xiii	No Δ	No Δ	+
xiv	No Δ	No Δ	-

Possible Outcomes and (In)Consistencies within the DFS Framework

Given possible changes in *L*, *K* and/or *T* relative to *L**, *K** and/or *T**, there are 27 potential outcomes – in terms of combinations of shifts of the *A(z)* schedule, pivots of the *B(z)* schedule, and the value of Θ. Table 1 lists these outcomes and identifies, in Panel D, the 14 that are inconsistent with the DFS model. An example of such inconsistency is a downward shift of the *A(z)* schedule – perhaps due to technological advancements in the foreign country relative to the home country – with no corresponding pivot of the *B(z)* schedule. The DFS model predicts that such a scenario would yield a decrease in Θ. Thus, an observed outcome of no change (or an increase) in Θ, is not consistent with the DFS model.

In the next section, we present our calibration exercises involving the DFS model. We have identified the possible outcomes here since observation of an outcome(s) that is not consistent with the predictions of the DFS model would call into question the model's usefulness.

DATA/VARIABLE CONSTRUCTION AND RESULTS FROM CALIBRATING THE DFS MODEL

Variable Construction

As has been noted, we begin our analysis by calibrating the DFS model for China relative to i) all countries, ii) the US, and, separately, to those countries classified as iii) high income, iv) middle income, v) upper middle income, vi) lower middle income, and vii) low income. The categorization of countries is based on the 1990 World Bank income classifications.[1] Countries were classified by their 1990 World Bank classifications, as this year is the nearest to the middle of the reference period. Further, the classification is static in that countries are categorized throughout the reference period to reduce variation caused by a country(ies) moving between cohorts. Data from the Penn World Table 7.0 [10] are used to complete the calibration exercises. Consideration of comparative statics requires data for capital stocks, labor supplies, and technologies for both China and the respective trading partners. Further, considering that the ratio of nominal wage rates, China-to-foreign, is depicted on the vertical axis of the DFS diagram, requires a measure of relative wages.

The capital stock series was constructed following the methodology employed in Hummels and Levinsohn [11]. For all countries, the 1960 capital stock value is assumed to equal to 2.5 times the country's real GDP value. In subsequent years, the capital stock is estimated as the sum of the capital stock estimate for the prior year less 13.33 percent depreciation plus any new investment: $K_{it} = [K_{it-1} \times (1 - 0.1333)] + INVEST_{it}$. Following this methodology, given the depreciation rate, by 1968 the entire initial capital stock has depreciated and the capital stock series/estimates employed in our analysis are based solely on the timing and the levels of capital investment.

---

[1] Classifications are available at: http://siteresources.worldbank.org/DATASTATISTICS/Resources/OGHIST.xls.

Labor supply values are difficult to obtain or estimate for many countries, particular for the early years in our reference period; however, when data are available, there is a strong correlation (0.98) between labor force values and population values [18]. Thus, to facilitate the inclusion of more countries in our data, we employ population values as a proxy variable for labor supplies [18].

Solow [17] residuals were estimated to quantify the levels of technology embodied in each country's output. Employing annual data over the 1968-2008 period for all 98 countries in our dataset, a two-factor (capital and labor) Cobb-Douglas production function was estimated. Due to the presence of panel-level heteroskedasticity and first-order serial correlation, the Feasible Generalized Least Squares technique was employed. The resulting coefficients were then employed in conjunction with annual estimates of labor and capital to estimate the corresponding levels of embodied technology. Specifically, $T_{it} = \left(\frac{real\ GDP}{L^{0.1364} \times K^{0.8706}} \right)_{it}$. Finally, nominal GDP per capita values are employed as a proxy for nominal wages. As such, the variable does not capture wage income solely nor does it represent variation in wages within an economy. However, GDP per capita is a measure of average income. Absent a better alternative measure, its use would seem an appropriate substitute. Table 2 presents descriptive statistics.

Table 2. Descriptive Statistics

	N countries; obs.	Labor: L	Capital: K	Technology: T	GDP per capita
All Countries (incl. China)	98; 4,018	19,579,284	539,084,289	1.6078	8,881
		(69,652,379)	(483,032,058)	(2.4866)	(10,254)
All Countries (excl. China)	97; 3,977	13,677,447	532,470,729	1.5835	8,954
		(36,227,406)	(468,944,387)	(2.4859)	(10,280)
China	1; 41	548,173,528***	3,534,580,073***	1.4119	1,570***
		(156,825,257)	(4,124,567,184)	(0.2423)	(1,588)
USA	1; 41	119,713,264***	9,607,399,804***	3.2836***	30,698***
		(22,924,971)	(4,048,101,260)	(0.1698)	(7,341)
High Income (incl. USA)	24; 984	14,240,180	551,055,017	2.7030***	23,831***
		(26,195,397)	(500,823,229)	(0.1371)	(8,515)
Middle Income	40; 1,640	8,428,057***	563,061,174	1.1152***	6,425***
		(12,408,130)	(510,365,007)	(1.3425)	(4,750)
Upper Middle Income	11; 451	12,441,490	691,705,364***	1.8340	11,362***
		(19,451,884)	(612,688,060)	(1.7510)	(5,637)
Lower Middle Income	29; 1,189	6,905,721***	514,265,102	0.8426***	4,552***
		(7,787,910)	(456,615,708)	(1.0269)	(2,516)
Low Income (excl. China)	33; 1,353	19,631,084	130,140,838***	1.2826***	1,198***
		(55,721,884)	(156,691,472)	(2.0454)	(1,297)

Standard deviations in parentheses. "***" denotes statistical significance from the corresponding "All Countries (including China)" mean value at the 1% level of significance.

Panel A: Relative Labor Supplies (L*/L)

Panel C: Relative Capital Stocks (K*/K)

Panel B: Relative Technology (T*/T)

Panel D: Relative Nominal Wages (w/w*)

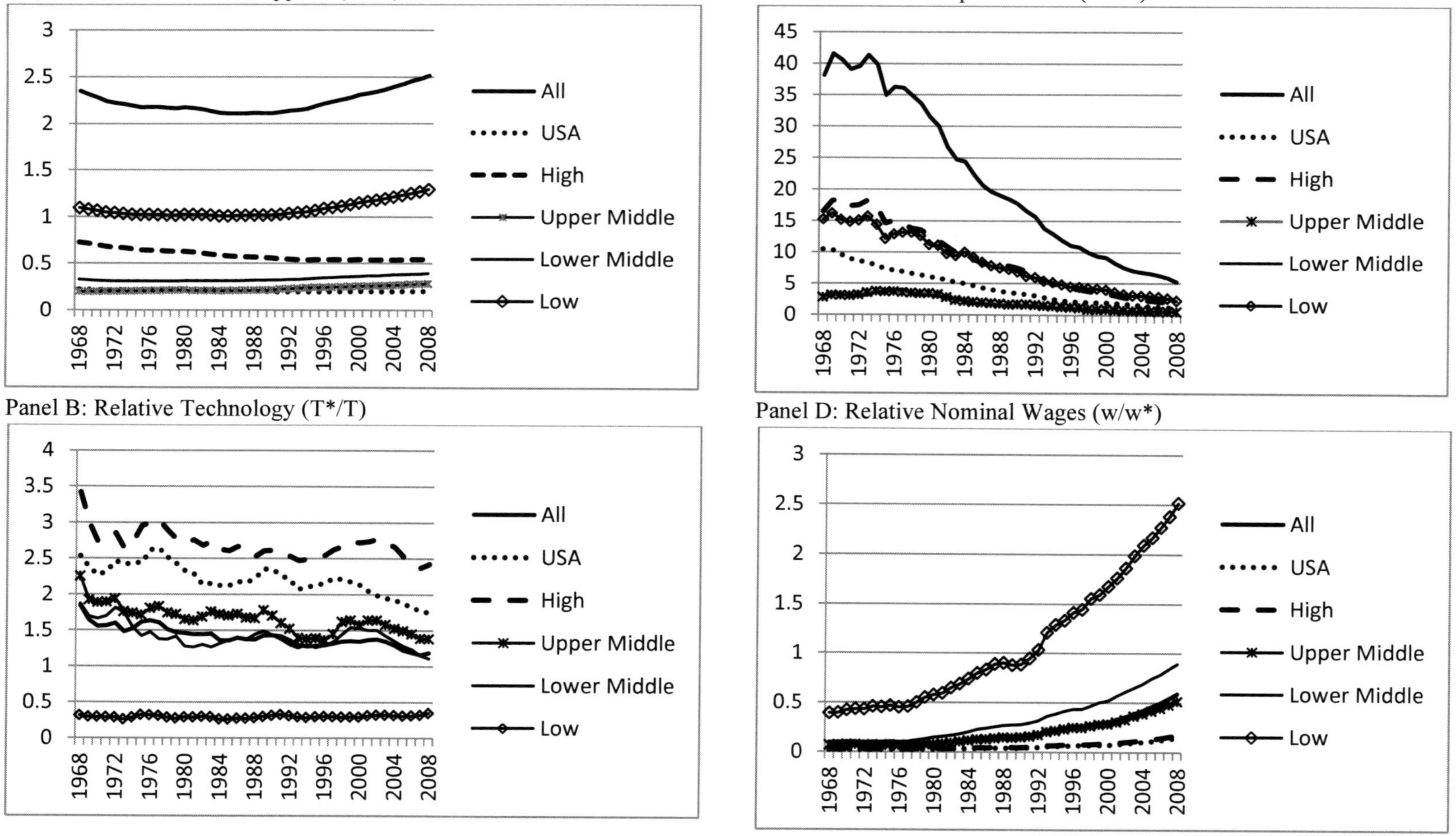

Figure 3. Relative Changes in Factor Endowments and Nominal Wages by Comparison Cohort, 1968-2008.

Calibration Results, by Cohort

Figure 3 illustrates the ratios for each of the four variables of primary interest over the reference period. The corresponding values for 1968, 1978, 1988, 1998, and 2008 are presented in Table 3. Focusing on the cohort of 97 trading partners (i.e., the cohort labeled "All"), we see that the ratio of foreign-to-China labor supplies (*L*/L*) increased from 2.35 to 2.52, a 7.24 percent increase, during the reference period. Similarly, the ratio of foreign-to-China capital stocks (*K*/K*) decreased 86.21 percent from 38.16 to 5.26. We also see that the ratio of foreign-to-China technology (*T*/T*) decreased from 1.85 to 1.19, a decline of 35.5 percent. Finally, the China-to-foreign ratio of nominal GDP per capita (*w/w**) increased by more than 933 percent from 0.06 to 0.59.

For the considered trading partner cohorts, we categorize observed dynamics into two groups. For the US and the cohort of high income countries, the calibration exercises indicate that the shifts in factor endowments are such that China has gained comparative advantage. For all other cohorts (i.e., all trading partners, middle income countries, upper middle income countries, lower middle income countries, and low income countries), the results of the exercise are ambiguous.

We first consider the changes noted above for the "All Countires (excl. China)" cohort. These changes are illustrated in Panel A of Figure 4. These same directional changes in labor supplies, capital stocks, embodied technologies, and nominal wages are found for all trading partners/cohorts considered except for the US and the high income country cohort. The increase in *L*/L* leads to an upward pivot of the *B(z)* schedule to *B(z)'*. The decreases in *K*/K* and *T*/T* shift the *A(z)* schedule upward since improved technology and more capital per worker would lower the unit labor requirement for China more so than for the foreign cohort. We also see that the ratio of China-to-foreign nominal GDP per capita values rises. The change in comparative advantage is ambiguous since we do not know if the upward shift in the *A(z)* schedule is somewhat minor, as represented by the move from *A(z)* to *A(z)'*, in which case China loses comparative advantage, or is larger, as is represented by the move from *A(z)* to *A(z)''*, in which case China gains comparative advantage.

Table 3. Observed Changes, 1968-2008, and Corresponding DFS Outcomes

All trading partners	Δ L*/L	Δ T*/T	Δ K*/K	ΔΘ
1968:	2.35	1.85	38.16	0.06
1978:	2.17	1.52	34.81	0.08
1988:	2.12	1.37	18.98	0.15
1998:	2.26	1.35	9.94	0.28
2008:	2.52	1.19	5.26	0.59
%Δ, 1968–2008:	7.24%	-35.50%	-86.21%	933.62%
Δ A(z), Δ B(z), Δ Θ:	+	+		+
DFS Outcome (from Table 1): **#11: Indeterminable change in comparative advantage.**				

US	Δ L*/L	Δ T*/T	Δ K*/K	ΔΘ
1968:	0.22	2.53	10.45	0.02
1978:	0.21	2.52	6.63	0.02
1988:	0.20	2.23	3.75	0.04
1998:	0.20	2.21	1.99	0.07
2008:	0.20	1.76	1.12	0.15

Table 3. (Continued)

All trading partners	Δ L*/L	Δ T*/T	Δ K*/K	ΔΘ
%Δ, 1968–2008:	-9.03%	-30.69%	-89.24%	809.44%
Δ A(z), Δ B(z), Δ Θ:	-	+		+
DFS Outcome (from Table 1): **#2: China gains comparative advantage.**				

High Income cohort	Δ L*/L	Δ T*/T	Δ K*/K	ΔΘ
1968:	0.73	3.42	16.47	0.02
1978:	0.63	2.89	13.78	0.03
1988:	0.57	2.53	7.93	0.05
1998:	0.54	2.67	3.75	0.08
2008:	0.54	2.43	1.79	0.17
%Δ, 1968–2008:	-25.13%	-29.00%	-89.15%	712.97%
Δ A(z), Δ B(z), Δ Θ:	-	+		+
DFS Outcome (from Table 1): **#2: China gains comparative advantage.**				

Middle Income cohort	Δ L*/L	Δ T*/T	Δ K*/K	ΔΘ
1968:	0.52	2.03	5.70	0.08
1978:	0.52	1.54	7.01	0.09
1988:	0.53	1.55	3.18	0.20
1998:	0.60	1.52	1.74	0.36
2008:	0.67	1.23	1.12	0.69
%Δ, 1968–2008:	28.90%	-39.25%	-80.39%	742.00%
Δ A(z), Δ B(z), Δ Θ:	+	+		+
DFS Outcome (from Table 1): **#11: Indeterminable change in comparative advantage.**				

Upper Middle Income cohort	Δ L*/L	Δ T*/T	Δ K*/K	ΔΘ
1968:	0.20	2.25	2.74	0.07
1978:	0.21	1.74	3.46	0.07
1988:	0.21	1.67	1.72	0.15
1998:	0.25	1.62	0.91	0.26
2008:	0.28	1.39	0.54	0.51
%Δ, 1968–2008:	43.51%	-38.38%	-80.42%	666.82%
Δ A(z), Δ B(z), Δ Θ:	+	+		+
DFS Outcome (from Table 1): **#11: Indeterminable change in comparative advantage.**				

Lower Middle Income cohort	Δ L*/L	Δ T*/T	Δ K*/K	ΔΘ
1968:	0.33	1.87	2.96	0.10
1978:	0.31	1.38	3.55	0.12
1988:	0.32	1.45	1.46	0.27
1998:	0.35	1.45	0.83	0.46
2008:	0.39	1.11	0.58	0.89
%Δ, 1968–2008:	20.14%	-40.53%	-80.36%	806.74%
Δ A(z), Δ B(z), Δ Θ:	+	+		+
DFS Outcome (from Table 1): **#11: Indeterminable change in comparative advantage.**				

Low Income cohort	Δ L*/L	Δ T*/T	Δ K*/K	ΔΘ
1968:	1.10	0.32	15.21	0.39
1978:	1.02	0.29	13.14	0.50
1988:	1.02	0.28	7.48	0.90
1998:	1.12	0.29	4.23	1.56
2008:	1.30	0.35	2.26	2.52
%Δ, 1968–2008:	18.35%	11.16%	-85.16%	543.80%
Δ A(z), Δ B(z), Δ Θ:	+	+/-?		+
DFS Outcome (from Table 1): **#11: Indeterminable change in comparative advantage.**				

Panel A: Ambiguous Change in China's Comparative Advantage relative to All, Upper Middle Income, Middle Income, Lower Middle Income, and Low Income Cohorts

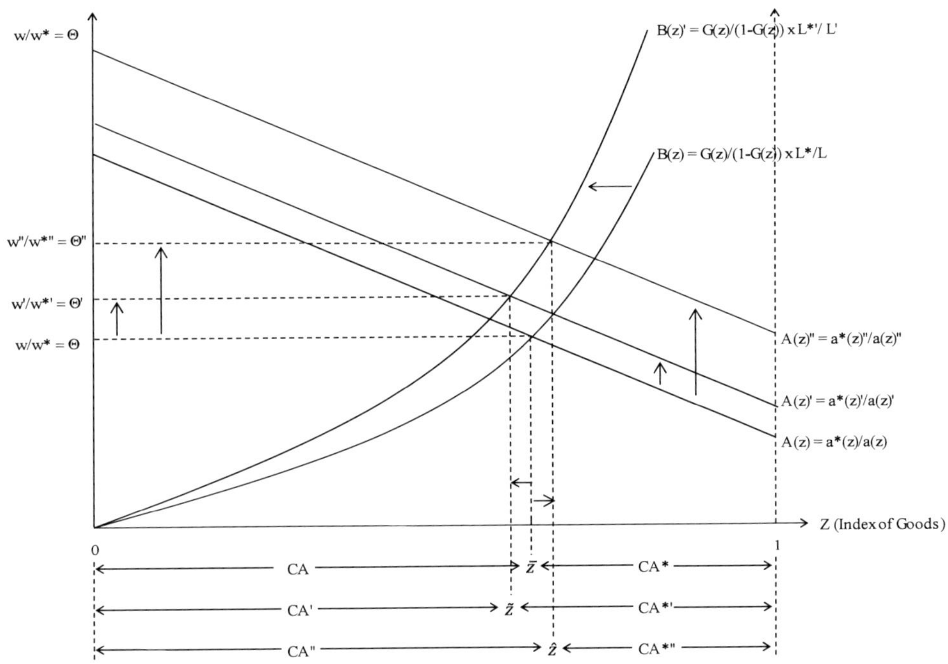

Panel B: Gain in China's Comparative Advantage relative to the USA and High Income Cohort

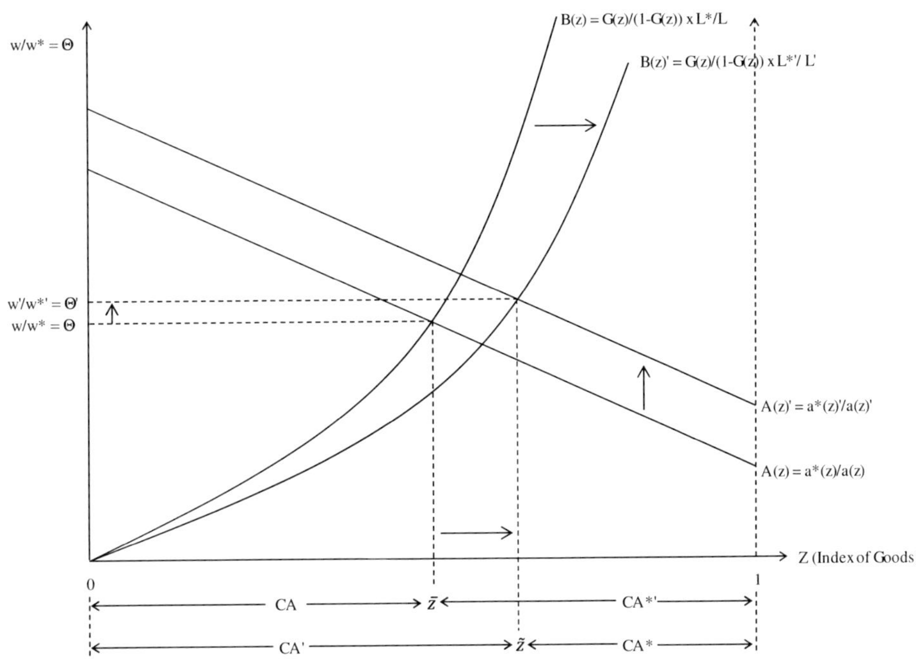

Figure 4. Predicted Change in China's Comparative Advantage, 1968-2008.

Again looking to Table 3 and focusing on the US, we see that the ratio of US-to-China labor supplies decreased over the reference period by roughly 9 percent. Thus, the *B(z)* schedule would pivot downward. The ratios of US-to-China capital stocks and technologies decreased by 89.2 percent and 30.7 percent, respectively, which would cause the *A(z)* schedule to shift up. Finally, the ratio of China-to-US nominal GDP per capita values increased by more than 809 percent. A like pattern of changes in relative factor endowments is observed when we compare China to the high income country cohort. The corresponding dynamics are illustrated in Panel B of Figure 4, showing China's gain in comparative advantage relative to the US (and to the high income country cohort) as represented by a move to the right along the horizontal axis from $\bar{z}$ to $\tilde{z}$.

As noted at the outset, the typical worker gains as a result of trade through greater purchasing power which results from the greater efficiency that is gained when production shifts following changes in factor endowments. However, it is also possible that some workers, as a result of the anticipated shifts in production, experience negative consequences (e.g., unemployment or reduced wages) due to trade. In the next section, we employ regression analysis to determine if Stolper-Samuelson effects, in the forms of lower industry employment or reduced average industry wages have been realized by US workers in response to increased trade. We analyze these effects for production and non-production workers separately, while placing particular emphasis on trade with China.

TRADE AND U.S. MANUFACTURING EMPLOYMENT AND WAGES

The Econometric Model

To produce our baseline estimation equations, we adopt a framework utilized by Mann [14], Freeman and Katz [8], and Kletzer [12]. The general-form equation is given as equation (1).

$$\Delta \ln L_{jt} = \beta_1 \Delta \ln D_{jt} + \beta_2 \Delta \ln\left(\frac{X}{S}\right)_{jt} - \beta_3 \Delta \ln\left(\frac{M}{S}\right)_{jt} + \beta_R \Delta \ln R_{jt} + \beta_V \Delta \ln V_{jt} \quad (1)$$

An analogous equation has the change in industry-level average wages $(\Delta \ln W_{jt})$ as the dependent variable. Δ is the difference operator, and ln denotes the natural logarithm. Equation (1) provides insight into the anticipated relationships between industry-level employment and average wages and the components of industry sales. Specifically, all else equal, employment (L) and wages (W) are expected to be positively related to increases in domestic demand (D) for domestic output. Similarly, a positive relationship is expected between increases in exports as a share of domestic shipments $\left(\frac{X}{S}\right)$ and both employment and wages. On the contrary, an increase in imports relative to domestic shipments $\left(\frac{M}{S}\right)$ is anticipated to be negatively related to wages and employment.

Modifying the general form equations to include i) a vector of time dummy variables, Ω_t, that control for unobservable variation in industry-level employment and/or average wages due to policy changes, ii) a vector of industry dummy variables, ϑ_j, that control for time-invariant industry-specific characteristics, iii) error terms, ε^1_{jt} and ε^2_{jt}, that are assumed to be independent and identically distributed, iv) a common intercept term, α_0, and v) to avoid possible multicollinearity problems when performing the regression analysis, the change in total industry-level exports (X) as a measure of foreign demand for domestic output and the change in the import penetration rate $\left(\frac{M}{D}\right)$ (i.e., imports as a share of total domestic market sales) in place of imports as a share of domestic shipments yields equations (2) and (3), which are our baseline estimation equations.

$$\begin{aligned}\Delta \ln L_{jt} &= \alpha_0 + \beta_1 \Delta \ln D_{jt} + \beta_2 \Delta \ln X_{jt} - \beta_3 \Delta \ln\left(\frac{M}{D}\right)_{jt} \\ &+ \beta_R \Delta \ln R_{jt} + \beta_V \Delta \ln V_{jt} + \beta_\Omega \Omega_t + \beta_\vartheta \vartheta_j + \varepsilon^1_{jt} \end{aligned} \tag{2}$$

$$\begin{aligned}\Delta \ln W_{jt} &= \alpha_0 + \gamma_1 \Delta \ln D_{jt} + \gamma_2 \Delta \ln X_{jt} - \gamma_3 \Delta \ln\left(\frac{M}{D}\right)_{jt} \\ &+ \beta_R \Delta \ln R_{jt} + \beta_V \Delta \ln V_{jt} + \beta_\Omega \Omega_t + \beta_\vartheta \vartheta_j + \varepsilon^2_{jt} \end{aligned} \tag{3}$$

To control for additional influences on employment, we expand the vectors $\Delta \ln V_{jt}$ and $\Delta \ln R_{jt}$, which include industry-level changes in technology, constructed as Solow residuals [17], and changes in capital-labor ratios that are also industry-specific. Industry capital-labor ratios are given as the value of plant and equipment divided by production employment. To control for business cycle fluctuations, the annual change in the manufacturing sector capacity utilization rate is included.

$$\begin{aligned}\Delta \ln L_{jt} &= \alpha_j + \beta_1 \Delta \ln DOM_{jt} + \beta_2 \Delta \ln EXP_{jt} + \beta_3 \Delta \ln IMPPEN_{jt} \\ &+ \beta_4 \Delta \ln CAPUTIL_t + \beta_5 \Delta \ln KL\ RATIO_{jt} + \beta_6 \Delta \ln TECH_{jt} \\ &+ \beta_\Omega \Omega_t + \beta_\vartheta \vartheta_j + \varepsilon_{jt} \end{aligned} \tag{4}$$

In equation (4), the vector L_{jt} includes industry production and non-production employment. DOM_{jt}, representing domestic demand, is equal to industry shipments less exports plus imports. Foreign demand is given by EXP_{jt}, while $IMPPEN_{jt}$ represents import competition. Equation (5) is an analogous estimation equation where the vector W_{jt} includes average industry wages of production and non-production workers.

$$\begin{aligned}\Delta \ln W_{jt} &= \alpha_j + \beta_1 \Delta \ln DOM_{jt} + \beta_2 \Delta \ln EXP_{jt} + \beta_3 \Delta \ln IMPPEN_{jt}` \\ &+ \beta_4 \Delta \ln CAPUTIL_t + \beta_5 \Delta \ln KL\ RATIO_{jt} + \beta_6 \Delta \ln TECH_{jt} \\ &+ \beta_\Omega \Omega_t + \beta_\vartheta \vartheta_j + \varepsilon_{jt} \end{aligned} \quad (5)$$

The relevant finding for US workers from the DFS calibration exercise presented in Section 3 is China's gain of comparative advantage. This suggests possible variation in the effects of exports and imports on domestic wages and employment across trading partners grouped by average income levels. More specifically, distilling the separate effects of, say, import competition by income cohort we may anticipate a stronger proportional influence on domestic employment if the import competition is from low income countries and a weaker, albeit still potentially negative, if from high income countries. Estimating modified versions equations (4) and (5) allow us to discern these cohort-specific effects.

Econometric Results

To examine the industry-level effects of trade on employment and average wages, data from the Annual Survey of Manufacturers [19; 20] for the years 2006 and 2007 have been appended to data for the years 1972-2005 that are from the NBER-CES Manufacturing Industry Database [1]. The resulting dataset includes US manufacturing industries categorized according to the 2002 NAICS classification system. Trade data, categorized according to the 1987 SIC classification system (1972-2001) are from Feenstra [4; 5] and Feenstra et al. [6]. Trade data for the years 2002-2007, categorized according to the 2002 NAICS classification system (2002-2007) are from the US ITC [21]. Capacity utilization rates for the US manufacturing sector are from the FRBSL [3]. All data series have been mapped to the 3-digit Census of Population Industrial Classification (CIC) system. The resulting dataset includes 75 3-digit manufacturing industries.[1] While the regression models we estimate are dynamic equations, Table 4 presents descriptive statistics for the static variables over the full reference period and for the first and final years of the reference period.

In the typical manufacturing industry during the typical year, there were roughly 2.5 production workers for every non-production worker. Annual wages were typically about 55.6 percent higher for non-production workers as compared to production workers. About two-thirds (67.8%) of the sector's exports went to high income trading partners. Another 28.2 percent went to middle income countries, 4.3 percent went to low- income countries, and 3 percent went to China. Similarly, about two-thirds of the sector's imports (67.2%) were sourced from high income countries, while 22.2 percent of imports were from middle income

[1] See Appendix B for industry listing.

countries, 10.6 percent were from low income trading partners, and 7.7 percent of imports were from China.

Comparing 2007 to 1972, we see a considerable decrease in the employment of production workers, a modest decrease in non-production worker employment, and slight increases in average annual wages for both production workers and non-production workers. Both exports and imports increased; however, the increase in imports (593%) was considerably greater than the increase in exports (382%). Exports to low income countries increased proportionally more (727%) than did exports to middle income (502%) or high income countries (323%). Likewise, imports from low income countries increased by a staggering 11,445 percent, while imports from middle income (1,280%) and high income countries (318%) increased proportionally less. Both exports and imports, at least in terms of manufactures, increased for all trading partner cohorts but shifted toward low income countries and, to a lesser extent, toward middle income countries and away from high income countries. It is noteworthy that both imports and exports increased proportionally more than did the size of the domestic market. Thus, the average import penetration rate increased as did the degree of import penetration that each cohort accounted for. Even so, it is the average import penetration rate from low income countries that increased, proportionally, the most: a near 50-fold (4,909%) increase from 0.17 in 1972 to 8.52 in 2007.

Table 4. Descriptive Statistics

	1972-2007 N = 2,700 (a)	1972 N = 75 (b)	2007 N = 75 (c)
Production Worker Employment	158,493 (166,004)	177,121 (175,531)	120,632 (131,237)
Non-production Worker Employment	62,718 (71,604)	57,631 (55,092)	51,333 (57,915)
Avg. Annual Production Worker Wages	31,785 (8,455)	32,655 (6,831)	33,224 (9,608)
Avg. Annual Non-production Worker Wages	49,430 (7,822)	49,896 (5,438)	52,550 (9,859)
Exports (2000 US$)	5,240 (9,530)	1,920 (3,070)	9,260 (14,800)
Exports to High Income Countries	3550 (6,540)	1,370 (2,300)	5,790 (9,600)
Exports to Upper Middle Income Countries	377 (730)	167 (297)	592 (1,140)
Exports to Lower Middle Income Countries	1100 (2,350)	300 (475)	2,220 (3,650)
Exports to Low Income Countries (excl. China)	227 (526)	79 (158)	653 (1,320)
Exports to China	159 (223)	0 (0)	1,339 (1,078)
Imports (2000 US$)	7,830 (16,900)	2,410 (4,520)	16,700 (28,000)
Imports from High Income Countries	5,260 (12,300)	2,080 (4,400)	8,680 (17,700)

Table 4. (Continued)

	1972-2007 N = 2,700 (a)	1972 N = 75 (b)	2007 N = 75 (c)
Imports from Upper Middle Income Countries	508	130	909
	(1,370)	(450)	(2,140)
Imports from Lower Middle Income Countries	1230	172	3,260
	(3,690)	(418)	(6,910)
Imports from Low Income Countries (excl. China)	832	33	3,810
	(2,760)	(116)	(7,470)
Imports from China	605	0.0000	2,964
	(1,080)	(0.0000)	(6,019)
Import Penetration Rate	0.1461	0.0583	0.2669
	(0.1565)	(0.0558)	(0.2271)
Import Penetration from High Income Countries	0.0931	0.0491	0.1248
	(0.0893)	(0.0524)	(0.1077)
Import Penetration from Upper Income Countries	0.0095	0.0029	0.0117
	(0.0172)	(0.0061)	(0.0160)
Import Penetration from Lower Income Countries	0.0204	0.0046	0.0452
	(0.0323)	(0.0120)	(0.0517)
Import Penetration from Low Income Countries (excl. China)	0.0231	0.0017	0.0852
	(0.0713)	(0.0091)	(0.1490)
Import Penetration from China	0.0131	0.0000	0.0671
	(0.0422)	(0.0000)	(0.1153)
Domestic Demand (2000 US$)	53,000	42,100	64,800
	(61,400)	(42,000)	(82,600)
Capital-Labor Ratio	218,755	296,653	221,399
	(326,132)	(324,046)	(251,711)
Technology	2.18	3.97	10.60
	(10.2)	(34.3)	(91.8)
Capacity Utilization Rate	79.70	83.41	79.07
	(3.84)	(0.00)	(0.00)

Non-weighted industry averages listed. Domestic demand, export, and import values in millions.

Estimating equations (4) and (5) allows determination of the respective influences of exports and import penetration on industry-level employment and average wages. We first estimate each regression model while allowing for separate effects for China and for all other trading partners. These results are presented in Table 5. To consider variation in the influences of exports to and import penetration from China and the cohorts that have been determined based on per capital income, we estimate modified versions of equations (4) and (5). Results are presented in Table 6. Due to the presence of panel-level heteroskedasticity and first-order serial correlation in the data, we employ the Feasible Generalized Least Squares estimation technique. Beginning with results presented in Table 5, we see that year-to-year increases in import penetration from China, correspond, all else equal, with reductions in both production worker employment and non-production worker employment (columns (a) and (b), respectively). Given the functional forms of the estimation equations, we can say that a one percent increase in import penetration from China for the typical industry corresponds with 0.28 percent and 0.86 percent decreases in production worker and non-production worker employment, respectively. A like increase in import penetration from other countries corresponds with a 0.21 percent decrease in production worker employment, a 0.69 percent decrease in non-production worker employment, and a 0.25 percent decrease in average annual wages for production workers (column (c)). For the same three estimations, we find that in response to a one percent increase in exports to China, non-production worker employment increases by 0.005 percent, while a like increase in exports to the rest of the world results in a 0.01 percent increase in production worker employment, a 0.02 percent increase in non-production worker employment, and a 0.001 percent decrease in average annual wages for production workers.

Considering the remaining variables in Table 5, we see that increased domestic demand corresponds with higher employment and higher average wages for both production and non-production workers. Increases in industry-level capital-labor ratios correspond with lower employment of both production workers and non-production workers but is positively related to average wages of production workers. Technological advances correspond with lower production worker employment and higher average wages for non-production workers. As the magnitudes of coefficient estimates and the pattern of statistical significance for these variables are consistent across Tables 5 and 6, we restrict our focus to the trade-related variables from this point forward.

Table 5. Estimated Trade-Induced Labor Market Dynamics

Dep. Var.:	Δ ln Prod. Employment$_{it}$ (a)	Δ ln Non-Prod. Employment$_{it}$ (b)	Δ ln Avg. Prod. Wages$_{it}$ (c)	Δ ln Avg. Non-Prod. Wages$_{it}$ (d)
Δ ln China Import Penetration Rate$_t$	-0.2849***	-0.8649***	0.2260	0.7355
	(0.0870)	(0.2194)	(0.9405)	(1.5348)
Δ ln All except China Import Penetration Rate$_{it}$	-0.2062***	-0.6877***	-0.2473***	0.0357
	(0.0295)	(0.0745)	(0.0319)	(0.0521)
Δ ln Exports to China$_t$	-0.0002	0.0050*	0.0015	-0.0026
	(0.0011)	(0.0029)	(0.0012)	(0.0020)
Δ ln Exports to all except China$_{it}$	0.0096***	0.0202***	0.0010***	-0.0005
	(0.0031)	(0.0078)	(0.0033)	(0.0054)
Δ ln Domestic Demand$_{it}$	0.1316***	0.2103***	0.1138***	0.0762***
	(0.0074)	(0.0188)	(0.0081)	(0.0131)
Δ ln Capital-Labor Ratio$_{it}$	-0.7655***	-0.2975***	0.1085***	0.0177
	(0.0098)	(0.0247)	(0.0106)	(0.0172)
Δ ln Technology$_{it}$	-0.0012**	0.0001	0.0003	0.0017*
	(0.0006)	(0.0014)	(0.0006)	(0.0010)
Δ ln Capacity Utilization Rate$_{it}$	-0.0222	0.0097	-0.0192	-0.1486
	(0.0967)	(0.2438)	(0.1045)	(0.1706)
Constant	-0.0035	-0.0034	-0.0149***	-0.0053
	(0.0053)	(0.0133)	(0.0057)	(0.0093)
Wald χ^2	19,213***	1,324***	1,762***	689***
Log Likelihood	5,694.62	3,431.48	5,503.55	4,305.66
Pseudo R^2	0.8871	0.3512	0.4188	0.2198

Robust standard errors in parentheses. "***", "**", and "*" denote significance from zero at the 1%, 5%, and 10% levels, respectively.

Table 6. Estimated Trade-Induced Labor Market Dynamics, Cohort-Specific Effects

Dep. Var.:	Δ ln Prod. Employment$_{jt}$ (a)	Δ ln Non-Prod. Employment$_{jt}$ (b)	Δ ln Avg. Prod. Wages$_{jt}$ (c)	Δ ln Avg. Non-Prod. Wages$_{jt}$ (d)
Δ ln China Import Penetration Rate$_t$	-0.2861**	-0.6793**	0.0644	-0.0503
	(0.1147)	(0.2893)	(0.1240)	(0.2022)
Δ ln Low Income Import Penetration Rate (excl. China)$_{jt}$	-0.3316**	-1.3992***	-0.4966***	0.1649
	(0.1353)	(0.3413)	(0.1463)	(0.2385)
Δ ln Lower Middle Income Import Penetration Rate$_{jt}$	-0.2210**	-0.4611*	0.0174	-0.1391
	(0.1019)	(0.2571)	(0.1102)	(0.1796)
Δ ln Upper Middle Income Import Penetration Rate$_{jt}$	-0.1449	-0.4658	-0.6008***	-0.2993
	(0.1296)	(0.3270)	(0.1401)	(0.2285)
Δ ln High Income Import Penetration Rate$_{jt}$	-0.1978***	-0.6729***	-0.2071***	0.0959
	(0.036)	(0.0908)	(0.0389)	(0.0635)
Δ ln Exports to China$_t$	0.0002	0.0013	0.0015	-0.0029
	(0.0018)	(0.0046)	(0.0020)	(0.0032)
Δ ln Exports to Low Income Countries (excl. China)$_{jt}$	0.00005	0.0042	0.0004	0.0002
	(0.0014)	(0.0036)	(0.0016)	(0.0025)
Δ ln Exports to Lower Middle Income Countries$_{jt}$	0.0046**	0.0122*	0.0001	-0.0010***
	(0.0020)	(0.0052)	(0.0022)	(0.0036)
Δ ln Exports to Upper Middle Income Countries$_{jt}$	-0.0032**	0.0004	-0.0018	0.001
	(0.0015)	(0.0039)	(0.0017)	(0.0027)
Δ ln Exports to High Income Countries$_{jt}$	0.0098***	0.0097	0.0086***	0.0064
	(0.0029)	(0.0073)	(0.0031)	(0.0051)
Δ ln Domestic Demand$_{jt}$	0.1303***	0.2078***	0.1144***	0.0783***
	(0.0074)	(0.0188)	(0.0081)	(0.0131)
Δ ln Capital-Labor Ratio$_{jt}$	-0.7655***	-0.2994***	0.1072***	0.0187
	(0.0098)	(0.0246)	(0.0106)	(0.0172)
Δ ln Technology$_{jt}$	-0.0012**	0.0001	0.0003	0.0017*
	(0.0005)	(0.0014)	(0.0006)	(0.0010)
Δ ln Capacity Utilization Rate$_{jt}$	-0.046	-0.0380	-0.0141	-0.1496
	(0.0972)	(0.2454)	(0.1051)	(0.1714)
Constant	-0.0031	-0.0037	-0.0148***	-0.0044
	(0.0053)	(0.0133)	(0.0057)	(0.0093)
Wald χ^2	19,304***	1,336***	1,779***	707***
Log Likelihood	5.699.73	3,435.49	5,508.28	4,312.42
Pseudo R^2	0.8875	0.3533	0.421	0.2241

See Table 5 notes.

Table 6 presents coefficient estimates from the regression models that have been modified to allow for variation in the influences of exports and import penetration across trading partner cohorts. The negative consequences of increased import penetration on employment of both production workers and non-production workers are greatest if the source of the rising import penetration is the low income trading partner cohort. A one percent increase in import penetration from low income countries corresponds with a 0.33 percent decrease in production worker employment and a 1.4 percent decrease in non-production worker employment. By comparison, given the same one percent increase in import competition from China, employment of production workers and non-production workers would decrease by 0.29 percent and 0.68 percent, respectively. Increased import competition from low, upper middle, and high income countries is also found to negatively influence average wages of production workers. With respect to increased exports, the pattern of significance is less clear. Higher exports to high income countries correspond with increased production worker employment and average wages. Likewise, increased exports to lower middle income countries correspond with increased employment for production and non-production workers alike. No significant effect, for employment or average wages, is reported for increased exports to China.

CONCLUSION

We have employed data that span the period from 1968 through 2008 to calibrate the DFS model of Ricardian comparative advantage. The calibration exercise has allowed us to explore changes in relative factor endowments (i.e., capital, labor, and technology) as the underlying basis for China's emergence as an international trading power. Our evaluation of the DFS model serves two purposes. By considering changes in China's factor endowments relative to those of the full cohort of 97 trading partners, the United States, and cohorts of trading partners that have been categorized based on World Bank income classifications, we gain insights regarding changes in comparative advantage. Results from the calibration exercises suggest that China has gained comparative advantage relative to the US and in comparison to the high income country cohort during the reference period. For all other cohorts, the change in China's comparative advantage is ambiguous.

The calibration exercises motivate our examination of the effects of trade on industry-level employment and average wages in the US manufacturing sector. Examining data for 75 3-digit CIC industries in the United States' manufacturing sector during the period from 1972-2007, we find relatively small, yet statistically significant, negative effects of rising import penetration from China on employment of production workers and of non-production workers. These effects, however, are not particularly pronounced relative to reported effects for countries categorized as low income or as middle income (i.e., lower middle income or upper middle income). We find no evidence of significant effects of trade with China (exports or imports) on average wages for production workers or non-production workers. Likewise, we do not report significant positive/offsetting employment effects that are attributable to increased US exports to China.

It is important to recognize that, due to more disaggregate data not being available, the analysis presented here involves the use of data that are classified at a relatively broad (i.e., 3-digit CIC) industry level. Heterogeneity across industries, and even across firms within industry classifications, along with period/year specific variation make it difficult, if not impossible, to infer precise employment and wage effects. As a result, we choose to be reserved in our interpretations and in our conclusions. That being said, we do report significant influences of greater exports and rising import competition on industry-level employment and average wages. Additional research is needed to discern more precise estimates of trade-induced employment effects.

Appendix A: Country Listing, by Income Classification

High Income (24): Australia, Austria, Belgium, Canada, Cyprus, Denmark, Finland, France, Hong Kong, Iceland, Ireland, Israel, Italy, Japan, Netherlands, New Zealand, Norway, Singapore, Spain, Sweden, Switzerland, Taiwan, United Kingdom, United States;

Upper Middle Income (11): Barbados, Brazil, Gabon, Greece, Korea (Republic of), Mexico, Portugal, South Africa, Trinidad & Tobago, Uruguay, Venezuela;

Lower Middle Income (29): Algeria, Argentina, Bolivia, Cameroon, Chile, Colombia, Costa Rica, Cote d`Ivoire, Dominican Republic, Ecuador, El Salvador, Fiji, Guatemala, Iran, Jamaica, Jordan, Malaysia, Morocco, Nicaragua, Panama, Paraguay, Peru, Philippines, Romania, Senegal, Syria, Thailand, Turkey, Zimbabwe;

Low Income (34): Bangladesh, Benin, Burkina Faso, Burundi, Central African Republic, Chad, China, Congo (Dem. Rep.), Egypt, Equatorial Guinea, Ethiopia, Gambia, Ghana, Guinea, Haiti, Honduras, India, Indonesia, Kenya, Madagascar, Malawi, Mali, Mauritania, Mozambique, Nepal, Niger, Nigeria, Pakistan, Rwanda, Sri Lanka, Tanzania, Togo, Uganda, Zambia.

Appendix B: CIC Industry Classifications

100 Meat Products; 101 Dairy Products; 102 Canned and preserved fruits and vegetables; 110 Grain mill products; 111 Bakery products; 112 Sugar and confectionery products; 120 Beverage industries; 121 Miscellaneous food preparations & kindred products; 130 Tobacco manufactures; 132 Knitting mills; 140 Dyeing & finishing textiles, except wool & knit goods; 141 Floor coverings, except hard surface; 142 Yarn, thread, and fabric mills; 150 Miscellaneous textile mill products; 151 Apparel and accessories, except knit; 152 Miscellaneous fabricated textile products; 160 Pulp, paper, and paperboard mills; 161 Miscellaneous paper and pulp products; 162 Paperboard containers and boxes; 172 Printing, publishing, & allied industries, except newspapers; 180 Plastics, synthetics, and resins; 181 Drugs; 182 Soaps and cosmetics; 190 Paints, varnishes, and related products; 191 Agricultural chemicals; 192 Industrial and miscellaneous chemicals; 200 Petroleum refining; 201 Miscellaneous petroleum and coal products; 210 Tires and inner tubes; 211 Other rubber products, and plastics footwear and belting; 212 Miscellaneous plastics products; 220 Leather tanning and finishing; 221 Footwear, except rubber and plastic; 222 Leather products, except footwear; 231 Sawmills, planning mills, and millwork; 232 Wood buildings and mobile homes; 241 Miscellaneous wood products; 242 Furniture and fixtures; 250 Glass and glass products; 251 Cement, concrete, gypsum, and plaster products; 252 Structural clay products; 261 Pottery and related products; 262 Miscellaneous nonmetallic mineral & stone products; 270 Blast furnaces, steelworks, rolling & finishing mills; 271 Iron and steel foundries; 272 Primary aluminum industries; 280 Other primary metal industries; 281 Cutlery, hand tools, and other hardware; 282 Fabricated structural metal products; 290 Screw machine products; 291 Metal forgings and stampings; 292 Ordnance; 300 Miscellaneous fabricated metal products; 310 Engines and turbines; 311 Farm machinery and equipment; 312 Construction and material handling machines; 320 Metalworking machinery; 321 Office and accounting machines; 322 Electronic computing equipment; 331 Machinery, except electrical, not

elsewhere classified; 340 Household appliances; 341 Radio, T.V., and communication equipment; 342 Electrical machinery, equipment, and supplies, not elsewhere classified; 351 Motor vehicles and motor vehicle equipment; 352 Aircraft and parts; 360 Ship and boat building and repairing; 361 Railroad locomotives and equipment; 362 Guided missiles, space vehicles, and parts; 370 Cycles and miscellaneous transportation equipment; 371 Scientific and controlling instruments; 372 Optical and health services supplies; 380 Photographic equipment and supplies; 381 Watches, clocks, and clockwork operated devices; 390 Toys, amusement, and sporting goods; 391 Miscellaneous manufacturing industries.

REFERENCES

[1] Becker, R.A. & Gray, W.B. (2009) NBER-CES Manufacturing Industry Database. Online. Available at: http://www.nber.org/data/nbprod2005.html.

[2] Dornbusch, R., Fischer. S., & Samuelson. P. (1977) "Comparative Advantage, Trade, and Payments in a Ricardian Model with a Continuum of Goods," *American Economic Review* 67(5): 823-839.

[3] Federal Reserve Bank of St. Louis (FRBSL) (2012) Capacity Utilization: Manufacturing (NAICS) (MCUMFN), Release: G.17 Industrial Production and Capacity Utilization. Online. Available at: http://research.stlouisfed.org/fred2/series/MCUMFN?cid=3.

[4] Feenstra, R.C. (1997) "U.S. Exports, 1972-1994, with State Exports and Other U.S. Data", NBER Working Paper no. 5990.

[5] Feenstra, R.C. (1996) "U.S. Imports, 1972-1994: Data and Concordances", NBER Working Paper no. 5515.

[6] Feenstra, R. C., Romalis, J. & Schott, P.K. (2002) "U.S. Imports, Exports and Tariff Data, 1989-2001", NBER Working Paper no. 9387.

[7] Frankel, J.A. & Romer, D. (1999) "Does Trade Cause Growth?", *American Economic Review* 89, 3: 379-399.

[8] Freeman, R.B. & Katz, L.F. (1991) "Industrial Wage and Employment Determination in an Open Economy," in *Immigration, Trade, and the Labor Market,* John M. Abowd and Richard B. Freeman, eds. Chicago, IL: University of Chicago Press.

[9] Heckscher, E. (1919) "The Effect of Foreign Trade on the Distribution of Income", *Ekonomisk Tidskriff* 497–512. Translated as chapter 13 in American Economic Association, *Readings in the Theory of International Trade,* Philadelphia: Blakiston, 1949, 272–300, and a new translation is provided in Flam and Flanders.

[10] Heston, A., Summers, R. & Aten, B. (2011) Penn World Table Version 7.0, Center for International Comparisons of Production, Income and Prices at the University of Pennsylvania (May). Online. Available at: https://pwt.sas.upenn.edu/.

[11] Hummels, D. & Levinsohn, J. (1995) "Monopolistic Competition and International Trade: Reconsidering the Evidence," *The Quarterly Journal of Economics* 110(3): 799-836.

[12] Kletzer, L.G. (2002) *Imports, Exports and Jobs: What does trade mean for employment and job loss?,* Kalamazoo, MI: W.E. Upjohn Institute for Employment Research.

[13] Krugman, P. (2008) "*International Trade Models.*" Lecture, International Economics, Lecture 18 from Princeton University, Princeton, September 18, 2008.

[14] Mann, C.L. (1988) "The Effect of Foreign Competition in Prices and Quantities on the Employment in Import-Sensitive U.S. Industries," *The International Trade Journal*, 2(4), 409-444.

[15] Ohlin, B. (1933) *Interregional and International Trade,* Cambridge, Mass.: Harvard University Press.

[16] Ricardo, D. (1817) *On the Principles of Political Economy and Taxation,* London: John Murray.

[17] Solow, R.M. (1957) "Technical Change and the Aggregate Production Function", *The Review of Economics and Statistics* 39(3): 312-320.

[18] World Bank (2012) World Development Indicators, Washington, DC: World Bank. Online: http://databank.worldbank.org.

[19] US Census Bureau (US Census) (2011) 2007 Economic Census. Series ID# EC0731SG1. Online. Available at: http://factfinder2.census.gov/faces/nav/ jsf/pages/ searchresults.xhtml?refresh=t.

[20] US Census Bureau (US Census) (2008) Annual Survey of Manufactures. Online. Available at: http://www.census.gov/manufacturing/asm/historical_data/index.html.

[21] US International Trade Commission (US ITC) (2012) Interactive Tariff and Trade DataWeb – Version 3.0. Online. Available at: http://dataweb.usitc.gov/.

In: Current Issues in International Trade
Editor: Gouranga G. Das

ISBN: 978-1-63321-405-7

Chapter 8

TRADE REFORM, ENVIRONMENT AND INTERMEDIATION: IMPLICATION FOR HEALTH STANDARD

Biswajit Mandal*

Department of Economics, University at Albany-SUNY, Albany, NY, US;
Visva-Bharati University, Santiniketan, India

ABSTRACT

The health standard of a region or economy significantly depends on environmental quality. And the informal sector has a striking role for overall environmental quality because sometimes producers prefer not to produce in the formal sector as formal production calls for stringent environmental and other governmental regulations. Under such circumstances the informal counterpart of the economy becomes heaven for those producers who do not want to abide by the rules. Extralegality of informal production, by definition, indicates the emergence of intermediation activity. In light of these concerns here I build a standard general equilibrium structure to capture these phenomena and to focus on the effects of trade reform. It has been shown in this paper that tariff reform may lead to greater usage of abatement technology under certain factor intensity assumption. However, interestingly, this cannot unambiguously ensure a better environmental quality in broader sense.

Keywords: Environment, International Trade; Intermediation; General Equilibrium

JEL classification: O13, F1, D73, D5

* Address for Correspondence : BISWAJIT MANDAL, Department of Economics & Politics, Visva-Bharati University, Santiniketan, India, 731235, Telephone: (+91) 03463262751-56 Extn. 405. E-mail: biswajiteco@gmail.com / bmandal@albany.edu.

1. INTRODUCTION

Broadly speaking, general health standards and health related problems are intertwined with the environmental standard of a country in particular. And on the other hand the nexus between trade and environment related issues are in the forefront of economic research for quite a long time. Huge numbers of papers are produced concerning the world wide panic of environmental degradation that may arise due to non-usage of environmentally sound technology of production. Trade theorists more often than not look at such concerns from the perspective of globalization. A representative sample consists Anderson and Neary (1992), Barrett (1994), Beghin et al., (1997), Conrad (1993), Copeland (1994), Hoel (1997), Markusen et al., (1993), Motta and Thisse (1994), Neary (2005), Rauscher (1994, 1997), Ulph (1997), Ulph and Ulph (1996) et al. Surprisingly a relatively less attempt (Chaudhuri and Mukhopadhyaya, 2011; Biswas et al., 2012; Chung and Chung, 2012) has been made to analyze an important aspect of developing economy in particular and world economy in general, corruption which naturally co-exists with trade and environment related problems. Therefore trade and environmental issue must have some inference for health standard of an economy which is almost a neglected area of research.

A-priori manufacturing production and industrial activities are the principal sources of pollution in both developed (DCs) and less developed countries (LDCs). DCs, with higher per capital income, prefer to use different regulatory framework to reduce environmental pollution by curbing production units or processes that pay little attention to the growing concern of environment. However, the scenario of LDCs are a bit different. Although the regulatory framework, its enforcement and the resources allocated to comply with legislation are generally limited in LDCs. On top of that increasing competition in domestic markets due to liberalization in trade and services has forced firms to reduce costs by any means and to upgrade their technologies to become more competitive.

Conventionally the relationship between environmental protection and private costs is quite straight forward, environmental regulations in different forms can only be met by additional investments and higher operative costs. Consequently economic growth rate is expected to be lowered. Furthermore, taking into account the unequal application of environmental regulations in different countries, we observe that a trade-off between environmental preservation and private competitiveness may often arise.

In this context it is very important to note that many have taken the policy implication of the so-called 'environmental Kuznets curve' (EKC). Poor countries can and perhaps grow themselves out of environmental problems rather than tackling them with stricter regulation at least for the time being. Critics also mention that the now rich countries have become clean at least partly by exporting the dirty production of products to other, poorer countries. This implies that the current poor countries will not be able to replicate fully this experience. Nevertheless, how some environmental policies even in the LDCs can push some firms to an isolated "free" zone where nobody is bothered about environment is taken into account in this paper. So use and non-use of abatement technology in production in the LDCs exist simultaneously. We will come back to this issue later.

Before we move to the brief description of the structure and basic results let me just put forth the interconnectedness of environment and health in a very simple way. Environmental pollution' encompasses the terms environment and pollution. Environment is the complete range of external conditions under which an organism lives. On the other hand, pollution means to make or render an undesirable change in the characteristics of the land, air or water that harmfully effect human life or other species. In addition to this, over the last three decades there has been increasing global concern over the public health impacts caused by environmental pollution, in particular, the global burden of disease. The World Health Organization (WHO) estimates that about a quarter of the diseases that mankind faces today occur due to prolonged exposure to environmental pollution. Most of these environment-related diseases are however not easily detected and may be acquired during childhood from the environment where they are raised and manifested later in adulthood. So the detrimental long-run effects of utilization of non-environment friendly technology in production on health in general are quite explicit.

As we mentioned before, sometimes stringent environmental regulation induces firms to go beyond the formal setup or sector and to continue production in the informal sector[1] where environmental strictures are not so binding or non-existent. Since informal production itself is not permitted by law, it becomes a happy hunting ground for extortionists who actually negotiate between producers and bureaucratic officials or government representatives. In exchange of this service they demand pecuniary benefit which by definition is DUP activities (Bhagwati, 1982) in nature. This paper focuses on such concerns in light of a reformatory trade policies in a general equilibrium theoretical model. And subsequently try to look at the possible ill effects on health, if any, of a reformatory trade policy. The basic results that I derive are as follows:

a. tariff reform may lead to greater usage of abatement technology under certain factor intensity assumption;
b. a tariff cut cannot unambiguously ensure a better environmental quality and health standard, per se, in broader sense.

The rest of the paper is arranged as follows. Section 2 builds the basic model and talks about the solution mechanism. Effects of tariff reform are discussed in Section 3. Section 4 concludes the paper.

2. The Model

There are three goods *X, Y* and *Z* produced in the neo-classical framework using four factors such as skilled labor *(S)*, unskilled labor (L) and two types of capital (K and T). K is

[1] Informal sector is an important ingredient of the contemporary world economy particularly in the developing regions as this segment occupies a formidable chunk of the unskilled labor force. This sector covers primarily the non-agricultural employment of unskilled labor. It accounts for 50-80% of total employment in South Asia, 30-50% in South East Asia, 40-50% in Africa, 55% in Latin America and Caribbean, 24% in Southern Europe, 10% in Western Europe, 18% in Canada and 8% in USA (ILO, 2002). Yet, informal sector's jobs are not considered as respectable ones. The main derogatory feature of informal sector is its extra-legality or illegality by law since it does not conform to government regulations. These units do not abide by labor regulations of the government, and do not pay taxes. In fact a large part of it would have vanished if they had to confront government regulations. The paucity of legal protection makes the informal sector an easy pray for extortion and corruption. It has been reported in Ethiopia that the urban informal sector of this rural country is comprised of almost one million people and is vastly distorted with extortion. While Morocco experiences an annual loss of \$ 3.6 billion because of lack of transparency related extortion/corruption/bribe (Drakard, 2009).

perfectly mobile across X and Y but T is specific to Z. X and Y are produced in the formal set up whereas Z is produced in the informal set up[2]. The point to be noted very carefully is that the moment producers shift from formal to informal sector they are denied the formal capital/credit represented by K. They bank on informal credit, T. In addition both X and Y require another intermediate input as abatement technology which is not needed in Z. That is the way we bring in informality and environment together. Furthermore, S is specific to X and gets Ws as wage. L is mobile between Y and Z. Unskilled labors (L) are unionized in Y. They get $\bar{W}$ as their wage. K gets identical return r across X and Y while T gets R in Z. Who are not fortunate enough to work in Y, have to go out of the formal segment. Producers of Z need to comply with some institutional and political menace as it is an extra-legal, if not illegal, activity. To combat such menace producers obtain service of intermediaries who actually watch out for institutional perils. Their marginal productivities in terms of the volume of goods are zero though they get positive return for their work[3]. However, without such an arrangement production of Z could not have taken place. We call sector Z as informal productive sector. Therefore, in a nutshell production can take place anywhere between formal and informal segments. Production in informal sector requires less costly labor as $\bar{W} > W$ but possible return to capital is higher as informal units are not entitled to get loans from legal or government recognized sources. On top of that they need to, however, rely on intermediation activity as informal production does not abide by environmental regulation. This is reflected by the non-existence of abatement cost and existence of cost of intermediation or extortion in form of α in tandem. α resembles an ice-berg kind of cost. Therefore the amount lost from Z is entirely spent for employing intermediators who actually negotiates with administrators for the survival of environment non-friendly sector Z. Intermediation is done only by unskilled labor. Let L_N be the people and N be the sector representing intermediation/extortion. The return to extortionists, W is identical with competitive informal wage, W. Perfect labor mobility between Z and N ensures this equality.

We have a small open economy with competitive markets for production as well as for extortions related intermediation or corruption. Competitive corruption market implies that the lost output due to intermediation is fully exhausted in paying out extortionists. Moreover, we have the standard neo-classical assumptions of constant returns to scale and diminishing return to factors. The following set of equations describes the model and the interpretations of symbols are usual and well used in trade models (Jones, 1965, 1971)[4]. Further, Y is the importable commodity and subject to a tariff t[5].

Competitive commodity market guarantees the following equalities:

[2] For details about the way we define informal sector see Marjit and Kar (2011).

[3] We can coin this sort of intermediations as directly unproductive profit-seeking activities (Bhagwati, 1982). This is the concept of corruption and/or related extortion that we are going to use in our model.

[4] The symbols that would be used extensively in this paper are: $P_j \Rightarrow$ price of the jth commodity (j= X, Y, Z); $W_S \Rightarrow$ skilled wage; $\bar{W} \Rightarrow$ unskilled formal wage; $W \Rightarrow$ unskilled informal wage; $r \Rightarrow$ rate of return to K; $R \Rightarrow$ rate of return to T; $a_{ij} \Rightarrow$ production requirement of the ith factor in one unit of jth commodity (i = S,L,K,T and j = X,Y,Z); S $\Rightarrow$ total supply of skilled labor; L $\Rightarrow$ total supply of unskilled labor; $L_N \Rightarrow$ number of unskilled labor employed in extortion; K $\Rightarrow$ total supply of capital, K; T $\Rightarrow$ total supply of capital, T.

[5] One can effortlessly disagree to argue that Y should not be the importable commodity for any developing economy as it uses unskilled workers. But we do not find any harm in assuming this. Here skilled good (X) is exportable. In order to avoid the possibility of complete specialization we have taken the remaining good (Y) as importable. Introduction of any other commodity as importable, instead of Y, would not matter much to the basic results of the paper.

$$W_S\, a_{SX} + r\, a_{KX} + \mu\, a_{CX} = P_x \tag{1}$$

$$\bar{W} a_{LY} + r\, a_{KY} + \mu\, a_{CY} = P_Y(1 + t) \tag{2}$$

$$W a_{LZ} + R\, a_{TZ} = P_Z(1 - \alpha) \tag{3}$$

μ is the per unit price or cost of abatement technology or cleansing act. a_{CX} and a_{CY} represent how much unit of abatement technology is required to produce one unit of environment friendly X and Y respectively. μ, a_{CX} and a_{CY} are given and constant.

Note that, $\alpha \in [0,1]$; a low α will mean lower fee of extortion and conversely.

We have mentioned earlier that N people are paid out of the amount lost from the value of Z. And in a competitive set up the value of output lost in Z must be identical to the payment made for extortionists. Thus,

$$\alpha . P_Z . Z = W L_N \tag{4}$$

Full employment of all the factors ensures the following:

$$a_{SX} . X = S \tag{5}$$

$$a_{KX} . X + a_{KY} . Y = K \tag{6}$$

$$a_{TZ} . Z = T \tag{7}$$

$$a_{LY} . Y + a_{LZ} . Z = L - L_N \tag{8}$$

We further know that $a_{CX} . X = C_X$ and $a_{CY} . Y = C_Y$. C_X and C_Y represent total amount of abatement technology used in X and Y respectively, and C means abatement technology together. So

$$\mu(a_{CX} . X + a_{CY} . Y) = \mu(C_X + C_Y) = \mu C \tag{9}$$

Subsequently health standard (H) is a function of environmental quality and thus in turn depends on Z which does not abide by environmental regulations. Therefore

$$H = f(Z);\ f'(Z) < 0 \tag{10}$$

This completes the structure of the model. Now let us solve for the unknown variables. Note that $\{t, \alpha, \bar{W}, K, T, L, S\}$ are exogenously given and we need to solve for $\{W_S, W, r, R, X, Y, Z, L_N \text{ and } C\}$ from equation (1) - (9). We have nine equations and nine unknown variables. Thus the system is solvable.

3. EFFECTS OF TARIFF REFORM

There is no wonder that restrictive trade policies are gradually becoming an issue of the past. Following WTO negotiation, an era of reform has set in and the entire developing world in some form or the another has responded to such transformation. Therefore to start with the analysis of trade reform we assume that the government has initiated the liberalization strategy and accordingly opted for a tariff cut in the importable sector. Following Jones (1965, 1971) and using the Heckscher-Ohlin nugget structure (developed in Jones and Marjit 2009) drawing from Gruen and Corden (1970) we can easily derive the values of X and Y consequent upon tariff cut.

$$\hat{X} = (-)\sigma_X \frac{\theta_{KX}}{\theta_{SX}} \frac{t}{\theta_{KY}} \hat{t} > 0 \text{ (as t falls)} \tag{11}$$

$$\hat{Y} = \sigma_X \frac{\theta_{KX}}{\theta_{SX}} \frac{\lambda_{KX}}{\lambda_{KY}} \frac{t}{\theta_{KY}} \hat{t} < 0 \tag{12}$$

Using (9) $$\hat{C} = \sigma_X \frac{\theta_{KX}}{\theta_{SX}} \frac{t}{\theta_{KY}} \hat{t} \left(\lambda_{CY} \frac{\lambda_{KX}}{\lambda_{KY}} - \lambda_{CX}\right) \tag{13}$$

Two opposing forces are working for the change in C. As t falls X increases and thus demand for and /or use of C rises. Whereas, a reduction Y acts in the opposite direction.

Hence

$$\left.\begin{aligned} &\hat{C} > 0 \; iff \; \left(\lambda_{CY} \frac{\lambda_{KX}}{\lambda_{KY}} - \lambda_{CX}\right) < 0 \\ &or, \frac{a_{CX}}{a_{KX}} > \frac{a_{CY}}{a_{KY}} \; or, \frac{a_{KX}}{a_{KY}} < \frac{a_{CX}}{a_{CY}} \end{aligned}\right\} \tag{14}$$

Therefore, if X uses the abatement technology more intensively than Y, a policy of tariff reform leads to more usage of abatement technology in the economy. It cannot, however, ensure a better environmental situation in the country. Because the moment Y falls, it relinquishes some unskilled labor and capital. Capital goes to X and raises the production. Labor goes to Z and N simultaneously. Thus if Z goes up, this will pollute the environment further. But, if entire labor force gets employed in N, then the extent of pollution in the economy will remain unchanged. In what follows we propose that:

PROPOSITION I: *If* $\frac{a_{CX}}{a_{KX}} > \frac{a_{CY}}{a_{KY}}$, *tariff reform leads to greater usage of abatement technology.*

Proof: See discussion above

Now let us move to the condition under which Z may rise, fall or remain constant. This would help us commenting on the overall quality of the environment and quality of health due to reform. Change in the production of either X and Y cannot influence the quality of environment as both are produced by using environmentally sound technology. Whether environmental effect is bad or good that naturally depends only on Z. And that consequently determines H.

Manipulating the system of equations a bit we get

$$\hat{Z} = S_X\hat{X} + S_Y\hat{Y} + S_Y^t(\hat{Y} + \hat{t}) \tag{15}$$

$$\hat{Z} > 0 \; iff \; S_X > \frac{S_Y^t}{\sigma_X}\frac{\theta_{SX}}{\theta_{KX}}\frac{\theta_{KY}}{t} + (S_Y + S_Y^t)\frac{\lambda_{KX}}{\lambda_{KY}}$$

where, $S_X = \frac{\beta.X}{(1-\beta).P_Z.Z}$ and $S_Y = \frac{\beta.Y}{(1-\beta).P_Z.Z}$ and $S_Y^t = \frac{t\beta.Y}{(1-\beta).P_Z.Z}$.

It is apparent from (15) that if the share of expenditure coming from X is sufficiently large, environmental quality of the economy would be worse off. The economic underpinning is as follows: since X expands and Y shrinks, the change in demand for Z is uncertain. Along with it as t falls the effective price of Y also falls indicating a less income from Y that can be spent on Z. Negative demand effect on Z is two-pronged: one for less production of Y and other for less price of Y. Hence equilibrium supply of Z will increase if and only if the share of X is sufficiently large to outweigh the negative demand effect generated from Y. Hence the following proposition is immediate.

PROPOSITION II: *Overall environmental quality and health standard will be degraded if* $S_X > \frac{S_Y^t}{\sigma_X}\frac{\theta_{SX}}{\theta_{KX}}\frac{\theta_{KY}}{t} + (S_Y + S_Y^t)\frac{\lambda_{KX}}{\lambda_{KY}}$.

Proof: See discussion above

CONCLUSION

In this paper I have developed a general equilibrium model of trade where both formal and informal sectors exist in tandem. Tight environmental guidelines lead to the emergence of informal sector which crucially hinges upon the intermediation done by extortionists. These people, essentially, make the informal production possible. It has been shown here that a policy of tariff cut may induce greater usage of abatement technology. However, the environmental quality and the health standard of the country may be worsened under a certain condition.

ACKNOWLEDGMENT

I am thankful to the Planning Unit, Visva-Bharati University for partial financial support. Financial support as C V Raman Fellow is also gratefully acknowledged. The usual disclaimer applies.

REFRENCES

Anderson, J.E. and J.P. Neary (1992): "Trade reform with quotas, partial rent retention, and tariffs," *Econometrica*, 60, 57-76.

Barrett, S. (1994): "Strategic environmental policy and international trade," *Journal of Public Economics,* 54, 325-338.

Beghin, J., Roland Holst, D., and D. van der Mensbrugghe (1997): "Trade and pollution linkages: Piecemeal reform and optimal intervention," *Canadian Journal of Economics,* 30, 442-455.

Bhagwati, J. (1982) - Directly Unproductive Profit Seeking (DUP) Activities. *Journal of Political Economy*, 90(5), pp 988-1002.

Biswas, A., Farzanegan, M.R. and Thum, M., (2012): Pollution, shadow economy and corruption: theory and evidence. *Ecological Economics* 75, 114–125.

Chang, Shu-Chen and Teng-Yu Chang, (2012) "Threshold Effects of Economic Growth on Air Pollution under Regimes of Corruption", *Economics Bulletin*, Vol. 32 No. 1 pp. 1046-1059.

Chaudhuri, Sarbajit & Mukhopadhyay, Ujjaini, 2011. "Foreign direct investment, environmentally sound technology and informal sector," MPRA Paper 31447, University Library of Munich, Germany.

Conrad, K. (1993): "Taxes and subsidies for pollution-intensive industries as trade policy," *Journal of Environmental Economics and Management,* 25, 121-135.

Copeland, B.R.(1994): "International trade and the environment: Policy reform in a polluted small open economy,"*Journal of Environmental Economics and Management*,26,44-65.

Drakard, M. (2009) – Corruption and Bribery as a way of life in Africa. *The Cutting Age*, 26th October, 2009.

Gruen, F. & M. Corden (1970) – *A tariff that worsens terms of trade*. In I. A. McDougall and R. H. Snapes (Eds) Studies in International Economics, Amsterdam: North-Holland.

Hoel, M. (1997): "Environmental policy with endogenous plant locations", *Scandinavian Journal of Economics,* 99, 241-259.

ILO (2002) - Men and Women in the Informal Economy. International Labour Organisation. 2002. ISBN 92-2-113103-3. Retrieved 2006-12-18.

Jones, R.W. (1965) – The Structure of Simple General Equilibrium Models. *Journal of Political Economy*, 73, pp.557-572.

Jones, R.W. (1971) – *A three-factor model in theory, trade and history*. In Bhagwati, J et al., (Eds) Trade, Balance of Payments and Growth, North- Holland, Amsterdam, pp. 3-21.

Jones, R.W. and S. Marjit (2009) - Competitive trade models and real world features. *Economic Theory,* 41(1), pp. 163-174.

Marjit, S. & S. Kar (2011) – The Outsiders: Economic Reform and Informal Labor in a Developing Economy, Oxford University Press.

Markusen, J.R., E.R. Morey and N.D. Olewiler (1993): "Environmental policy when market structure and plant locations are endogenous," *Journal of Environmental Economics and Management,* 24, 68-86.

Motta, M. and J.F. Thisse (1994): "Does environmental dumping lead to delocation?", *European Economic Review,* 38, 563-576.

Neary, J. P (2005): International Trade and the environment: theoretical and policy linkage.

Porter, M.E. and C. van der Linde (1995): "Toward a new conception of the environment Competitiveness relationship," *Journal of Economic Perspectives,* 9, 97-118.

Rauscher, M. (1994): "On ecological dumping," *Oxford Economic Papers,* 46, 822-840.

Rauscher, M. (1997): *International Trade, Factor Movements, and the Environment*, Oxford: Clarendon Press.

Ulph, A. (1997): "Environmental policy and international trade," in C. Carraro and D. Siniscalco (eds.): *New Directions in the Economic Theory of the Environment*, Cambridge: Cambridge University Press, 147-192.

Ulph, A. and D. Ulph (1996): "Trade, strategic innovation and strategic environmental policy: A general analysis," in C. Carraro, Y. Katsoulacos and A. Xepapadeas (eds.): *Environmental Policy and Market Structure*, Dordrecht: Kluwer Academic, 181-208.

In: Current Issues in International Trade
Editor: Gouranga G. Das

ISBN: 978-1-63321-405-7

Chapter 9

CONSTRUCTING TRADE BARRIER INDEX FOR SELECTED COUNTRIES OF SOUTH ASIA

***Dripto Mukhopadhyay*[1] *and Sanjib Pohit*[2]**
[1]Vice President, Indicus Analytics
[2]Professor AcSIR and Senior Principal Scientist
CSIR—National Institute of Science, Technology and Development Studies,
New Delhi, India

ABSTRACT

External trade from South Asian countries is relatively lower than that of the other regions of the world. However, it has been noticed that trade within South Asian region is minuscule compared to trade external to this region. One of the key determinants for this trend is believed to be trade barriers within the region. This paper has made an attempt to understand the extent and nature of trade barriers and their impact on trade activities with the region by constructing a trade barrier index.

The study concludes with evidence, based on primary survey data from five South Asian countries, that trade barriers play a significant adverse role in within-region trade. The trade barriers also increase cost of transactions significantly in form of bribery and damages.

Keywords: South Asia, Trade Barrier Index, Principal Component Analysis

INTRODUCTION

Over the past two decades, economies across the world have witnessed greater regional and economic integration due to gradual reduction in tariff and nontariff barriers across nations. Independent nation states, such as those in Europe, have given way to economic

[1]Indicus Analytics Pvt. Ltd, Nehru House, 2nd Floor, 4-Bahadur Shah Zafar Marg, New Delhi 110002 INDIA Email: dripto.mukhopadhyay@gmail.com
[2]CSIR-NISTADS, Room No. 10, Pusa Gate Dr. K.S. Krishnan Marg, New Delhi 110012 INDIA. Email: spohit@gmail.com; spohit@nistads.res.in

communities; while, in other countries, regional agreements regarding trade, investment, and mobility of people have greatly reduced the barriers to cross-border economic engagement. Most of the countries have adopted outward-looking economic policies to promote growth and employment through expanding export-oriented activities. All countries nowadays court multinationals to promote growth and increase the productivity of investment. Typically, multinationals locate production process across nations to reap benefits from lower cost of production and raw materials. This necessitates movement of parts, components, semi-manufactured goods, and sub-assemblies across the nation at a fast pace with minimal impediments/cost.

Furthermore, increased competitive pressure in today's world has made all firms to be cost-conscious. Outsourcing to lower-cost firms and countries has become a major source of cost reduction. Reduced inventory costs through just-in-time manufacturing and an efficient supply chain management has been another effective instrument for cost reduction. With worldwide fall in tariff levels, efficiency of supply chains and associated logistics costs has become a core determinant of competitiveness of both firms and countries. This trend is now very much evident in the First World economies as well as in fast-growing East Asian economies. The high degree of intra-region trade is very much a facet of this trend. This is a manifestation of a low degree of impediment in trading among regional partners.

The scenario in South Asia is in stark contrast to this worldwide trend. Intraregional trade in South Asia is abysmally low, roughly standing at about 5 percent of the total trade of the South Asian economies. By contrast, intraregional trade accounts for roughly 65 percent of the European Union's total trade; it is 51 percent in the North American Free Trade Agreement (NAFTA) area, 25 percent in the Association of South East Asian Nations (ASEAN), and 16 percent in the Latin American trade bloc. This has occurred despite the fact that South Asian economy nowadays has become outward looking and has signed the South Asia Free Trade Agreement.

South Asia is often perceived as having very poor external supply chains—inefficient ports, long delays, cumbersome customs procedures, etc. The published international surveys, such as the World Bank's "Doing Business," have tended to confirm the perceptions. South Asia has performed poorly on all "trading across border" measures, requiring more documents, time, and cost than either developed countries or East Asia. A regional integration agenda can never be successful without proper trade facilitation practices. This is especially true for the SMEs who are often the major driving force for the intraregional trade in South Asia. Hence, identification of trade barriers is crucial if South Asia is to reap benefit from trade integration exercise. This has not yet received the desired attention, but increasingly gaining prominence in policy circles.

In recent years, World Bank has been publishing the logistics' barrier index for all the countries of South Asia on an annual basis. Certainly, this is a positive development highlighting the trade facilitation problems of the South Asian countries. However, these indices focus on each country's barrier with respect to the rest of the world. The nature of impediments in trading within themselves is not highlighted in these indices. If we go by literature on trade facilitation problems in respect of South Asian countries, impediments in trading among themselves is believed to be much more than in trading with countries outside the region (Das and Pohit, 2006; De, Prabir, Abdur Rob Khan and Sachin Chaturvedi, 2008). However, there is dearth of quantitative studies highlighting the extent of trade barriers among South Asian countries and its relative position among themselves. This paper is an attempt in this direction.

To be specific, our aim is to construct the indices of trade barrier for major South Asian countries, namely India, Bangladesh, Sri Lanka, Pakistan, and Nepal. It must be noted that the paper (trade barrier indices) focuses solely on the perspective of trade relation between India and rest of the major aforementioned South Asian countries

DATA AND METHODOLOGY

It is obvious that secondary information is not sufficient to construct the said trade barrier index for South Asia. For this reason, primary surveys were conducted in each of these five South Asian countries, namely India, Bangladesh, Sri Lanka, Pakistan, and Nepal, to collate information for constructing trade barrier index. The respondents to our surveys were exporters, importers, and freight-forwarding agents, who were engaged in trade between India and her South Asian partner countries. We have used a structured questionnaire to solicit information on impediments. The respondents were asked to provide their perception about the impediments in a scale of 0 to 5, where 0 represents no impediment and 5 stands for very high impediment. The impediments have also been classified by modes of transports such as road, rail, sea, and air. Information has also been collated on various categories of impediments under each modes of transport. Additionally, respondents were also asked to report whether changes occurred during the past 5 years on a scale of 0 to 5, where 0 represents no change and 5 represents very significant change. In all, we have collated about 70 respondents (filled in questionnaires) for impediments for trade between India and her South Asian partner countries. In other words, we have four sets of respondents of about 140 each, representing those engaged in trading between India and Nepal, India and Bangladesh, India and Sri Lanka, and India and Pakistan. Each set of respondents is further divided into two equal groups. One group composed of respondents within India, while the other composed of those in the corresponding partner country. This method of collating information enabled us to capture the degree of impediments neutrally.

To rank the countries in terms of barriers to trade, it is essential to reduce the relevant factors or variables into one single measure or a composite index for a specific country. Thus, composite index can be defined as a linear combination of variables, assigning equal or different weights to the variables. These weights can be determined subjectively or with the help of statistical or econometric technique to make it objective in nature. In many cases, equal weights are used to construct a composite index where it is assumed that each and every variable is equally important in explaining the phenomenon.[3] Sometimes, subjective weights are also used when importance of the variables is known *a priori* and is imposed externally. However, assigning equal weights to variables or assigning weights subjectively are generally characterized with biased result.

According to our questionnaire of impediments, the parameters were grouped into broad parameters, sub-parameters, and sub-sub-parameters. As Table 1 indicates, the broad parameters are organized under the following heads, namely (a) general barriers, (b) road transport–related barriers, (c) rail transport–related barriers, (d) sea transport–related barriers, and (e) air transport–related barriers. Each of these broad parameters was further divided into several sub-parameters and some of them were further sub-divided into sub-sub-parameters.

[3] In fact, this is the approach that has been followed by World Bank's logistics' index.

The list of broad parameters and sub-parameters along with number of sub-sub-parameters is given in Table 1(see Annex 1 for further details).

Table 1. List of Broad Parameters, Sub-Parameters, and Number of Sub-Sub-Parameters

Broad Parameters	Sub-Parameters	Number of Sub-Sub-parameters
General	Efficiency in processing of Pre-shipment/ pre-arrival documents	0
	Meeting Standards	0
	Business Mobility	2
	Competence of the logistics industry	2
	Trade Policy	4
	Availability and efficiency of banks for processing documents	0
	Availability and effectiveness of insurance facilities	0
Road Transport	Physical Transport	0
	Bilateral Transport Protocols	0
	Customs and Documentation	10
	Infrastructure at LCS	7
	Transaction costs	5
	Delivery times	2
Rail Transport	Physical Transport	0
	Bilateral Transport Protocols	0
	Customs and Documentation	10
	Infrastructure at LCS	7
	Transaction costs	5
	Delivery times	2
Sea Transport	Physical Transport	0
	Bilateral Transport Protocols	0
	Customs and Documentation	10
	Infrastructure at LCS	7
	Transaction costs	5
	Delivery times	2
Air Transport	Physical Transport	0
	Bilateral Transport Protocols	0
	Customs and Documentation	10
	Infrastructure at LCS	7
	Transaction costs	5
	Delivery times	2

Our survey has provided us perceptions of exporters/importers of relevant perspectives at the level of the sub-sub-parameters. First, we have used average values of each of sub-sub-parameters to arrive at an index for the sub-parameters. At a next step, we have used the index values for sub-parameters for obtaining values at a broad parameter level. At the final stage, we have constructed the composite index of trade barriers for each of the perspectives, as mentioned earlier, using values of broad parameters. To arrive at a composite trade barrier index, we have used the well-trusted principal component analysis. This method is extensively used by regional scientists because of its optimality property. The procedure of the principal component analysis is described briefly in Annex 2.

The first principal component, which has adequate explanatory capacity within the model, has been used to form the composite index. This is characterized by a property of having the largest sum of squared correlations among variables and hence is best suited for the given purpose. Since weights are determined solely by relationships among variables, the procedure completely removes bias on part of the researcher during analysis stage.[4]

Analysis of Results

At the outset, it must be noted that composite index, computed through principal component analysis, is essentially a relative measure. An individual score only shows its relative strength compared to others and does not depict its magnitude in an absolute sense. The index was computed using standardized data and hence had a mean value of zero and standard deviation as 1. Since this is a comparative measure across countries, we have classified the countries under study in three groups. These groups are countries with relatively higher trade barriers, average trade barriers, and lower trade barriers, rather than considering them as single data points. The groups were formed based on mean and standard deviation as obtained from the data.

Table 2 presents pair-wise correlation coefficients of indicators used to arrive at the final composite index of trade barriers. It is important to note that these correlation coefficients are not the result of any causal relationships since the variables are assumed to be independent of each other. The pattern of the correlation matrix suggests that all variables included in the model revealed moderate-to-high correlation, barring a few.

We have confirmed the statistical validity of inclusion of all these variables in our model through statistical tests. In our analysis, we have used the Kaiser–Meyer–Olkin Measure of Sampling Adequacy (KMO). The value of this statistics ranges from 0 to 1. In our model, the KMO statistic is found to be 0.67, which suggests that correlation coefficients, on the whole, are adequately suitable to make the analysis justifiable.

We already mentioned that the first principal component of the model has been considered to form the composite index of trade barriers. The model has derived five principal components since five variables were included in it. The strength of each factor in representing the model is computed by corresponding eigenvalues, which basically indicate the explanatory capacity of a particular component. The percentage of variance explained by the first principal component is found to be about 45 percent.

[4]For observations where numbers were missing for certain variable, we replaced the same with the mean value so that the variable is not dropped from analysis.

Table 2. Correlation Coefficients between Broad Parameters

Broad parameters	General	Road Transport	Rail Transport	Sea Transport	Air Transport
General	1.00	0.47	0.53	0.26	0.24
Road Transport	0.47	1.00	0.33	0.46	-0.38
Rail Transport	0.53	0.33	1.00	0.38	0.37
Sea Transport	0.26	0.46	0.38	1.00	-0.09
Air Transport	0.24	-0.38	0.37	-0.09	1.00

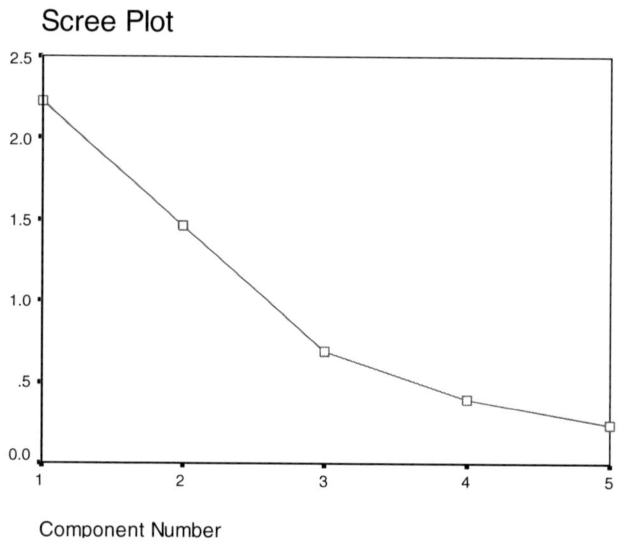

Figure 1. Scree Plot.

These statistics along with the scree plot are indicative of the fact that the first principal component is suitable enough to be used for computing the composite index of trade barrier.[5] Earlier, we have discussed the importance of weights assigned to each variable. In many cases, indices are constructed using equal weights to every variable or some subjective weights decided by the researcher. Since these two approaches do not take into account relative importance of variables, they may not represent the phenomenon that is being tried to capture through the index.

Table 3. The Weights of the Indicators for the Final Composite Index

Indicator	Weight	Relative weight (%)
General	0.783	25.34
Road Transport	0.729	23.59
Rail Transport	0.784	25.37
Sea Transport	0.674	21.81
Air Transport	0.120	3.90

[5]A scree plot shows the contribution of the components in the model. It suggests that the components have less contribution to the model from the point the curve becomes smooth.

Table 4. The Final Composite Index

Country/Perspective	Composite Index of Trade Barriers	Rank Based on Composite Index	Level of Trade Barrier
India's perspective of Bangladesh	-0.39	5	Average
India's perspective of Pakistan	-0.75	7	Lower
India's perspective of Nepal	0.28	3	Average
India's perspective of Sri Lanka	-0.76	8	Lower
Bangladesh's perspective of India	-0.44	6	Average
Sri Lankan perspective of India	0.46	2	Average
Nepal's perspective of India	1.41	1	Higher
Pakistan's perspective of India	-0.21	4	Average

Table 5. Weighted Composite Index for General and Road Transport Parameters

Country/Perspective	Composite Index of Trade Barriers	Rank Based on Composite Index	Level of Trade Barrier
Nepal's perspective of India	0.810	1	Higher
Pakistan's perspective of India	0.144	2	Average
Bangladesh's perspective of India	0.064	3	Average
India's perspective of Bangladesh	-0.076	4	Average
India's perspective of Pakistan	-0.318	5	Average
India's perspective of Nepal	-0.624	6	Lower

By contrast, PCA defines weights based on correlation across variables. If the indicators are chosen properly, the objective weights derived through PCA for index computation provides the right direction and relative position for each variable. The weights given in Table 3 are derived through Varimax Rotation of variables based on the property of maximizing correlation squares across variables. Table 3 shows the relative weights of variables used in our analysis. As we see from the table, general trade barriers, road transport, and railway transport are assigned higher weights compared to sea transport and air transport. These variables have higher correlation also with the final trade barrier index. These weights were used to combine variables linearly to arrive at the composite index. The composite scores were classified into three groups based on the mean and standard deviation across the countries/perspectives. The composite score for each perspective is given in Table 4. One should remember while interpreting scores that these are relative in nature and should be interpreted as "higher the index value, higher is the level of trade barrier of the country." Given the nature of the composite index, it is better to study these in groups instead of comparing in terms of the magnitude of the composite index. It appears from the data in Table 4 that Indian traders face the least impediments in trading with Sri Lanka. On the contrary, the maximum impediments were faced by Nepalese traders.

We have used trade barriers related to all the transport modes in our analysis. However, road transport between India and Sri Lanka and sea transport between India and Nepal is not a reality. The proxies are used for these two instances to allow comparison across all the five countries. To have a clear understanding of the fact that whether these proxies could alter results in terms of trade barrier index, we have also constructed trade barrier index only with the help of barriers related to general and road transport parameters. Sri Lanka had been excluded since it did not have any road connectivity with India. However, the new composite index including these two broad parameters also shows a similar trend (see Table 5). This is a weighted composite index of the first five components since explanatory capacity of individual components are not large enough to be considered as representative exclusively for constructing the composite index.

VALIDATION OF RESULTS

In the previous section, we have ranked countries based on the level of trade impediments. Naturally the question arises whether our results portray the reality. Further, we attempt to do the same. Table 6 represents correlations between the trade barrier index and the broad indicators used for construction of the index. Relatively higher correlations are noted with road transport and sea transport. The literature on trade barriers suggests that the impediments not only affect trade flow across countries, but also increase transaction costs significantly. Generally, transaction costs reflect in the form of bribe (speed money) and damages.

During our survey, information was solicited on these two components. Since the amount of bribery or damages depend on several externalities such as product being traded and its nature, consignment value, and similar ones, the questionnaire sought information on percentage of speed money of the total consignment value to maintain parity across traders in intra- and intercountry analysis. Damage-related transaction costs were also captured in a similar fashion.

Table 6. Relationship between Trade Barrier Index and the Broad Indicators

Broad Parameters	Correlation Coefficients Trade Barrier Index
General	0.178
Road Transport	0.491
Rail Transport	0.106
Sea Transport	0.358
Air Transport	-0.362

Table 7. Relationship of Trade Barrier Index with Bribe and Damages

Country/Perspective	Composite Index of Trade Barriers	Average % Bribe	Average % Damage
India's perspective of Bangladesh	-0.39	3.50	3.05
India's perspective of Pakistan	-0.75	3.13	3.79
India's perspective of Nepal	0.28	3.33	3.74
India's perspective of Sri Lanka	-0.76	2.84	3.23
Bangladesh's perspective of India	-0.44	2.60	0.13
Sri Lankan perspective of India	0.46	6.13	3.78
Nepal's perspective of India	1.41	4.45	11.60
Pakistan's perspective of India	-0.21	0.92	1.81

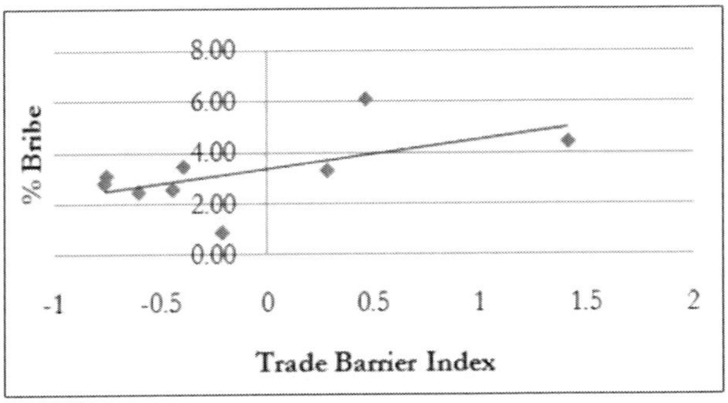

Figure 2. Relation between Trade Barrier and Bribe.

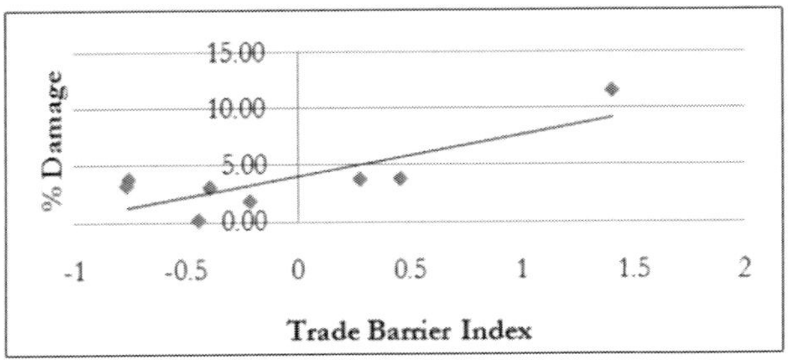

Figure 3. Relation between Trade Barrier and Damage.

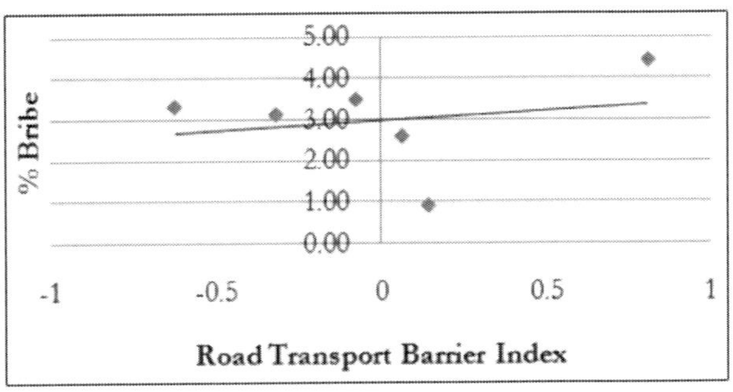

Figure 4. Relation between Road Transport Barrier Index and Bribe.

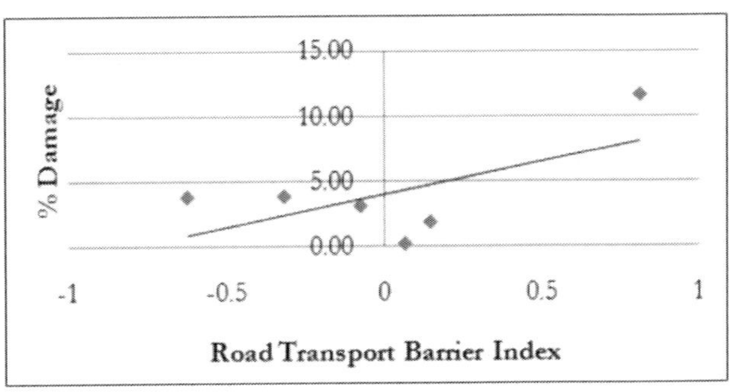

Figure 5. Relation between Road Transport Barrier Index and Damage.

We have computed average value for each of the country/perspective under study. Table 7 provides a snapshot of average percentage of bribes and damages along with the index of trade barrier for respective perspectives. The relationship between trade barrier index with incidence of bribery and damages faced by the exporters/importers is also shown in Figures 2 and 3. Both scatter diagrams clearly depict strong positive relationships between trade barrier indices with the transaction costs, as mentioned earlier. We have also computed correlation coefficients between two transaction costs and the trade barrier index. The correlation coefficient between trade barrier index and percentage of bribery is 0.59 and the coefficient between trade barrier index and damage is 0.79. The higher the trade barrier, higher was the average percentage bribery and the same also was true for damages. A similar relationship is also evident in case of trade barrier index for road transport with bribery and damages with correlation coefficients of 0.19 and 0.61, respectively (see Figures 4 and 5). This strongly suggests that poor road transport facilities affect the trade significantly through substantially high damage incidences. Therefore, any step toward reducing trade barriers will result in significant reduction in transaction cost in form of bribery and damages.

RELATIONSHIP OF INDEX VALUES AND CHANGES IN TRADE BARRIERS

The reduction in impediments between countries under study would undoubtedly boost intra–South Asian trade. It is generally believed that impediments have declined in recent years (Taneja, 2013). To understand changes in the trade barrier–related issues, information was also solicited from respondents about the extent of changes on a scale of 0 to 5. We have computed average change reported for each broad parameter for every perspective selected for this study based on the responses. The relationships between trade barrier index and changes reported on the trade barriers during past 5 years for broad parameters are presented Tables 8 and 9. The correlation coefficients depict a negative relationship between changes in trade barrier reported and trade barrier index values except for air transport and sea transport. This indicated that the higher the changes in trade barriers, the lower the trade barrier index values. However, we need to consider this phenomenon as more of an indicative one rather than a robust statistical result. The reason behind the same is that nonapplicability of some of the facilities for specific countries resulted in reduction of data points for analysis purpose at the parameter level.[6]

To overcome this problem, we have undertaken the same analysis at country/perspective level. The correlations between changes in trade barriers during the past 5 years as reported by traders for all broad parameters and the barrier index related to those parameters of a specific country/perspective are presented in Table 10. Barring the case of Nepal, a clear negative relationship is observed. Figure 6 presents the same relationship for all countries put together. Scatter diagram obtained from Figure 6, as well as correlation coefficient of -0.23 obtained from data for all countries together, suggests that changes envisaged by the trading community has reduced trade barriers in general. However, this result should be treated as an indicative trend and not as a statistically valid trend, since the number of observations for each country was limited.

[6]For example, rail and road transport facilities were not applicable for trade between India and Sri Lanka.

Table 8. Correlation between Broad Parameter Index and Changes in Those Parameters in the past 5 Years

Parameter	Correlation with Changes in Past 5 Years
General	-0.84
Road transport	0.16
Rail transport	-0.46
Sea transport	0.02
Air transport	0.58

Table 9. Correlation between Overall Trade Barrier Index and Changes in Broad Parameters in the Past 5 Years

Changes in Parameters in the Past 5 Years	Correlation with Overall Index
General	-0.57
Road transport	0.07
Rail transport	-0.36
Sea transport	-0.70
Air transport	-0.72

Table 10. Correlation between Parameter-wise Trade Barrier Indices and Changes in Same in the Past 5 Years

Country-specific perspective	Correlation
India's perspective of Bangladesh	-0.73
India's perspective of Pakistan	-0.31
India's perspective of Nepal	-0.33
India's perspective of Sri Lanka	-0.85
Bangladesh	-0.29
Pakistan	-0.68
Sri Lanka	-0.61
Nepal	0.95

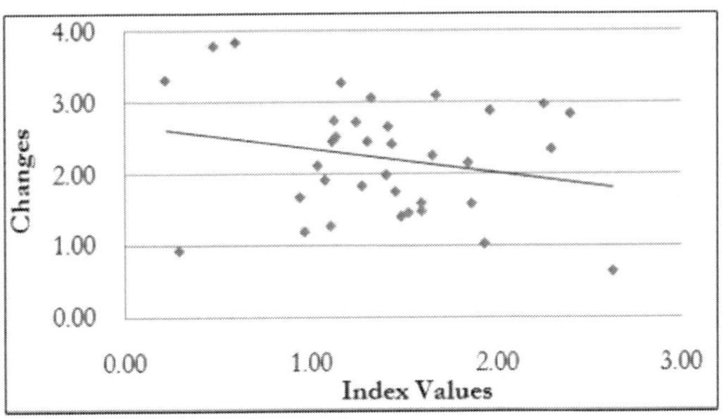

Figure 6. Relationship between Trade Barrier Index Value and Changes - All Perspectives

KEY TAKE-AWAY

Deviating from the world trend, South Asian economies apparently trade more with countries outside the region than among themselves. Though better trade relations can result in higher economic growth of the countries within South Asian region and also can play an instrumental role in reducing poverty, the countries prefer to maintain status quo in terms of their trade relations with neighboring countries. A few studies did highlight the impediment to trade that act as deterrent to trading activities within South Asian region. This study is in the same vein and makes an effort to identify trade barriers and develop a measure to quantify them in five major states in South Asian region. The countries selected for the study are India, Pakistan, Sri Lanka, Bangladesh, and Nepal. The trade barrier index that has emerged through this study is predominantly relating to India-centric trade. We have captured trade barriers that Indian stakeholders faced during trade with Pakistan, Sri Lanka, Bangladesh, and Nepal and those that stakeholders in these four countries faced while trading with their Indian counterparts. The study focused completely on feedback from stakeholders, that is, exporters, importers, and freight-forwarding agencies, engaged in trade activities between India and these four countries. A total of 560 responses were considered for computing the index.

Creating a trade barrier index was itself a challenge since majority of the elements involved were nonquantifiable in nature. To overcome this bottleneck, we identified parameters in a manner that allowed us to convert perceptions into quantifiable scores. A few steps created and followed in trade barrier index computation ensured capturing the entire trade environment and its facilitating elements of each country in a holistic manner. The index had been constructed in a few stages so that one can understand the extent of trade barriers from a micro to a macro perspective. The index values at each stage were used as raw data at the next stage for index computation. This has enabled us to measure trade barriers at every stage along with an overall macro perspective. We have used multistage principal component analysis, which is one of the most robust methodologies that could be used for this purpose. Since this methodology assigns weights in an objective manner based on correlations across variables, it minimizes the scope for biased results. Our finding on inward trade to India suggests that trade from Nepal to India faced highest level of trade barriers, followed by trade from Sri Lanka to India. In case of outward trade from India, India to Nepal is on a higher side compared with other countries. However, these varied for sub-parameters and sub-sub-parameters. This also varies from country to country. However, when we look from an overall perspective of these five South Asian countries, few striking characteristics emerge, which have significant relevance from policy viewpoint. Most of the traders have mentioned the following issues as key trade barriers, irrespective of outward from India or inward trade to India:

- Absence of competent logistic facilities for trade activities
- Nontransparent trade policies
- LCS infrastructure for all modes of transport with relatively lower infrastructure in case of air transport
- Transport cost for all modes of transport modes
- Significant delay in consignment delivery
- Customs facilities and procedures, though not as high as those mentioned earlier

A couple of other interesting points emerged through this study were amounts spent on bribery is correlated positively with trade barrier index. This suggests that imposing barriers to trade promotes unethical practices through bribery etc., which not only deprives the respective governments' revenue earning, but also increases cost of trading substantially for the stakeholders. The same trend is true for damages of consignments due to trade barriers. Correlation coefficients between trade barrier with bribery and damages were 0.59 and 0.79, respectively. From welfare point of view, significant welfare loss is caused because of existing trade barriers in South Asian region. If the countries can reduce trade barriers within the South Asian region through bilateral or multilateral dialogues, dependence of these countries on trade with countries external to the region will be minimized to a large extent, particularly for the smaller economies. This can also generate significant economic and welfare gain for these countries that are also virtually struggling for GDP growth as well as eradication of poverty and other development goals.

ANNEX 1. DETAILED LIST OF PARAMETERS

Broad Parameter	Sub-Parameters	Sub-Sub-parameters
GENERAL	Efficiency in processing of Preshipment/ prearrival documents	
	Meeting Standards	
	Business Mobility	a) Obtaining visas
		b) Business travel
	Competence of the logistics industry (Transport operators, Customs brokers, Freight Forwarders, Clearing Agents)	a) Small operators
		b) Large operators
	Trade Policy	a) MFN
		b) Port Restrictions
		c) Implementation of Quotas
		d) Rules of Origin
	Availability and efficiency of banks for processing documents (e.g., L/C, insurance and foreign exchange)	
	Availability and effectiveness of insurance facilities	
ROAD TRANSPORT	Physical Transport	
	Bilateral Transport Protocols	
	Customs and Documentation	a) Number of documents required to clear goods
		b) Processing of documents by customs
		c) Testing
		d) Efficiency in processing of documents by health/technical control agencies
		e) Competence of customs officials
		f) Customs awareness of Trade Policy
		g) Transparency of Border Administration
		h) Classification of products

Annex 1. (Continued)

Broad Parameter	Sub-Parameters	Sub-Sub-parameters
		i) Excessive checks due to security measures
		j) Effectiveness of EDI facilities
	Infrastructure at LCS	a) Access to the LCS
		b) Availability of Services at the LCS
		c) Quality of Services at the LCS
		d) Congestion at border/ LCS
		e) Availability and use of Information Technology (computers, Internet, etc)
		f) Availability of power
		g) Physical Security
	Transaction costs	a) Transport Costs
		b) Port/LCS Charges
		c) Handling charges
		d) Inspection charges
		e) Bribes (Unofficial costs)
	Delivery times	a) Delays from scheduled delivery times
		b) Damages due to delays in delivery
RAIL TRANSPORT	Physical Transport	
	Bilateral Transport Protocols	
	Customs and Documentation	a) Number of documents required to clear goods
		b) Processing of documents by customs
		c) Testing
		d) Efficiency in processing of documents by health/technical control agencies
		e) Competence of customs officials
		f) Customs awareness of Trade Policy
		g) Transparency of Border Administration
		h) Classification of products
		i) Excessive checks due to security measures
		j) Effectiveness of EDI facilities
	Infrastructure at LCS	a) Access to the LCS
		b) Availability of Services at the LCS
		c) Quality of Services at the LCS
		d) Congestion at border/ LCS
		e) Availability and use of Information Technology (computers, Internet, etc.)
		f) Availability of power

Broad Parameter	Sub-Parameters	Sub-Sub-parameters
		g) Physical Security
	Transaction costs	a) Transport Costs
		b) Port/LCS Charges
		c) Handling charges
		d) Inspection charges
		e) Bribes (Unofficial costs)
	Delivery times	a) Delays from scheduled delivery times
		b) Damages due to delays in delivery
SEA TRANSPORT	Physical Transport	
	Bilateral Transport Protocols	
	Customs and Documentation	a) Number of documents required to clear goods
		b) Processing of documents by customs
		c) Testing
		d) Efficiency in processing of documents by health/technical control agencies
		e) Competence of customs officials
		f) Customs awareness of Trade Policy
		g) Transparency of Border Administration
		h) Classification of products
		i) Excessive checks due to security measures
		j) Effectiveness of EDI facilities
	Infrastructure at LCS	a) Access to the LCS
		b) Availability of Services at the LCS
		c) Quality of Services at the LCS
		d) Congestion at border/ LCS
		e) Availability and use of Information Technology (computers, Internet, etc.)
		f) Availability of power
		g) Physical Security
	Transaction costs	a) Transport Costs
		b) Port/LCS Charges
		c) Handling charges
		d) Inspection charges
		e) Bribes (Unofficial costs)
	Delivery times	a) Delays from scheduled delivery times
		b) Damages due to delays in delivery

Annex 1. (Continued)

Broad Parameter	Sub-Parameters	Sub-Sub-parameters
AIR TRANSPORT	Physical Transport	
	Bilateral Transport Protocols	
	Customs and Documentation	a) Number of documents required to clear goods
		b) Processing of documents by customs
		c) Testing
		d) Efficiency in processing of documents by health/technical control agencies
		e) Competence of customs officials
		f) Customs awareness of Trade Policy
		g) Transparency of Border Administration
		h) Classification of products
		i) Excessive checks due to security measures
		j) Effectiveness of EDI facilities
	Infrastructure at LCS	a) Access to the LCS
		b) Availability of Services at the LCS
		c) Quality of Services at the LCS
		d) Congestion at border/ LCS
		e) Availability and use of Information Technology (computers, Internet, etc.)
		f) Availability of power
		g) Physical Security
	Transaction costs	a) Transport Costs
		b) Port/LCS Charges
		c) Handling charges
		d) Inspection charges
		e) Bribes (Unofficial costs)
	Delivery times	a) Delays from scheduled delivery times
		b) Damages due to delays in delivery

ANNEX 2. METHODOLOGY—PRINCIPAL COMPONENTS ANALYSIS

This approach develops a composite index by defining a real-valued function over the relevant variables would permit defining the potentials of the districts objectively. A set of assumptions behind our method of construction of a composite index is given below:

1. the condition of weak Pareto rule demands that when a district registers values of indicators uniformly higher than those of the other districts—the former should have a higher ranking than the latter ones;
2. the condition of nondictatorship implies that no single indicator should be considered so significant as to determine the final ordering all by itself;
3. the condition of unrestricted domain implies that the method should be capable of giving the final ranking for all possible data matrices;
4. the final condition is that of independence from irrelevant alternatives, which demands that while ranking two districts, the decision must be guided by the values of the indicators for these units under study alone and not by any other irrelevant phenomenon;

With these general assumptions, the composite index is defined as

$$C_i = W_1x_{11} + W_2x_{12} + W_3x_{13} + \ldots\ldots\ldots\ldots + W_nx_{1n}$$

or, $C_i = \sum W_i x_{ij}$, where C_i is the composite index for the ith observation, W_j is the weight assigned to j^{th} indicator, and x_{ij} is the observation value after elimination of the scale bias.

From the above-stated formula of the composite index, it is evident that to compute the composite index two major components are to be known, that is, the weights assigned to the indicators and the observation values after eliminating of the scale bias for the available indicators. These two have been discussed further in detail.

Elimination of Scale Bias

The variables chosen for any analysis are usually measured in different units and are generally not additive. Hence it is necessary to convert them to some standard comparable units such that the initial scale chosen for measuring them do not bias the results. The method that was adopted to achieve this is by standardizing the variables is as follows:

$$x_{ij} = (X_{ij} - X_m / \sigma)$$

where x_{ij} is the scale-free observation, X_{ij} is the original observation, and X_m is the mean of the series and σ is the standard deviation.

The transformed series now would be scale free and would have a mean of zero and a standard deviation of unity.

Assigning Weights Objectively Using Factor Analytic Model

Once the bias of measurement is removed from the observations, the crucial problem that remains is that of assigning appropriate weights to the selected indicators. If one has sufficient insight into the nature and magnitude of interrelationships among the variables and their implications, one might choose to determine the weights on the basis of independent judgment. This way of constructing an index stands exposed to subjectivity. Assigning equal weight (or no weight) would imply assumption of equal correlation of each indicator with the composite index of importance, which would hardly be a realistic approach in this case. Therefore, in this analysis, the weights for individual indicators have been assigned on the basis of the factor analytic model.

Factor analysis is a tool used to construct a composite index in such a way that the weights given maximize the sum of the squares of correlation (of the indicators with the composite index). The application of factor analysis or principal component analysis in this specific case has been accepted in "objective ranking" of the regions. This method enables one to determine a vector known as the first principal component or factor, which is linearly dependent on the variables, having the maximum sum of squared correlation with the variables.

The weights to the indicators are chosen in such a way that the principal components satisfy two conditions:

a) The number of principal components is equal to the number of indicators and they are uncorrelated or orthogonal in nature.
b) The first principal component or P_1 absorbs or accounts for the maximum possible proportion of variation in the set of the indicators. This is the reason why it serves as the ideal measure of composite index.

Method Outlined[7]

Step 1: We start by taking the simple correlation coefficients of k numbers of indicators. These correlation coefficients may be arranged in a table, which is called the correlation table.

The elements of the diagonal would be unity as they are the self-correlation, that is, the correlation of each X_i with itself ($r_{xixi} = 1$ for all the i's). The correlation matrix is symmetrical, that is, the elements of each row are identical to the elements of the corresponding columns, since $r_{xixj} = r_{xj\,xi}$.

Correlation Table of the set of K Variables					
	X_1	X_2	X_3	X_k	$\Sigma^k{}_i r_{xixj}$
X_1	$r_{x1\,x1}$	$r_{x1\,x2}$	..	$r_{x1\,xk}$	$\Sigma^k{}_i\, r_{x1xi}$
X_2	$r_{x2\,x1}$	$r_{x2\,x2}$	..	$r_{x2\,xk}$	
"	..	..	..	..	
"	..	..	..	..	
X_k	..	..	..	..	
"	$r_{xk\,x1}$	..	..	r_{xkxk}	
$\Sigma^k{}_i\, r_{x1xj}$	$\Sigma^k{}_i r_{xix1}$	$\Sigma^k{}_i r_{xix2}$	$\Sigma^k{}_i r_{xix3}$	$\Sigma^k{}_i r_{xixk}$	$\Sigma^k{}_i \Sigma^k{}_i r_{xixj}$

Step 2: Sum of each column (or row) of the correlation table is computed, obtaining k number of sums of simple correlation coefficient.

[7] J. Johnston (1984)

$\Sigma^k{}_i r_{xixj} = \Sigma^k{}_i r_{xixj}$

Step 3: We compute the sum total of the column (or row) sums

$\Sigma^k{}_i \Sigma^k{}_j r_{xixj}$

and we take its square roots.

Step 4: Finally, we obtain the factor loadings for the first principal component P_1 by dividing each column (or row) sum by the square root of the grand total.

$a_{ij} = (\Sigma^k{}_i r_{xixj}) / (\sqrt{\Sigma^k{}_i \Sigma^k{}_i r_{xixj}})$

It should be clear that the loadings thus obtained are the correlation coefficients of the respective indicator with the composite index.

Step 5: The P_1 or the first principal component is constructed in the following way

$P_1 = a_{11} x_1 + a_{12} x_2 + \ldots\ldots\ldots\ldots + a_{1k} x_k$

Step 6: The sum of the squares of the loading of the principal component is called the latent root (or eigenvalue) of this component and are denoted by the Greek letter l with the subscript of the principal component to which it refers. For example, the latent root of the first principal component P_1 is

l_I= [latent root of P_1]
$= \Sigma^k{}_i 1^2{}_I$
$= \underline{1}^2{}_1 + 1^2{}_2 + \ldots + 1^2{}_k$

The sum of the latent root of all the principal components would be equal to the number of indicators:

$\Sigma^k{}_i l_i = k$

The importance of the latent root or the eigenvalue lies in the fact that it expresses the percentage of variation in the set of indicator the principal component explains. If, for example, $l_1 = 2.797$ and the number of variables are 8, then the P_1 expresses:

$l_I / k = (2.797/8)*100 = 35\%$ of the variations of the set of 8 variables.

Tests of significance of the loadings:

The loadings in our study have been tested based on the levels of significance of the Pearson's correlation coefficients.

REFERENCES

Chinpal, Rauniar, 2009. "Trade Facilitation: Indo-Nepal," presented in the Workshop on Trade Facilitation in South Asia, 26-27 June, ICRIER, Delhi, India.

Das, S and Sanjib Pohit (2006) "Quantifying the Transport, Regulatory and Other Costs of Indian Overland Exports to Bangladesh," The World Economy, Vol. 29, No. 9, 1227-1242.

De, Prabir, Abdur Rob Khan and Sachin Chaturvedi, 2008."Transit and Trade Barriers in Eastern South Asia: A Review of the Transit Regime and Performance of Strategic Border-Crossings," Asia Pacific Research and Training Network on Trade, Working Paper series, no. 56.

ESCAP, 2003. "Transit Transport Issues in Landlocked and Transit Developing Countries," Landlocked Developing Countries Series, No. 1, 2003.

Johnston, J. (1984), Econometric Methods, 3rd edn. McGraw-Hill, New York.

Pohit,Sanjib, 2009. "Trade Barrier Index," presented in the Workshop on Trade Facilitation in South Asia, 26-27 June, ICRIER, Delhi, India.

Taneja, Nisha and Sanjib Pohit, 2006. "India-Nepal Informal Trade: Estimation & Qualitative Assessment," ArthaVijnana, March-June, Vol. XL VIII, No. 1 & 2, pp. 119-146.

Taneja, Nisha, Shravani Prakash. Pallavi Kalita (2013) "India's Role in Facilitating Trade under SAFTA", ICRIER Working Paper 263.

World Bank, 2008.Trade and Transport Facilitation in South Asia: System in Transition, Vol. I and II, Report no. 44061-SAS.

World Bank.Logistics Performance Index-Connecting to Compete, various issues, http:/www.worldbank.org.

World Bank.Doing Business, various issues, http://www.doingbusiness.org.

PART III: METHODOLOGIES AND POLICY APPLICATIONS

In: Current Issues in International Trade
Editor: Gouranga G. Das

ISBN: 978-1-63321-405-7

Chapter 10

CGE MODELLING AS A FRAMEWORK FOR ABSORBING SPECIALIST INFORMATION: LINKING AN ENERGY MODEL AND A CGE MODEL TO ANALYSE U.S. ENERGY POLICIES

Peter B. Dixon and Maureen T. Rimmer
Centre of Policy Studies, Victoria University, Australia

ABSTRACT

Computable general equilibrium (CGE) models are widely used in analyses of issues in trade, public finance, macro stimulus, environment, energy, labour markets and microeconomic reform. The defining features of these models are explicit behaviour by agents, and linkages between agents through their roles as customers for each other's services and competitors for the economy's resources. Most CGE models are based on standard economic assumptions (e.g. constant returns to scale, pure competition, utility maximization, cost minimization) implemented with standard economic data sources (e.g. input-output tables and national accounts published by government statistical agencies). However, there is a large body of specialist theory and data that is not part of the standard CGE toolkit. This chapter shows how specialist information can be brought to bear in a CGE framework. We take an example from the energy area and show how information from a specialist energy model, NEMS, can be transferred into a CGE model, USAGE, to deliver policy results that retain the strengths of both modelling techniques.

1. INTRODUCTION

The field of computable general equilibrium (CGE) modelling started over 50 years ago with the seminal work the Norwegian economist Leif Johansen (1960, 1974). His work and most CGE modelling since then has been based on standard economic assumptions (e.g. constant returns to scale, pure competition) implemented with standard economic data sources (e.g. input-output tables and national accounts published by government statistical agencies).

There is a large body of specialist theory and empirical information in the areas energy and environmental engineering that can be brought to bear in a CGE framework. Current CGE practice with respect to specialist material is to create special-purpose models which have elaborate treatments of the issue of interest and rudimentary treatments of the rest of the economy. The weakness of these special-purpose models is that they cannot generate economy-wide insights. They cannot tell us how policy changes in the area of interest will affect different sectors of the economy, nor can they tell us how developments in the rest of the economy impinge on the area of interest. This chapter shows how information from a specialist energy model, NEMS, can be transferred into a CGE model, USAGE, to deliver policy results that retain the strengths of both modelling techniques

The chapter is organized as follows. In the remainder of this introductory section we define CGE modelling and provide some background material on USAGE. Then we describe the NEMS model. Section 2 sets out a selection of NEMS results and Section 3 describes how these are absorbed into USAGE. Sections 4 and 5 describe integrated USAGE-NEMS simulations. Concluding remarks are in Section 6.

1.1. What is CGE Modelling?

CGE modelling is a form of economy-wide modelling. Economy-wide models emphasize the links between different parts of the economy. The first economy-wide model was Leontief's (1936) input-output model which quantified links between industries as suppliers and customers for each other's products. In Leontief's input-output world, an increase in household demand for cars stimulates the motor vehicle industry, which in turn stimulates the steel industry, which in turn stimulates the iron ore and coal industries. CGE modelling extended Leontief's framework by introducing links through competition for scarce resources. As originally recognized by Johansen (1960), an industry may be harmed by the expansion of other industries through shortages of labour and capital. In Johansen's CGE world, expansion of industry i generates benefits for industry j through Leontief's input-output linkages but these benefits may be offset through increases in the costs to j of primary factors.

Another link between industries encapsulated by modern CGE models occurs through the exchange rate which connects import-competing and export-oriented industries. This is important in analysing tariff policy. With cuts in protection, import-competing industries contract, lowering the exchange rate and allowing expansion of export-oriented industries.

1.2. The USAGE Model

USAGE (US Applied General Equilibrium) is a dynamic CGE model of the U.S. economy.[1] A USAGE simulation of the effects of a shock to the economy (e.g. a change in energy policy) requires two runs of the model: a baseline run and a policy (or perturbation)

[1] USAGE was developed at the Centre of Policy Studies in collaboration with the U.S. International Trade Commission. Its theoretical structure is similar to that of Australia's MONASH model, Dixon and Rimmer (2002). Recent published applications of USAGE include Dixon and Rimmer (2011), Dixon et al. (2013) and Zahniser et al. (2012).

run. The baseline is intended to be a plausible forecast while the policy run generates deviations away from the baseline caused by the shocks under consideration.

As in all CGE models, optimizing behaviour governs decision-making by firms and households. Industries minimize costs subject to constant-returns-to-scale production functions and input prices that they treat as given. Households also take prices as given and choose their consumption bundle to maximize utility subject to their budget constraint. Domestic and imported goods are treated as imperfect substitutes. Export demands for U.S. commodities are modelled as inversely related to their foreign-currency prices. Explicit recognition is given to tax, transport and other margins that separate purchasers prices from producer prices. The model can be run at various levels of aggregation. For this chapter we adopted a version with 120 industries.

USAGE has three types of dynamic mechanisms: capital accumulation; liability accumulation; and lagged adjustment processes. An industry's capital stock at the start of year $t+1$ is its capital at the start of year t plus its investment during year t minus depreciation. Investment during year t is determined as an increasing function of the expected rate of return on the industry's capital. Liability accumulation is specified for the public sector and for the foreign accounts. Public sector liability at the start of $t+1$ is public sector liability at the start of t plus the public sector deficit incurred during t. Net foreign liabilities at the start of $t+1$ are specified as net foreign liabilities at the start of t plus the current account deficit in t plus the effects of revaluations of assets and liabilities caused by changes in price levels and the exchange rate. Lagged adjustment processes are specified in USAGE for labour market variables. For example, wages adjust sluggishly to eliminate gaps between supply and demand for labour.

1.3. The NEMS Model

NEMS (National Energy Modelling System) is a dynamic model of U.S. energy demand and supply.[2] It was built by the Energy Information Administration in the U.S. Department of Energy. NEMS specifies annual movements in a huge number of energy-related variables over a projection period usually set at 25 years. The variables include: imports, exports and production of 12 grades of coal with production disaggregated by type of mine (surface or underground) and 14 regions; imports, exports and production of crude oil with production disaggregated by 12 regions; production of 8 types of renewable energy; generation of electricity by about 20 generation technologies in 15 regions; and residential, commercial, industrial and transportation demands for energy to satisfy hundreds of end-use requirements, e.g. heating and cooling in three types of residence in 9 regions, and fuel for cars and trucks of 6 sizes and 20 vintages with 63 fuel-using technologies. Major driving variables in NEMS projections are the world price of oil and U.S. GDP growth. Econometrically estimated trends in technologies also play an important role.

As with USAGE, NEMS is used to produce baseline forecasts and policy runs. The policy runs are concerned with the effects of changes in energy-related variables away from their baseline paths. These variables include world oil prices, energy producing and using

[2] NEMS is explained in DOE/EIA (2009). Technical documentation can be found in reports referred to there.

technologies and government regulations in the energy sector such as limitations on greenhouse gas emissions.

NEMS simulations underlie the widely used and respected EIA publication, Annual Energy Outlook.

2. NEMS Results

Here we set out some NEMS results for a business-as-usual or baseline run for the period 2010 to 2035 and for a policy run incorporating a greenhouse gas policy inducing a substantial replacement of coal by natural gas in the generation of electricity. Table 1 shows a selection of NEMS baseline results. Corresponding policy results are in Table 2. Spreadsheets from which we derived the tables were supplied by the Department of Energy.[3]

NEMS results in the tables that we transferred to USAGE are shaded. The first transferred results are those in the total row for "Power sector non-fuel costs (Billion 2009$)". We interpret these as referring to expenditures by the power sector on an array of goods and services with the same structure as investment expenditures by the USAGE Electric services industry.[4] Without further information, we cannot make use of the breakdown of these costs given in the tables.

From the next segments of Tables 1 and 2 we can make use of the NEMS results for inputs of Natural gas and Steam coal to the power sector. We also use the total row for "Power Sector Fuel Use by Fuel Type (billions of MMBTU)" as a measure of the output of electricity. This involves the assumption that transmission losses are constant through time as a share of energy input. The remaining items in this segment of the tables are not sufficiently informative to allow a useful transfer to USAGE.

From the third segment of the tables we use the results for the prices of Natural gas, Other coal (which we assume is Steam coal, a major input to electricity generation) and Electricity. It would be possible to use some of the other prices but none of them refer to products that are major inputs to electricity generation or to products whose prices are significantly different between the NEMS baseline and policy runs.

Comparison of the two tables reveals that the main energy-related effect of the greenhouse policy incorporated in Table 2 is a substantial replacement of coal by natural gas in the generation of electricity. For 2035, Table 1 shows a baseline input to the power sector of steam coal which greatly exceeds that of natural gas (21.64 compared with 7.99 in billion MMBTU). In the policy simulation the position is reversed with the input of coal being less than that of natural gas (9.31 compared with 12.50 billion MMBTU). With increased use of natural gas in the policy simulation, NEMS shows an increase in the price of natural gas: $\$_{2009}$9.28 per MMBTU in Table 2 for 2035 compared with $\$_{2009}$9.02 per MMBTU in Table 1.

With reduced use of steaming coal (Other coal) in the policy simulation, NEMS shows a reduction in price: $\$_{2009}$2.05 per MMBTU in Table 2 for 2035 compared with $\$_{2009}$2.43 in Table 1. The replacement of coal by natural gas in electricity generation increases the cost of electricity. For 2035, the NEMS baseline shows the electricity price at $\$_{2009}$27.18. For the policy run the electricity price in 2035 is $\$_{2009}$31.86.

---

[3] In the material sent to us by DOE the two runs were referred to as BAU11 and CorePX15.

[4] This industry in USAGE covers electricity generation and distribution.

Table 1. NEMS baseline run

	2010	2015	2020	2025	2030	2035
Power Sector Non-fuel Costs (Billion 2009$)						
Overnight capacity investments	-	0.64	7.60	8.97	8.80	7.37
Retrofit and capital additions	8.41	10.44	8.34	8.36	8.98	8.50
Power sector fixed O&M costs	21.47	22.40	22.70	22.78	23.44	24.07
Power sector non-fuel variable O&M costs	8.09	8.26	8.70	9.94	10.26	10.39
Total	***37.97***	***41.74***	***47.33***	***50.05***	***51.49***	***50.33***
Power Sector Fuel Use by Fuel Type (billions of MMBTU)						
Liquid Fuels	0.45	0.43	0.45	0.46	0.47	0.48
Natural Gas	7.61	7.05	6.97	6.69	7.34	7.99
Steam Coal	19.49	17.98	18.99	20.73	21.23	21.64
Nuclear Power	8.39	8.77	9.22	9.22	9.22	9.19
Renewable Energy	3.84	5.17	5.52	5.83	6.19	6.51
Electricity Imports	0.12	0.11	0.09	0.07	0.04	0.05
Total	***40.10***	***39.72***	***41.45***	***43.21***	***44.69***	***46.07***
Average All Sector Delivered Prices by Fuel Type (2009$/MMBTU)						
Liquefied Petroleum Gases	18.03	21.70	23.88	25.47	26.45	26.70
E85	24.89	26.41	28.75	29.64	30.42	30.95
Motor Gasoline	22.07	26.00	28.20	29.64	30.39	30.93
Jet Fuel	15.76	18.91	22.07	23.58	24.73	25.43
Distillate Fuel Oil	20.54	21.86	25.11	26.71	27.50	28.11
Residual Fuel Oil	11.26	13.13	14.96	16.38	17.13	16.94
Natural Gas	6.90	6.55	7.00	7.80	8.35	9.02
Metallurgical Coal	6.19	6.05	6.34	6.46	6.52	6.57
Other Coal	2.31	2.19	2.20	2.28	2.35	2.43
Coal to Liquids	0.00	1.79	1.90	1.84	1.98	2.12
Electricity	28.05	26.21	26.04	26.17	26.50	27.18

Table 3 shows the NEMS policy deviations that are fed into USAGE together with the USAGE variable names: prealCL, prealES, etc. are USAGE notation for the policy-induced percentage deviations in real prices of coal, electricity etc. where real prices are prices for commodities relative to the price of GDP; x0dom(ES) is the percentage deviation in the output of electricity; x1ci(i,j) is the percentage deviation in the input of commodity i to industry j; and d_realinvES is the extra non-fuel costs in the electricity power sector caused by the policy. With the exception of d_realinvES, the shocks for all of the variables in Table 3 can be deduced directly from Tables 1 and 2. For example, the percentage deviation in 2035 in the real price of coal shown in Table 3 is -15.52. This is the percentage gap between the policy price of coal (2.05 in Table 2) and the baseline price (2.43 in Table 1). For d_realinvES, we could have calculated the shocks as the differences between the entries in Tables 2 and 1 for total power sector non-fuel costs. However, these differences are rather volatile. Consequently we preferred to use differences between 5-year average results from NEMS. For example, the 2015 shock shown in Table 3 for d_realinvES was calculated as the difference between the NEMS policy results averaged for 2013, 2014, 2015, 2016 and 2017, and the NEMS baseline results averaged for these years.

Table 2. NEMS policy run

	2010	2015	2020	2025	2030	2035
Power Sector Non-fuel Costs (Billion 2009$)						
Overnight capacity investments	-	0.19	23.76	33.70	27.17	27.67
Retrofit and capital additions	8.41	8.42	6.17	6.04	27.28	21.94
Power sector fixed O&M costs	21.47	22.01	21.76	23.75	26.91	29.76
Power sector non-fuel variable O&M costs	8.07	7.96	8.95	9.22	11.32	15.01
Total	***37.94***	***38.58***	***60.65***	***72.71***	***92.67***	***94.37***
Power Sector Fuel Use by Fuel Type (billions of MMBTU)						
Liquid Fuels	0.45	0.45	0.46	0.45	0.45	0.45
Natural Gas	7.77	8.56	9.06	9.20	10.48	12.50
Steam Coal	19.26	15.72	14.48	13.41	11.32	9.31
Nuclear Power	8.39	8.77	9.11	9.83	11.29	12.56
Renewable Energy	3.85	5.57	7.18	8.51	9.32	9.26
Electricity Imports	0.12	0.11	0.09	0.07	0.03	0.05
Total	***40.04***	***39.39***	***40.58***	***41.67***	***43.09***	***44.33***
Average All Sector Delivered Prices by Fuel Type (2009$/MMBTU)						
Liquefied Petroleum Gases	18.03	21.55	23.68	25.28	26.16	26.61
E85	24.89	26.41	28.83	29.58	30.43	31.00
Motor Gasoline	22.07	26.00	28.23	29.62	30.36	30.97
Jet Fuel	15.76	18.99	22.02	23.53	24.68	25.28
Distillate Fuel Oil	20.54	21.93	25.01	26.66	27.44	27.96
Residual Fuel Oil	11.26	13.08	14.88	16.40	17.00	17.14
Natural Gas	6.99	7.36	8.06	8.48	9.02	9.28
Metallurgical Coal	6.16	6.03	6.34	6.51	6.63	6.55
Other Coal	2.29	2.17	2.07	2.07	2.07	2.05
Coal to Liquids	0.00	1.80	1.78	1.67	1.63	1.66
Electricity	28.10	25.86	26.48	27.58	29.24	31.86

3. Changes to USAGE to Absorb NEMS Results

We made three sets of changes to a normal version of USAGE to facilitate the absorption of results from NEMS.

3.1. New Variables

First we added to the USAGE code definitions of percentage changes or changes in variables that were not already in the code and for which NEMS provides usable results.[5] These variables were: the real prices for coal, electricity, natural gas and natural gas distribution; and the extra non-fuel costs in the electricity power sector. The real price variables are straightforward and can be seen in the modified USAGE code as:

[5] USAGE computations are performed with GEMPACK software, see Horridge et al. (2013) and Harrison et al. (2014). Models are presented to GEMPACK in equations that are linear in percentage changes or changes in the variables.

Equation E_prealCL
prealCL = p0dom(*"Coal"*) -p0gdpexp;
Equation E_prealNG
prealNG= p0dom(*"NaturalGas"*) -p0gdpexp;
Equation E_prealNGD
prealNGD = p0dom(*"NatGasDistrb"*) -p0gdpexp;
Equation E_prealES
prealES = p0dom(*"Electricserv"*) - p0gdpexp;

To handle extra non-fuel costs incurred by the Electric services industry, we added the following equation to the USAGE code:

Equation E_d_realinvES
d_realinvES = 0.01*QMAKE_DUM*x0dom(*"DummyInd"*);

This requires explanation.

Table 3. Policy-induced deviations from NEMS imposed on USAGE variables

	2010	2015	2020	2025	2030	2035
Real prices (% deviation)						
prealCL, Coal	-0.51	-1.03	-6.04	-9.40	-11.74	-15.52
prealES, Electricity	0.21	-1.32	1.68	5.38	10.34	17.22
prealNG, Natural gas	1.27	12.49	15.14	8.70	8.00	2.85
prealNGD, Natural gas distrb.	1.27	12.49	15.14	8.70	8.00	2.85
Output (% deviation)						
x0dom(ES), Electricity	-0.16	-0.82	-2.09	-3.55	-3.57	-3.78
Inputs to Electricity (% deviation)						
x1ci(Coal,ES), Coal	-1.17	-12.55	-23.74	-35.30	-46.68	-57.00
x1ci(NG,ES), Natural gas	2.15	21.46	29.99	37.41	42.72	56.45
x1ci(NGD,ES), Natural gas distrb.	2.15	21.46	29.99	37.41	42.72	56.45
Additional non-fuel costs in Electricity (change, 2009$m)						
d_realinvES	0.00	-307.73	14016.21	21424.76	31673.04	36043.75

The variable x0dom("DummyInd") is the percentage growth between two periods in the output of a dummy industry which has a cost structure reflecting that of investment in the electricity industry. About 50 per cent of these costs are accounted for by purchases from the construction industry. The sales of the dummy industry are entirely to the electric services industry.

QMAKE_DUM is the level of output in the dummy industry. Thus the right hand side of equation E_d_realinvES is the increase in the output of the dummy industry between two periods. By giving d_realinvES a shock, we force the output of the dummy industry to increase by an amount reflecting this shock.

The database for our simulations refers to 2005. In this database QMAKE_DUM is set at a small amount, $1 billion. In the baseline, QMAKE_DUM stays at $1 billion throughout the simulation period: d_realinvES is set at zero for each 5-year interval forcing x0dom("DummyInd") to come out at zero. In the policy run, d_realinvES is given shocks reflecting extra policy-induced expenditures in the electric services industry. Referring to the last row in Table 3, we see that the shock for d_realinvES in 2015 is -$\$_{2009}$307.73 million. The shock in 2020 is $\$_{2009}$14,323.94m. This is necessary to bring the extra policy-induced expenditure up from -307.73m in 2015 to 14,016.21m in 2020. The shock in 2025 is 7,408.55m. This bring the extra policy-induced expenditure up from 14,016.21m in 2020 to 21,424.76m in 2025, and so on. With all of the sales of the dummy industry being to the electric services industry, the shocks in the policy run force the electric services industry to undertake extra expenditures of -307.73m in 2010, extra expenditures of 14,016.21m in 2020, extra expenditures of 21,424.76m in 2025, etc. The structure of these extra expenditures reflects the structure of the inputs to the dummy industry, that is, the structure of investment expenditures by the electric services industry.

3.2. Closure Changes

All of the variables mentioned in Table 3 are naturally endogenous, that is they are normally explained in a CGE model such as USAGE. However, for our purposes we need to make them exogenous so that they can be shocked with the movements implied in the NEMS baseline and policy runs. Corresponding to each of the required unnatural exogenizations, we must make an unnatural endogenization. The swaps that we made between the exogenous and endogenous categories are shown descriptively in Table 4 and in USAGE notation in Table 5.

In making the swaps, the first principle we applied is that when a commodity price is exogenized, then a cost-changing variable must be endogenized. The cost-changing variables that we chose to endogenize were all-input-saving technical changes in the relevant industries. These technical change variables move all inputs up or down by a uniform percentage so that unit costs can be adjusted to bring them into line with the exogenously set prices. An alternative possibility is to endogenize rates of return on capital. If NEMS indicated a high price for natural gas, for example, then USAGE could have absorbed this by allowing the natural gas industry to have high rates of return, that is pay high rentals on its capital. However, we don't think that this is realistic. In the long run, the natural gas industry is likely to make normal rates of return. We assume that high prices in the NEMS policy run reflect greater natural gas output and a consequent requirement to exploit higher-cost gas deposits.

The second principle that we applied was that exogenization of a commodity supply requires endogenization of a demand-shift variable. To allow exogenization of the output of electric services, we endogenized a variable in USAGE that causes a uniform percentage shift across users in the demand for electricity. Thus, for example, if the demand specification for electricity in USAGE generated a decrease in demand for electricity of 5.27 per cent, but the exogenously specified decrease in output was 3.78 per cent, then the endogenous *demand* shift variable would increase demand by every user of electricity by 1.57 per cent.[6]

The third principle was that exogenization of a commodity input to the production process of an industry requires endogenization of a technology variable for that industry

[6] -5.27 = 100*(1-0.0378)/1.0157 -1).

representing input-using or saving technical change specific to the relevant commodity. Thus, USAGE accepted the NEMS policy results showing decreased use of coal and increased use of natural gas in the electric services industry by generating input-saving technical changes in the industry for coal and input-using technical changes for natural gas. Similarly, USAGE accepted the NEMS policy results for increased non-fuel costs by generating large input-using technical changes in the electric services industry for the dummy commodity (the output of the dummy industry described in the previous subsection).

Table 4. Exogenizing naturally endogenous variables

Endogenized variables	Exogenized variables
All-input-saving tech change in electric services (ES)	Real price of electric services
All-input-saving tech change in natural gas (NG)	Real price of natural gas
All-input-saving tech change in natural gas distrib. (NGD)	Real price of natural gas distribution
All-input tech-saving tech change in Coal	Real price of coal
Demand shift for ES	Output of electric services
Demand shift by ES for Coal	Input of coal to electric services
Demand shift by ES for NG	Input of natural gas to ES
Demand shift by ES for NGD	Input of natural gas distribution to ES
Demand shift by ES for product of dummy industry	Additional non-fuel costs in ES

Table 5. Exogenizing naturally endogenous variables: USAGE notation

Endogenized variables	Exogenized variables
ff_a1("Electricserv")	prealES
ff_a1("NaturalGas")	prealNG
ff_a1("NatGasDistrb")	prealNGD
ff_a1("Coal")	prealCL
fa1c("Electricserv")	x0dom("Electricserv")
fa1ci("Coal", "Electricserv")	x1ci("Coal", "Electricserv")
fa1ci("NaturalGas", "Electricserv")	x1ci("NaturalGas", "Electricserv")
fa1ci("NatGasDistrb", "Electricserv")	x1ci fa1ci("NatGasDistrb", "Electricserv")
fa1c("DummyInd")	d_realinvES

The effects of the policy (the transition from Table 1 to Table 2) on the unnaturally endogenized variables are given in Table 6. Concentrating on 2035, we can see a 1.57 per cent shift in demand for electricity [fa1c("Electricserv") = 1.57]. This indicates that to reconcile the NEMS result for the effect of the policy on the output of electricity in 2035, USAGE needed to introduce an extra 1.57 per cent demand for electricity by all users of electricity. On the cost side for electricity, USAGE required an 8.92 per cent all-input-using technical change [ff_a1("Electricserv") = 8.92] to achieve the NEMS result for the policy-induced increase in the price of electricity. This tension between the NEMS and USAGE ideas about the price of electricity probably indicates that we have not taken enough of the NEMS results into USAGE for inputs to electricity. We may not have needed a technical deterioration as large as 8.92 per cent had we been able to use the NEMS results for nuclear and renewable electricity.

For coal, USAGE requires an all-input-saving technical change of 14.55 per cent in 2035 [ff_a1("Coal") = -14.55] to hit the NEMS result for the policy-induced reduction in the price of coal (-15.52 per cent, see Table 3). USAGE does not naturally imply a long-run reduction in the price of coal merely on the basis of a long-run reduction in demand for coal. In the long run, a reduction in demand for coal in USAGE simply makes the coal industry smaller. To pick up the apparent long-run upward-sloping supply curve built into the NEMS modelling of the coal industry, USAGE requires input-saving (cost-reducing) technical change. This allows USAGE to cope with the NEMS result that a policy-induced reduction in demand for coal generates a long-run reduction in its price.

For natural gas, the explanation of the positive result for ff_a1("NaturalGas") in 2035 (2.62 per cent) is similar but opposite to the coal result. NEMS implies a long-run upward-sloping supply curve for natural gas whereas USAGE implies a flat long-run supply curve. To cope with the NEMS result that a policy-induced increase in demand for natural gas generates a long-run increase in price, USAGE requires input-using (cost increasing) technical change.

Table 6. NEMS/USAGE tensions: USAGE results for endogenized shift variables (% deviations)

	2010	2015	2020	2025	2030	2035
All-input-using tech change						
ff_a1("Coal")	-0.49	-0.95	-5.71	-8.89	-11.04	-14.55
ff_a1("Electricserv")	-0.17	-6.26	-8.37	-4.16	0.27	8.92
ff_a1("Naturalgas")	1.07	10.40	12.59	7.29	6.77	2.62
ff_a1("NatGasDistrb")	0.35	3.78	3.97	1.53	0.73	-1.51
Demand shift for Electricity						
fa1c("Electricserv")	-0.15	-1.17	-2.18	-4.01	-1.58	1.57
Demand shift in Electricity for inputs						
fa1ci("Coal", "Electricserv")	-0.74	-4.41	-14.24	-30.35	-45.52	-59.68
fa1ci("NaturalGas", "Electricserv")	2.63	32.63	46.40	48.71	47.33	49.48
fa1ci("NatGasDistrb","Electricserv")	2.56	31.45	44.63	46.84	45.53	47.58
Demand shift for Dummy product used only in Electricity						
fa1c("DummyInd")	0.28	-31.84	2498.71	4059.32	6233.65	6676.53

The major input to the natural gas distribution industry in USAGE is natural gas. By 2035, the policy-induced increase in the price of natural gas implied by NEMS is sufficient from the point of view of USAGE to more than explain the NEMS result for the increase in the price for natural gas distribution. Thus, for the natural gas distribution industry, USAGE requires a small (-1.51 per cent) all-input-saving technical change to allow it to hit the exogenously imposed increase in the price of natural gas distribution.

As expected, USAGE requires a large coal-saving technical change in the production of electricity [fa1ci("Coal","Electricserv") = -59.68 in 2035] to accommodate the NEMS-imposed reduction in the use of coal in the industry. Similarly, it requires large natural-gas-using technical changes in the production of electricity. Finally, very large technical changes in the electricity industry in favour of using the dummy product [fa1c("DummyInd")=

6,676.53 in 2035] are required to accommodate the policy-induced increases in non-fuel costs implied by the NEMS policy.

3.3. Other Changes to the USAGE Model

Previous applications of USAGE have generally been in year-on-year mode (that is the model produces results for year t, year t+1, year t+2, etc) or in long-run mode where the model produces a result for a single year far into the future, for example, starting from a database for 2005, the model produces a result for 2022. For the current project we modified the model so that it produced results for years spaced at 5-year intervals: starting from a database for 2005 the model produces results for 2010, 2015, etc. We had two reasons for using 5-year intervals. The first was to allow us to project far into the future (to 2035) with a manageable amount of computation (only 6 years, 2010, 2015, ..., 2035 rather than the 25 years which would have been necessary had we adopted a year-on-year mode). The second was to avoid what appeared to be some year-on-year instability in the NEMS results, instabilities that would have been difficult to handle in USAGE in year-on-year mode.

Table 7. USAGE macro baseline

Per cent growth, 5 years ending:	**2010**	**2015**	**2020**	**2025**	**2030**	**2035**
Private consumption, real	5.61	20.62	15.09	15.16	15.28	15.33
Investment, real	-18.32	17.16	14.85	14.91	12.3	11.65
Public consumption, real	8.37	7.73	7.73	7.73	7.73	7.73
Exports, real	27.37	28.92	23.68	22.84	24.03	23.66
Imports, real	2.95	19.03	20.03	20.01	20.01	20.01
GDP, real	4.75	19.24	14.25	14.25	14.25	14.25
Employment	-3.02	9.77	4.77	4.77	4.77	4.77
Capital	0.37	15.71	10.15	11.07	11.21	11.31
Total factor productivity	6.62	7.04	7.37	7.25	7.26	7.28
Percent of GDP						
Current account deficit	3.79	3.48	3.33	3.11	2.55	1.91
Net foreign liabilities	21.89	48.35	56.12	60.82	61.33	59.05
Public sector deficit	7.09	5.28	4.95	4.33	3.56	2.62
Public sector debt	61.82	72.20	77.93	80.33	79.24	74.77

Another modification that we made to USAGE concerned the electricity services industry. Rather than having several electricity generation industries (coal-fired, gas, nuclear, etc) we aggregated so that the model had just one electricity-producing industry (electric services). NEMS tells us about inputs to electricity, the output of electricity, investment in electricity and the price of electricity. We judged that this information could be taken into USAGE via a single electricity industry and that the multiple-electricity-industry approach in standard versions of USAGE would add nothing useful to the NEMS-USAGE link.

We made a third modification in light of results from our initial linked NEMS-USAGE simulation. The simulation indicated an unrealistically large boost in the output of crude oil from the NEMS policy. We traced this to a high assumed value for the elasticity of substitution in the electricity services industry between crude oil and natural gas. When this elasticity was reduced from its initial value of 1.0 to 0.0, the unrealistic result for crude oil disappeared.

4. The USAGE Baseline

Table 7 shows the USAGE baseline for macroeconomic variables. The results for 2010 are realized growth between 2005 and 2010: private consumption in 2010 was 5.61 per cent higher than in 2005; investment was 18.32 per cent lower, etc. In making a forecast for 2015 we assumed that the economy would recover from the current recession. This allows fast growth in employment, GDP and other macro variables between 2010 and 2015. Beyond 2015, we assumed that the economy grows steadily, with employment and GDP growth at the rates implied in the Energy Information Administration's (EIA) *Annual Energy Outlook, 2011*.

In accordance with experience of the last few decades, we assume that trade grows quicker than GDP. Over the forecast period, we assume that foreign investors will enforce a gradual decline in the U.S. current account deficit as a share of GDP. This will be imposed by the rest of the world through a downward adjustment in the U.S. real exchange rate. Decline in the current-account/GDP ratio means that exports will grow quicker than imports. We also assume that the public-sector deficit will decline as a share of GDP. This will be brought about by slow growth in public sector expenditure relative to growth in GDP. Despite reductions in the current account deficit and the public sector deficit as shares of GDP, net foreign liabilities and the public-sector debt will continue to grow as shares of GDP.

In creating the USAGE baseline we built in the NEMS baseline results for all the highlighted variables in Table 1.

5. The USAGE Policy Run: Effects of the NEMS Policy

5.1. Macro Effects

Table 8 shows the macro effects of the NEMS policy. We concentrate on the results for 2035, starting with real GDP.

As can be seen from the table, the NEMS policy translated into a macroeconomic outcome via USAGE, generates a reduction in GDP in 2035 of 0.45 per cent. That is, the policy makes GDP 0.45 per cent lower in 2035 than it would have been in the absence of the policy.

Why 0.45 per cent? A useful equation for understanding GDP effects is

$$y = a + S_{\ell} * \ell + S_k * k \tag{1}$$

where

y is the policy-induced percentage deviation in GDP;

ℓ and k are the policy-induced percentage deviations in aggregate employment (L) and capital (K);

a is the policy-induced percentage deviation in total factor productivity; and

S_ℓ and S_k are the labour and capital shares in GDP.

Table 8. Macro effects of the NEMS policy: results from USAGE

Percentage deviation in:	2010	2015	2020	2025	2030	2035
Private consumption, real	-0.04	-0.20	-0.39	-0.39	-0.54	-0.61
Investment, real	0.00	0.01	-0.05	-0.12	-0.20	-0.27
Public consumption, real	0.00	0.00	0.00	0.00	0.00	0.00
Exports, real	-0.01	0.08	0.19	0.18	0.21	0.10
Imports, real	-0.02	-0.11	-0.11	-0.06	-0.07	-0.09
GDP, real	-0.02	-0.11	-0.24	-0.26	-0.37	-0.45
Employment	0.00	0.00	0.00	0.00	0.00	0.00
Capital	0.01	0.12	0.09	0.01	-0.07	-0.14
Total factor productivity	-0.02	-0.13	-0.25	-0.25	-0.35	-0.42
Percent of GDP: policy less baseline						
Current account deficit	0.00	0.01	0.01	0.01	0.01	0.01
Net foreign liabilities	0.01	0.07	0.02	0.02	0.26	0.21
Public sector deficit	0.00	-0.01	-0.01	0.00	0.01	0.01
Public sector debt	0.02	0.08	0.13	0.07	0.17	0.21

We assume that the policy has no effect on aggregate employment. The policy will affect the distribution of employment across industries, but we would expect wage adjustments over the medium term to eliminate any noticeable aggregate employment effect of energy policies. As will be explained shortly, the policy reduces aggregate capital. With the capital share in GDP being about 20 per cent, the reduction in K of 0.14 per cent shown in Table 8 contributes about -0.03 per cent to GDP. So in terms of equation (1), the main part of the answer as to why the policy reduces GDP by 0.45 per cent must be a total factor productivity effect, the *a*-term in (1).

Inputs to the electricity industry in the baseline for 2035 represent 2.33 per cent of GDP. Thus the policy-induced increase in the cost of electricity of 17.22 per cent (Table 3) is equivalent to a loss of total factor productivity worth -0.40 per cent of GDP (= 0.0233*17.22). This, together with the capital contribution explains a reduction in GDP of 0.43 per cent (= 0.40 +0.03). What about the other 0.02 per cent reduction in GDP (the gap between 0.45 and 0.43)? We traced this to the effects of the policy-induced technical changes for coal, natural gas and natural gas distribution (the ff_a1 results for these industries in Table 6) acting on sales of these commodities outside the electricity industry.

Why does the policy reduce the capital stock? The answer is that we assume for the medium term that the policy has no effect on rates of return on capital throughout the economy. These rates of return are determined by international interest rates, exchange rate expectations and risk premia. For the medium term we would not expect the policy to have any identifiable effect on these variables. By contrast, we would expect the policy to reduce real wages: the policy is equivalent to a technical deterioration which reduces the value of the marginal product of labour. With capital (the internationally mobile factor) not taking a hit, but with labour (the immobile factor) taking a hit, the cost of using capital rises relative to the cost of using labour. This induces an increase in L/K. With L fixed by assumption, K must decline.

With a reduction in K, the policy induces a reduction in investment (0.27 per cent in 2035, Table 8) and with a reduction in GDP, the policy induces a reduction in private consumption (0.61 per cent, Table 8). We assume that the policy has no effect on public consumption. Together, the reductions in investment and private consumption amount to a reduction in expenditure worth about 0.49 per cent of GDP. With the decline in GDP being 0.45 per cent there must be an induced improvement in the real balance of trade (X-M must increase). This is shown in Table 8 by a small increase in exports (0.10 per cent) and a small reduction in imports (0.09 per cent).

The policy has only minor effects on the deficit and debt variables listed in the last four rows of Table 8. All of these variable increase in relation to GDP. This is mainly because the policy reduces GDP rather than increases the two deficits.

The final question that we consider in relation to the results in Table 8 is: why does private consumption fall relative to GDP (0.61 per cent compared with 0.45 per cent)? The ingredients for answering this question are in Table 9. First, as shown in Table 9, the policy causes a reduction (0.17 per cent) in the terms of trade (the price of exports relative to the price of imports). This is mainly because the policy causes an increase in the price of natural gas (a commodity for which there are significant imports). This is not offset by the reduction in the price of coal (a commodity for which there are almost no imports or exports). The fall in the terms of trade reduces the amount of gross national expenditure (GNE, which includes imports but not exports) that can be supported by any given level of GDP (which includes exports but not imports). Thus, a fall in the terms of trade tends to reduce the consumption/GDP ratio. Another contributing factor is that the policy increases the price of consumption goods relative to the prices of other components of GNE. Notice in Table 9 that the policy-induced deviation in 2035 in the price deflator for private consumption is zero[7] whereas the deviations in the price deflators for public consumption and investment are both negative (-0.27 and -0.43 per cent in 2035). With nominal consumption being modelled as an exogenous fraction of nominal household disposable income and with nominal household disposable income being an approximately constant fraction of nominal GDP, an increase in the price of private consumption relative to the prices of other components of GNE tends to reduce real private consumption relative to real GDP.[8]

But what explains the deviations in the prices of private consumption, public consumption and investment? As mentioned earlier, the price of labour falls relative to the costs of using capital (notice that the deviation in the real wage rate in 2035 is -0.65 per cent).

[7] In our simulations the price deflator for consumption is the numeraire.

[8] A helpful identity for understanding this argument is:

$$\frac{C}{Y} = \left(\frac{P_c C}{HDY}\right) * \left(\frac{HDY}{P_y Y}\right) * \left(\frac{P_y}{P_{gne}}\right) * \left(\frac{P_{gne}}{P_c}\right)$$

The first fraction on the RHS is fixed by assumption. The second fraction is approximately fixed via the behavioural assumptions in USAGE. The third fraction falls in response to the decline in the terms of trade. The fourth fraction also declines since the price of consumption rises relative to other components of GNE.

This increases the cost of capital intensive goods relative to that of labour-intensive goods. The goods and services that predominate in investment expenditures (e.g. construction) and public consumption (e.g. government services) are labour intensive relative to those that predominate in private consumption.

5.2. Industry Effects

Table 10 shows the effects of the NEMS policy on output in a selection of USAGE industries, the biggest losers and winners.

Coal is the outstanding loser. About 70 per cent of U.S. coal is absorbed by the electricity industry. As shown in Table 3, the policy reduces the use of coal as an input to electricity by 57 per cent in 2035. Via USAGE, this translates into a reduction in coal output of 40.61 per cent (Table 10). This is approximately 70 per cent of 57 per cent.

The next biggest loser from the NEMS policy is railroad services (an output deviation of -6.60 per cent in 2035, Table 10). About 11 per cent of railroad services are devoted to the transport of coal to the electricity industry. The 57 per cent reduction in the coal/electricity flow explains most of the USAGE result for the contraction of railroad services. The rest of the contraction reflects the overall reduction in economic activity (the 0.45 per cent reduction in GDP).

The output of the electricity industry contracts (3.19 per cent[9]) as a result of the policy-induced 17.22 per cent increase in its price. The increase in the electricity price has an adverse effect on Aluminium smelting, a trade-exposed electricity-intensive industry. Nitro-phosphorus fertilizer is also trade-exposed. Its adverse result in Table 10 is explained not by the increase in the price of electricity but by the increase in the price of natural gas, a major input to this industry.

Table 9. Macro effects of the NEMS policy: further results from USAGE to explain why private consumption falls relative to GDP

Percentage deviation in:	2010	2015	2020	2025	2030	2035
Private consumption, real	-0.04	-0.20	-0.39	-0.39	-0.54	-0.61
GDP, real	-0.02	-0.11	-0.24	-0.26	-0.37	-0.45
Price deflator for private cons	0.00	0.00	0.00	0.00	0.00	0.00
Price deflator for investment	-0.02	-0.13	-0.22	-0.19	-0.25	-0.27
Price deflator for public cons	-0.03	-0.17	-0.30	-0.27	-0.38	-0.43
Price deflator for GNE	-0.01	-0.05	-0.08	-0.07	-0.09	-0.10
Terms of trade	-0.02	-0.24	-0.35	-0.23	-0.27	-0.17
Price deflator for GDP	-0.01	-0.09	-0.13	-0.11	-0.14	-0.13
Real wage rate (priv cons deflated)	-0.05	-0.29	-0.49	-0.44	-0.59	-0.65

9 The output of the electricity commodity contracts by 3.78 per cent, Table 3. However the electricity industry produces not only electricity but also some natural gas distribution. This secondary product cushions the output contraction in the electricity industry.

At the other end of Table 10, the main winners from the policy are the natural gas industries (natural gas, natural gas distribution and natural gas transportation). These industries are stimulated directly by the policy-dictated increase in their sales to the electricity industry. The favorable result for mining (excludes coal, oil and gas) is also natural-gas-related. According to the USAGE database, the mining industry provides drilling and other investment services to the natural gas industry. Via this link, mining is stimulated by increased investment in natural gas.

Table 10. Effects on industry outputs of the NEMS policy: USAGE results (% deviations from baseline)

Industry	2010	2015	2020	2025	2030	2035	Comment
30 Coal	-0.90	-9.46	-17.64	-26.32	-34.10	-40.61	Direct effect
88 Railroad services	-0.21	-1.89	-3.33	-4.75	-5.88	-6.60	Coal transport
100 Electric services	-0.19	-1.16	-2.42	-3.40	-3.36	-3.19	Price increase
78 Aluminium smelter	-0.06	0.01	-0.25	-0.55	-1.08	-1.82	Trade exposed electricity user
58 Nitro-phosphorus fertiliser	-0.42	-4.04	-5.51	-3.62	-3.75	-1.45	Trade exposed NG user
33 Construction	-0.03	-0.38	-0.05	0.21	0.45	0.62	Extra ES construction
117 Export education	0.06	0.55	0.90	0.77	0.95	0.80	Trade exposed
102 Natural gas distribution	-0.70	-6.79	-8.21	-4.00	-3.35	0.91	Direct effect
27 Commercial fishing	0.05	0.41	0.79	0.77	1.01	0.97	Trade exposed, no Electricity
29 Mining (excludes coal, oil & gas)	0.23	1.68	2.02	1.42	1.41	1.33	Investment sales to NG (drilling)
101 Natural gas transportation	-0.02	-0.79	-1.03	0.53	1.06	3.44	Transports NG
32 Natural gas	0.03	-0.82	-1.05	1.82	2.80	7.03	Direct effect

Commercial fishing and export education (services provided to foreign students) are among the winners from the policy because neither of these industries is electricity intensive and both are highly trade-exposed. They benefit from policy-induced real devaluation, encapsulated in the reduction in the real wage rate (0.65 per cent, Table 9).

Construction appears among the winners in Table 10 (an output deviation of 0.62 per cent in 2035) despite the overall contraction in investment (0.27 per cent in 2035, Table 8). The reason is that construction is directly stimulated by the policy-induced increase in non-fuel expenditures by the electricity industry.

CONCLUSION

Enormous amounts of detail about energy economics and engineering are built into models such as NEMS. This includes information on energy products disaggregated into fine categories and about the longevity and productivity of major power plants, the cost of new generating capacity, the contribution of individual power plants to base-load and peak-load capacity, transmission losses, and many other important features of the power sector. However, energy models do not provide a picture of how changes in the energy sector affect the rest of the economy.

Direct incorporation into economy-wide models of energy detail at the level available in energy models is well beyond the current state of the art in economy-wide modelling. However direct incorporation is not required. This chapter demonstrates the feasibility of translating results from a detailed energy model into economy-wide implications by passing energy results through a CGE model. An illustrative example was given using the NEMS energy model and the USAGE CGE model.

Linking a detailed energy model and a CGE model requires modifications of the CGE model. First, variables must be added to the CGE model to absorb shocks from the energy model. Second, closure changes must be made to allow naturally endogenous energy variables in the CGE model to become exogenous so that they can be shocked onto paths generated by the energy model. Third, dummy industries may be required in the CGE model to handle lumpy energy investment expenditures projected from the energy model. CGE modellers must also cope with a large amount of unfamiliar technical information. For example, in making the NEMS-USAGE link, we had to deal with an initially bewildering array of energy units such as joules, MMBTUs, kilowatt-hours and terawatt-years. However the payoff from a successful energy-CGE link is considerable. It introduces a level of realism to the CGE model that is respected by energy specialists. In this way the results from the CGE model gain credibility in influential policy advising organizations such as the U.S. Department of Energy.

The NEMS-USAGE link described in this chapter could be extended relatively easily in two ways. First, more information could be taken from NEMS into USAGE. For example, in future research we could include output paths for nuclear and renewable electricity among the variables transferred from NEMS to USAGE. We anticipate that if this were done, then the apparent tension between the NEMS and USAGE determinations of the price of electricity would be reduced. Second, many more results could be generated by USAGE including employment by industry, occupation and region, and exports and imports by commodity. A third, more difficult, extension would be to build in a feedback from USAGE to NEMS. If USAGE suggests that a NEMS policy causes a significant change in GDP growth , for example, then this should be fed back to NEMS. What makes this difficult is that we would need either the capability to rerun NEMS or a high level of cooperation/coordination with a NEMS team.

The linking methodology described in this chapter is widely applicable. For example, in a study using Australian energy and CGE models, Adams and Parmenter (2013) derived comprehensive results for the effects on Australian industries and regions of proposed greenhouse policies. In our own work we recently applied the linking methodology in a project for the U.S. Department of Transportation (DOT) concerned with the economy-wide effects of increased expenditure on U.S. highways. DOT ran their detailed highway model (HERS, the Highway Economic Requirements System) to work out the implications of increased highway expenditure for: fuel consumption and maintenance of cars and trucks; travel times; road fatalities; and road maintenance and safety costs. We translated the HERS results into implications for macroeconomic and industry variables by adding new road-related variables to USAGE and adopting a closure that allowed us to shock USAGE variables onto HERS paths. Another example of linking concerns energy security involving large scale replacement of U.S. oil imports by domestically produced ethanol. In this example, information was introduced to USAGE from a detailed model of ethanol production and use technologies. The ethanol model included technical details that are normally overlooked in CGE modelling such as the role of the "blend wall" [the idea that vehicles must be modified to accept fuel with an ethanol/gasoline ratio of more than about 0.10, see Tyner et al. (2011)]. In all these examples, the linking methodology allowed the CGE model to generate new insights.

REFERENCES

Adams, P. D. & Parmenter, B. R. (2013). "CGE modeling of environmental issues in Australia", chapter 11 in P.B. Dixon and D.W. Jorgenson (editors) *Handbook of CGE Modeling*, Elsevier, Amsterdam, 553-657.

Dixon, P. B. & Rimmer, M. T. (2002). *Dynamic General Equilibrium Modelling for Forecasting and Policy: a Practical Guide and Documentation of MONASH,* Contributions to Economic Analysis 256, North-Holland Publishing Company, Amsterdam, xiv+338.

Dixon, P. B. & Rimmer, M. T. (2011), "You can't have a CGE recession without excess capacity", *Economic Modelling*, Vol. *28*(1-2), January-March, 602-13.

Dixon, P. B., Koopman, R. B. & Rimmer, M. T. (2013). "The MONASH style of CGE modeling: a framework for practical policy analysis", chapter 2, in P.B. Dixon and D.W. Jorgenson (editors) *Handbook of Computable General Equilibrium Modeling*, Elsevier, Amsterdam, 23-102.

DOE/EIA. (2009). *The National Energy Modeling System: An Overview*, available at http://www.eia.gov/oiaf/aeo/overview/.

Harrison, J., Horridge, J. M., Jerie, M. & Pearson, K. R. (2014). *GEMPACK manual*, GEMPACK Software, ISBN 978-1-921654-34-3, available at http://www.copsmodels.com/gpmanual.htm .

Horridge, M., Meeraus, A., Pearson, K. & Rutherford, T. (2013). "Software platforms: GAMS and GEMPACK", chapter 20, , in P.B. Dixon and D.W. Jorgenson (editors) *Handbook of Computable General Equilibrium Modeling*, Elsevier, Amsterdam, 1331-82.

Johansen, L. (1960). *A Multisectoral Study of Economic Growth*, Contributions to Economic Analysis 21, North-Holland Publishing Company, Amsterdam, x+177.

Johansen, L. (1974). *A Multisectoral Study of Economic Growth, second enlarged edition*, Contributions to Economic Analysis 21', North-Holland Publishing Company, Amsterdam, x+274.

Leontief, W. W. (1936). "Quantitative Input-Output Relations in the Economic System of the United States", *The Review of Economics and Statistics*, Vol. *18*(3), August, 105-125.

Tyner, W. E., Dooley, F. J. & Viteri, D. (2011). "Alternative pathways for fulfilling the RFS mandate", *American Journal of Agricultural Economics*, Vol. *93*(2), 465-72.

Zahniser, S., Hertz, T., Dixon, P. B. & Rimmer, M. T. (2012). "Immigration policy and its possible effects on U.S. agriculture and the market for hired farm labor: a simulation analysis", *American Journal of Agricultural Economics*, vol. *94*(2), January, 477-82.

In: Current Issues in International Trade
Editor: Gouranga G. Das

ISBN: 978-1-63321-405-7

Chapter 11

WHEN MODELLERS BEHAVE LIKE LAWYERS: HAVE WE LOST THE PLOT?

Alan A. Powell*

Department of Econometrics and Business Statistics,
Monash University, Melbourne, Australia

ABSTRACT

Australia has made outstanding contributions to the use of quantitative economic models in public policy discussions. That leading role is now threatened by the increasing use of econometric modellers in an advocacy, lawyer-like role, rather than as impartial sources of the best available technical advice. This development became inevitable once it became fashionable in Canberra during the mid-1980s to deny the existence of public goods and to force the funding of economic intelligence garnering increasingly into the private sector. This paper argues that we are all the losers.

Keywords: Applied general equilibrium, policy analysis, econometrics professional standards

1. INTRODUCTION

Recent times have seen an increasingly befuddled press become at once mesmerized by, yet simultaneously sceptical about, the nowadays commonplace use of quantitative economic models to support arguments in policy debate. The clash between the policy position on the

---

* Corresponding author: Emeritus Professor Alan Powell, Department of Econometrics and Business Statistics, Monash University, Melbourne 3800, Australia. Email: alan.powell@monash.edu.

This chapter is basically the text of the paper that I presented to the Australasian Meeting of the Econometric Society, University of Melbourne, July 2, 1997. As the issues raised herein have persisted (or indeed, have become more serious over time), I have not updated the text other than to give more recent references to some of the modelling. I am grateful for comments on the original paper to Matthew Peter and to Ken Wallis (who broadly agreed with me). My debt to the latter for pointing me towards the key U.K. references in the subject matter of this paper is large. The sole responsibility for the views expressed, and for any errors or omissions of fact, rests with me.

protection of passenger motor vehicles taken by the government of the State of South Australia versus the view of the federal government's Industry Commission provides a stark example (see Deans and Jacobsen): the former's arguments were bolstered by simulations with the second generation Murphy Model, MM2 (Powell and Murphy 1997), and other proprietary models, while the latter relied heavily on the MONASH model (Adams and Dixon, 1995; Adams et al., 1994; Dixon and Rimmer, 2002).

Not that there is anything wrong with, nor surprising about, the idea that different modellers might produce simulations suggesting different policy conclusions. Even in the case of modellers using precisely the same model, this can happen, and indeed has happened relatively frequently with Australia's first fully public-domain policy model, ORANI (Dixon et al., 1982). The different results in such cases will be relatively easily traced to the modeller's different choices about one or more of:

- data (the provenance of all quantitative modelling is based on the factual evidence or data base to which it appeals)
- parameters (these are the magnitudes of key constants that determine behaviour in the model)
- relevant equations (models consist of sets of equations, among which only a few will usually be crucial in determining a particular model result)
- closure (this is the decision about which variables are to be taken as given, and which are to be determined by the model)
- shocks (the changes in policy or external circumstances that are to be analysed) altered by the user without seeking special assistance from the model builder.

In non-technical language, this says that the two modellers have made different assumptions, each viewing her/his choice as the more 'reasonable' (read: 'relevant to the real world'). With the crucial assumptions identified, they can be debated. In the case where different models are involved, the work during its short life of the Economic Modelling Bureau of Australia (EMBA) in organizing a series of models comparisons conferences was helpful for establishing some of the reasons for the differences between the simulation properties of the models, as were some conferences that pre-dated the Bureau's activity in this field.

The 1989 conference run by Mark Upcher under the joint auspices of the Treasury and the ANU's Centre for Economic Policy Research was especially fruitful at teasing out the differences between the Australian module of the McKibbin-Sachs Global (MSG) model and the then extant version of the Murphy Model (see Parsell, Powell and Wilcoxen (1991)). This was possible only because the (then) youthful model builders (Warwick McKibbin and Chris Murphy) were prepared to devote substantial amounts of time to assisting the investigators (Bruce Parsell, Peter Wilcoxen and myself) mounting the model comparison. I believe:

(a) that this type of interaction is roughly what could be expected under the institutional arrangements that prevailed in England where the major econometric model builders were funded by a common patron, the Macroeconomic Modelling Consortium, which comprised the Economic and Social Research Council (ESRC), the Treasury and the Bank of England, and was managed by the ESRC. The Consortium required, as a condition for funding the research, that the model builders should interact in this intensive way with the ESRC's Macroeconomic Modelling Bureau under Ken Wallis' leadership at the University of Warwick. Results from models that had not been checked out independently were simply not admissible in the policy debate. The Bureau was also required to include under its purview the Treasury model, which is in the public domain by law and of which updated versions are released annually. From time to time, other models (e.g., those of the Bank of England and of Oxford Economic Forecasting) also were deposited voluntarily with the Bureau to meet the requirement for admissibility in the policy debate. (More detail on the structure of the macroeconomic modelling industry in the United Kingdom, including a comparison from an industrial organization point of view with France and the United States, will be found in Smith (1994)).

Under current Australian conditions, however, I find it difficult to believe:

(b) that the proprietors of any well established commercial model (not even the very same McKibbin and Murphy who gave such excellent cooperation to a models comparison conference in 1989) could be motivated to put the necessary amount of time and effort into this type of exercise. Because the instigators of Australian models comparisons work lack the teeth of the ESRC's modelling bureau, it will only be possible to coax or cajole the modellers into providing the profession with the documentation and access required for independent scrutiny: the bottom-line requirements of the commercial imperative will not allow otherwise.

Of itself this need not stifle the policy debate, nor lead to serious damage to quantitative economic modelling as an accepted and useful (though, of course, partial) tool for helping policy makers in their deliberations. But this sanguine perspective is based on the premise that the commercially based models compete against other models that are supported publicly and which are fully exposed, messy interstices and all, to rigorous peer group review. The supporting arguments for this conclusion are set out in the sections below.

This short paper is written in the hope that it will stimulate discussion among modellers and their clientele – especially their public-sector clientele – as how to get the best out of formal quantitative models as an input to policy discussions. Section 2 explains why models used for public policy discussion must be properly documented. It reviews the requirements for modelling work to be accorded scientific standing, and identifies economies of scope and scale in model production. The institutional implications of the latter are discussed, as well as the (in my view, exemplary) U.K. response to them. Section 3 continues the institutional theme, summarizing lessons gleaned over two decades at the Impact Project. Section 4 explains why fully publicly documented and accessible models are still needed. The principal points of the paper are summarized in the concluding Section 5.

2. Why Full Public Disclosure Is Necessary

Economics, perhaps more than any other line of social inquiry, aspires to the status of a science. Our inability as economists to conduct controlled experiments puts us at a disadvantage. But instead of minimizing this disability, all too often we have accentuated it by failing to implement those straightforward measures that are taken as routine in the physical sciences. In particular – and as was forcefully pointed out by Dewald, Thursby and Anderson (1986) – too often we have not even taken the standard precautions needed to ensure that our work can be replicated.

The requirement of replicability supplies the first reason for maintaining a detailed record of any research undertaking. The researchers themselves have finite memories; without detailed written records even they, in many instances, would not be able to reproduce their own work at a later date. But should they put this record in the public domain?

Scientific Status of Modelling Work

Independent replication by others is widely and wisely accepted as an absolutely basic requirement of scientific work. This is why it is incumbent on researchers to publicly document both their methods and materials sufficiently to allow other workers to reproduce reported results. If this condition is not met, the results are not accorded scientific standing and are not taken seriously by other scientists.

Already we perceive a tension here in the current Australian climate: if models which are used to support public policy arguments lie outside the public domain, how can these arguments provide a credible basis for decision making? What is required to ensure replicability? In the issue carrying the paper by Dewald et al. cited above, the editors of the *American Economic Review* announced that it was their policy to publish papers

> 'only where the data used in the analysis are clearly and precisely documented, are readily available to any researcher for purposes of replication, and where details of the computations sufficient to permit replication are provided' (p. v).

In the case of economy-wide modelling work, this can amount to a tall order. To take just one well known example — the ORANI model — a listing of the model's data base and parameter file runs to 646 pages (Kenderes and Strzelecki, 1991). The equations of the model itself, their interpretation and illustrative simulations are documented in a 372-page monograph (Dixon, Parmenter, Sutton and Vincent, 1981), in publicly available working papers, and in a journal literature too voluminous to cite here.

Economies of Scale and Scope in Modelling

Given that a practical policy and/or forecasting model involves a very heavy investment in intellectual effort, data garnering and documentation, it would be amazing if economists did not recognize the potential for economies of scale and scope. The realization of such economies requires model builders to see most of the model's core ingredients — such as its standard or default equation listing, data base and parameter file — as public goods. Around such publicly (or semi-publicly) available tools we would expect a community of modellers to develop. And indeed the last two decades saw such a community develop around the models (especially ORANI) at the Impact Project, whose example proved compelling enough to inspire one courageous individual to attempt something similar on a global scale (Hertel 1994).

The perspective that I am taking here views the resources available to support research as too few, and the issues to be analysed as too pressing, for opportunities to be squandered by engaging in the wrong sort of replication while failing to attend to the right sort of replication as outlined above. By the 'wrong' sort of replication I mean unnecessary duplication: that is, two or more individuals or groups making separate demands on research resources to produce essentially the same product, be it a data-base, a parameter file, or a core model. The extent to which model building has been privatized in Australia arguably has reached this socially wasteful stage. What is more, the previously publicly provided infrastructure is aging, conditions of access are becoming worse, and documentation lags are increasing.

Institutional Impediments and Institutional Innovation

Most of the resistance to sharing resources in modelling can be traced to just two sources: (1) *funding difficulties* and (2) the *academic imperative*. If a common, open-access research facility is to be created, how does one elicit enough cooperation among the potential clientele to ensure that attempted free-riding does not sink the venture? If academic recognition, promotion and tenure seem to be more available to 'loners' who keep their research cards very close to their chests, how can a community of modellers develop around a common modelling resource base?

On the question of funding, leaving matters to the private sector will fail to reap the rewards that demonstrably come from cooperation. Leaving it to the private sector most likely will lead to proprietary models where almost all of the incentives are to share nothing – only if we are exceptionally lucky might we see the formation of one or more research consortia backed by some of the larger players.

For the latter to work, all putative members of a research consortium must recognize that without cooperation all are likely to be worse off. Having faced up to this, they must then agree to behave as responsible members of their modelling community. This implies meeting a share of the funding where possible, and agreeing that modelling infrastructure developed in-house will be shared by consortium members. If the backers are exceptionally publicly spirited, they just may agree to sharing their model with the community at large. But there has been very little of this type of activity in Australia (or indeed, anywhere else).

The academic imperative will remain an obstacle as long as promotion and tenure committees – not to mention referees and editors of journals in applied economics – continue to reward novelty at the expense of the usefulness of research outputs. Over time I hope that we will see more academic researchers and editors realize that a quality piece of applied analysis which builds on an existing core model and database offers better professional opportunities than implementing some new twist for its own sake on a toy model with data of doubtful provenance and questionable relevance to any real world problem.

The United Kingdom came to terms with these institutional failings in the early 1980s when a parliamentary committee stated that it 'was not satisfied that the [then] present arrangements produce[d] the most useful model-based evidence for the Committee, for Parliament, or the public.' The Committee went on to note:

> 'neither in evidence to the Committee nor in published work is there any sustained systematic process of inter-model comparison, tracking down the reasons for differences

between models and the justification of them ... There is no general access to models for users outside the forecasting teams, or any means by which they can themselves make inter-model comparisons in which they may be interested. There is no generally agreed process of testing... '

(Treasury and Civil Service Committee of the House of Commons session 1980-81, Chapter 10)

These observations provided the momentum that ultimately led to the establishment of the ESRC Macroeconomic Modelling Bureau at Warwick in 1983, and to its maintenance as the quality assurance device for the U.K. profession. It was able to discharge this role because of its independence, and the requirement already alluded to that publicly financed modellers deposit their complete models (including databases) with the Bureau. The latter is then in a position to 'undertake direct comparisons across models of the U.K. economy at all stages ...' (Wallis, 1993b, p. 227).

3. Lessons from the Impact Project Experience

The Australian community of policy modellers with an orientation towards applied general equilibrium was largely created at the Impact Project. Many key figures of the community either participated in some way in the development of the ORANI or the MONASH model under Peter Dixon and associates, or else attended training courses organized by the Project. Such training courses provide the ultimate public exposure of a model. From the viewpoint of those attending, the principal advantages are that such a course

- gives quick access to the core model, data base and computing system;
- establishes contact with a network of researchers having overlapping interests;
- gives hands-on experience with manipulating a state-of-the-art model for policy analysis; and
- serendipitously achieves many of the aims of refresher courses in economic theory and policy analysis.

From the viewpoint of the profession, the detailed knowledge of the model gained on a course is taken back into the institution or firm employing the course graduate, so that accurate knowledge of how the model works becomes diffused among the model-using clientele.

The story of the success of the family of ORANI-based models has been documented at length in Powell and Lawson (1990), Vincent (1990), Powell and Snape (1993) and Dee (1994). This success would not have been possible without generic software allowing modellers routinely to modify those parts of the ORANI theory that were not adequate to the task in hand, to eliminate unnecessary detail by aggregating over sectors/agents not currently under focus, and to amplify sectors of current interest by adding additional equations and data. The GEMPACK software suite developed by Ken Pearson and associates (see Harrison and Pearson, 1996) put all of this on a routine basis.

Apart from the importance of modelling flexibility to the clientele, and of human capital formation through training courses, other 'lessons' gleaned from Impact's two decades of experience (as summarized by Powell and Lawson, 1990, or Powell and Snape, 1993) suggest that a project which aims to provide the infrastructure for a focused modelling community:

1. should not be run entirely within a university, nor entirely within the client agencies;
2. should be accompanied by full public documentation of data, methods, and results;
3. should have detailed involvement of the policy clientele in the design stage of model building;
4. should be at full arm's length from executive government.

The last of these recommendations involves putting some space between the practitioner who is supplying the tools and the practitioner who is crafting the policy advice. The credibility of the tools should not be left too vulnerable to misjudgments by policy analysts or to the political popularity of particular policy recommendations based on them. Item 3 above, on the other hand, emphasizes that a policy-oriented model will be of limited use if no policy adviser uses it with enthusiasm.

As we have noted above, item 2 is simply a criterion for scientific work: results must be capable of replication. Where conflicting interests are at stake, it is unreasonable to expect opponents to accept the reasonableness of assumptions or the internal consistency of simulations without full documentation; moreover, they can be relied upon to invest considerable resources into unearthing any shoddy work. And in any event, abiding by best scientific practice is the assurance of quality control. Item 1 recognizes complementarities between the discipline of a civil service environment, which encourages working to a pre-announced research program, and the creativity of the academic environment, which often does not.

Finally, sponsors need to be convinced that a model, including its database/parameter file and computer systems, like any capital good, is subject to both depreciation and obsolescence. An on-going resource commitment is necessary for updating and refurbishment.

4. Continuing Need for Well Documented, Publicly Accessible Models

Well documented models in the public domain are capable of being well understood and used by participants in policy debates who are fully at arm's length from the model builders; such models consequently form a reference standard to which all modelling in a given discussion can be related. If a commercial model with relatively restricted public accessibility is used in debate and is claimed to be superior in some way to publicly documented and accessible models, the onus would then be on the user of the commercial model to point out the differences by fully exposing at least those parts of the commercial model that are under contention. If the supply of publicly documented and accessible models becomes sparse or non-existent, however, there is no reference standard and little chance that debates among modellers on technical matters will generate anything but confusion and public ridicule, a result which the Press can be relied upon to promote with glee.

It became fashionable in Canberra during the mid-1980s to deny the existence of public goods and to force the funding of economic intelligence garnering increasingly into the private sector. This has created opportunities for many talented modellers to set up shop as service providers. Several of them understandably packed up the tool kit built in the public and academic sectors and proceeded to add value and to differentiate the product to suit the conditions of the market place. Those left behind in academia and in the public sector faced an increasingly hostile climate in which developmental work was claimed not to be a matter of public concern since competition among private model proprietors would serendipitously provide the modelling infrastructure. Clients in the public sector need only purchase products off the shelf and all would be well.

Antecedents of Existing Models and the Knowledge Base for Modelling

The first point to make in rebuttal of the above view is that all of the current Australian models that are highly regarded by the profession – or if not the models themselves, then at least their direct lineal antecedents – were initially (and usually substantially) developed in academia or in public institutions. If seminal work in private-sector models is occurring (and there is some), it is hard to see how it can spread at all rapidly to the rest of the profession: the commercial imperative obviously is a substantial impediment. No private proprietor will willingly place a model fully in the public domain if her/his livelihood depends upon reaping rents from it.

Frankly, I find this situation alarming. The current tendency of Australian governments to purchase economic modelling services 'off the shelf' means that all model proprietors are focused on pleasing their clients (in itself a good thing) in the narrow context of whatever issue is current (a serious danger to clear thinking and honest scientific work). It would be far too easy for modellers whose livelihoods depend on pleasing the client, either consciously or unconsciously, to tune their models to the client's requirements, irrespective of the empirical provenance of the parameter values and other model settings that they feel compelled to adopt in the light of the client's expressed needs and preferences. This is known in semi-technical language as fudge-factoring: that is, endogenizing the assumptions to produce the required result.

In case any should take offence at the implications of the above paragraph, let me make it clear that the validity of the point of view that I am expressing here does not require one to believe that such lapses from grace actually take place. For proper public policy formation in a democracy it is necessary that all arguments supporting a given policy option are based on honestly stated premises. The ordinary citizen may read that Dr X or Professor Y is a highly acclaimed modeller and that her/his model implies that the government should do Z. Such a citizen is entitled to assume that any modeller with high prestige in the profession will be addressing the issue as honestly and dispassionately as she/he can. The citizen is also entitled to assume that the standards of the profession promote such objectivity by utilizing the ordinary common-sense precaution of independent peer-group scrutiny and evaluation. In a world dominated by privately financed models, there can be no such guarantee.

From the kind of scenario I have painted above it is not hard to imagine the situation deteriorating to the point where quantitative economic modellers become regarded by the clientele as not much more than 'hired mouths' – once it becomes widely accepted that non-publicly accessible models provide acceptable fuel for policy disputes, the temptation to use modellers as lawyers will be irresistible. And so much the more so as non-experts in modelling become fully aware that the available factual evidence rarely is strong enough to support one model specification or set of parameter values definitively to the exclusion of all others.

Summary and Conclusion

Underlying my arguments above have been three propositions. I regard the truth of the first as self-evident, and the desirability of the remaining two as clear. They are:

(1) No modeller will willingly place a model fully in the public domain if her/his livelihood depends upon reaping rents from it.
(2) Only models in the public domain are readily open to independent authentication. By independent authentication I mean that an independent professional is able to check the computer implementation of the model against a full description of it provided by the model builder.
(3) No model which has not been independently authenticated should have standing in public policy discussions.

Conditional on the truth of (1), a strict interpretation of the desiderata (2) and (3) would exclude most contemporary Australian models from the policy debate.

Above I have softened (2) and (3) to allow as admissible models that are well enough documented for the profession to have a good general grasp of the main mechanisms present in them, provided elements that are crucial to contentious points in the policy debate are fully publicly exposed. I have argued that such a relaxation of standards is more manageable and less dangerous if we have well defined, publicly documented and accessible models available as a reference standard; and moreover, that the infrastructure on which private models are built has been developed almost exclusively in the public and/or academic sectors. The difficulties that modellers in these sectors are experiencing in obtaining funding means that the infrastructure is deteriorating and that the base from which most private modellers will have to work in the future may be of inferior quality.

I have noted the economies of scale and scope that underlie major modelling projects, and concluded that 'leaving it to the market' is not likely to produce an efficient outcome. I have also pointed out that the academic imperative mitigates against serious developmental work in applied modelling. This view is shared by Ron Smith (whose views derive from British, rather than Australian, experience):

> 'My ... conclusion is that a free market solution (which includes public sector clients buying the outputs they require from either vertically integrated or separate producers) is unlikely to generate adequate investment in basic research and development. The immediate rewards of model development work to the clients (decision-makers and academics) are too low for them to provide enough resources to motivate the teams.'

Finally, I have commented that the denial of the public-goods aspects of policy models by many bureaucrats since the mid-1980s has been destructive, and threatens Australia's outstanding international reputation as an intelligent user of modelling in the making of real policy decisions. With an increasing tendency to see modellers as 'hired guns' – that is, as lawyers – we are in danger of losing the plot.

REFERENCES

Adams, P. D. & Dixon, P. B. (1995). Prospects for Australian Industries, States and Regions: 1993-94 to 2001-02, *Australian Bulletin of Labour*, *21*, 87-108.

Adams, P.D., Dixon, P. B., McDonald, D., Meagher, G. A. & Parmenter, B. R. (1994). Forecasting for the Australian Economy Using the MONASH Model, *International Journal of Forecasting*, *10*, 181-189.

Centre of Policy Studies. (1994). MONASH Model — MONASH94 issued by the Centre of Policy Studies, Monash University, Clayton 3168 Vic. Australia, as part of the documentation for the November 1994 MONASH Training Course.

Deans, A. & Jacobsen, G. (1997). SA challenges IC on cuts to car tariffs, *Australian Financial Review*, April 30th.

Dee, P. (1994). General Equilibrium Models and Policy Advice in Australia , paper presented at the IFAC Workshop on Computing in Economics and Finance, Amsterdam, June 8-10.

Dewald, W. G., Thursby, J. G. & Anderson, R. G. (1986). Replication in Empirical Economics, *American Economic Review*, *76*, 587-603.

Dixon P. B., Parmenter, B. R., Sutton, J. & Vincent, D. P. (1982). *ORANI: A Multisectoral Model of the Australian Economy* (Amsterdam and New York: North Holland Publishing Company).

Dixon, P. B., Malakellis, M. & Rimmer, M. T. (1997). The Australian automotive industry from 1986-87 to 2009-10: analysis using the MONASH model, a report to the Industry Commission, May, x+84

Dixon P. B. & Rimmer, M. T. (2002). *Dynamic General Equilibrium Modelling for Forecasting and Policy* (Amsterdam and New York: North Holland/Elsevier).

Dixon P. B. & Jorgenson, D. W. (2013). *Handbook of Computable General Equilibrium Modeling* (Amsterdam and New York: North Holland/Elsevier).

Harrison, W. J. & Pearson, K. R. (1996). Computing Solutions for Large General Equilibrium Models , *Computational Economics*, *9*, 83-127.

Hertel, T. W. (ed.) (1997). *Global Trade Analysis: Modeling and Applications* (New York and Cambridge, U.K.: Cambridge University Press).

Hertel, T. W. (1994). Taking IMPACT Abroad: The Global Trade Analysis Project, paper presented at the IFAC Workshop on Computing in Economics and Finance, Amsterdam, June 8-10.

Kenderes, M. & Strzelecki, A. (1991). Listing the 1986-87 ORANI Database, Industry Commission Research Memorandum No. OA-569, Belconnen, ACT, December.

Parsell B. F., Powell, A. A. & Wilcoxen, P. J. (1991). The Effects of Fiscal Restraint on the Australian Economy as Projected by the Murphy and MSG2 Models: A Comparison, *Economic Record*, *67*, 97-114.

Powell, A. A. & Murphy, C. W. (1997) *Inside A Modern Macroeconometric Model – A Guide to the Murphy Model*, second revised and enlarged edition (Berlin, Heidelberg and New York: Springer-Verlag), xviii + 454.

Powell, A. A. & Snape, R. H. (1993). The Contribution of Applied General Equilibrium Analysis to Policy Reform in Australia, *Journal of Policy Modeling*, *15*, 393-414.

Powell, A. A. & Lawson, T. (1990). A Decade of Applied General Equilibrium Modelling for Policy Work, Ch. 8 in L. Bergman, D. Jorgenson and Erno Zalai (eds.), *General Equilibrium Modeling and Economic Policy Analysis* (Cambridge, MA: Blackwell) 241-90.

Smith, R. (1994). The Macromodelling Industry: Structure, Conduct and Performance, Ch. 5 in Stephen G. Hall (ed.), *Applied Econometric Forecasting Techniques* (Hemel Hemstead, Hertfordshire: Harvester Wheatsheaf) 68-88.

Vincent, D. (1990). Applied General Equilibrium Modelling in the Australian Industries Assistance Commission: Perspectives of A Policy Analyst, Ch. 9 in L. Bergman, D. Jorgenson and E. Zalai (eds.), *General Equilibrium Modeling and Economic Policy Analysis* (Cambridge, MA: Blackwell, 1990), 291-350.

Wallis, K. F. (1993a). On Macroeconomic Policy and Macroeconometric Models, *Economic Record*, *69*, 113-130.

Wallis, K. F. (1993b). Comparing Macroeconometric Models: A Review Article, *Economica*, *60*, 225-237.

In: Current Issues in International Trade
Editor: Gouranga G. Das
ISBN: 978-1-63321-405-7

Chapter 12

CGE-BASED ANALYSIS OF TRADE POLICIES: CAPTURING THE "DEVIL" IN THE DETAILS

Badri G. Narayanan *
Purdue University, US

ABSTRACT

For decades, Computable General Equilibrium (CGE) analysis has been criticised by policy analysts for its usually aggregated analysis, with sectors that usually comprise hundreds of sub-sectors that are of interest to practicaly policy specialists (Lloyd and MacLaren, 2004). Few CGE modelers have come up with tools and methods to address this issue. In this chapter, we review many recent methods to disaggregate sectors, factors, household types and regions in CGE models. These methods can play a critical role in policy analysis the trade of US with other countries.

INTRODUCTION

The choice of the tool for disaggregated CGE-based trade policy analysis depends on the situation under consideration. If one is merely interested in the trade of disaggregated sectors (not production structure), one could employ models nested partial and general equilibrium (PE-GE) models such as the one developed by Narayanan, Hertel and Horridge (2010), in conjunction with the TASTE tool (Horridge and Laborde, 2008) for example; if one is interested in the input-output structure as well, one could use tools such as SPLITCOM, using assumptions on production structure and consumption, such as the way it is done in Narayanan and Khorana (2011). TERM framework developed at the Centre of Policy Studies (CoPS), Monash University in Australia (presently at Victoria University, Melbourne, Australia), is an example of the tool for disaggregating regions. Several papers such as Narayanan and Walmsley (2011) and Mirza, Narayanan and van Leeuwen (2009) provide examples of way to deal with factor disaggregation. Disaggregation of household types as

* Corresponding author: Email: badri@purdue.edu.

well as government transfers can be dealt with in a framework developed by Walmsley and Minor (2012). These tools and methodologies are reviewed in this chapter, with examples from US trade policy issues with emerging economies, based on the existing literature.

Section 2 of this chapter discusses the literature on extending CGE models to detailed sectors, focusing on trade and tariff issues alone. Section 3 suggests ways to disaggregate sectors in such a way that the input-output structure at the disaggregated level is also captured. Section 4 describes the methods to deal with disaggregation of factors. Section 5 shows how sub-regional models can be developed, starting from multi-country models. Section 6 explains ways to disaggregate households and government expenditure in a multi-country CGE framework and Section 7 concludes.

General Equilibrium at the Tariff-Line Level Trade Policies

Examination of the impacts of tariff changes at a disaggregated level is important for many reasons, such as the following:

(a) ***Variations in tariffs:*** Significant variations in tariff rates at different tariff lines for many commodities cause serious aggregation bias in aggregate-sector-based studies. Those interested in aggregate impacts can use a specialized technique, such as the Trade Restrictiveness Index (TRI), to account for these differences (eg., Anderson and Neary, 1996), however, the appropriate index will depend on the objective in mind. For example, see Bach and Martin (2001) for an aggregation methodology that factors in expenditure, input costs and tariff-revenue; Anderson and Neary (2003) for Mercantilist TRI (MTRI); and Anderson (2008) for the consequences of atheoretic tariff aggregation in trade policy modeling.

(b) ***False Competition:*** The aggregation of sectors may result in ‘false competition’: Two countries that do not compete in a third market at the disaggregated level (e.g., one exports engine blocks and one does auto transmissions), may appear as competitors at an aggregate (auto parts) level. Welsch (2006), for example, finds that intra-industry specialization of the countries over the years leads to the reduction in the heterogeneity of aggregate commodity groups and hence the decline in estimated Armington elasticities.

(c) ***Sub-Sector-specific trade policies:*** Many policies are framed for specific products that are not identified among the relatively aggregated sectors. Finally, most trade policy negotiations are conducted at highly disaggregated “tariff lines”. Narayanan and Vashisht (2008) for example, evaluate the impact of Free Trade Agreement (FTA) that has been negotiated between India and Thailand. This involves tariff cut proposals at HS-6 level. This is why there has been a strong preference for partial equilibrium (PE) analysis (e.g. Ramos et al. 2007 and Evans et. al 2007) as negotiations begin to get seriously under way. Although there have been attempts to model, for example, as many as 500 sectors in a Computable General Equilibrium (CGE) framework by Dixon and Rimmer (2004), they are still far more aggregate than what is required for tariff-line negotiations.

On the other hand, while comprehensive PE models may show approximate welfare measures for small exogenous changes (Kokoski and Smith, 1987), they are unable to offer a comprehensive assessment of the impact of trade policy reforms on economy-wide welfare, wages, employment and other variables of interest to policy makers. These policy indicators are typically produced by Computable General Equilibrium (CGE) models. This paper utilizes a combined PE-GE approach to trade policy analysis, thereby permitting us to contrast the PE, GE and combined PE-GE predictions for bilateral trade flows as well as aggregate welfare and other economy-wide variables of interest.

One of the first attempts to perform a somewhat disaggregated analysis in a CGE framework was made by Basevi (1966, 1968). However, there has been a surge in research efforts aimed at linking PE and CGE models only recently. This has been common in the poverty/micro-simulation literature (Herault, 2007; Hertel et. al., 2007b), in sub-regional economic modeling (Madsen and Jensen-Butler, 2004) as well as in the application of econometrics to CGE models (Han and Woodland, 2003; Hertel et. al., 2007a; Bhattarai and Whalley, 1999; Arndt et. al., 2002; and McKitrick, 1998). More recently, authors have begun to link CGE and PE models for disaggregated trade policy analysis. In particular, Grant, Hertel and Rutherford (2007) have proposed a partial/general equilibrium (PE/GE) framework, building on the GTAP-in-GAMS global CGE model (Rutherford and Paltsev, 2000) and focusing on the treatment of tariff rate quotas, which cannot readily be aggregated for use in a normal CGE model. Narayanan et al. (2010) draws inspiration from this work; likewise implementing a PE/GE model within the GTAP modeling framework (Hertel, 1997).

The PE/GE framework involves several steps to implement. The first step is to develop a detailed partial equilibrium model for the disaggregated sectors, often along the lines of the benchmark CGE model. The idea is to focus on the trade and tariff policies, which are more easily available at the tariff-line level. Narayanan et al. (2010), for example, introduces Armington nests across sources and between domestic and imported products, at the disaggregated level. Thus, one can perform simulations related to tariff and trade policies at the disaggregated level. Secondly, they aggregate these disaggregated sectors to aggregated sectors that have the typical CGE treatment. This is facilitated by Constant Elasticity of Substitution (CES) and Constant Elasticity of transformation (CET) nests.

The box below summarises the differences between the standard CGE treatment and the approach suggested in PE and PE/GE models developed in Narayanan et al. (2010). In the standard GTAP model, there is no substitution between various commodities, at any level of aggregation; however, a CES structure is assumed in the PE and PE-GE models for substitution between disaggregated commodities within an aggregated sector, at the level of total domestic consumption by the aggregate regional household, which comprises firms, government and households. Armington substitution between domestic and imported commodities takes place for each agent separately in the standard GTAP model, while in the PE-GE model, this happens at the aggregate user level (regional household). Armington nest across the sources, however, is defined at the regional household level in both the standard model and the PE-GE variant. Much like the CES assumption for the consumption, there is a CET nest defined for production at the disaggregated level.

Box 1. Comparison of the Salient Features in Different Models

Feature	Standard GTAP Model	PE and PE-GE Models
Substitution among domestic composite commodities' consumption	No such feature	An aggregate user substitutes between disaggregate commodities
Substitution between domestic and imports	Each firm and final user separately substitutes domestic and imports at sector-level	An aggregate user substitutes domestic and imports at both sector and sub-sector levels.
Substitution between imports from different sources	An aggregate user substitutes imports from different sources at the sector-level	An aggregate user substitutes imports from different sources at both sub-sector and sector-levels.
Transformation of domestic commodities production	Each domestic firm makes its own sector-level output	Each domestic firm makes a mixture of sub-sectors that are transformed from the aggregate sector-level production

Source: Narayanan et al. (2010)

Box 2 below provides a sample excerpt of the code for the disaggregated sectors part of this model, focusing on the international trade-related aspects. The complete model and archive that can be readily run with the RunGtap interface is available on Global trade analysis project (GTAP) model website, in the technical paper series (No: 29).

Box 2. An Excerpt from the Model Code (TABLO File)

Equation E_QXSK
 # Regional demand for disaggregated imported commodities by source (HT 29) # (all,k,SSECT_COMM21)(all,r,REG)(all,s,REG)
qxsk(k,r,s)= -amsk(k,r,s) + qimk(k,s)- ESUBMK(k) * **[pmsk(k,r,s)** - amsk(k,r,s) - pimk(k,s)];

Equation E_QXS
 # Regional demand for disaggregated imported commodities by source (HT 29) # (all,i,SPLT_COMM)(all,r,REG)(all,s,REG)
VIWS(i,r,s) * qxs(i,r,s) = sum{k,SSECT_COMM:MPSP_COMM(k)=i, VIWSK (k,r,s) * qxsk(k,r,s)};

Equation E_PMSK
 # Eq'n links domestic and world prices (HT 24) # (all,k,SSECT_COMM)(all,r,REG) (all,s,REG)

```
pmsk(k,r,s) = tmk(k,s) + tmsk(k,r,s) + pcifk(k,r,s);

Equation E_PCIFK
#Eq'n links FOB and CIF prices for k shipped from region r to s (HT 26')#
(all,k,SSECT_COMM)(all,r,REG)(all,s,REG)
pcifk(k,r,s) = FOBSHRK(k,r,s) * pfobk(k,r,s)+ TRNSHRK(k,r,s) * ptransk(k,r,s);

Equation E_PFOBK
# Eq'n links agent's and world prices (HT 27) # (all,k,SSECT_COMM)(all,r,REG)
(all,s,REG)
pfobk(k,r,s) = pmk(k,r) - txk(k,r) - txsk(k,r,s);

Equation E_PIMK
# Price for aggregate imports (based on HT 28) # (all,k,SSECT_COMM)(all,s,REG)
pimk(k,s) = sum{r,REG, MSHRSK(k,r,s) * [pmsk(k,r,s) - amsk(k,r,s)]};

Equation E_PCIF
(all,i,SPLT_COMM)(all,r,REG)(all,s,REG)
VIWS(i,r,s) * pcif(i,r,s)=sum{k,SSECT_COMM:MPSP_COMM(k)=i, VIWSK(k,r,s) *
pcifk(k,r,s)};

Equation E_PFOB
(all,i,SPLT_COMM)(all,r,REG)(all,s,REG)
VXWD(i,r,s) * pfob(i,r,s)=sum{k,SSECT_COMM:MPSP_COMM(k)=i,
VXWDK(k,r,s) * pfobk(k,r,s)};

Equation E_TMS
(all,i,SPLT_COMM)(all,r,REG)(all,s,REG)
VIMS(i,r,s)*tms(i,r,s)=sum{k,SSECT_COMM:MPSP_COMM(k)=i, VIMSK(k,r,s) *
tmsk(k,r,s)};

Equation E_PMS
(all,i,SPLT_COMM)(all,r,REG)(all,s,REG)
VIMS(i,r,s)*pms(i,r,s)=
sum{k,SSECT_COMM:MPSP_COMM(k)=i, VIMSK(k,r,s) * pmsk(k,r,s)};

Equation E_PIM
(all,i,SPLT_COMM)(all,s,REG)
VIM(i,s)*pim(i,s)=sum{k,SSECT_COMM:MPSP_COMM(k)=i,     VIMK(k,s)     *
pimk(k,s)};

Equation E_QIM
(all,i,SPLT_COMM)(all,s,REG)
VIM(i,s)*qim(i,s)=sum{k,SSECT_COMM:MPSP_COMM(k)=i,     VIMK(k,s)     *
qimk(k,s)};
```

Equation E_PTRANS
(all,m,MARG_COMM)(all,i,SPLT_COMM)(all,r,REG)(all,s,REG)
VTMFSD(m,i,r,s)*ptrans(i,r,s)=
sum{k,SSECT_COMM:MPSP_COMM(k)=i, VTMFSDK(m,k,r,s) *ptransk(k,r,s)};
! Equating qtmfsdk to GTAP-level!

Equation E_QTMFSDK
(all,m,MARG_COMM)(all,k,SSECT_COMM)(all,r,REG)(all,s,REG)
qtmfsdk(m,k,r,s)=qtmfsd(m,MPSP_COMM(k),r,s);
! Calculating flow-specific transport cost index at k-level!

Equation E_PTRANSK
 # Generates flow-specific modal average cost of transport index (cf. HT7) #
(all,k,SSECT_COMM)(all,r,REG)(all,s,REG)
ptransk(k,r,s)

= **sum{m,MARG_COMM,** VTFSD_MSH(m,MPSP_COMM(k),r,s) * **[pt(m)** - atmfsdk(m,k,r,s)]};
! Equating atfk to GTAP-level!

Equation E_ATFK (all,k,SSECT_COMM) atfk(k)=atf(MPSP_COMM(k));
! Equating atallk to GTAP-level!

Equation E_ATALLK
(all,m,MARG_COMM)(all,k,SSECT_COMM)(all,r,REG)(all,s,REG)
atallk(m,k,r,s)=atall(m,MPSP_COMM(k),r,s);
! Generating atmfsdk from GTAP-level and HS6 level variables!

Equation E_ATMFSDK
 # Generates flow-specific average rate of technical change #
(all,m,MARG_COMM)(all,k,SSECT_COMM)(all,r,REG)(all,s,REG)
atmfsdk(m,k,r,s) = atm(m) + ats(r) + atd(s) + atfk(k) + atallk(m,k,r,s);

Equation E_AMS
(all,i,SPLT_COMM)(all,r,REG)(all,s,REG)
VIWS(i,r,s)*ams(i,r,s)=
sum{k,SSECT_COMM:MPSP_COMM(k)=i, VIWSK(k,r,s) * amsk(k,r,s)};

Equation E_TM
(all,i,SPLT_COMM)(all,s,REG)
VXW(i,s)*tm(i,s)=sum(k,SSECT_COMM:MPSP_COMM(k)=i, VXWK(k,s) * tmk(k,s));

Equation E_TX
(all,i,SPLT_COMM)(all,r,REG)

```
VXW(i,r)*tx(i,r)=sum(k,SSECT_COMM:MPSP_COMM(k)=i,    VXWK(k,r)    *
txk(k,r));
! Aggregating txs from HS6 level!

Equation E_TXS
(all,i,SPLT_COMM)(all,r,REG)(all,s,REG)
VXWD(i,r,s)*txs(i,r,s)=
sum{k,SSECT_COMM:MPSP_COMM(k)=i, VXWDK(k,r,s) * txsk(k,r,s)};
```

The standard GTAP model, PE model and PE-GE model have differences in closures. This is because of the construct of these models. Box 3 below provides a summary of comparisons of all these three closures. The simple PE closure assumes the total output and consumption at the aggregated sector level are exogenous and have no link with the GE model. By fixing these variables exogenously, Narayanan et al. (2010) draws a sharp distinction between the PE and PE/GE models. All variables at the aggregate level pertaining to the sectors other than the one being disaggregated, which is autos in this case, are also exogenized. All technical change variables at the aggregate level and tax/tariff change variables and import- augmenting technical change at disaggregate level are exogenous and fixed in this PE closure. A salient feature of this framework is that the welfare decomposition is extended to the disaggregated levels, so one can trace the welfare effects to changes at such levels.

General Equilibrium For Disaggregated Sectors

Section 2 discussed about a framework that could be employed when a modeler is merely interested in trade and tariff policies for disaggregate sectors. However, in many instances, one may be interested in other aspects of CGE modeling as well. For example, one may be concerned with domestic policies or input-output framework at the disaggregated levels. In such cases, the only way is to disaggregate the sectors in the database used for the modelling. Several alternative types of assumptions may be required herein, since the complete input-output dataset with all taxes and other data at disaggregate levels is seldom available.

Splitcom is a tool developed by Mark Horridge, to disaggregate sectors in GTAP Data Base. When one uses this tool, one can probably just feed in the readily available trade and tariff data from TASTE and then allow the rest of the dataset to be equally distributed across the disaggregated sectors. A more careful modeler would introduce disaggregated production, consumption and input-output data in conjunction with this tool, but realistically, one can collect data on production and trade and infer consumption as a residual and then assume an input-output structure based on practicalities. For example, Narayanan and Khorana (2011) assume that cotton textiles split out from textiles sector consumes all cotton split out from plant-based fibers sector and none of the other plant-based fibers; vice-versa is assumed for non-cotton textiles. They have a similar set of assumptions to define the input-output structure of coffee production and raw coffee sectors, which are split from other food products and other crops, respectively, among the GTAP sectors.

BOX 3. CLOSURES USED IN DIFFERENT MODELS

PE Model	GE Model	PE-GE Model
Exogenous: Changes in total output and demand in all sectors and regions. Changes in all price, tax and quantity variables for non- Auto sectors at *i* level. Changes in import tax and import-augmented technical-change (amsk) variables at *k-level.* Slack variable for tradeables market-clearing at *k-level.* **Endogenous:** All other price, tax and quantity changes and slack variables.	**Exogenous:** Changes in endowment output, world price index for primary factors, distribution parameters for savings, government and private consumption and population. Slack variables for consumer goods, endowments, income, profits, savings price and tradeables' market clearing; All technical and tax change variables. **Endogenous:** All other price and quantity changes and slack variables.	**Exogenous:** Changes in endowment output, world price index for primary factors, distribution parameters for savings, government and private consumption and population. Slack variables for consumer goods, endowments, income, profits, savings price and tradeables' market clearing; Slack variables for different prices, quantities and welfare-count-variables are exogenous for non-Auto sectors. All technical and tax change variables at *i* level, except export/import tariffs and *ams* at aggregated level, that are exogenous for other aggregated sectors. **Endogenous:** All other price, tax, technical and quantity changes and slack variables.

One may also employ econometric tools to estimate the input-output structure at the disaggregated levels, as outlined in Peterson (2008). For this, one needs complete input-output tables for a set of countries, whose coefficients may be regressed against economic variables such as production and GDP, and then those for the countries that need disaggregation may be estimated using these equations.

Another alternative is to merely impose the shares from an available input-output table that has all the disaggregate sectors, on the aggregate sector in question, to split the latter into disaggregated sectors. This may be done by employing entropy theoretic methods to hit the target shares and matrix rebalancing techniques to ensure that the input-output tables are balanced after any such adjustment. Such methods are outlined in Narayanan and Walmsley (2008) and Narayanan et al. (2012).

DISAGGREGATING FACTORS IN CGE MODELS

Typically, in large CGE models, there are four or five factors: land, labor (skilled/unskilled), capital and natural resources. However, policy-makers would be interested in many more factors, for several reasons. Agricultural policy-makers, for example, may gain a lot of insight when the land is divided into several Agro-Ecological Zones (AEZ), with the possibility of shifting production from one type to another. Even development economists may find such a proposition useful, since this helps trace the roots of inequality, distribution, etc. In the GTAP framework, this has been dealt with in detail.

Labor economists are not usually satisfied with one or two categories in labor as a factor. There have been many CGE models developed at country-levels, with several labor categories, but as a first attempt in multi-country CGE, Tsigas and Wintergarten (2010) develop a methodology to include five labor categories; Mirza et al. (2010) illustrate the usefulness for such detail in labor, by showing that the US labor market effects of Chinese expansion differed across these categories. Similarly, capital may be divided into domestic and foreign capital categories, for example, to analyze FDI policies.

AEZs and labor types offer relatively simplistic examples of factor disaggregation. However, we may come across more difficult policy questions for research. For example, Narayanan and Walmsley (2011) examine the issue of labor standards, taking child labor as an example. In order to allow for differential treatment of commodities produced using child labor, mere fragmentation of labor types to allow for child labor as a separate factor is not enough; commodities need to be split into two sets: one that uses child labor for production and another that does not. This is done at all levels of nests in the GTAP model.

Linking Global CGE with "Sub-Regional" Models

While global CGE models have become popular in the past couple of decades owing to the importance of global policy and environmental issues, regional, national and local CGE models are also widely used by the domestic policy-makers. Global reach of economic issues has now gained so much importance that even local policies can have global consequences and vice versa. For example, increased textile trade in a country resulting from a free trade agreement may affect the states/districts that produce a lot of exported textiles, thus having implications for the local policies affecting logistics, transportation, infrastructure, etc.

Thus, linking of global CGE models like GTAP with local CGE or PE models is an important aspect of spatial disaggregation in global CGE modelling. Horridge has developed The Enormous Regional Model (TERM) to facilitate such detailed modelling. One major hurdle for such models is the lack of data. TERM framework helps the users assume shares in the sub-regions, based on stylised facts and national datasets. When real data is available, it can be readily used herein.

Multi-Country CGE Models with Multiple Households

One major problem in CGE models is the absence of details on the types of households as well as the disaggregation of governmental undertaking sectors and income transfers. MYGTAP is a new framework that has been developed by Minor and Walmsley (2013) to address this issue. Using this framework, one can disaggregate the households into several categories and assume behavioral parameters to account for interactions between such categories. Governmental transfers to poor households is an example policy issue for which we need such disaggregated household types, coupled with detailed treatment of government's utility function. These features are essential to analyse policies in developing countries in particular.

CONCLUSION

Flair for disaggregation is dominant in all walks of research today. It is indeed essential to pay attention to details in CGE-based policy analysis exercises. However, a lot of thought needs to go into the choice of methodological frameworks. If one is interested merely in the trade policies for detailed sectors and not their input-output linkages or domestic policies, the framework outlined in section 2 is recommended; otherwise, one should employ the tools briefed in section 3. For disaggregating factors, one may refer to section 4; further, to choose between straightforward splitting of factors alone and a much more detailed treatment of factors as well as their use in different split sectors, policies in question should be deeply examined for suitability with either assumptions. Global-local models may be developed using tools listed in section 5, while detailed institutions and households may be modeled using the ideas outlined in section 6.

A major challenge arising from disaggregation of any sort is the complexity involved in deciphering the results of models. Britz et al. (2012) discusses this aspect in a few major CGE models and suggests machine learning tools to help the modelers understand such complex model results. In fact, the enormous volume of results is another motivation to be choosy with the kind of framework needed. While it is always tempting to integrate all types of details in a single model, practicalities should determine the priorities among competing as well as complementary model features.

On the other hand, the results may be sensitive to the aggregation of any part of the model, discussed in previous sections, which is a reasonable motivation to have an all-encompassing model. As several papers discussed in this chapter show, even the aggregate results are sensitive to whether or not we do the disaggregation in different parts of the model. Therefore, an alternative way of dealing with this dilemma is to suppress the details as needed while analysing the results.

REFERENCES

Anderson, J. E. (2008). "Consistent Trade Policy Aggregation". *National Bureau of Economic Research*, Working Paper No: 14046, accessible at http://www.nber.org/papers/w14046.pdf.

Anderson, J. E. & Neary, J. P. (2003). "The Mercantilist Index of Trade Policy". *International Economic Review*, *44*(2), 627-49.

Anderson, J. E. & Neary, J. P. (1996). "A New Approach to Evaluating Trade Policy". *Review of Economic Studies*, *63*(1), 107-25.

Anderson, J. E. & van Wincoop, E. (2004). "Trade Costs". *Journal of Economic Literature*, *42*(3), 691-751.

Anderson, J. E. (1998). "Trade Restrictiveness Benchmarks". *The Economic Journal, 108*(449), 1111- 25.

Arndt, C. & Pearson, K. R. (1998). "How to Carry Out Systematic Sensitivity Analysis via Gaussian Quadrature and GEMPACK". GTAP Technical Paper No. 3, Center for Global Trade Analysis, Purdue University, West Lafayette.

Arndt, C., Robinson, S. & Tarp, F. (2002). "Parameter Estimation for a Computable General Equilibrium Model: A Maximum Entropy Approach". *Economic Modelling, 19*(3), 375-98.

Bach, C. F. & Martin, W. (2001). "Would the right tariff aggregator for policy analysis please stand up?". *Journal of Policy Modelling, 23*(6), 621-35.

Basevi, G. (1968). "The Restrictive Effect of the US Tariff and its Welfare Value". *The American EconomicReview, 58*(4), 840-52.

Basevi, G. (1966). "The United States Tariff Structure: Estimates of Effective Rates of Protection of United States Industries of United States Industries and Industrial Labor". *The Review of Economics and Statistics, 48*(2), 147-60.

Batra, A. (2006). "Asian Economic Integration". Working Paper No: 186, Indian Council for Research on International Economic Relations, New Delhi.

Beghin, J. C. & Kherallah, M. (1994). "Political Institutions and International Patterns of Agricultural Protection". *The Review of Economics and Statisitics, 76*(3), 482-9.

Beghin, J. C. & Fang, C. (2002). "Protection and Trade Liberalization under Incomplete Market Integration". *American Journal of Agricultural Economics, 84*(3), 768-73.

Bhattarai, K. & Whalley, J. (1999). "The Role of Labour Demand Elasticities in Tax Incidence Analysis with Heterogeneous Labour". *Empirical Economics, 24*(4), 599-619.

Boussard, J., Gerard, F., Piketty, M. G., Ayouz, M. & Voituriez, T. (2006). "Endogenous Risk and Long Run Effects of Liberalization in a Global Analysis Framework". *Economic Modelling, 23*(3), 457-75.

Bouët, A., Decreux, Y., Fontagne, L., Jean, S. & Laborde, D. (2004). "The MacMap-HS6 Database: A Consistent Picture of Applied Protection Across the World". Working Paper 2004-22, Centre d'Etudes Prospectives et d'Informations Internationals CEPII, Paris.

Chadha, R. (2005). *Sectoral Study of Automobiles.* Report by National Council for Applied Economic Research and Tariff Commission, Government of India, New Delhi.

Dimaranan, B. V., ed. (2006). *Global Trade, Assistance, and Production: The GTAP 6 Data Base.* Center for Global Trade Analysis, Purdue University, West Lafayette.

Dixon, P. B. & Rimmer, M. T. (2004). "The US Economy from 1992 to 1998: Results from a Detailed CGE Model". *The Economic Record,* 80 (Special Issue): S13-S23.

Evans, D., Gasiorek, M. & Robinson, S. (2007). "A Comparative Analysis of Shallow and Deep Integration of China and India into the Global Economy: A Research Agenda and First Application of the Disaggregated TAPES Partial Equilibrium Model to China". Paper presented at Tenth Annual Conference on Global Economic Analysis, Center for Global Trade Analysis, Purdue University, West Lafayette, June 7-9.

Francois, J., Van Meijl, H. & Van Tongeren, F. (2005). "Trade Liberalization in the Doha Development Round", *Economic Policy,* April, 349-391.

Gaston, N. & Trefler, D. (1997). "The Labour Market Consequences of the Canada-U.S. Free Trade Agreement". *The Canadian Journal of Economics, 30*(1), 18-41.

__. (1994). "Trade and Wages: Evidence from U.S. Manufacturing". *Industrial and Labor Relations Review, 47*(4), 574-93.

Gohin, A. (2005). "The Specification of Price and Income Elasticities in Computable Genral Equilibrium Models: An Application of Latent Separability", *Economic Modelling, 22* (5), 205-25.

Goldberg, P. K. (1995). "Product Differentiation and Oligopoly in International Markets: The Case of the U.S. Automobile Industry". *Econometrica, 63*(4), 891-951.

Grant, J., Hertel, T. W. & Rutherford, T. (2007). "Extending General Equilibrium to the Tariff Line: US Dairy in the Doha Development Agenda." Paper presented at Tenth Annual Conference on Global Economic Analysis, Center for Global Trade Analysis, Purdue University, West Lafayette, June 7-9.

Han, S. & Woodland, A. D. (2003). "An Inter-temporal General Equilibrium Econometric Model for a Small Open Economy with Application to Australia", *The Economic Record, 79*(244), 1-19.

Herault, N. (2007). "Trade Liberalisation, Poverty and Inequality in South Africa: A Computable General Equilibrium-Microsimulation Analysis", *The Economic Record, 83*(262), 317-28.

Hertel, T. W. (ed.) (1997). *Global Trade Analysis: Modeling and Applications.* Cambridge University Press.

Hertel, T. W., Hummels., D., Ivanic, M. & Keeny, R. (2007a). "How Confident Can We be of CGE- based Assessments of Free Trade Agreements?" *Economic Modelling, 24*(4), 611-635.

Hertel, T. W., Keeny, R., Ivanic, M. & Winters, A. (2007b). "Why is'nt the Doha Development Agenda More Poverty Friendly?" GTAP Working Paper No: 37. Center for Global Trade Analysis, Purdue University, West Lafayette.

Hillberry, R. H. (2002). "Aggregation Bias, Compositional Change and the Border Effect," *The Canadian Journal of Economics, 35*(3), 517-30.

Horridge, J. M. (2005). "Splitcom: Programs to disaggregate a GTAP Sector". Center for Policy Studies, Monash University, Melbourne, Australia. November. Available online at https://www.gtap.agecon.purdue.edu/resources/splitcom.asp

Horridge, J. M. & Laborde, D. (2008). "Tariff Analytical and Simulation Tool for Economists: TASTE", *mimeo.*

Huff, K. & Hertel, T. W. (2001). "Decomposing Welfare Changes in GTAP." GTAP Technical Paper No: 05. Center for Global Trade Analysis, Purdue University, West Lafayette.

ICRA. (2003). *Report on the Competitiveness of Indian Auto Industry*, Society of Indian Automobile Manufacturers, Automotive Component Manufacturers Association of India (ACMA) and Investment Information and Credit Rating Agency of India (ICRA), New Delhi.

ICRA. (2004a). *The Thailand & ASEAN India Free Trade Agreement: Implications for the Indian Auto Industry*, Automotive Component Manufacturers Association of India (ACMA) and Investment Information and Credit Rating Agency of India (ICRA), New Delhi.

ICRA. (2004b). *The MERCOSUR-India Preferential Trade Agreements -- Implications for the Indian Automotive Industry*, Automotive Component Manufacturers Association of India (ACMA) and Investment Information and Credit Rating Agency of India (ICRA), New Delhi.

ICRA. (2005). *Implications of an FTA with South Africa for the Indian Auto Industry*, Automotive Component Manufacturers Association of India (ACMA) and Investment Information and Credit Rating Agency of India (ICRA), New Delhi.

Iyer, H. (2004). "The Bangkok Agreement: Prospects of Trade Expansion in Asia-Pacific Region" in UNESCAP, ed., *Bulletin on Asia-Pacific Perspectives: 2003-04*. United Nations Economic and Social Commission for Asia and the Pacific, Bangkok, 55-68.

Jensen, H. G. & Sandrey, R. (2006). "A Possible SACU/China Free Trade Agreement: Implications for the South African Manufacturing Sector". Working Paper No. 8/2006, Trade Law Centre for Southern Africa TRALAC, Stellenbosch.

Kawai, M. & Wignaraja, G. (2007). "ASEAN+3 or ASEAN+6: Which Way Forward?". Discussion Paper No: 77, Asian Development Bank Institute, Tokyo.

Kokoski, M. F. & Smith, V. K. (1987). "A General Equilibrium Analysis of Partial-Equilibrium Welfare Measures: The Case of Climate Change". *The American Economic Review*, *77*(3), 331-41.

Kumar, A. G. & Saini, G. K. (2007). "Economic Co-operation in South Asia: The Dilemma of SAFTA and Beyond". Working Paper No: 2007-017, Indira Gandhi Institute of Development Research, Mumbai.

Lloyd, P. J. & Maclaren, D. (2004). "Gains and Losses from Regional Trade Agreements: A Survey", *The Economic Record*, *88*(251), 445-67.

Lai, H. & Zhu, S. C. (2004). "The Determinants of Bilateral Trade", *The Canadian Journal of Economics*, *37*(2), 459-83.

Madsen, B. & Jensen-Butler, C. (2004). "Thoeretical and Operational Issues in Sub-regional Economic Modelling, Ilustrated Through the Development and Application of the LINE Model", *Economic Modelling*, *21*(3), 471-508.

Malcolm, G. (1998). "Adjusting Tax Rates in the GTAP Data Base". GTAP Technical Paper No:12, Center for Global Trade Analysis, Purdue University, West Lafayette.

Malakellis, M. (1998). "Should Tariff Reductions be Announced? An Intertemporal Computable General Equilibrium Analysis", *The Economic Record*, *74*(225), 121-38.

McDougall, R. M. (2002). "A New Regional Household Demand System for GTAP". GTAP Technical Paper No: 20, Center for Global Trade Analysis, Purdue University, West Lafayette.

McKitrick, R. R. (1998). "The Econometric Critique of CGE Modeling: the Role of Functional Forms", *Economic Modelling*, *15*(4), 543-73.

McKinsey. (2005). *Vision 2015 for the Indian Automotive Components Industry*, Automotive Component Manufacturers Association of India (ACMA) and McKinsey and Company, New Delhi.

Ministry of Heavy Industries and Public Enterprises. (2006). *Automotive Mission Plan 2006-2016: A Mission for Development of Indian Automotive Industry*, New Delhi.

Narayanan, B. G. & Vashisht, P. (2008). "Determinants of Competitiveness of Indian Auto Industry". Working Paper No: 201, Indian Council for Research on International Economic Relations, New Delhi.

Olarreaga, M. & Soloaga, I. (1998). "Endogenous Tariff Formation: The Case of Mercosur". *The World Bank Economic Review*, *12*(2), 297-320.

Pearson, K. R. & Horridge, J. M. (2005). "Hands-on Computing with RunGTAP and WINGEM to Introduce GTAP and GEMPACK". GTAP Resource No: 2692. Center for Global Trade Analysis, Purdue University. West Lafayette.

Pearson, K. R., Hertel, T. W. & Horridge, J. M. (2005). "AnalyseGE: Software Assisting Modellers in the Analysis of Their Results". Center for Policy Studies, Monash University, Melbourne.

Pomfret, R. (1985). "Categorical Agregation and International Trade: A Comment". *The Economic Journal*, *95*(378), 483-5.

Ramos, M. P., Bureau, J. & Salvatici, L. (2007). "Shipping the Good Beef Out: EU Trade Liberalization to Mercosur Exports". Working Paper 07/17, The Agricultural Trade Agreements Project (TRADEAG).

Ray, E. J. (1987). "The Impact of Special Interests on Preferential Tariff Concessions by the United States". *The Review of Economics and Statistics*, *69*(2), 187-93.

Rutherford, T. F. & Paltsev, S. V. (2000). "GTAPinGAMS and GTAP-EG: Global Datasets for Economic Research and Illustrative Models", Department of Economics, University of Colorado, September, available at http://www.mpsge.org/papers/gtaptext.pdf.

Trefler, D. "Trade Liberalization and the Theory of Endogenous Protection: An Econometric Study of U.S. Import Policy". *The Journal of Political Economy*, *101*(1), 138-60.

Tyers, R. & Yang, Y. (2004). "The Asian Recession and Northern Labour Markets", *The Economic Record*, *80*(248), 58-75.

USITC. (2009). "The Economic Effects of Significant U.S. Import Restraints". Publication No: 4094. Investigation No: 332-325. United States International Trade Commission, Washington D.C. August, Available online at http://www.usitc.gov/publications/332/ pub4094.pdf

Weerahawa, J. & Meilke, K. (2007). "Indo-China Relationships: Implications for the South Asian Economies". Paper presented at the Symposium of IATRC (International Agricultural Trade Research Consortium), Beijing, July 8-10.

Welsch, H. (2006). "Armington Elasticities and Induced Intra-industry Specialization: The Case of France, 1970-1997". *Economic Modelling*, *23*(3), 556-67.

Willenbockel, D. (2004). "Specification Choice and Robustness in CGE Trade Policy Analysis with Imperfect Competition", *Economic Modelling*, *21*(6), 1065-99.

Winston, A. P. (2009). "Enhancing Agriculture and Energy Sector Analysis in CGE Modelling: An Overview of Modifications to the USAGE Model". General Paper No: G-180. Center for Policy Studies, Monash University, Melbourne, Australia. January. Available online at http://www. monash.edu.au/policy/ftp/workpapr/g-180.pdf

World Bank. (2006). "World Development Indicators". World Bank, Washington D.C.

Young, L. and S.P. Magee. 1986. "Endogenous Protection, Factor Returns and Resource Allocation", *The Review of Economic Studies*, *53*(3), 407-19.

In: Current Issues in International Trade
Editor: Gouranga G. Das
ISBN: 978-1-63321-405-7

Chapter 13

CGE METHODOLOGY AND TRADE-TECHNOLOGY NEXUS REDUX: ILLUSTRATIONS AND SYNTHESIS FOR MODELLING AND POLICY ANALYSIS

Gouranga G. Das*

Department of Economics, Hanyang University Erica Campus,
Kyunggi-Do, South Korea

"...our interests are to a considerable extent explorative in a more intrinsic sense; the motive of action is in part curiosity as to what the result will be, and hence depends on partial ignorance of the result when the action is performed."

-Frank Knight, What is Truth in Economics? Journal of Political Economy, 1940, Vol. XLVIII.

"Reducing barriers to trade is not enough to fulfill the development promise of Doha. Trade must be part of a larger development strategy for each country, a strategy that includes attention to macroeconomic policy, infrastructure, education, and health as well as to accountable and responsible governance. These elements of investment climate take time to develop but are essential for growth and poverty reduction and are crucial to make a sound strategy pay its growth and poverty reduction dividends."

—Nicholas Stern, Chief Economist and Former Senior Vice President, World Bank, Global Economic Prospects-Realizing the Development Promise of Doha Agenda: 2004.

* With the usual disclaimer, I acknowledge that I have benefited from interactions with Professors Peter Dixon, Ken Pearson from the Victoria University, Melbourne, USA and Professor Alan Powell, Monash University, Australia. Substantially significant discussion in this chapter is entirely new except the reproduction of few selected tables and one figure based on my earlier journal publication (Das 2001 and 2002a). This chapter has made use of few tables and diagrams (*redux*) as and when necessary.

ABSTRACT

Choice of appropriate methodological framework, like CGE, theoretical or econometric analysis, depends on the issue or theme that modellers research. Giving illustrations from the trade-endogenous growth literature, the chapter presents a semi-endogenous growth model and its implementation in a computable general equilibrium GTAP model of trade. After reviewing general features of two CGE models, it illustrates an implementation to argue that the partial treatment of technology diffusion achieves the desired objective of mechanics behind trade-led technology flows. It offers a relatively big picture of trade-induced learning, and growth, contingent on absorption capacity and structural congruence. The model has room for improvement. However, the framework offers simple operational feasibility, but not at the cost of losing the inherent dynamics.

Keywords: CGE, absorption, ORANI, GTAP, intra-industry trade, Technology, Capture, Closure.

1. INTRODUCTION AND OVERVIEW

As the first pithy remark unfolding the chapter signifies, research, in general, is exploratory by nature and hence, methodological appropriateness is important for investigation of the issues in hand. Driven by the research question, researchers harp on a framework to analyse the conjectures. Given no single and unique predominance of a framework, the one that suits the purpose is adopted. The second quote relates to the general theme of the book (i.e., trade-development issues) and its broader implications. In particular, the second one implies that trade strategy should be integrated with the growth-development strategy as both internal and external factors are crucial for economic performance.

This chapter's intention is to demonstrate the application of a particular genre of models for carrying out policy analysis pertaining to a particular research theme.[1] Subsequently, the article presents a semi-endogenous growth and development model based on applied general equilibrium (AGE/CGE) framework to show its application to address trade-growth-development nexus via trade-induced learning. In this context, I must mention that we find a continuous tussle between the choice of methodological framework and the theme or, the research question. As Sen (p. 617, 2008) has argued, based on works by Arrow, Hicks, Keynes, Morishima, and others, "[one] priority is that of 'separation' with a focus on segregating distinct questions sharply, and then analysing them separately. A very different priority is that of integration which looks particularly for interrelations between distinct issues.... ...The discipline, however, needs both." Thus, despite the drive for analytical convenience it is necessary to balance the macro 'big' picture as well as the micro or distinct factors capturing the partial picture. Complete understanding of the complex reality requires— as Sen has argued along the style of Morishima—investigation of 'significantly identified partial pictures' as a basis of integrative broader framework. Issue of trade at the firm or, regional or national level is at best partial unless macro synergy is recognized. I discuss such aspect with the help of illustrations from the literature on trade, growth, technology linkages. I have shown that: general equilibrium models with microfoundations

[1] That does *not* mean that this is the *only one* in hand. As there is profusion of literature, there could be plenty.

purport to capture that aspect. The reason for taking that theme is: although trade in goods and services are dealt essentially at the micro level, issue of economic development and growth linked to this micro details needs to be seen at the macro level in a larger framework and wider context. Hence, referring to the second quote opening this chapter, trade-development aspect needs to be viewed widely as a component of the broader strategy and public policy. As traditional and modern trade theory involves impacts on goods market, labor market, and other factors with implications for sectoral, industrial as well as macroeconomic phenomena, this article focuses on methodology of applied general equilibrium (AGE) or computable general equilibrium (CGE) framework. However, for parsimony I consider one prototypical model and describe its general treatment of production and investment (for the purpose in hand). The issues such as migration, capital flows, foreign direct investment, land-use changes, and climate change could be handled in such framework (among others). In keeping with the gradual shifting of paradigm in the area of trade theory and empirics, here I choose one aspect of trade and economic growth for illustrating in a leading global trade model, by altering the extant structure.[2] In particular, I present an illustrative example of operationalizing trade-mediated technology diffusion in an extended global trade model.

2. THE THEME AND THE CONTEXT

Trade and Growth Interconnections

The commission on growth and development, appointed for by the World Bank and led by Robert Solow and Michael Spence along with expert commissioners from developing economies, submitted the Spence Commission Report (May, 2008) on the 'growth strategies for sustained growth and development'. Drawing on the idiosyncratic regional growth experiences and the historical trajectories of development episodes and associated contributing factors, the report highlights, *inter alia*, the importance of pursuing context- and case-specific policies such as those related to trade and industry development, environment, education, knowledge creation, technological improvement, inequality, etc; in particular, it emphasizes the preponderant role of engagement in the global economy as well as extending the knowledge frontier via investment in human capital, institutional quality, R&D and learning. Quantitative evidence shows an upsurge in global trade, especially in new manufactured products intensive in technology. Growth of Intra-industry trade in manufactures among the developed nations, between the North and the South, as well as among rapidly industrialising dynamic developing nations, shows the relevance of product cycle theory of trade and technology-based dynamic comparative advantage. The index of such trade (IIT) in manufactures is given by the Grubel-Lloyd index (1975) [GL(U)]:

[2] This illustration is simple and more complex issues could be mounted with substantial alterations. That is beyond the scope of a single-volume and hence, is not elaborated here. One could see Hertel (1997) and www.gtap.agecon.purdue.edu for more resources.

$$GL(U) = 1 - \sum_{i=1}^{n} \frac{|X_i - M_i|}{\sum_{i=1}^{n} X_i + M_i}$$

where

X_i = exports (in value terms) of product group i.
M_i = imports (in value terms) of product group i.

It gives the aggregate index over all commodities i = 1.... ... ... n, with minimum mathematical complexity (Greenaway 1983). Based on Das (2002a), we present the extent of such trade for developing nations.[3] The following table shows the cross-country evidences of such trade.[4]

Table 1. Country-Wise Aggregate Intra-Industry Trade Index (in Manufactures) with Different Country- Groups & Different Macro-Aggregates, 1990

Country Name	ID (IIT index with devld country	IG (IIT index with devlg. Country	IW IIT index with World	Total (X+M) in miln.$ Total export & import with World	PCGNP In U.S. Dollars	TCONC T(X+M)
Mexico	0.49	0.57	0.53	54877.957	2490	0.2308
Singapore	0.5	0.79	0.73	113520.278	11160	3.2809
Sri Lanka	0.2	0.18	0.24	4526.072	470	0.6243
Indonesia	0.14	0.38	0.25	47512.386	570	0.4428
Yugoslovia	0.64	0.2	0.7	33306.192	3060	0.4046
Korea Republic	0.48	0.43	0.53	134859.408	5400	0.5705
Tunisia	0.26	0.37	0.31	8974.433	1440	0.81
Turkey	0.25	0.6	0.38	35260.088	1630	0.3654
Chile	0.09	0.29	0.16	15544.33	1940	0.5593
Cyprus	0.11	0.38	0.18	26236.106	8020	4.7702
India	0.4	0.38	0.43	41657.974	350	0.1637
Thailand	0.37	0.54	0.45	56375.383	1420	0.7032
Portugal	0.47	0.09	0.5	41826.55	4900	0.7361
Colombia	0.2	0.38	0.26	12353.578	1260	0.3004
Hongkong	0.4	0.36	0.51	111499.647	11490	1.8686
Israel	0.73	0.38	0.64	27376.384	10920	0.5146
Venezuela	0.3	0.52	0.41	23583.569	2560	0.4886
Argentina	0.41	0.55	0.58	16428.193	2370	0.1762
China	0.29	0.67	0.57	115436.543	370	0.3164
Ecuador	0.07	0.14	0.06	4518.257	980	0.4153

[3] The discussion is based on Das (2002a) and I reproduce Table 1
[4] Based on Das (2002a), Table 5.

Country Name	ID (IIT index with devld country	IG (IIT index with devlg. Country	IW IIT index with World	Total (X+M) in miln.$ Total export & import with World	PCGNP In U.S. Dollars	TCONC T(X+M)
Paraguay	0.44	0.16	0.2	2307.307	1110	0.4387
Greece	0.27	0.56	0.34	27787.821	5990	0.4799
Brazil	0.49	0.39	0.54	53871.983	2680	0.1301
Zimbzbwe	0.23	0.46	0.3	3322.439	640	0.6257
Philippines	0.26	0.34	0.36	21132.432	730	0.4818
Pakistan	0.08	0.15	0.09	12877.825	380	0.3628
Malaysia	0.5	0.72	0.6	58702.269	2320	1.3845
Mauritius	0.16	0.21	0.18	2916.717	2250	1.3956
Bangladesh	0.06	0.29	0.36	3774.835	210	0.165
Kenya	0.06	0.55	0.82	3156.348	370	0.4186

Source:

(a) World Development Report, 1992, Table-3 : Structure of Production Handbook of International Trade & Development Statistics, UNCTAD; Table-6.1 : Basic Indicators

(b) World Debt Tables, Vol.2 (Country Tables), 1992-93 & World Bank Publications.

(c) World Development Report, 1992.

Below, Tables 2 and 3 are based on a Global Trade Analysis Project (GTAP) database underlying a global trade CGE model (developed at Purdue University, USA. This is based on an Australian precursor ORANI model, using General equilibrium software GEMPACK developed at Monash University, Australia.

Table 1 depicts that for the developed countries such trade in manufactures are more with the developed and newly industrializing economies (NIEs), whereas for the less developed or the developing economies the trade is more with the countries at similar income levels. Per capita GNP is an indicator for income level or development status. In 1990s, as table 1 presents we see a change in trade patterns in dynamic emerging economies of East Asia. Table 2 updates the pattern for 2007-2008, and the recent picture shows the rise in intensity of such trade across both the developed and the developing world.

All these tables support the evidence for the emergence of non-traditional tradeable sector based on industrialization strategy, as part of trade policy pursued by the countries with different development spectrum. Quite clearly, we can observe differential accelerations of trade in heterogeneous manufactured goods among the developing countries. That is supported by the findings in Table 3 where revealed comparative advantage (RCA) in product categories across selected GTAP regions is calculated.[5] The RCA scores conform well with a priori expectations that industrialized countries like the U.S., Germany, France, Belgium, and others have higher registered values for such indices in electronic, high-tech manufactures, whereas the NIEs also score higher values in contrast to the relatively follower regions (laggards) like Bangladesh, Pakistan, Africa, and others.

---

[5] The reason for using GTAP database is that it's a trade model with comprehensive datasets for many regions and sectors and thus, for comprehensiveness and coherence it is more useful than utilizing diverse data sources. Of course, there are data from UNCTAD, WTO, or other sources, but GTAP is well-known for ready-to-use features.

Table 2. Grubel-Lloyd Intra-Industry Trade Indexes for Selected Regions and Sectors

GSC2 sectors with codes	GSC2 Regions and GTAP Codes	Australia	China	Hong Kong	Japan	Korea	Taiwan
27 tex	Textiles	0.35	0.84	0.74	0.99	0.45	0.23
28 wap	Wearing apparel	0.25	0.14	0.77	0.06	0.68	0.60
29 lea	Leather products	0.61	0.14	0.02	0.09	0.69	0.52
31 ppp	Paper products, publishing	0.48	0.67	0.66	0.73	0.98	0.68
32 p_c	Petroleum, coal products	0.69	0.84	0.00	0.22	0.87	0.61
33 crp	Chemical, rubber, plastic products	0.54	0.80	0.24	0.81	0.88	0.96
34 nmm	Mineral products nec	0.58	0.58	0.06	0.85	0.68	0.85
35 i_s	Ferrous metals	0.79	0.45	0.11	0.34	0.95	0.88
36 nfm	Metals nec	0.29	0.61	0.50	0.75	0.68	0.39
37 fmp	Metal products	0.50	0.39	0.31	0.83	0.58	0.36
38 mvh	Motor vehicles and parts	0.55	0.62	0.01	0.21	0.29	0.92
39 otn	Transport equipment nec	0.59	0.95	0.00	0.47	0.58	0.95
40 ele	Electronic equipment	0.23	0.87	0.23	0.75	0.70	0.71
41 ome	Machinery and equipment nec	0.43	0.91	0.37	0.53	0.96	0.94
42 omf	Manufactures nec	0.64	0.12	0.37	0.90	0.73	0.54

Source: Author's calculation using GTAP Database Version 6.

GSC2 sectors with codes	Malaysia	Singapore	Thailand	India	Sri Lanka	Canada	USA	Mexico	Argentina	Brazil	Belgium
27 tex	0.84	0.75	0.66	0.24	0.67	0.72	0.58	0.94	0.64	0.93	0.89
28 wap	0.34	0.66	0.08	0.03	0.09	0.65	0.18	0.48	0.64	0.93	0.79
29 lea	0.87	0.75	0.30	0.24	0.31	0.25	0.16	0.82	0.46	0.22	0.98
31 ppp	0.61	0.95	0.97	0.48	0.23	0.55	0.91	0.41	0.58	0.58	0.85
32 p_c	0.93	0.63	0.12	0.89	0.08	0.76	0.63	0.31	0.09	0.70	0.84
33 crp	0.92	0.90	0.99	0.96	0.68	0.87	0.98	0.54	0.69	0.54	0.99
34nmm	0.89	0.77	0.73	0.93	0.65	0.79	0.82	0.99	0.72	0.95	0.92
35 i_s	0.49	0.42	0.40	0.96	0.07	0.83	0.60	0.71	0.66	0.35	0.80
36 nfm	0.58	0.61	0.33	0.34	0.14	0.62	0.64	0.75	0.83	0.73	0.97
37 fmp	0.89	0.60	0.88	0.46	0.30	0.86	0.76	0.79	0.50	0.94	0.91
38 mvh	0.64	0.32	0.90	0.87	0.07	0.90	0.54	0.79	0.98	0.90	0.96
39 otn	0.61	0.48	0.50	0.62	0.40	0.81	0.83	0.71	0.85	0.95	0.73
40 ele	0.57	0.96	0.80	0.43	0.45	0.78	0.79	0.83	0.09	0.53	0.84
41 ome	0.75	0.77	0.96	0.66	0.34	0.83	0.91	0.85	0.53	0.55	0.91
42 omf	0.51	0.78	0.65	0.76	0.84	0.71	0.41	0.99	0.34	0.99	0.99

GSC2 sectors with codes	Netherlands	Sweden	Switzerland	Botswana	South Africa	Denmark	Finland	France	Germany	UK
27 tex	0.67	0.64	0.86	0.86	0.81	0.88	0.64	0.85	0.88	0.64
28 wap	0.16	0.39	0.27	0.73	0.94	0.68	0.56	0.60	0.54	0.40
29 lea	0.15	0.41	0.39	0.44	0.84	0.61	0.51	0.73	0.50	0.44
31 ppp	0.83	0.32	0.78	0.13	0.84	0.72	0.15	0.89	0.96	0.75
32 p_c	0.69	0.78	0.02	0.03	0.09	0.85	0.82	0.76	0.42	0.95
33 crp	0.87	0.91	0.79	0.31	0.87	0.87	0.85	0.90	0.80	0.95
34 nmm	0.69	0.94	0.72	0.02	0.81	0.76	0.74	0.98	0.91	0.93
35 i_s	0.99	0.73	0.73	0.16	0.24	0.62	0.73	0.94	0.92	0.97
36 nfm	0.95	0.99	0.93	0.16	0.19	0.76	0.78	0.81	0.99	0.80
37 fmp	0.93	0.86	0.94	0.07	0.74	0.90	0.98	0.87	0.89	0.82
38 mvh	0.64	0.74	0.32	0.43	0.87	0.61	0.74	0.85	0.58	0.71
39 otn	0.97	0.87	0.58	0.20	0.50	0.42	0.63	0.88	0.86	0.98
40 ele	0.70	0.86	0.68	0.10	0.35	0.75	0.71	0.93	0.90	0.97
41 ome	0.91	0.86	0.68	0.19	0.75	0.84	0.89	0.98	0.73	0.96
42 omf	0.61	0.76	0.87	0.04	0.56	0.81	0.63	0.89	0.91	0.96

Source: Author's calculation using GTAP Database Version 6 using Gempack software.

From these tables, it is evident that although such trade based on monopolistic competition, product diversification, and increasing returns to scale are much common between the developed nations, over the years the gradual rise of such trade shows export diversification of the less-developed countries (LDCs) adopting active trade-led industrialization strategies and consequently, moving up the ladder of product diversification. Das (2014) has documented the rise of Four Asian 'Tigers', viz., South Korea, Hong Kong, Taiwan and Singapore to establish themselves as the high performing Asian economies (HPAEs). This has been facilitated by export-promotion, import-substitution as well as domestic macroeconomic policies supporting gross domestic capital formation, human capital, and the rise in savings. Rise of the Southern Emerging Economies or Southern Engines of Growth, viz., BRICSAM (Brazil, Russia, India, China, South Africa, and Mexico) has enabled them to 'enrich' their export basket so that the share of 'low-quality' exports with inferior technology content has decreased, whereas quality-upgrading of exports with better technology embodiment has resulted in increased trade in differentiated products in manufactures from countries such as, South Korea, Taiwan, Hong Kong, Singapore. Recently joining the bandwagon are the BRICSAM countries.

Table 3. Revealed Comparative Advantage indexes for GTAP Sectors and Regions (%)

GSC2 Regions and GTAP Codes		1 aus	2 nzl	4 chn	5 hkg	6 jpn	7 kor	18 ind	19 lka	21 can	22 usa	23 mex	30 bra	38 bel	39 dnk	40 fin	41 fra	42 deu	43 gbr	47 lux	48 nld	51 swe	76 bwa
GSC2 Sector and codes																							
27 tex	Textiles	0.19	0.32	2.25	1.22	0.69	2.57	4.26	3.66	0.36	0.50	0.98	0.49	1.08	0.61	0.24	0.68	0.68	0.50	1.18	0.33	0.26	0.35
28 wap	Wearing apparel	0.13	0.34	4.27	2.98	0.05	0.79	3.89	15.60	0.26	0.25	1.71	0.17	0.52	0.58	0.24	0.49	0.39	0.32	0.26	0.09	0.17	0.29
29 lea	Leather products	0.40	0.90	6.55	0.10	0.05	0.94	2.11	1.98	0.07	0.17	0.30	3.00	0.79	0.27	0.15	0.62	0.29	0.29	0.14	0.07	0.12	0.17
30 lum	Wood products	0.62	2.38	1.85	0.02	0.06	0.11	0.34	0.14	3.66	0.53	1.32	1.89	0.67	1.70	2.79	0.62	0.74	0.27	0.67	0.12	2.24	0.12
31 ppp	Paper products, publishing	0.43	1.85	0.41	0.38	0.26	0.54	0.24	0.18	3.28	1.05	0.30	1.76	0.93	0.61	9.20	1.05	1.21	0.89	0.79	1.23	4.31	0.12
32 p_c	Petroleum, coal products	0.55	0.17	0.59	0.00	0.15	1.62	1.32	0.14	0.70	0.61	0.23	1.32	1.05	0.41	0.98	0.52	0.23	0.58	0.00	3.13	0.86	0.04
33 crp	Chemical, rubber, plastic products	0.45	0.81	0.63	0.09	0.89	0.96	1.03	0.55	0.78	1.08	0.43	0.63	1.84	1.00	0.63	1.45	1.31	1.27	1.16	1.60	1.02	0.12
34 nmm	Mineral products nec	0.55	0.23	1.41	0.04	0.95	0.52	1.01	0.75	0.69	0.97	0.87	1.19	1.33	0.59	0.72	1.18	1.22	0.90	1.71	0.47	0.79	0.02
35 i_s	Ferrous metals	0.86	0.41	0.39	0.05	1.54	1.53	1.17	0.04	0.58	0.38	0.51	2.35	1.79	0.43	1.94	1.27	1.15	0.71	7.64	1.01	1.79	0.06
36 nfm	Metals nec	5.80	1.54	0.40	0.35	0.58	0.66	0.49	0.07	1.73	0.58	0.41	1.47	0.93	0.26	0.96	0.62	0.92	1.00	1.67	0.74	0.67	2.05
37 fmp	Metal products	0.34	0.56	1.71	0.10	0.74	0.94	1.33	0.17	1.07	0.90	0.95	0.60	0.95	0.94	0.92	0.90	1.46	0.87	1.39	1.49	1.49	0.07
38 mvh	Motor vehicles and parts	0.45	0.08	0.09	0.00	2.29	1.10	0.13	0.01	2.35	0.86	2.06	1.02	1.53	0.18	0.30	1.41	2.30	0.82	0.27	0.46	1.34	0.20
39 otn	Transport equipment nec	0.41	0.22	0.53	0.00	1.22	1.75	0.30	0.20	1.48	2.01	0.21	1.83	0.26	0.30	1.26	2.29	1.22	1.36	0.33	0.47	0.44	0.04
40 ele	Electronic equipment	0.13	0.08	1.53	0.26	1.73	2.28	0.12	0.09	0.44	1.08	1.81	0.33	0.34	0.34	1.82	0.60	0.64	1.07	0.67	0.41	0.87	0.01
41 ome	Machinery and equipment nec	0.34	0.36	1.04	0.17	1.73	0.75	0.36	0.16	0.87	1.29	1.66	0.53	0.67	1.07	1.20	1.00	1.61	1.00	0.70	0.37	1.27	0.09
42 omf	Manufactures nec	0.45	0.54	4.25	0.40	0.70	0.55	4.60	2.08	0.36	0.63	0.48	0.4	2.67	0.35	0.19	0.62	0.49	1.28	0.21	0.86	0.26	29.01

Source: Author's calculation using GTAP Database Version 6 using Gempack simulation software.

Further, manufactured exports from the LDCs have expanded at a rate substantially faster than the world trade in manufactures. Some fast growing developing countries have made progress in upgrading the product composition of their manufactured exports (UNCTAD, Handbook of International Trade and Development Statistics, Various Issues). As per Das (2002a), "[among] the developing regions, South and South East Asian countries continue to be the major dynamic exporters of manufactures to the DCs. The strong orientation of exports of manufactures from the developing countries in South and South East Asia and Latin America is for the market of the U.S. The European Economic Community (EEC) has relied less than the U.S. and Japan on imports of manufactures from developing countries relative to other foreign sources of supply (excluding intra-EEC trade). Only South and South East Asia have, among the developing regions, gained significant importance as the sources of imports of manufactured products for the U.S., the EEC and Japan. Developing countries have been important outlets for manufactured products from the DCs." Also, the study shows that with economic development and more trade integration such trade in hi-technology intensive manufactures increases, and with further trade liberalization, scope of transfer of technology via intermediates increase.

Issues Unearthed from the Stylized Facts

Following Das (2002a), "[As] the process of economic growth and development proceeds, the composition of production and exports of these less-developed economies (LDCs) shift towards more diversified and technically sophisticated goods. Exports of labour-intensive consumer goods begin to decline. Consumer goods industries such as synthetic textiles and motor vehicles, and producer goods industries, producing either intermediate goods such as chemicals, steel and refined petroleum, or capital goods such as machinery and transport equipment--all these industries almost always involve large economies of scale, based either on the scale of the plant, or on the size of the production run. Different factors such as the minimum efficient size of plant, increasing returns to scale, and indivisibilities in the production process play an important role in manufacturing production in these countries."

With further progress towards a higher stage of growth and development, the developing countries can increasingly participate in such trade. For that to happen, much laggard poor countries need to adopt, adapt, and assimilate sophisticated technologies via skill and human capital formation. Such trade in sophisticated products with considerable product heterogeneity requires technology upgrading, learning, and assimilation. Trade-induced learning could come from learning-by-exporting, learning-by-importing, or both. According to Stiglitz (2003), "globalization can be a very powerful force for developing countries, enabling the technology gap and the knowledge gap that separates the developed from the less developed countries to be overcome." Nevertheless, he continues, "if that promises to be achieved, I do think that there will have to be fundamental reforms in the institutions and in the policies governing globalization in the world today." In particular, it has been emphasized that the success stories of East Asian miracle and the other newly industrializing nations owe much to the concerted efforts by the government directed towards 'closing the technology gap'. According to Pack and Westphal (1986, p.105), "effort is required in using technological information and accumulating technological knowledge...to create new technology. This takes the form of investments in.....effective use of knowledge."

Also, World Bank's World Development Report (1999) documents that

"even a follower country needs a labour force with a relatively high level of technical education, especially when technologies are changing rapidly" (see p.42, ibid.)

According to this report, three main tasks for closing 'knowledge gaps' between the technology creator and the recipient countries are [see p.25]:

(i) "Acquiring and adapting global knowledge—and creating knowledge locally
(ii) "Investing in human capital to increase the ability to absorb and use knowledge, and
(iii) "Investing in technologies to facilitate both the acquisition and the absorption of knowledge."

No doubt, these three tasks are complementary and 'mutually reinforcing' in nature in the sense that effective absorption of advanced technology acquired from the origin requires an educated, skilled work force. During this process of assimilation specialization pattern shifts to sophisticated goods with new vintage technology and hence, income level increases as these 'new vintage goods' are exported to countries with higher demand and high income level. Thus, trade opens the scope of implied or linked comparative advantage (Hausmann et al. 2014).

Now coming to the aspect of an operational point of view, all these above arguments suggest that it is important to incorporate these factors within any model of technology diffusion. So far as the issues of empirical measurement of knowledge flow are concerned, in the literature technology flows have been identified through intersectoral input-output transactions. This strand of empirical literature attempts to quantify technology spillover via the construction of technology flow matrices based on the R&D intensity of sectors. The models developed by Grossman and Helpman (1990, 1991), Young (1991), Jones (1995) have explored the possible interlinkages between invention, technology diffusion, learning, growth and productivity. Amongst those models of previous vintage, the ones developed by Eaton and his co-workers had also an empirical dimension. Eaton and Kortum (1996, 1999) modelled world growth where innovation was fully endogenous depending on the factors affecting R&D and diffusion. In another version of the *'semi-endogenous* 'model, technology creation is exogenously specified as opposed to the fully endogenous growth models.

All told, we see that the meaningful exploration of embodied technology transmission and its absorption can be suitably studied in a *general equilibrium framework*. For the illustrative purpose, therefore, this analysis draws heavily on the methodologically appealing applied general equilibrium (AGE or CGE, interchangeably) framework. By confining our discussion within the issue of technology transfer via hi-tech intermediates, we ascribe important role to the factors facilitating learning effects via technology absorption. In fact, in Section below I propose an analytical framework which belongs to the latter paradigm of models of new growth theory. On the theoretical plane, CGE-based multi-sectoral analysis involves formulating sectoral indexes of technological embodiment and incorporating the structural equation for technology transmission. Because technology perturbation is externally taken, the TFP growth in a sector of interest and the magnitude of the sector-specific TFP shock has to be taken from history (data). Experiments can focus on the followings: analysing the impact of the exogenous technological shock in the donor country (i) on itself; (ii) on the recipient sectors in the destinations; and (ii) the inter-sectoral differentials in the magnitude of assimilation of the transferred technology from the origin. Although discussions are limited to international trade —only one of the conduits for knowledge dissemination from developed to less developed countries—other candidates like the disembodied technology flows, foreign direct investment (including joint ventures), and geographical distance via gravity models are not researched. Keeping the focus static, neither have I taken stock of the dynamic aspects of technology diffusion. Thus, for investigative convenience, from methodological standpoint *a la* Sen (2008), the implications of embodied technology transfer is explored in a CGE framework *without* necessarily losing out much intellectually, by separating the technology creation aspect. As we will see, this partial treatment gives a *reasonably complete* understanding of the big picture of the issue in hand while keeping the treatment of endogeneity of technology aside. Before embarking on illustrative implementation, I present general features of such models for pedagogic purpose.

We need new analytical framework for capturing the features of empirical plus analytical methodology in the literature on trade and innovation. General Equilibrium theoretical model based on Jones (1965) can capture such effect theoretically. Typical features of such models are variable input-output coefficient, and price-average cost relationship at sectoral level (Das 2009). These offer qualitative effects *without* explicit numerical assessment of the policy shocks.

For policy implications, numerical calculations give precise directions of change due to exogenous perturbations in the economic systems. However, for numerical policy analysis CGE/AGE models are simulated for quantification via numbers. For instance, in order to analyse the effects of technological change modellers need to exogenize or endogenize the technical progress parameters in the production function. In order to model technology flows via trade and investment, we need to delineate a sensible mechanism of such transmissibility of technological knowledge, and its absorption for effective adoption. Thus, modelling the aspects of new trade theory with macroeconomic effects via innovation-led growth needs different modelling technique or, innovative approaches. We intend to provide illustrations of such mechanism in an augmented version of a popular CGE trade model (Das 2002a). As will be shown, the reproduction of results exemplifies a stylized model functioning. Before embarking on such mission, below we discuss the basics of such models with some commonality of structural presentation.

3. CGE Model and Its Prototypes: Synthesis of Two Typical Models

Brief Overview of General Features

General equilibrium (GE) models are the economy-wide models with *"endogenous" relative* prices. Standard assumption of optimising behaviour forms the basis of simulation of consumption and production decisions, and the model does not determine *absolute price* level, rather determines the price level relative to a '*numeraire*' as fixed up in the model. These comprise systems of simultaneous nonlinear equations (Dixon et al. 1992). Usually the equations are derived from the microfoundations of economic behaviors. The first order conditions are used as basic structural form equations of the model. They are usually static or comparative-static; although some dynamic general equilibrium models like the 'growth' models can be considered. Another genre of models is the disaggregated 'sectoral' models focusing on particular sectors and industries only. Theorists such as Debreu discussed the problems of existence, uniqueness and stability of solutions with analytical methods. As opposed to the general equilibrium models, the partial equilibrium models concentrates on one industry or, one product ignoring the interactions among the constituents of the system. In the GE- models price system acts as a signalling device to producers, consumers, and all economic agents. The agents respond to these signals in their pursuit of maximising welfare, which, in turn, maximises society's welfare led by an 'invisible hand'. The solution is a Paretoan Welfare Optimum. Fiction of a Walrasian 'auctioneer', as expounded by Leon Walras, is important for market-clearing to achieve an equilibrium solution of the system. The *'auctioneer'* calls out successive vectors of prices and quantities, and *'planned'* responses of the agents to this 'call' is observed until it yields 'true' equilibrium vectors where plan fulfilment of all the agents are achieved. This 'auctioneer' mechanism is indicative of an *'iterative' simulation or 'trial and error' process* of solving the sets of non-linear equations. In reality, this might imply quantity-signalling as the rule of the game in the absence of a flexible price system. The non-existence of an *"auctioneer"* often leads to *'coordination failure'* in the real world, and the intervention in the market system via *economic policy or planning* ensures avoidance of such 'failures'. They provide the services of such 'auctioneer'[68].

The *CGE-models*[69] are a bit different from them in the sense that they provide *numerical solutions* to the problem and thus, have an empirical basis. These are primarily based on computer-aided solutions. One line of research is based on the *Social Accounting Matrices(SAM)*. A software system called HERCULES was developed for facilitating the solution of this type of model. This software uses the GAMS system to provide a user-friendly interface for input and output. The second one is based on Johansen's (1960)[70] procedure of *linearizing* the non-linear equations for solving the general equilibrium models. Here, the non-linear models are converted to models in variables which are linear in rates of change of the variables. Australian CGE model ORANI is in this genre of models. This comparative-static model can be used to study the effects of policy changes on a disaggregated basis. This linearization increases the computational efficiency greatly.

The *Johansen type* models are solved in a *linearized* form where *variables are rate of growth* (as opposed to their levels presentation). *Five groups of equations* are broadly present: consumption, production, prices, market-clearing, and miscellaneous. The consumer and

[68] Vide Philpott, Bryan (1992) *General Equilibrium Modelling For Policy Analysis and Economic Planning*, Paper for International System on Forecasting, Research Project on Economic Planning Working Paper # 102, Victoria University of Wellington, August 1992.

[69] This is based on the chapters 3 and 1 of the book by *D.A. Kendrick, Models for analysing Comparative Advantage. Advanced studies in Theoretical and Applied Econometrics, Volume 18, Kluwer academic Publishers, 1990.*

[70] L. Johansen, A Multi-Sectoral Model of Growth, North-Holland , 1960.

producers behaviors are based on standard Neo-classical *optimizing behaviour* which give rise to *consumer demand* equations (for commodities) and *producer demand* equations (for factors). The price equations determine 'domestic' prices from the input-output relationships and from the world prices and exchange rates. The market-clearing equations ensure the equality between demand and supply in both the factor and the goods markets.

Consumption by agents are distributed on commodities differentiated by source viz., domestic and imported/foreign. There are consumption functions for each commodity and source. These are outcome of *two-stage optimisation* where at the top level it is assumed that there is no substitution possibility between the commodities *(fixed coefficient form)*. At the bottom level, there is substitution possibilities between the goods from different sources so that the utility derived from the consumption of each commodity type is a *multiplicative function* of the consumption of that commodity from different sources i.e., domestic and imported. But this utility enters at the top level in a fixed coefficient functional from so that there is no substitution between these different commodities, for example, say, between clothes and food. This results in a consumption function where the arguments are only the prices of domestic and imported commodity, not the prices of other commodities. The substitution between domestic and imported commodities depends on their *relative prices*. Consumption is constrained by the *budget* availability.

The *production functions* are based on the *two-tier* structure as well. These two aspects are: (a) the relationship between the *activity level* and *inputs* of each industry; (b) the relationship between the *activity level* and the *commodity output* in each industry. This allows *multi-product specification of each industry.*

The activity level is determined by a *Leontief fixed-coefficient* production function where a *Cobb-Douglas combination* of primary factor inputs to an industry is combined with a *Cobb-Douglas conjugate* of commodity from domestic and foreign sources. This allows no substitution possibilities between the factors and commodity inputs. There are possibilities of substitution between different factors and commodities from diverse sources. Having determined the activity level of an industry, the production levels are computed by doing a *standard optimisation exercise* where producers maximize value of output of a commodity by an industry *subject to an activity level* for that industry.

The price equations are basically ensuring *zero-profit condition* in production, and also relating domestic prices with international prices via the exchange rate. Market clears for factors as well as goods. *Labour* is mobile between sectors, while *capital* is usually not. Miscellaneous identities include: trade equation, wage equation, consumer price index, etc. derived to describe the macroeconomic environment properly[71]. In what follows, we discuss with parsimony the features of two leading CGE models—ORANI model for the Australian Government's policy making, and a well-known multi-regional, multi-sectoral trade model, namely, the Global Trade Analysis Project (GTAP) model developed at the Centre for Global trade analysis at Purdue University in conjunction with Monash University's Centre of Policy Studies (CoPS) software-suite General Equilibrium modelling Package (GEMPACK)—for their functioning features.

---

[71] All these discussions are based on chapter 4 of Kendrick (1990).

COMPARATIVE STATICS, CLOSURE AND INVESTMENT: AN EXPOSITORY DISCUSSION BASED ON ORANI AND GTAP

Nature of the Models

Prior to discussing the notions of saving and investment in the ORANI and GTAP-framework, it is important to consider the time-dimension of the model[72]. Selection of the length of run and the nature of analysis (static, dynamic, or comparative-static) determine the choice of "closure" for specifying a macro-environment for an experiment. These are comparative-static, GE-models where we compare the new equilibrium position of the economy with the old one after some changes in the system are introduced via the experiment-specific shocks. These are usually policy shocks in a policy-oriented study.

In particular, taking t=0 and t=T as two periods separated in time, we introduce shock(s) at t=0 and maintain them through till the 'snapshot' year t=T. We do not explicitly model the paths of adjustment or movements of these variables in the transition period although some relations between the value of some variables in the interim period and the equilibrium reached at the solution period can be envisaged. One or more sustained shocks are introduced at t=0 into the time-path(s) of one or more exogenous variables. Consequent upon this disturbance, the change of the endogenous variables in the new equilibrium state is considered without reference to the way in which the new state has been reached. In simulation, we compare at one point of time, the deviation of the endogenous variables from the 'control' or 'base' scenario. The initial time t=0 is the period when we introduce the shock/s which we maintain at least until snapshot period t=T. The 'base-case' or 'control scenario' comprises the initial period and the snapshot period without the shock/s. The comparison between the two 'STATIC' equilibria viz., the one attained with the sustained shocks (along the shocked path), and the one that would have been reached without the shock/s (along the control path) at the same time-period (i.e., t=T) gives the magnitude of change[73] that is ascribed to the shocks.

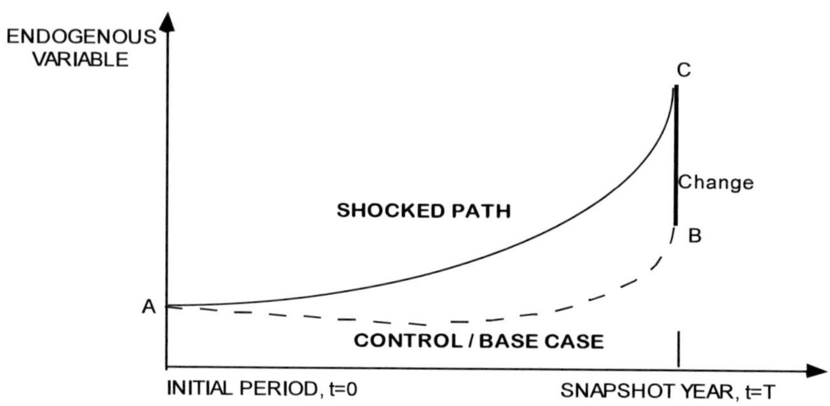

Figure 1. Comparative-Static equilibrium of Base-Case and Simulated change under exogenous shock.

[72] This discussion is based on Horridge, Mark (1985): Long-Run Closure of ORANI: First implementation, WP# OP-50, IMPACT Project.

[73] Vide Horridge, J.M. et al. (1993) 'ORANI-F: A General Equilibrium Model of the Australian Economy', *Economic and Financial Computing* ,Vol. 3, No. 2, summer,

In the diagram above, the percentage change in the endogenous variable in year T that is due to the shocks injected at t=0 is given by [100* (C-B)/B]. The entire discussion about saving and investment is situated in this comparative-static framework.

Length of Run and Closure in ORANI

ORANI is a large comparative-static applied general equilibrium model of the Australian economy comprising over 100 industries and commodities, and 8 labor occupations. ORANI-F and MONASH are the models based on this generic version, but containing dynamic relationships between the variables. The vector of capital-stocks of industry at the current time 't' is assumed to be determined by the investments made in the previous years prior to 't'; current net investment (at time 't') determines the vector of capital-stocks in the next period (in time "t+1"). Future capital-stocks equal current capital stocks plus current net investment. In the *short run*, it is assumed that industry-specific capital stocks are fixed after the policy changes whereas in the *long-run* the policy changes affect the capital-stocks. We study the changes in equilibrium values of the variables following a shock in both the runs.

Now the problem is to specify the macroeconomic environment by choosing a '*closure*'. Choice of '*closure*' means closing a model by decision about the *exogenous-endogenous split* amongst the set of variables describing the system of equations for the model which contains more variables than the number of equations. This hinges upon the decision about which length of run is regarded as suitable for the problem being solved. As such, there is no clear-cut definition of short run and /or, long run; depending on the purpose in hand, one defines the length of run as short or long, and accordingly chooses a closure. This is due to the fact that there is no discernible pattern of adjustment of different variables under different or identical policy shocks. Since the rate of adjustment varies, it is often advisable to define the 'run' by considering the expected time-period of important adjustments of the endogenous candidates following a policy shock.

In the *short run*, *ORANI*[74] considers next period capital-stock, K_{t+1}, as *'endogenous'* and current period industry capital-stock, K_t, as *'exogenous'*. Since on the supply-side of the economy, the level of capital-usage is fixed by fixing capital in each industry, the short-run effects are to be felt not in the sizes of their capital-stock. This means that the burden of adjustment should fall on the 'rate of return' of industries. Therefore, it has to be made *'endogenous'* given the macroeconomic environment. We compute the changes in the rates of return compatible with an assumed (or, no change) change in the sizes of industry capital-stocks given the policy shocks.

In the *long run*[75], we allow for *capital reallocation effects* so that it is a sufficient time period for capital *(after the policy shock)* to adjust. That is, the sizes of industry capital stocks adjust to policy changes. Initially, there are changes in rates of return, but the capital formation and the consequent changes in capital-stock will *restore* the rates of return to their initial or some *exogenously specified* value. Thus, the pertinent point is to compute the change in the current period capital-stock consistent with an assumed (fixed or, set to zero) change in

[74] DPSV (1982), Ch.3, Pg. 64.
[75] ibid., Pg. 66.

the industry rates of return. When mobility of capital is allowed and changes in the industry *'capital-stocks'* are also possible following a shock, industry *'investments'* are also prone to change so that with *'given'* rate of return and perfectly elastic supply of investible funds, economy-wide level of capital formation is likely to change. Therefore, each industry's investment can be tethered to its capital formation. Aggregating across industries, it may happen that the economy's level of investment has changed. Thus, aggregate level of investment is *endogenised* and the economy-wide rate of return is *exogenous* for a policy shock. We compute the change in the endogenous variable (capital-stock) that would be necessary to be compatible with the assumed change (or, zero change) in the exogenous variable (rates of return).. Given the comparative-static nature, we compare the two equilibria at a given point of time. We compare the state of equilibrium of the endogenous variable(s) along the control or base path (evolved during the elapsed time from t=0 to t=t+1 with no shocks whatsoever) with the equilibrium position attained along the shocked path.

Investment in ORANI[76]

Production of Fixed Capital

In this static model, investment is on the demand side; like expenditure, its composition affects the composition of aggregate demand. It does not affect the supply side unlike in a dynamic model, where it varies from year to year. Creation of new capital stock in each industry leads to investment. Production of new units of fixed capital for use in an industry say, *'j'* leads to production of industry capital of type *'j'*. Given the level of fixed capital creation for industry *'j'*, demands for inputs is determined. The production of this 'given' units of fixed capital leading to capital creation follows a nesting structure where derived demands for inputs (non-primary) are determined from the solution of a cost-minimization problem. Given the level of investment for capital formation of type *'j'* in each industry, problem is to choose the least-cost combination of domestic and imported inputs to produce the composite-input used for producing the given level of capital goods. Thus, at the bottom level of the nest, the problem is to minimize the cost of imperfect substitutes non-primary factor inputs from domestic and abroad subject to a level of output of effective input of *CES-composite* inputs. At the next level, the total cost of the effective (direct) composite-commodity inputs are minimized where these are combined using a *Leontief production technology* to yield the given level of capital goods in each industry. Important thing to note is that although the primary factors do not enter into the production functions of the capital goods sector directly, they contribute to capital formation via the inputs of construction used heavily for the creation of fixed capital. Moreover, the technological coefficients vary from industry to industry across $j=1,2,3,.....,h$ and the production functions are different for each industry producing each capital type. This gives rise to *variations of composition* of units of fixed capital across *'j'* industries. We now turn to the determination of 'levels' of units of capital goods to be produced in each industry

[76] ibid., Pg. 94.

Allocation of Investment across industries [77]

In ORANI, it is implicitly assumed that some macroeconomic policy changes lead to a given change (exogenously specified) in aggregate investment. Only the effects of a shock on spreading of such current aggregate investment expenditure over using industries are considered. This is based on:

a) current rate of return (RORC) on fixed capital at period '0', net of fixed depreciation.
b) capital in industry 'j' takes one period (some length of time) to be installed, and available for production so that in this model this is not readily available for production. Thus, productive capacity of the industries is not altered.
c) declining expected rate of return, EROR(1), (the assumption being that the investors, careful enough about the possible consequences of an expanding capital-stock in industry 'j', expect an increase in the capital stock in any industry 'j' to cause a fall in its rate of return in the next period). This expected decline depends on some elasticity parameter measuring elasticity of next period 'ror' in response to present period 'ror', RORC(0). If there is no presumed change in the capital stock in future from its existing level [Kj(0)], the current and expected '*ror*' are equivalent. EROR (1) is a declining function of [Kj(1)/Kj(0)] as shown in the diagram below.
d) allocation of aggregate investment expenditure across industries in such a way that the 'ror' expected (in the snapshot/solution period for which the simulation is run) are all equalized. This is valid for some of the industries whose investment is treated as 'endogenous' within ORANI. Thus, it is pertinent for a short run which is 'long' enough for some industries to adjust and the economy-wide 'ror' is a simple average of these ror's. Investments in these industries are determined by the model's implications about relative ror.

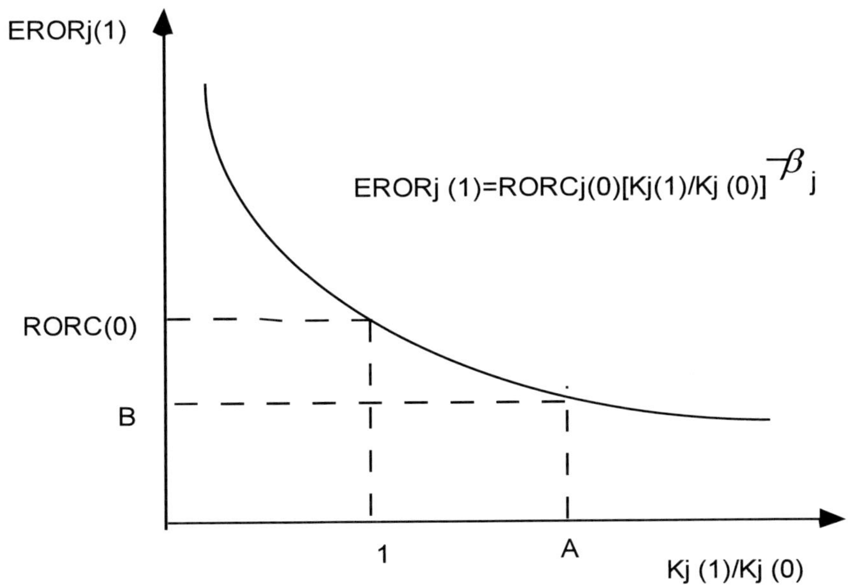

Figure 2. Expected Rate of Return Schedule for Industry "j'.

[77] ibid., PP. 118-122.

e) for some industries, where the above theory is not appropriate, allocations occur in such a way so that the growth in investment in industry 'j' relative to that of the entire industry investment does not change; thus,investment in these industries move with real aggregate investment;. This is also dependent on the closure rule adopted and the length of the run. Choice of the elements of the set of industries in these two cases is largely user-determined.

f) Capital-stock at the end of the period is determined by the current capital-stock and the current level of investment. Assumption is that the current capital-stock incorporates fully the effects of past investments.

Concepts of Saving and Investment in GTAP

Global Saving and Global Investment

Each region has a representative regional household. In this model, 'saving' enters into the regional household's (a hypothetical construct) per capita utility function as a *'commodity'*. Thus, in the *standard* GTAP *closure*, the regional household collects the entire income generated in the economy and distributes it over three sources of final demand viz., saving, private household expenditures, and government expenditures (see Hertel ed. 1997). Like the other two components, the demand for 'saving' is determined endogenously by maximisation of per capita utility function subject to income (which is sum total of allocations over private consumption, government consumption, and saving). Therefore, saving is like a homogeneous, "*real*", physical commodity. Each region has its local *'saving' commodity*. Since there is no money in the model, we conceive of this as a 'real' quantity like 'units' of commodities.

The Global Bank, as a collector of all these regional *'real'* commodities, assembles a portfolio of saving from different regions (both private and government), and creates a global saving pool. All these 'saving' commodities are aggregated to form a composite homogeneous good, and a price (*PSAVE*) is set by the global bank as a Walrasian auctioneer. PSAVE is taken as the *numeraire* of the model. The Global economy as a whole may be realistically assumed to be 'closed'. If all firms earn zero profit, all other markets are in equilibrium, and the households (private and government) are on their budget constraints, then the market for this 'saving' commodity will automatically clear following *Walras' Law*. This will guarantee equilibrium in the Global economy as a whole. That is, the supply of this composite good (*walras_sup*) matches the demand for aggregate saving (*walras_dem*). This is guaranteed by calculating separately these two and checking their equality. This also gives a consistency check for correct implementation of the model. A slack variable (*walraslack*) is introduced and endogenized to check whether its value is zero in the post-solution period.

Demand in each region for this 'saving' commodity is generated by the demand for investment or capital formation/creation. Therefore, instead of being a leakage from the circular flow, the 'saving' is now mobilised and put into circulation as investment through capital creation and/or, purchase of capital goods. Thus, this portfolio of regional saving commodities is basically a composite investment good (financed by the saving of the regional households) and providing investible funds. Now, for ensuring the balance into the system, the global bank distributes this composite investible 'fund' (i.e., the 'saving' commodity composite with price *PSAVE*) to the 'savers' (who are price-takers) according to their demand for 'saving'. At this point, it is important to note that although different regions have different 'shares' in the global pool of 'saving', the model does not have any mechanism incorporating ownership of capital, allocation of shares, and dividends in this basket. Zero pure-profit requires that PSAVE be a weighted average of the price of each region's capital goods [pcgds(r)].

Investment Allocation Mechanism[78]

We now turn to the alternative mechanisms of allocating these composite investible 'funds' by the Global Bank to the regions so as to ensure equality between "global saving" and "global investment". This is, however, related to the implementation of the model where a particular environment, regarded as suitable for the problem being studied, is specified. Typically, the allocation over regional investment of this saving pool is done by adopting one of two alternative mechanisms depending on the 'length of run' or '*time*' dimension of the analysis. The basic idea of the allocation of saving commodity depends on the nature of the "closure" that one wants to specify for the macroeconomic environment, and this choice of the exogenous-endogenous split, in turn, depends on the 'time-frame' of analysis. Thus, specification of the macro-environment by adopting a particular 'closure' (depending on the short, medium, and/or, long-run nature of the problem) governs the methods of distribution of investible 'funds'. Depending on which length of run is considered as appropriate for the experiment, the particular value of a "binary" coefficient (RORDELTA) is chosen to select one of the alternative mechanisms of allocation of funds. The two channels for determining Gross regional investment [REGINV(r)] are as below[79].

Equilibration of Rate of Return [ror(r)] Mechanism

This method equilibrates rates of return across the regions, expected in the snapshot (or solution) period, to apply in the period following the solution period. These expected rates of return are (RORE(r)). This is essentially related to the short run equilibrium in the capital market. In the solution period, these RORE(r)'s are set equal to the prospective global average rate of return [RORG] so that in the percentage-change form, we can write as:

rore(r)=rorg

RORG is defined as the average of all these RORE(r). Thus, investible 'funds' have been allocated to equate all the prospective rates of return to a common value. This short run is 'long' enough for investment decisions to be taken and for investment demand to affect the composition of output in the solution period. However, it is not long enough for the newly created capital to augment capacity. Since it involves some gestation lag for new investment to be installed and available for production, the productive capabilities of the industries in the model are unaffected in the period when simulation is carried out. Productive capital-stock 'on-line' for use in production is constrained by the capital stock available (exogenous) at the beginning of the period of simulation. Investment, thus, has a limited role in the model.

[78] The discussion is based on Ch 2 of Hertel, et al. eds. GTAP: Modelling and Applications and DPSV (1982).

[79] Vide Walmsley, Terry (1997) 'Long-Run Simulation of GTAP: initial simulation in APEC for a Horridge-Style Closure'. CoPS (Monash University)/IMPACT Working paper.

However, as it is a component of final demand, it affects economic activity in the solution period via its impact on the profile of demand structure.

The sum of regional demands for the capital formation across the regions equals the global supply of saving. We have a stock-flow identity relating the beginning of the solution period capital-stock [KB(r)] to the end of period capital-stock [KE(r)] as given below:

$$KE(r)=KB(r)*[1-DEP(r)]+REGINV(r)$$

In percentage change form, it is written as

$$ke(r)=INVKERATIO(r)*qcgds(r)+[1-INVKERATIO(r)]*kb(r)$$

We have *exogenously fixed* regional supplies of capital-stocks *at the beginning of the solution period* so that the services of capital utilized during this period are proportional KB (r). With *full capacity utilization*, the flow of capital services in region 'r' from these stocks is written, in percentage change form, as

$$ksvces(r)=kb(r)$$

Now, ksvces(r) is the (*exogenous*) change in the *flow* of capital services in the *solution period*. ke(r) is endogenised and it determines the changes in gross regional investment qcgds(r) via the equation above. As we have seen above, the change 'globalcgds' in investible 'funds' is distributed across regions to ensure the equality rore(r)=rorg. In this short run closure, although regional aggregate capital stocks are fixed, industry capital stocks change and adjust to the shock. As kb(r) is *substantively* exogenous, it is consistent with the short run analysis of the effects of the shock.

The shock will have impacts throughout the intermediate period till the snapshot period. Changes here mean deviation from 'control' or 'base case' scenario. Thus, changes in the regional capital-stocks refers to deviation from the 'control' path of capital so that regional capital-stocks in use are kept at their control equilibrium values so that kb(r)=0 i.e., the deviation from the base case is 'zero'. In the solution period, changes in regional investment qcgds(r) are due only to changes in demand and production. If any shock increases demand for the products of a region, then that is transmitted to an increase in the demand for capital goods in the producing region via an increase in rental prices given those regional capital stocks in use are at their control values.

Even though regions have fixed capital (and therefore fixed shares in global capital) in this closure, they can gain or lose share in the global investment. It has been noted above that prospective rates of return (for the period following the solution period) are driven to equality across regions by the allocation of the investment pool. The shallower is the downward slope of the schedule connecting the prospective future rates of return with the prospective proportional expansion (relative to the solution period) in a region's capital stock, the greater will be the share of investment captured by that region. This shallowness is measured by the value of RORFLEX(r) in GTAP notation which is the relevant parameter of the schedule mentioned above. The sensitivity and hence the magnitude of changes in regional gross investment depends on the values of parameter, RORFLEX(r), which is defined as a measure of the rate of expected decline of 'ror' in the next period, [RORE(r)], in response to the augmentation of the capital-stock (assumption being that the investors are careful and expect an increase in the capital stock of a region to lead to a fall in its rate of return). RORFLEX (r) shows the percentage decline in RORE(r) from the level 'ror' for an increase in annual investment equivalent to 1% of the capital stock. If it is high, RORE(r) is sensitive to current investment and conversely, lower value means greater volatility of regional investment. β_r in Figure 3 below is the above-mentioned parameter.

Fixed Regional Portfolio Mechanism

The second method assumes that the regional composition of the global capital stock is unaltered. As before, the global rate of return [rorg] is a weighted average of regional expected rates of return [rore(r)] with weights being the shares of regional net investment [NETINV(r)] in Global net investment [GLOBINV]. Here no reallocation of shares in investment is considered, but inter-industry capital mobility within a region is allowed. Thus, 'globalcgds' is equal to (the percentage change in) regional net investment in region 'r' for every 'r'. This closure is described as the *'partial long run equilibrium'* or *'medium run'* closure in the GTAP literature.

Implementation of the Alternative Mechanisms

One can set the investment allocation mechanism using a 'binary' parameter RORDELTA for switching between the two closures depending on the nature of the analysis e.g., the length of run. If RORDELTA is equal to '1', option 1 is chosen and if it is set to 'zero', option 2 is selected. The default setting in the parameter file is changed according to our purpose.

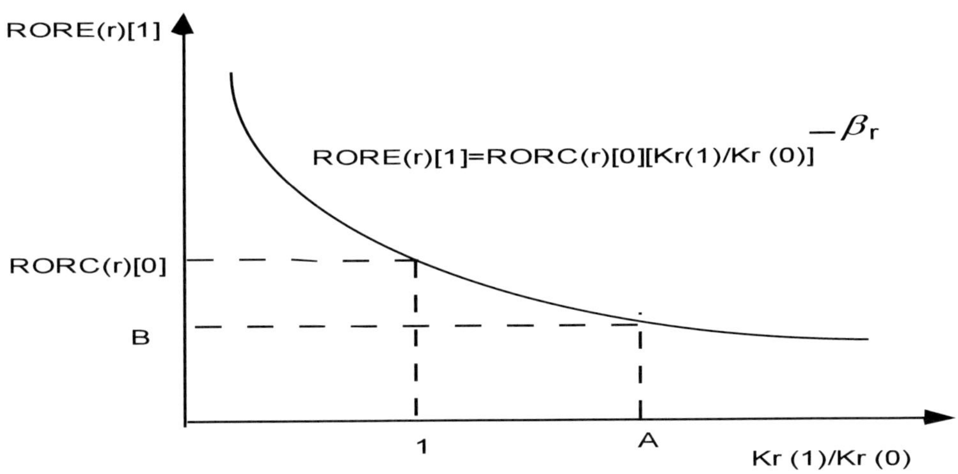

Figure 3. Expected rate of Return Schedule for Region "r".

Analyzing Trade-Growth-Development Issues: Illustrative Results from a Trade-Technology Nexus CGE Model

Stylized Evidence

Based on our discussion about rise in trade in manufactured and sophisticated products intensive in technology giving emergence of intra-industry trade—as presented in Tables 1, 2, and 3—here, we consider core technology clusters for sake of convenience without considering all detailed sectoral analysis. Such list of technology clusters is given in Table 4. These sectors are: Bio-technology (BT), Nanotechnology (NT), Transport Equipment (TE), Fabrication (FT), Consumption Goods (CG) and International Transport Services (ITS)—all exhibiting higher growth in trade (see Table 5). Das (2002b) explored the interlinkages between trade in hi-technology goods and the role of human capital. According to Das (2007), the average annual growth rates for world trade in such clusters are 12%, 6%, 10%, and 11% respectively for ICT, Biotechnology, Nanotechnology, and Transport equipment. Das (2014) shows that the regional growth rates during 1992—2007 in such clusters from G7, EU and OECD nations are: 5.3%, 6.9%, and 4.9% respectively for ICT clusters, whereas for Nanotechnology cluster growth rates are: 8.3% (G7), 10% (EU), and 8.9% (OECD). For Biotechnology, these numbers are: 2.4% (G7), 4% (EU), and 4.9% (OECD). Table 5 highlights the importance of trade in technologically sophisticated products in recent years and thus, lends support to the conjecture based on previous discussion on changes in specialization pattern and evolution of dynamic comparative advantage. This is attributed to gradual shifting to high value-added trade share in the export basket (Bustos 2011, Hausmann et al. 2014, Das 2014).

Globalization and trade opens up vistas for technological spillover due to exposure to advanced trade partners' technologies. But the effective assimilation depends on the structural features, and skill endowment. To understand this mechanism, we need to spell out a mechanism with an operational viewpoint and adopt 'right' methodology. I now present the model mechanism and then, move onto implementation based on the GTAP prototype of static CGE.

A Stylized Model

As discussed at the outset, trade in manufactures and hi-tech product has been a driving force for the organization of production networks across the globe. Not only that, trade in services has been substantial thanks to E-commerce and trade facilitation, aided by the emergence of Information and communication technologies (ICT). Thus, innovation in technology-intensive products has become important. The emerging economies or the Southern Engines of Growth (BRICSAM) have gradually shifted and evolved due to diversifying and acquiring dynamic comparative advantage in a globalized production networks. This has, no doubt, led to the emergence of off-shore North-South outsourcing. Even, the rise of regional production networks via intra-South regional cooperation is gaining weight (Das and Han 2013).

Without going into the details of such global production sharing or value-chain slicing (as it is not the subject of this chapter and discussed elsewhere in this book), in this chapter I discuss an important aspect of such trade-linked production relationship influencing heavily the economic growth of the developing regions. This chapter purports to show the practical implementation aspect of CGE/AGE models and utilizing such models for addressing the leading issues in economic development under the aegis of globalization. I reproduce some illustrative stylized model results for exhibiting the aspect of adapting extant methodology to suit the research objective.[80] All these CGE models depend heavily on simulation software packages. GAMS and GEMPACK are two widely used solution tools.

Table 4. Concordance of GTAP sectors with technology clusters

Technology clusters	Elements	GSC1 Identifier
ICT Cluster	Electronic equipment, Machinery and equipment nec, Manufactures, NEC	ELE, OME,OMF
Consumer Goods	Sugar cane, sugar beet, Plant-based fibers, Crops nec, Bovine cattle, sheep and goats, horses, Animal products nec, Raw milk, Wool, silk-worm cocoons, Fishing, Bovine meat products, Meat products nec, Vegetable oils and fats, Dairy products, Processed rice, Sugar, Food products nec, Beverages and tobacco products, Wearing apparel, Leather products Wood products, Paper products, publishing, Petroleum, coal products	C_B,PFB, OCR,CTL, OAP,RMK, WOL, FSH, CMT, OMT, VOL, MIL, PCR, SGR OFD, B_T, WAP, LEA, LUM, PPP, P_C
Biotechnology Cluster (BT)	Paddy rice, Wheat, Cereal grains nec, Vegetables, fruit, nuts Oil seeds, Forestry	PDR, WHT, GRO, V_F, OSD, FRS
Nanotechnology Clsuter (NT)	Coal, Oil, Gas, Minerals nec, Textiles, Chemical, rubber, plastic products, Mineral products nec	COA, OIL, GAS, OMN, TEX, CRP, NMM
Transport Equipment	Motor vehicles and parts, Transport equipment nec	MVH, OTN
Fabrication	Ferrous metals, Metals nec, Metal products	I_S, NFM, FMP
Services	Electricity, Gas manufacture, distribution; Water, Construction, Trade, Transport nec, Water transport, Air transport, Communication, Financial services nec, Insurance, Business services nec, Recreational and other services, Public Administration, Defense, Education, Health, Dwellings	ELY, GDT, WTR, CNS, TRD, OTP WTP, ATP, CMN OFI, ISR, OBS ROS, OSG,DWE

Source: Based on GTAP and OECD (1997), Science, Technology and Industry–Scoreboard of Indicators. pp. 40-41.

[80] This section is heavily based on some of the results of implementation from Das (2001).

Table 5. Trade in technology clusters for aggregated GTAP regions in 2008 (in US$)

	1 ConsumerGood	2 AgBioTech	3 ElectronicIT	4 Nano_Matrls	5 TransportTec	6 Metal_MedTec
1 G7	496306	75672	1405047	922728	875677	423884
2 OtherEU	248685	35308	307293	409709	161473	154953
3 Brazil	35551	15616	16755	36536	19334	18490
4 Russia	14039	6394	8204	196642	6211	46774
5 India	33254	5206	26095	41782	5364	16088
6 China	220732	6781	453534	86170	37680	93880
7 Hkg_Twn	36533	254	162276	42902	7800	29879
8 SouthKorea	20030	245	162585	61231	61165	30006
9 SouthEAsia	108364	23319	320331	208020	25289	40929
10 RSA	29921	1326	1880	2852	309	1005
11 ECA	115646	16903	136021	127719	89203	96607
12 SouthAfrica	13186	4267	10034	25863	6510	31426
13 LAC	50803	32837	12285	141980	11962	50185
14 Mexico	23466	5126	91057	51024	45311	16980
15 OthrOECD	47439	6945	72505	111937	10010	55124
16 MENA	31019	8160	40854	611895	7883	28195
17 SSA	8614	9292	1185	128747	2049	4955

Source: Author's calculation based on aggregation of GTAP Version 7 Time series trade data.

The following diagram based on Das and Powell (2001) summarily presents a stylized trade-mediated technology-diffusion model with the factors of technology adoption built into the model.

This transmitted improvement is higher, the higher are the values of skill-induced absorption capacity of destination‘s’ (AC_s) and structural similarity or congruence (SS_{rs}). The recipient-specific AC-index AC_s (where $0 \leq AC_s \leq 1$) and the binary structural similarity index SS_{rs} (where $0 \leq SS_{rs} \leq 1$) interactively determine a “capture parameter” θ_s, measuring the efficiency with which the knowledge embodied in bilateral trade flows from source ‘r’ is *captured* by the recipients ‘s’:

$$\theta_s = AC_s . SS_{rs}$$

The realised productivity level from the potential streams of latest technology is dependent on $\theta_s \in [0,1]$ with $\theta_s = 1$ implying full realisation of the foreign technology-induced productivity improvement. Exports from source ‘r’ to destination‘s’ determine an “*Embodiment index*” E_{rs}. The latter, together with AC_s and SS_{rs} determine the value of a “*Spillover Coefficient*” $\gamma_s(E_{rs}, AC_s, SS_{rs})$ via the spillover function γ_s. θ_s and E_{rs} jointly determine the value of the 'Spillover Coefficient' $\gamma_s(E_{rs}, \theta_s)$ for the destination 's'. More specifically,

$$\gamma_s \; E_{rs}, \theta_s \; = E_{rs}^{\;1-\theta_s} \;, \; 0 \leq \theta_s \leq 1$$

The functional form implies: $\gamma_s(E_{rs}, \theta_s) \leq E_{rs} \leq 1$ for $0 < \theta_s < 1$, $0 \leq E_{rs} \leq 1$ and $\frac{\partial \gamma'_s}{\partial \theta_s} = -E_{rs}^{-\theta_s}[1 + \ln \gamma_s] < 0$. Also, $\frac{\partial^2 \gamma_s}{\partial \theta_s^2} = [(\ln E_{rs})^2 . E_{rs}^{\;1-\theta_s}] > 0$ i.e., γ_s is a convex function of θ_s. Thus, the γ_s function shows *increasing* marginal returns to θ_s.[81]

Mathematically, the transmission equation for productivity improvement from 'r' to 's' is:

$$ava(s) = \gamma_s(E_{rs}, \theta_s).\ ava(r)$$

where ava(s) and ava(r) are respectively the percentage improvements in the productivity 'levels' (Hicks-Neutral Technical Progress parameters) in the value-added nest of the production function of regions 'r' and 's' (the lower case variables conventionally represent the percentage-changes in the corresponding 'level' variables in GEMPACK-based GTAP model).

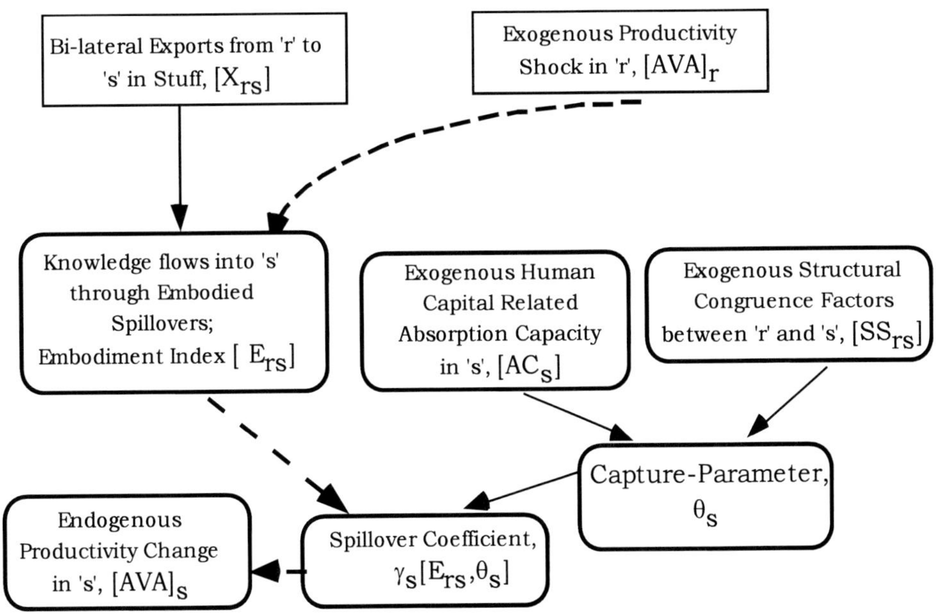

Figure 4. Principal pathways for trade-mediated technology diffusion mechanism in a stylized model (Based on Das and Powell (2001).

[81] Determinants AC and SS of θ_s are both bounded in [0,1] and *strictly exogenous*.

As mentioned elsewhere in this book and in the preceding discussion, GTAP model is implemented using Windows version [WINGEM] of GEMPACK (**G**eneral **E**quilibrium **M**odelling **Pack**age) software suite (run interactively) developed at Monash University's Centre of Policy Studies/IMPACT Project.[82]

Equation above in the notation of the GTAP-system of equations is:

$$ava(i,s)= [VXWD(i,r,s)/VOW(i,s)]^{(1-AC_s.SS_{rs})} . ava(i,r)$$

where i ∈ TRAD_COMM. TRAD_COMM contains traded commodity 'Stuff' only, VXWD(i,r,s) is the value of exports of tradable commodity 'i' from 'r' to 's' evaluated at world *'fob'* prices [i.e., X_{rs} in equation]; VOW (i,s) is the value of output of tradable commodity 'i' in 's' evaluated at world *'fob'* prices [i.e., Y_s]. The model is encoded in TABLO language for GEMPACK software. As discussed above, while no reallocation of regional shares in global investment is permitted, inter-industry capital mobility within a region is allowed with a medium-run, or partial long-run equilibrium standard closure in the GTAP literature (Hertel ed. 1997). This is known as the *medium-run, or partial long-run equilibrium* standard closure in the GTAP literature. In all standard closures of GTAP, the regional labor endowments are exogenous, while in the current closure new investment does not add to the capital stock available in the solution period[83]. However, as investment is a component of final demand, it affects economic activity in the solution period via its impact on the demand. In the case of our 1×3 macro aggregation of GTAP, these compositional influences are limited to the sourcing of "Stuff" from different regions in the assembly of locally-specific capital goods. The additional parameters introduced in the parameter file are HK(s) and SS(r, s). HK(s) represents AC_s. Their values are set arbitrarily. *Assuming* that the EU is more 'similar' to the US in both SS and AC than to the ROW, higher values are assigned for these exogenous variables in case of the EU as compared to the ROW; that is, $AC_{EU} > AC_{ROW}$ and $SS_{EU,US} > SS_{ROW,US}$.

GTAP Implementation

The economic model is the one described in Hertel (ed.) [1997] with an additional behavioral equation, two new parameters and two new coefficients, plus some additional national accounting identities. We have three regions, viz., USA (the presumably most developed region), the European Union (EU, the next in the status of growth and development), and the composite Rest-of-the World (ROW, the least-developed clubbed in one). Thus, the choice of the regions is governed by the theme of differentials in technology propagation contingent on human capital-induced absorption capacity and physical capital similarity or, structural homogeneity of the regions. The model is a '*macro*' model with three trading regions in the sense that there is *essentially* one good (namely, "Stuff") *but differentiated* across three geographically separated trading regions. This product

[82] Currently in February 2014, this centre has moved to Victoria University, Melbourne, Australia.

[83] We use 'solution period' and 'snapshot' period interchangeably to mean the period (occurring sometime after the shock) for which the simulation is run and solution is obtained. The solution is presented as the percentage deviation in the snapshot period in a variable of interest *relative* to its value *in that period* in a base-case or control scenario in which no shocks occur. See the discussion in preceding section on CGE modelling features.

differentiation (due to implicit technological differences across the developed and the less developed countries) opens up the scope for trade due to price differences, thanks to cost-divergences a la differentials in technological progress. As discussed in the previous sections on 'new' trade theory, here we see that trade is happening within the 'Stuff' sector due to product heterogeneity within the same industry.

In our implementation, we define one region at a time as the source of invention—set named 'SRC'. The countries other than the source belong to the set named 'REG_NOT_SRC'. These two sets are subsets of the set of all regions–REG. Table 6 gives the encoding of the spillover equation only in the TABLO[84] language.

Below we consider an arbitrary 2% TFP shock in the US (assumed to be the source of technology creation, and the most developed of all these three regions) in the "Stuff" sector. In the closure used here, prices, quantities of all non-endowment commodities, and regional incomes are *endogenous*, while policy variables, other technical change variables, and population [POP(r)] are *exogenous* to the model.

Explanation of Simulation Results

Table 7 summarises the impact of the perturbation on the macro variables.[85] With fixed supplies of land, labor and capital and no factor-bias, a 2% TFP-shock in 'Stuff' in the US leads to an increase in output in that sector and real GDP at factor cost of exactly 2%. After the HNTP shock, we *effectively* have 2-percent more of each factor after allowing for the improvement in its quality. Thus, in the snapshot period, one-hundred input-hours of composite *real* value-added are equivalent to one hundred and two quantity units of composite value-added measured in terms of constant efficiency units. Hence, there has been no change in the usage of primary factors of production (as measured in conventional units) between the base case and the shocked solution. This leads to a zero percentage change in value-added (not quality adjusted) by factors of production [row 6, Table 7]. However, real value-added (measured in constant efficiency units) increases in all the three regions. We observe that there has not been full transmission of technical change from the source to the destinations–the EU and the ROW. Table 8 suggests that the value of the spillover coefficient depends more strongly on θ_s than on E_{rs} *alone*. Thus, whilst trade is the prime vehicle for transmission of knowledge-flows, AC_s and SS_{rs} (and hence, θ_s) are critical for *'effective'* transmission of technology from 'r' to's'. This is supported by the fact that even when E_{rs} has lower values, the magnification by θ_s can lead to a high rate of capture of the technological improvement.

[84] TABLO is an algebraic language for writing economic models and for defining the associated sets, equations, coefficients, and variables for subsequent solution specifically compatible with the GEMPACK software suite (see Harrison and Pearson, 1996). Table 6 notations are declarations in that language of the set elements of concerned variables.

[85] Adapted from Das (2001).

Table 6. Key Technology Spillover Equation in the TABLO Source file

```
Equation MOD_EMB_SPLOVER

! This equation gives the Embodied Spillovers via Trade in the recipients!
(all, i, TRAD_COMM) (all, r, SRC) (all, s, REG_NOT_SRC)
ava(i,s)=[(VXWD(i,r,s)/VOW(i,s))^(1-HK(s)*SS(r,s))]*ava(i,r);
```

Table 7. Simulated regional effects of technological change in the USA on selected macroeconomic variables[(a)]

Percentage change in:	USA	EU	ROW
1. Technological Change [TFP]	2.00	1.07	0.05
2. Output of STUFF [qo]	2.00	1.07	0.05
3. Supply price of STUFF [ps]	-0.30	-0.19	+0.12
4. Output of sector CGDS	0.08	0.19	0.25
5. Price of investment goods	-0.26	-0.17	+0.09
6. Real Value-added in Stuff (in conventional units)	0.00	0.00	0.00
7. Price of Value-added [pva] (in conventional units)	1.68	0.86	0.19
8. Real Value-added in Stuff [in constant efficiency units]	2.00	1.07	0.05
9. Price of Value-added [in constant efficiency units]	-0.31	-0.20	+0.14
10. Nominal GDP from Income Side (market prices)	1.67	0.86	0.19
11. Nominal GDP from Expenditure Side (market prices)	1.67	0.86	0.19
12. Nominal GDP at Factor Cost	1.68	0.86	0.19
13. Real GDP from Income side (at market prices)	1.99	1.06	0.06
14. Real GDP from Expenditure side (at market prices)	1.99	1.06	0.06
15. Real GDP at Factor Cost	2.00	1.07	0.05
16. Price Index of GDP from Income side (market prices)	-0.31	-0.20	+0.14
17. Price index of GDP from expenditure side (market prices)	-0.31	-0.20	+0.14
18. Price Index of GDP at Factor Cost [(a)]	-0.31	-0.20	+0.14

(a) These values are for percentage changes of level variables from their control values (post- shock).

Table 8. Values of embodiment-index, spillover coefficient and capture-parameter [(a)]

GTAP Regions	Embodiment Index (E_{rs})	Spillover Coefficient (γ_s)	Capture-Parameter (θ_s)
EU	0.014	0.540	0.855
ROW	0.020	0.023	0.030
USA	1.000	1.000	1.000

(a) Values shown relate to the pre-shock situation.

Thus, the EU with higher values of both AC_s and SS_{rs}, does better than the ROW at capturing the TFP improvement occurring in the US despite the ROW having a higher value of E_{rs}. Consequently, in Table 7 we see a greater improvement in technology in the EU (1.07) as compared to that in the ROW (0.05).

Table 9 shows that in all three regions, '*Xpe*' is the most important source of the change in the terms-of-trade (TOT). The changes in regional export volumes can be ascribed to two-fold movements: *along* the export demand schedule and *shifts* of the demand curve. As the individual regions as exporters of Stuff face downward sloping foreign demand curves for their region-specific Stuffs, a fall in the price of exports in the USA and the EU (as opposed to a rise in the case of the ROW) is consistent with the percentage rises in exports from the USA and the EU which are larger than the percentage expansion of exports from the ROW to both of these regions. In part, this has been caused by the movements *along* the export demand curve governed by the changes in price relativities between regions.

Now, the expansion in activity level (i.e., increase in regional aggregate import demand) in each region results in outward *shifts* of the regional export demand curves. These changed trading conditions entail allocation of demand for *aggregate* composite imports of Stuff by a region across different sources of imports depending on the *relative price* changes. Given the expansionary effect on demand for *all* imports of Stuff [*qim (stuff,r)*] by any region 'r' due to the increase in *intermediate input demand* for it by firms producing Stuff and capital goods, as well as that in *final demand* by the public and private sectors, changes in relativities between the price of imported Stuff from any source 'k' (*pms (stuff,k,r)*) and the aggregate import price index (*pim (stuff, r)*) confronting 'r' determine changes in the source-specific import demand by any region.

As products are differentiated by origin, divergences between the export prices for Stuff produced in any region and the average world price for Stuff have given rise to changes in the TOT. Taking any region 'r' as the destination of exports of Stuff from two sources viz., 's' and 'k', *given* the Armington elasticity, the expansionary effect on aggregate imports of stuff (*qim (stuff, r)*) and the import share of 'k' in aggregate imports of 'r', then import of Stuff from 's' to 'r' [*qxs (i,s,r)*] depends on the changes in relativities between the price of imports of stuff from 'k' vis-a-vis that from 's'[86]. We discuss the change in *composition* of bilateral export sales which is contingent on these shock-induced relative price effects.

Table 9. Decomposition of percentage changes in regional TOT[(a)]

GTAP Region	World price effect (Wpe) (1)	Export price effect (Xpe) (2)	Import price effect (Mpe) (3)	Total TOT effect [tot(r)] (4)= (1)+(2)–(3)
USA	0.00	-0.23	+0.12	-0.35
EU	0.00	-0.12	+0.09	-0.21
ROW	0.00	+0.18	+0.01	+0.17

(a) We have rounded percentage changes to 2 decimal places.

Aggregate imports into the USA increase by 1.0108 percent. In the US, the market shares of the EU and the ROW in aggregate imports of tradable Stuff are 18 and 82 percent

[86] In GTAP, we assume that imports of region 'r' from region 's' are exactly the same as the exports of region 's' to 'r'. Hence, the percentage change in demand for exports of 'i' from 's' to 'r' can be expressed as:
qxs(i, s, r)=qim(i, r)– ESUBM*MSHRS (i, k, r)*[pms (i, s, r)–pms(i, k, r)] , where k ≠ s.
where MSHRS (i, k, r) is the share of imports from 'k' to 'r' in aggregate imports from both 'k' and 's' to 'r' and ESUBM (=5 in the database) is the Armington elasticity for imports from sources 'k' and 's'. Thus, we can write MSHRS (i, k, r)+ MSHRS (i, s, r)=1.

respectively. A relatively large decline (0.183%) in the price of imported Stuff from the EU to the US as compared to a rise (0.104%) in case of imports from the ROW to the US causes a 2.2 percent increase in imports of Stuff in the US from the EU, whereas imports from the ROW to the US rise by 0.75 percent only. Given identical Armington elasticities across all the regions (all equal to 5), this translates into an increase in demand for Stuff from the EU even though initially the EU has a lower export share in the US than the ROW. In the case of the EU, aggregate imports increase by 0.4951 per cent, while the market shares of the US and the ROW in total imports are 20 and 80 percent respectively. The decline in '*pms*' for the US (0.29%) as opposed to an increase (0.1%) in case of the ROW translates into a relatively larger increase of exports from the US (2.1%) to the EU than in case of the ROW (0.10%). In its own market, the ROW (a composite region) supplies 52 % of its total import demand whereas the US and the EU supply 22 and 26 % respectively[87].

Our foregoing discussion documents that for each region, marginal productivity of 'raw' primary composite factor inputs (in conventional units), real value-added in *effective units* and production of Stuff go up exactly by the same percentage as the TFP improvement. Effective price of the value-added (quality-adjusted) declines in the USA and the EU and rises in the ROW. More pronounced TFP changes lead to a more productive primary factor composite and to *falling costs* in the US and the EU. Stuff is produced combining the value-added composite and composite material inputs of Stuff using the Leontief technology at the top nest of the production tree (where intermediate inputs and value-added are *not* substitutable). Due to the expansionary effect of an increased demand, increased production of Stuff entails an equivalent increase in *intermediate input demand* [*qf (stuff, stuff, r)*]going into its *own* production in each region—i.e., 2, 1.07 and 0.05% in the US, the EU and the ROW respectively (Table 10).

The percentage falls in the price indexes for purchases of domestic 'Stuff' as intermediate input [*pfd (stuff, stuff, r)*]—0.3 % in the US and 0.19 % in the EU—are relatively larger than percentage increments in price indexes of composite imports of foreign-sourced Stuff [*pfm (stuff, stuff, r)*]—0.05 in the US and 0.02 in the EU. Given *qf (stuff, stuff, r)*, the decline in relative price of domestic vis-a-vis foreign sourced Stuff—0.35 % in the US and 0.21 % in the EU—leads to substitution in favour of domestic intermediate stuff.[88] Thus, the Armington structure causes a larger percentage increase in intermediate input demand for *domestic* Stuff [*qfd (stuff, stuff, r)*] i.e., 2.07 and 1.13 % in the US and the EU respectively. For demand for the composite import of Stuff [*qfm (stuff, stuff, r)*], these are 1.19 (for the US) and 0.604 (for the EU).[89]

[87] For ROW as composite region supplying in its own market, the equation is:
qxs (i, s, r)= qim (i, r)–ESUBM∗MSHRS (i, k, r)∗[pms (i, s, r) – pms (i, k, r)]
– ESUBM∗MSHRS (i, j, r)∗[pms (i, s, r) – pms (i, j, r)] where s ≠ j ≠ k are different *sources* of exports to *destination* 'r'. In case of intra-regional exports, r = s, say, then the above equation can be expressed as:
qxs (i, r, r)= qim (i, r)–ESUBM∗MSHRS (i, k, r) ∗ [pms (i, r, r) – pms (i, k, r)]
– ESUBM∗MSHRS (i, j, r) ∗ [pms (i, r, r) – pms (i, j, r)] where r ≠ j ≠ k.

[88] Intermediate input demand for domestic Stuff by firms producing Stuff can be written as:
qfd = qf–ESUBD∗ [1–FMSHR]∗[pfm–pfd] where FMSHR is share of composite import of Stuff going into its production. Analogously, firms' demand for imported Stuff is given by:
qfm = qf–ESUBD∗ [FMSHR]∗[pfd–pfm]. ESUBD (=2.5 in the database) is the Armington elasticity.

[89] These calculations are: for USA, 1.19=2–2.5 × 0.922 × (+0.35); for EU, 0.604=1.07–2.5 × 0.8866 × (+0.21).

Table 10. Simulated regional effects of technology shock on Stuff [a]

Percentage change in:	USA	EU	ROW
1.Output of Stuff	2.00	1.07	0.05
2.Supply Price of Stuff	-0.30	-0.19	+0.12
3.Share of domestically-sourced stuff	0.92	0.89	0.85
4.Share of foreign-sourced stuff	0.08	0.11	0.15
5.Demand for imported Stuff as an input	1.18	0.59	0.41
6. Demand for domestic Stuff as an input	2.07	1.13	-0.02

(a) Figures are rounded upto 2 decimal places.

The decline in relative price of composite imports vis-a-vis domestic Stuff by 0.17 % in the ROW results in a 0.41 % increase in intermediate input demand for imported Stuff whereas intermediate input demand for domestic Stuff falls by 0.01 %. In all regions domestically-sourced stuff has a much larger share than the foreign-sourced stuff in its production. The supply price of Stuff depends on the *pva* components and price of intermediate Stuff. Now, the price of value-added in constant efficiency units falls in the US and the EU, and rises in the ROW. Also, the price of intermediate input Stuff falls in the US and the EU, and rises in the ROW. Consequently, the zero-pure-profits equation determines that the industry price of composite tradable Stuff falls in the USA and the EU, and rises in the ROW.

SUMMARY AND CONCLUSION

In this chapter, two comparative-static CGE model (prototypes) are briefly reviewed in terms of their structures and treatments of investment, saving, and expected rates of return, and closure for setting the macroeconomic environment for a particular policy simulation. The single-region multi-sectoral ORANI model of the Australian Economy is a widely used model for policy analysis and is a methodological breakthrough outside the North American Tradition (see, for example, Dixon and Jorgenson 2013, and Dixon and Rimmer in this book in Chapter 10). GTAP model developed by Hertel and his colleagues (Hertel and Tsigas 1997) is essentially based on the ORANI and MONASH models. However, it is a multi-regional, global trade model with extension on trade accounts. Thus, the latter is suitable for trade related analysis. Given the current evolution of trade patterns, when the developing countries are moving up the economic ladder and catching up to converge with the G7 nations, and the post-2008 financial crisis period is experiencing emergence of the Southern engines of growth, North-South trade is taking a new dimension. The contour of trade is now North-South-South or, a triangular mode of relationship. Learning by trading is an important element of product-sophistication and quality-ladder model via technology flows (Coe and Helpman 1995, Coe et al. 1997, Barro and Lee 1995, Young 1991). In sum, this article shows that the issue of trade-led growth is a conditional one, and trade-induced learning hinges on the internal factors.

In order to illustrate the mechanism in a modified CGE framework, I presented results based on an augmented version of the GTAP CGE model (Das and Powell 2001). Embodied technology spillovers through bilateral trade linkages have been analyzed within the GTAP framework (Das 2002b, 2007 and 2014). The analysis is embedded in a setup where each region produces a traded 'Stuff' along with a non-traded capital good. However, the Armington (1969) assumption of product differentiation by origin opens the scope for international trade in the source-specific 'Stuff'. Embodied technology spillover occurs via bilateral trade in Stuff between source (viz., the USA) and destination (viz., the EU and the ROW). Absorption capacity (AC) and structural congruence (SS) jointly determine a capture-parameter which, together with the trade volume, *endogenizes* the spillover coefficient. We considered an exogenous 2% value-added augmenting TFP shock in the source country, the US. Following the shock, the higher value of the capture parameter in the EU allows this region to realise a high percentage of the potential productivity improvement, whereas the ROW experiences a relatively less pronounced TFP improvement despite a larger proportional stimulus in imports from the US than that from the EU. The TFP shock leads to an increase in the marginal productivity (in conventional units) of the 'raw' primary factor composite in all three regions whilst the effective price of value-added (quality-adjusted) declines in the US and the EU. Owing to the Armington structure and identical Armington elasticities across uses and the regions, the relatively larger percentage falls in the price indexes for the purchases of domestically sourced Stuff as compared to the percentage rises in the price indexes of composite imports of foreign-sourced stuff, resulted in substitution in favour of domestic stuff in the US and the EU. On the other hand, the decline in the relative price of foreign composite imports and an increase in the price of domestic stuff in the ROW cause substitution in favour of imported Stuff.

This chapter discusses two prototype CGE model and their shared features. Also, it introduces a current theme based on the endogenous growth theory—linking trade, technology diffusion, and absorption via human capital—and implements in a 'macro' model with one good differentiated across geographies. This generates the scope ofintra-industry trade in that singleton sector. The augmented CGE model offered insights on globalization and development. The model is illustrative and intuitive. In particular, *the purpose* of illustrating the necessity of model building, its modification as per the requirement, and adaptation to incorporate research theme/s is achieved via reproduction of some of the established results. Success in model building—as this chapter highlights—depends on the methodological appropriateness governed by research priority and analytical convenience, even sometimes at the sacrifice of much finer details. Attention should, therefore, be given on: the currency of the topic, the finesse of the model, and care for *not* losing the plot in favour of unnecessary methodological complexity of a tall order.

References

Armington, P. (1969). "A Theory of Demand for Products Distinguished by Place of Production, IMF Staff Papers, No. 16, 179-201.

Barro, Robert J. & Xavier, Sala-I-Martin. (1995). *Economic Growth*, New York: McGraw-Hill.

Bustos, P. (2011). Trade Liberalization, Exports, and Technology Upgrading: Evidence on the impact of MERCOSUR on Argentinian Firms. *American Economic Review*, 304-340.

Coe, D. T. & Helpman, E. (1995). "International R&D Spillovers", *European Economic Review*, No.39, 859-887.

Coe, D. T., Helpman, E. & Hoffmaister, A. W. (1997), "North-South R&D Spillovers", *The Economic Journal*, No. *107*, 134-149.

Das, Gouranga G. and Alan A. Powell (2001). "Absorption Capacity, Structural Similarity and Embodied Technology Spillovers in a 'Macro' model: An Implementation within a Computable General Equilibrium Framework."— *The Korean Journal of Policy Studies*, Volume *16*, No. 1, 111-132, Seoul National University, South Korea.

Das, Gouranga G. (2002a). "Cross-Country Analysis of Empirical Evidences of Intra-industry Trade in Manufactures for Dynamic Asian and Other Developing Economies: Implications for Economic Growth and Development" —*The Korean Journal of Policy Studies*, Volume *17*, Number 2, 49-75.

Das, Gouranga G. (2002b). Trade, Technology and Human Capital: Stylized Facts and Quantitative Evidence. *The World Economy*. *25*(2), 257-281.

Das, Gouranga G. (December 2007). "Who leads and who lags? Technology Diffusion, E-commerce and Trade Facilitation in a model of Northern hub vis-à-vis Southern spokes." – *Journal of Economic Integration*, Vol 22. No 4, 929-972.

Das, Gouranga G. (2009). A Hybrid Production Structure in Trade: Theory and Implications. *International Review of Economics*, Springer, Online Version: September 2009, Vol. *56*, No. 4, 359-375.

Das, Gouranga G. & Hongyul, Han. (April 2013). "Trade in Middle Products between South Korea and China: A Survey on Extent of Off-shoring, 276-310." Invited Book Chapter in: Bardhan, Kroll and Jaffe (University of California Berkeley, USA) (Editors-in-Chief), Oxford Handbook on Off-shoring and Employment. Oxford University Press, (University of California, Berkeley and Oxford).

Das, Gouranga G. (March 2014). What role for 'learning? A North-South Tale of Enrichment Effect. *Romanian Journal of Economic Forecasting*. Vol. 17 (1). Pp 67-85.

Dixon P. B., Parmenter, B. R., Powell, A. A. & Wilcoxen, P. J. (DPPW). (1992). Notes and Problems in Applied General Equilibrium Analysis (Amsterdam and New York: North Holland Publishing Company).

Dixon P. B., Parmenter, B. R., Sutton, J. & Vincent, D. P. (DPSV). (1982). ORANI: A Multisectoral Model of the Australian Economy (Amsterdam and New York: North Holland Publishing Company).

Dixon P. B. & Jorgenson, D. W. (2013). *Handbook of Computable General Equilibrium Modeling*, (Amsterdam and New York: North Holland/Elsevier).

Eaton, Jonathon. & Samuel, Kortum (1996). " Trade in Ideas: Patenting and Productivity in the OECD." *Journal of International Economics*, *40*, 251-278.

———& ———(1999). "International Technology Diffusion: Theory and Measurement." *International Economic Review*, *40*(3), 537-570.

Grubel, H. G. & Lloyd, P. J. (1975). "Intra-Industry Trade: The Theory and Measurement of International Trade in Differentiated Products." Macmillan, London.

Greenaway, D. (1983). "Intra-Industry Trade and Inter-Industry Trade in Switzerland", *Review of World Economics*, Band 199, Heft 1, 1983.

Grossman, G. M. & Elhanan, Helpman (May 1990). "Trade, Innovation and Growth." *American Economic Review*, *80*(2), 86-103.

Grossman, G. M. & Elhanan, Helpman (1991). Innovation and Growth in the Global Economy. Cambridge, MA, The MIT Press.

Harrison, W. Jill & Pearson, K. R. (1996). "Computing Solutions for Large General Equilibrium Models Using GEMPACK", *Computational Economics*, Vol. *9*, 83-127.

Hausmann, Ricardo., Hidalgo, C., Stock, D. & Yildirim, M. (January 2014). Implied Comparative Advantage. Centre for International Development, **CID Working Paper No. 276**. Harvard University.

Hertel, Thomas W. (ed.). (1997). *Global trade Analysis: Modeling and Applications* (New York and Cambridge: Cambridge Ujniversity Press).

_________ & Marinos, E.Tsigas, (1997). "Structure of the Standard GTAP mModel", Chapter 2 in Hertel (ed.) cited above.

Jones, C. I. (1995). "R&D-Based models of Economic Growth." *Journal of Political Economy*, *103*, 759-84.

Jones, R. W. (1965). The structure of simple general equilibrium models. *Journal of Political Economy*, *73*, 557–572

Pack, H. & Larry E. Westphal. (1986). "Industrial Strategy and Technological Change: Theory versus Reality." *Journal of Development Economics*, *22*, 87-128.

Sen, Amartya. (2008). *The Discipline of Economics. Economica*. *75*, 617-628.

World Bank Commission on Growth and Development. (May 2008). The Growth Report. Strategies for Sustained Growth and Inclusive Development (Spence Commission Report). Washington DC. USA.

Stiglitz, Joseph. (2003). Globalization, Technology, and Asian Development. *Asian Development Review*. Vol. *20* (2). 1-18.

World Bank. (1992). *World Development Report 1992: Development and the Environment.* Washington D.C., Oxford University Press.

____________(1999). *World Development Report 1998/9: Knowledge for Development.* New York, Oxford University Press.

Young, A. (1991). "Learning by Doing and the Dynamic Effects of International Trade." *Quarterly Journal of Economics*, *106*. 369-405.

INDEX

#

20th century, xii

A

abatement, xvi, 151, 152, 153, 154, 155, 156, 157
abolition, 40
access, xvii, 6, 203, 205, 206
accessibility, 207
accounting, xii, xix, 39, 57, 77, 81, 148, 252
ACs, 250, 252, 253, 254
activity level, 239, 255
adaptation, xi, xix, 69, 258
adjustable peg, 82
adjustment, 4, 17, 185, 194, 220, 240, 241
administrators, 154
adulthood, 153
advancement, xviii
adverse effects, xvi
advocacy, 201
aerospace, 90, 93, 94
Afghanistan, 89
Africa, vii, xiii, xiv, xxiii, 10, 55, 56, 57, 58, 60, 61, 62, 63, 64, 65, 66, 67, 68, 98, 153, 158, 225, 231
age, 7
agencies, xvii, 99, 172, 183, 207
aggregate demand, 3, 4, 9, 10, 11, 12, 13, 17, 21, 242
aggregation, 102, 103, 185, 214, 215, 222, 250, 252
agriculture, 200
Algeria, 148
allocative efficiency, xv, 104
alternative hypothesis, 76
analytical framework, xi, xiii, xix, 3, 4, 56, 236, 237
annual rate, 128
antidumping, 28
arbitrage, 24
Argentina, 7, 11, 89, 125, 148, 230, 232
arrest, 9, 12, 24
ASEAN, xiv, 27, 28, 29, 31, 37, 38, 39, 41, 42, 43, 44, 45, 46, 47, 48, 49, 50, 51, 52, 53, 54, 89, 162, 224, 225
Asia, vii, xiii, xiv, 3, 6, 8, 9, 10, 26, 27, 28, 29, 31, 32, 34, 39, 40, 41, 47, 48, 49, 60, 61, 67, 98, 108, 162, 180, 225, 235
Asian countries, xvii, 29, 34, 37, 40, 162, 163
Asian crisis, 7, 11
assessment, 43, 96, 215, 237
assessment procedures, 96
assets, 5, 6, 69, 185
assimilation, 235, 236, 237, 248
asymmetry, 74, 113
atmosphere, 24
Austria, 148
autarky, xi
authentication, xviii, 209
authenticity, xviii
authority, 5
Automobile, 224
avoidance, 238

B

bail, 6
balance of payments, 8, 10, 11, 17
balance sheet, 6
Bali round of trade negotiations, xii
Bangladesh, 88, 148, 163, 167, 168, 171, 172, 180, 231
bank failure, 6
Bank of England, 202
banking, 4, 5, 6, 7, 10, 11, 107
banking sector, 5, 6, 10, 11, 107
banks, 5, 6, 164
Barbados, 125, 148

barriers, xvii, 6, 10, 96, 104, 107, 123, 161, 162, 163, 165, 167, 168, 170, 172, 173, 227
base, 43, 102, 105, 198, 202, 204, 205, 206, 209, 240, 242, 246, 252, 253
base year, 105
basic research, 209
behaviors, 238, 239
Beijing, xxiv, 226
Belarus, 98
Belgium, xxii, 148, 231, 232
benchmarks, 55
benefits, 42, 88, 99, 104, 129, 162, 184
Bhagwati, 153, 154, 158
Bhutan, 89
bias, 112, 123, 124, 126, 165, 177, 214, 253
Bilateral, 27, 43, 47, 48, 97, 164, 225
bilateral relationship, 88
blend wall, 200
boilers, 35, 36, 38
Bolivia, 125, 148
Botswana, 233
bounds, 79
Brazil, xii, 7, 8, 89, 93, 95, 96, 103, 125, 148, 231, 232, 233, 250
breakdown, 60, 186
bribes, 170
Britain, 129
budget deficit, 28
Burkina Faso, 148
Burundi, 148
business cycle, 8, 13, 141

C

calibration, 128, 129, 134, 137, 142, 147
Cambodia, 57, 60, 61, 64, 65
Cameroon, 148
candidates, 237, 241
capital account, 8, 10, 11, 24
capital accumulation, 40, 104, 185
capital controls, 24
capital flows, xii, xiv, xv, xvii, 3, 4, 6, 7, 8, 9, 10, 11, 12, 16, 17, 23, 24, 229
capital goods, 31, 40, 42, 88, 235, 242, 244, 246, 252, 255
capital inflow, 9, 12, 107
capital intensive, 57, 60, 197
capital mobility, 7, 24, 247, 252
capital outflow, 12
capitalism, 29
Caribbean, 98, 153
case study, 113
catalyst, 66
catching-up, xiv, 63
categorization, 134
category a, 60, 62
cattle, 249
causal relationship, 165
Census, 32, 33, 129, 142, 150
Central African Republic, 148
central bank, 5, 9
Chad, 148
challenges, 40, 90, 210
chemical(s), 29, 31, 35, 36, 38, 39, 40, 43, 58, 62, 63, 90, 96, 148, 235
chemical industry, 29, 31
Chicago, 126, 149
child labor, 221
childhood, 153
Chile, 84, 89, 125, 148, 230
Chinese firms, 66
CIA, 122
circular flow, 244
circulation, 244
CIS, 98
civil service, 207
classification, 57, 60, 62, 90, 134, 142, 151
clean technology, xviii
cleavage, 38
clients, 208, 209
climate, xvii, 9, 23, 24, 204, 208, 227, 229
climate change, xvii, 229
closure, xviii, 107, 199, 202, 219, 240, 241, 244, 245, 246, 247, 252, 253, 257
clothing, 31, 57, 65
clustering, 31
clusters, 248, 249, 250
coal, xviii, 148, 184, 185, 186, 187, 188, 191, 192, 193, 195, 196, 197, 198, 232, 234, 249
coffee, 57, 219
coherence, 231
collaboration, xxi, 90, 184
Colombia, 125, 148, 230
commerce, xi, xii, xv, xvii, 248, 259
commercial, xviii, 185, 203, 207, 208
commodity, xix, 8, 10, 37, 60, 61, 62, 67, 80, 96, 154, 187, 190, 196, 197, 199, 214, 239, 242, 244, 245, 252
communication, xii, xv, 103, 120, 149, 248
communication systems, xv, 120
communication technologies, 248
communism, 6
community(s), xx, 162, 170, 204, 205, 206, 207
comparative advantage, xii, xiv, xvi, 29, 31, 39, 55, 56, 57, 61, 63, 64, 65, 66, 67, 69, 95, 104, 127,

128, 129, 130, 131, 133, 137, 138, 140, 142, 147, 229, 231, 236, 248
competition, xix, 39, 41, 42, 142, 146, 147, 152, 183, 184, 208, 214
competitive advantage, 64, 66
competitive markets, 130, 154
competitiveness, 11, 12, 28, 29, 31, 39, 41, 67, 81, 90, 152, 162
competitors, 37, 73, 183, 214
complexity, 57, 222, 230, 258
composites, 107
composition, xiv, xvi, xx, 10, 14, 17, 55, 56, 57, 65, 113, 235, 242, 245, 247, 255
compression, 17
computation, 167, 172, 193
computer, 93, 95, 207, 209, 238
computer systems, 207
computing, 57, 148, 166, 172, 206
conception, 158
concordance, 102
conference, xxii, xxiii, 67, 202, 203
configuration, xiii
conformity, 96
Congo, 148
Congress, iv
congruence, 228, 250, 258
connectivity, 87, 168
Consensus, xxiii
constant prices, 72, 73
constituents, 238
construction, xvi, 168, 176, 189, 197, 198, 236, 242
consumer goods, 34, 60, 220, 235
consumer price index, 79, 239
consumers, 129, 130, 238
consumption, xix, 9, 11, 12, 17, 19, 21, 22, 33, 34, 41, 107, 114, 185, 193, 194, 195, 196, 197, 213, 215, 216, 219, 220, 238, 239, 244
consumption function, 239
containers, 148
Continental, 126
contour, xiii, xvi, 257
convergence, xii, xiv, 67, 88
cooling, 185
cooperation, xiii, 101, 107, 199, 203, 205
coordination, xiii, 24, 199, 238
copper, 57, 60
corporate sector, 104
correlation(s), 74, 76, 135, 144, 165, 167, 168, 170, 172, 178, 179
correlation coefficient, 76, 165, 170, 178, 179
corruption, 152, 153, 154, 158
cosmetics, 57, 148
cost, xi, 6, 9, 17, 69, 95, 114, 115, 118, 129, 130, 154, 155, 161, 162, 170, 172, 173, 183, 186, 189, 190, 191, 192, 195, 196, 197, 198, 218, 228, 237, 242, 253
cost minimization, 183
Costa Rica, 125, 148
costs of production, 41
cotton, 65, 219
country of origin, 121
covering, xii, xvii
CPI, 73
creativity, 207
crises, xiii, xiv, 4, 6, 7, 11
criticism, xviii
crops, 219
crowding out, 41
crude oil, 34, 185, 193
CT, 248
Cuba, xii, 125
culture, xv, 120
cumulative distribution function, 115
currency, xiv, 7, 11, 12, 14, 72, 73, 82, 112, 113, 126, 185, 258
current account, 10, 11, 12, 14, 15, 16, 17, 22, 28, 74, 77, 82, 185, 194
current account balance, 14
current account deficit, 10, 11, 12, 14, 17, 22, 28, 82, 185, 194
current account surplus, 14, 28
customers, 183, 184
customs procedure, xii, 162
customs-related impediments, xii
Cyprus, 98, 148, 230

D

damages, xvii, 161, 168, 170, 173
danger, 208, 210
data analysis, 3, 4, 13, 72, 77
database, xxi, 34, 43, 44, 48, 63, 65, 90, 96, 102, 189, 193, 198, 205, 207, 219, 231, 255, 256
debts, ix
declining industries, 29
decomposition, xiii, 3, 4, 13, 21, 73, 219
decoupling, 26
deficit, 11, 14, 28, 41, 185, 193, 194, 195, 196
deflator, 197
demand curve, 255
democracy, 208
denial, 209
Denmark, 148, 233
Department of Energy, 185, 186, 199
Department of Transportation, 199

Departments of Agriculture, xxiv
dependent variable, 121, 140
deposits, 190
depreciation, 74, 75, 134, 185, 207, 243
deregulation, 8
derived demand, 242
devaluation, 12, 72, 77, 82, 198
developed countries, xvi, 6, 8, 29, 34, 40, 63, 152, 162, 231, 233, 235, 237, 253
developed nations, 229, 233
developing countries, xii, 3, 4, 6, 7, 8, 9, 10, 11, 12, 24, 27, 29, 37, 40, 47, 61, 66, 67, 69, 222, 231, 235, 257
developing economies, xiv, 3, 4, 5, 8, 11, 62, 231
developing nations, 6, 7, 8, 12, 229, 230
deviation, 24, 165, 187, 189, 194, 195, 196, 197, 198, 240, 246, 252
dialogues, 173
dichotomy, 75
differential treatment, 221
differentiated products, xii, 233
diffusion, xiv, xix, 100, 228, 229, 236, 237, 250, 251, 258
diminishing returns, 55, 56, 57, 66
direct investment, 158
disability, 203
disaster, 9
diseases, 153
dispersion, xi
disposable income, 196
dissatisfaction, xviii
distillation, 35, 36
distortions, 76
distribution, 9, 47, 62, 67, 103, 115, 117, 124, 186, 188, 191, 192, 195, 197, 198, 220, 221, 245, 249
distribution function, 115
distribution of income, 9
diversification, xiv, 61, 66, 233
diversity, 67
division of labor, 29, 37, 40
Doha, xii, 88, 223, 224, 227
domestic capital, 233
domestic demand, 8, 9, 10, 12, 17, 21, 22, 23, 140, 142, 145
domestic economy, 9, 11, 31
domestic markets, 3, 4, 8, 11, 12, 24, 31, 152
domestic policy, 221
Dominican Republic, 125, 148
DOT, 199
double counting, 42
drawing, 156
dual exchange rate, 77
dumping, 28, 158

E

E85, 187, 188
earnings, 10
East Asia, xiv, 22, 24, 26, 28, 29, 31, 32, 34, 39, 41, 47, 48, 49, 56, 60, 61, 62, 64, 153, 162, 231, 235
economic activity, 197, 246, 252
economic cooperation, 87
economic crisis, 8, 13
economic development, xii, xvii, 37, 67, 68, 229, 235, 249
economic downturn, 6
economic growth, xi, xv, xvii, xxiii, 6, 9, 21, 42, 55, 56, 57, 66, 67, 128, 152, 172, 229, 235, 249
economic growth rate, 152
economic integration, 161
economic performance, 10, 228
economic policy, 238
economic power, 29
economic reform(s), xv, xvi, 74, 75, 128
economic relations, xvi, 29, 88, 99, 107
economic systems, 237
economic theory, xvii, 206
economic welfare, 103
economics, xi, xii, xvii, xxii, xxiii, 55, 66, 128, 198, 205
economies of scale, 40, 204, 209, 235
Ecuador, 125, 148, 230
editors, 200, 204, 205
education, xiv, xviii, xxi, xxii, 40, 198, 227, 229, 236
effective exchange rate, xv, 71, 72, 73, 77, 82
Egypt, 148
El Salvador, 125, 148
elasticity of demand, 73
electricity, xviii, 185, 186, 187, 188, 189, 190, 191, 192, 193, 194, 195, 197, 198, 199
emerging markets, 7, 8, 9
emigration, 101
empirical methods, xii
employment, xvi, 60, 127, 128, 129, 130, 131, 140, 141, 142, 143, 144, 145, 146, 147, 149, 153, 155, 162, 194, 195, 199, 215
Enabling Clause, 89
encoding, 253
encouragement, ix
endogeneity, 237
endowments, 41, 63, 128, 147, 220, 252
energy, xvii, 34, 89, 183, 184, 185, 186, 195, 198, 199
energy input, 186
energy security, 199
enforcement, 152
engineering, xvii, 184, 198

England, 202
entropy, 220
environment(s), xv, xvi, xviii, xxii, xxiv, 7, 11, 28, 40, 101, 105, 107, 152, 154, 155, 156, 158, 172, 183, 207, 229, 240, 245
environmental degradation, 152
environmental issues, 200, 221
environmental policy, 158, 159
environmental protection, 152
environmental quality, xvi, 151, 153, 155, 157
environmental regulations, 152, 155
environmental standards, xvi
equality, 107, 154, 239, 244, 245, 246
Equatorial Guinea, 148
equilibrium, xiii, xvi, xvii, xviii, xix, xxiv, 103, 104, 107, 114, 131, 151, 153, 157, 183, 201, 206, 213, 214, 215, 228, 231, 236, 237, 238, 240, 241, 242, 244, 245, 246, 247, 252, 260
equipment, 34, 35, 36, 37, 38, 43, 47, 54, 60, 141, 148, 232, 234, 235, 248, 249
equity, 17
equity market, 17
ethanol, 200
Europe, xiii, xiv, xv, xvi, 3, 4, 6, 8, 9, 10, 98, 153, 161
European Union (EU), xix, 32, 45, 46, 52, 56, 60, 61, 62, 68, 87, 88, 90, 91, 92, 96, 98, 101, 102, 103, 104, 105, 106, 113, 126, 162, 226, 248, 252, 253, 254, 255, 256, 257, 258
evidence, 17, 37, 42, 56, 61, 62, 66, 76, 126, 147, 158, 161, 202, 205, 209, 229, 231
evolution, xii, xvi, xx, 6, 66, 74, 248, 257
exchange rate, xv, 11, 12, 71, 72, 73, 74, 75, 77, 81, 82, 83, 85, 184, 185, 194, 195, 239
exchange rate policy, 82
exclusion, 61, 209
exercise, xvii, xviii, 3, 4, 13, 17, 21, 23, 79, 96, 112, 137, 142, 147, 162, 203, 239
expenditures, 60, 186, 190, 197, 198, 199, 244
expertise, xxiii
export competitiveness, 32, 37
export market, 10, 12, 29, 41, 42, 90, 118
export promotion, 29, 40
exporter(s), 8, 9, 10, 73, 90, 120, 122, 123, 163, 165, 170, 172, 235, 255
export-led growth, xiv
exposure, 6, 153, 206, 248
externalities, 168

F

Fabrication, 248, 249
factor analysis, 178
factor cost, 253
factor endowments, xii, 128, 137, 140, 147
factor market, xix, 107
factories, 64, 67
families, 11
family members, ix
FDI, xii, xiv, xvii, 7, 11, 12, 16, 17, 23, 25, 26, 29, 31, 39, 40, 41, 42, 43, 47, 62, 63, 67, 97, 98, 99, 100, 107, 221
FDI inflow, 17, 97, 99, 100
fear, v, 47
federal government, 202
Federal Reserve, 149
fever, xx
fibers, 65, 219, 249
Fiji, 148
financial, xiii, xiv, xxiii, 3, 4, 5, 6, 7, 8, 10, 11, 12, 13, 26, 28, 41, 100, 111, 157, 257
financial crisis, xiii, 3, 4, 5, 12, 41, 257
financial innovation, 6
financial institutions, 5, 6
financial markets, 5, 11, 12, 28
financial sector, 5, 10, 11, 13
financial support, 111, 157
financial system, xxiii, 7
Finland, xxii, 148, 233
fiscal deficit, 6
fish, 38
fishing, xviii, 198
fixed costs, 112, 114, 119, 120
fixed exchange rates, 12
flexibility, xiii, 124, 206
fluctuations, 34, 73, 82, 141
food, 105, 148, 219, 239
food products, 219
footwear, 29, 31, 39, 57, 64, 65, 148
force, 62, 89, 128, 162, 189, 190, 201, 207, 235, 236, 248
forecasting, xxii, 204, 206
forecasting model, 204
foreign companies, 33
foreign direct investment, xi, 56, 229, 237
foreign exchange, xv, 8, 9, 11, 12, 17, 29, 71, 82, 88
foreign exchange market, xv, 71
foreign firms, 101
formal sector, xvi, 151
formation, xiii, 8, 17, 20, 23, 37, 40, 205, 206, 208, 233, 235, 241, 242, 244, 246
formula, 177
France, 5, 91, 97, 98, 101, 148, 203, 226, 231, 233
free market economy, 82
free trade, xi, xv, 88, 104, 112, 113, 122, 221
fruits, 148

fuel consumption, xviii, 199
full capacity, 246
full employment, 107
funding, 201, 202, 205, 207, 209
funds, 7, 12, 242, 244, 245, 246

G

G-20 countries, xii
Gabon, 148
GATS, 89
GATT, xii, xvii, 89
GDP deflator, 121
GDP per capita, 135, 137, 140
GE model, 215, 219, 231
generic drugs, 95
genre, xviii, xix, 228, 238
geography, xii, 69
Germany, 37, 90, 91, 93, 95, 96, 97, 98, 100, 101, 158, 231, 233
gestation, 245
global consequences, 221
global economy, xii, 27, 66, 128, 229
global interactions, xii
global recession, 3, 4, 5, 8, 9, 24
global scale, 204
global trade, xi, xii, xv, xx, 229, 231, 257
globalization, xi, xii, xiii, xvii, xix, xx, 6, 10, 24, 29, 41, 42, 73, 152, 235, 249, 258
GNP, 84, 91, 92, 105, 231
goods and services, 10, 14, 69, 186, 197, 229
governance, 66, 227
government expenditure, 100, 107, 214, 244
governments, 6, 8, 87, 93, 99, 101, 105, 107, 173, 208
grades, 185
graph, 69
gravity, xv, xvi, 111, 112, 113, 114, 118, 120, 121, 122, 123, 124, 126, 237
Great Depression, 5, 6, 7
Great Recession, 26
Greece, 5, 148, 231
greenhouse, 186, 199
greenhouse gas, 186
greenhouse gas emissions, 186
Grenada, 125
gross domestic product (GDP), xiv, xv, 9, 11, 14, 17, 21, 22, 23, 24, 25, 71, 72, 74, 77, 80, 82, 100, 112, 121, 128, 134, 135, 137, 140, 173, 185, 187, 193, 194, 195, 196, 197, 199, 220, 253, 254
gross investment, 246
grouping, 57, 63
growth accounting, 17, 21
growth models, 57
growth rate, 6, 13, 32, 33, 34, 37, 73, 76, 79, 80, 82, 90, 248
growth theory, 236, 258
Guatemala, 125, 148
guidelines, 157
Guinea, 148
Gulf war, 82
Guyana, 125

H

Haiti, 125, 148
health, xv, xvi, 10, 149, 151, 152, 153, 155, 156, 157, 227
health services, 149
heterogeneity, xx, 113, 123, 214, 235, 253
heteroskedasticity, 123, 135, 144
high performing Asian economies, xii, 233
highways, 199
history, xii, 7, 56, 158, 237
homes, 148
homogeneity, 252
Honduras, 125, 148
honesty, xviii
Hong Kong, 56, 91, 148, 232, 233
horizontal integration, 40
horses, 249
host, 31, 39, 41, 100
House, 161, 206
household sector, 12
housing, 5, 6
hub, 259
human, xiv, 60, 61, 62, 153, 206, 229, 233, 235, 236, 248, 252, 258
human capital, 60, 61, 62, 206, 229, 233, 235, 236, 248, 252, 258
hunting, 153
hybrid, xiv, 40
hydrocarbons, 89
hypothesis, 47, 56, 64, 69, 72, 80

I

Iceland, 148
ICRA, 26, 224, 225
ID, 150, 230, 231
ideal, 73, 178
identification, 122, 162
identity, 21, 196, 246
idiosyncratic, 229
image, xiv

IMF, xvii, xxii, 5, 25, 48, 77, 82, 258
imitation, 56, 62, 66, 69
import penetration, xvi, 127, 141, 143, 144, 145, 146, 147
import substitution, 29, 40
imported products, 215
imports, 10, 17, 21, 22, 28, 32, 34, 36, 42, 43, 58, 59, 60, 61, 62, 68, 69, 72, 80, 84, 90, 96, 107, 116, 117, 128, 129, 141, 142, 143, 147, 185, 194, 196, 199, 200, 216, 217, 230, 235, 255, 256, 257, 258
improvements, xviii, 251
impulses, 82
incidence, 7, 170
income, xvi, xx, xxi, 9, 10, 37, 39, 41, 47, 104, 107, 114, 118, 127, 128, 130, 134, 135, 137, 140, 142, 143, 144, 146, 147, 152, 157, 196, 220, 221, 231, 236, 244
income distribution, xxi
income inequality, xx, 9
income transfers, 221
increasing returns, xii, 56, 112, 233, 235
independence, 87, 99, 177, 206
independent variable, 72
indirect effect, xv
individuals, 205
indivisibilities, 235
Indonesia, 39, 57, 60, 61, 64, 65, 93, 95, 148, 230
industrial organization, 203
industrial policy(s), xiv, 31, 37, 39, 40
industrial relations, 29, 34, 40
industrial transformation, 39
industrialization, xiv, 11, 27, 28, 29, 31, 39, 40, 41, 47, 62, 66, 69, 231, 233
industrialized countries, 11, 231
inefficiency, xv, 107
inequality, xvi, 221, 229
inflation, 11, 12, 74
informal sector, xvi, 90, 151, 153, 154, 157, 158
infrastructure, xv, 120, 172, 205, 207, 208, 209, 221, 227
ingredients, xiv, 196, 204
initiation, 81
institutions, 6, 208, 222, 235
integration, xiv, 6, 10, 11, 17, 24, 31, 64, 71, 76, 79, 113, 162, 228, 235
integrity, xviii
intelligence, 201, 207
interdependence, 31
interest rates, 195
interface, 216, 238
intermediaries, 154
internal consistency, 207
internalizing, 80
International Labour Organisation, 158
International Monetary Fund, xvii, xxii, 5, 71, 121
international trade, xv, xvii, xxiv, 3, 4, 7, 9, 14, 23, 63, 66, 67, 69, 72, 90, 107, 112, 115, 124, 126, 127, 128, 158, 159, 216, 237, 258
interrelations, 228
intervention, 158, 238
intra-regional trade, xvii, 8, 29
inventions, 101
investment rate, 6
investment ratio, 24
investors, 194, 243, 247
invisible hand, 238
Iran, 148
Ireland, 5, 98, 126, 148
iron, 34, 35, 36, 57, 65, 184
islands, 122, 124
isolation, 128, 129
Israel, 148, 230
issues, xi, xiii, xv, xvi, xvii, xix, xx, xxi, 67, 80, 102, 112, 113, 124, 152, 170, 172, 180, 183, 201, 205, 214, 221, 228, 229, 236, 249
Italy, 5, 93, 94, 95, 148

J

Jamaica, 125, 148
Japan, xiv, xv, xxii, xxiii, 9, 28, 29, 31, 32, 37, 39, 40, 41, 42, 43, 44, 45, 46, 47, 48, 50, 51, 52, 53, 54, 55, 60, 67, 87, 89, 91, 96, 97, 100, 101, 102, 103, 104, 105, 106, 148, 232, 235
joint ventures, 237
Jordan, 148
justification, 206

K

Kenya, 148, 231
Keynes, 25, 26, 228
Keynesian, xiii, 3, 4, 8
kinks, 76
Korea, xiv, xxii, xxiii, 7, 27, 28, 29, 31, 32, 37, 39, 40, 41, 42, 43, 44, 45, 46, 47, 48, 49, 50, 51, 52, 53, 54, 89, 91, 96, 97, 148, 230, 232, 233

L

labor force, 128, 135, 153, 156
labor market(s), xvi, xix, 41, 127, 221, 229
labour force, 236
labour market, 183, 185
landlocked countries, 121, 122, 124

languages, xv, 120
Latin America, vii, xv, 6, 7, 10, 11, 98, 111, 112, 113, 121, 123, 125, 126, 153, 162, 235
laws, xvi
laws and regulations, xvi
lawyers, xviii, 208, 210
LDCs, xx, 152, 233, 235
lead, 6, 8, 11, 12, 64, 99, 100, 103, 111, 151, 153, 157, 158, 203, 205, 243, 247, 253, 256
leadership, 203
leakage, 244
learning, xv, 57, 62, 228, 229, 235, 236, 257, 259
legal protection, 153
legality, 153
legislation, 152
lending, 6
liberalisation, 67
liberalization, xii, 8, 11, 24, 71, 72, 77, 78, 82, 152, 156
liberation, 88
lifetime, v
light, xii, xiv, 31, 69, 88, 124, 151, 153, 193, 208
linear model, 238
liquidity, 6
loans, 5, 154
logistics, xv, 47, 87, 99, 104, 105, 162, 163, 164, 221
longevity, 198
love, v

M

machine learning, 222
machinery, 34, 37, 43, 57, 60, 93, 148, 235
macroeconomic effects, xii, 237
macroeconomic environment, xviii, 40, 239, 241, 245, 257
macroeconomic policy(s), 8, 227, 233, 243
macroeconomics, xxiii
magnitude, xvi, 4, 8, 9, 17, 21, 24, 80, 105, 121, 124, 165, 167, 177, 237, 240, 246
majority, 172
Malaysia, 37, 42, 43, 44, 47, 54, 57, 60, 61, 64, 65, 89, 148, 231, 232
man, 65
management, 162
manpower, 100
manufactured goods, 7, 9, 11, 65, 67, 162, 231
manufacturing, xiii, xiv, xvi, 7, 10, 24, 28, 29, 32, 37, 39, 40, 41, 56, 57, 67, 90, 105, 127, 128, 129, 141, 142, 147, 149, 150, 152, 162, 235
marginal product, 154, 196, 256, 258
market access, 88
market share, 29, 32, 37, 41, 42, 63, 64, 255
market structure, 34, 158
material handling, 148
materials, 43, 63, 204
mathematics, xxiii
matrix, xix, 165, 178, 220
matter, xiii, 154, 201, 208
Mauritania, 148
Mauritius, 97, 231
measurement, xii, 177, 236
meat, 57, 249
medical, 35, 36, 38
merchandise, xv, 17, 32, 34, 72, 80, 87, 89, 102, 107, 121
MERCOSUR, 89, 224, 258
meta-analysis, 126
metals, 34, 35, 36, 38, 43, 44, 45, 46, 50, 51, 52, 53, 54, 232, 234, 249
methodology, xvi, xvii, xviii, xix, 21, 111, 112, 121, 134, 172, 199, 214, 221, 229, 237, 248, 249
Mexico, 7, 11, 32, 103, 125, 148, 230, 232, 233, 250
migrants, 11, 113
migration, xi, xvii, 229
military, 88
millwork, 148
mission, 237
mixed economy, 82
model specification, 72, 209
modelling, xxiv, 84, 183, 184, 192, 199, 200, 201, 202, 203, 204, 205, 206, 207, 208, 209, 219, 221, 237, 239, 252
models, xv, xvii, xviii, xix, xx, xxiv, 72, 78, 112, 124, 154, 158, 183, 184, 185, 198, 199, 201, 202, 203, 204, 205, 206, 207, 208, 209, 213, 214, 215, 219, 220, 221, 222, 228, 236, 237, 238, 239, 240, 241, 249, 253, 257, 260
modifications, xii, 199
mold, xi
momentum, xvi, 6, 82, 206
monetary policy, 5, 40
monopolistic competition, xii, xv, 114, 233
Morocco, 148, 153
motivation, 56, 222
Mozambique, 148
multinational corporations, xii
mutation, xx

N

NAFTA, 102, 103, 162
nation states, 161
national expenditure, 196
national income, 21, 39

natural gas, xviii, 186, 188, 190, 191, 192, 194, 195, 196, 197, 198
natural resources, 60, 69, 107, 220
negative consequences, 140, 146
negative effects, 73, 147
negative relation, 170
negotiation, 40, 88, 91, 156
NEMS, xvii, 183, 184, 185, 186, 187, 188, 189, 190, 191, 192, 193, 194, 195, 197, 198, 199
Nepal, 89, 148, 163, 167, 168, 170, 171, 172, 180
net investment, 241, 247
Netherlands, 93, 95, 97, 98, 148, 233
neutral, 104
New Zealand, 148
Nicaragua, 125, 148
Nigeria, 93, 95, 148
non-linear equations, 238
non-participating countries, xv
nontariff barriers, 161
normal distribution, 120
North America, xvii, 98, 162, 257
North American Free Trade Agreement, 162
Northeast Asia, 39, 41, 48
Norway, 148
null, 76
null hypothesis, 76

O

objectivity, 208
Oceania, 98
OECD, xv, xxiii, xxiv, 3, 4, 8, 11, 28, 33, 34, 43, 44, 48, 87, 90, 91, 95, 97, 98, 99, 100, 101, 102, 107, 108, 248, 249, 259
officials, 153
offshoring, 7
oil, 40, 57, 60, 61, 62, 72, 103, 185, 194, 198, 200, 249
omission, 111, 112, 124
open economy, xxiii, 22, 154, 158
openness, xvi, xxi, 39, 72
opportunities, 41, 47, 205, 208
optimism, xx
organic chemicals, 62
organism, 153
outsourcing, xix, xx, 7, 66, 248
overlap, 37
ownership, 245

P

Pacific, vii, xiv, 26, 27, 41, 67, 180, 225
Pakistan, 88, 148, 163, 167, 168, 171, 172, 231
Panama, 125, 148
Paraguay, 89, 125, 148, 231
Pareto, 117, 124, 177
parity, 12, 168
Parliament, 205
participants, 207
pathways, xviii, 200, 251
PCA, 167
peer group, 203
perfect competition, 130
permit, 176, 204
Peru, 125, 148
petroleum, 61, 65, 102, 103, 106, 148, 187, 188, 232, 234, 235, 249
pharmaceutical, 34
Philadelphia, 127, 149
Philippines, 148, 231
phosphorous, xviii
phosphorus, 197, 198
physical sciences, 204
plants, 57, 198
plastic products, 232, 234, 249
plastics, 34, 65, 148
plausibility, xviii, xx
PMS, 217
policy issues, xix, 214
policy makers, xviii, 24, 56, 203, 215
policy making, 239
policy reform, 31, 71, 74
policy variables, xvi, 253
policymakers, xiii
political instability, 82
pollution, 152, 156, 158
poor performance, 61
population, 104, 135, 220, 253
population growth, 104
portfolio, 7, 9, 12, 23, 244
portfolio investment, 7
Portugal, 5, 129, 148, 230
positive relationship, 140, 170
poverty, xvii, xxi, 172, 173, 215, 227
poverty reduction, 227
power plants, 198
preservation, 152
President, 88, 161
prestige, 208
price changes, 255
price deflator, 196
price effect, 255
price elasticity, 72
price index, 114, 117, 220, 255, 256, 258
primary products, 42, 61, 62

principal component analysis, 165, 172, 176, 178
principles, 128
private costs, 152
private firms, 12
private sector, 9, 12, 87, 99, 105, 107, 201, 205, 208, 255
probability, 56, 62, 113, 120, 121, 122, 124
producer goods, 235
producers, 37, 62, 103, 129, 151, 153, 154, 209, 238, 239
product market, 103
production function, 21, 135, 185, 237, 239, 242, 251
production networks, xiii, xiv, xix, 31, 41, 248
production technology, 242
productive capacity, 243
productivity growth, 21, 25
profit, 103, 115, 118, 154, 239, 244, 245
profitability, 114
project, xix, xxi, 193, 199, 207, 216
proliferation, xiii, 28
propagation, xv, 252
proposition, 157, 221
prosperity, 10
protection, 28, 103, 184, 202
protectionism, 28
prototype(s), 248, 257, 258
public concern, 208
public domain, xvii, xviii, 203, 204, 207, 208, 209
public finance, 183
public goods, 201, 204, 207
public health, 153
public policy, xviii, 40, 201, 203, 204, 208, 209, 229
public sector, 12, 99, 185, 194, 208, 209
publishing, 103, 148, 162, 232, 234, 249
pulp, 148
purchasing power, 140

Q

quality assurance, 206
quality control, 207
quantification, 88, 237
question mark, 22
questioning, xviii
questionnaire, 163, 168
quotas, 157, 215

R

race, xi
radio, 65
rate of return, 154, 185, 241, 242, 243, 245, 247
raw materials, 162
real estate, 5, 6, 10
real terms, 121, 128
real wage, 195, 196, 198
realism, 199
reality, 32, 37, 63, 107, 167, 168, 228, 238
recession, 5, 6, 7, 8, 9, 10, 11, 13, 17, 20, 22, 24, 194, 200
recognition, xxi, 87, 96, 185, 205
recommendations, 207
recovery, xiii, 5, 8, 9, 13, 14, 17, 18, 20, 21, 40
recycling, 63
referees, 205
reform(s), viii, xiv, xvi, 39, 47, 71, 72, 73, 80, 82, 84, 85, 99, 128, 151, 153, 156, 157, 158, 183, 211, 215, 235
regional cooperation, xvii, 248
regional integration, 47, 162
regionalization, 126
regions of the world, 161
regression, xvi, 64, 122, 127, 140, 141, 142, 144, 146
regression analysis, xvi, 127, 140, 141
regression model, xvi, 142, 144, 146
regulations, 82, 151, 152, 153, 186
regulatory framework, 152
rejection, 76
relative prices, 69, 72, 237, 239
relaxation, 209
relevance, xx, 172, 205, 229
remittances, 11
renewable energy, 185
rent, 157
replication, xviii, 204, 205, 207
reproduction, 227, 237, 258
Republic of the Congo, xxiii
reputation, 209
requirements, 60, 129, 185, 203, 208
researchers, xvii, 204, 205, 206, 228
reserves, 8, 9, 11, 12, 17, 82
residuals, 135, 141
resins, 148
resistance, 117, 118, 205
resources, xii, 104, 107, 152, 183, 205, 207, 209, 224, 229
response, 8, 9, 17, 21, 41, 140, 145, 196, 203, 243, 246
responsiveness, xvii, 83, 107
restrictions, xi, 6, 72
retail, 50, 51, 54
returns to scale, 103, 154, 183
revenue, 173, 214
rewards, 205, 209

RFS, 200
risk(s), 5, 6, 56, 195
Roberto Azevedo, xii
Romania, 148
root(s), xiv, 72, 76, 77, 80, 179, 221
Royal Society, xxi
rubber, 148, 232, 234, 249
rubber products, 148
rules, 96, 151
Russia, vii, xv, 6, 7, 87, 88, 89, 90, 91, 92, 93, 94, 95, 96, 97, 98, 99, 100, 101, 102, 103, 104, 105, 106, 107, 108, 233, 250
Rwanda, 148

S

safety, 10, 199
Samsung, 48
SAS, 180
savings, 5, 6, 28, 40, 107, 220, 233
scale economies, 115
scarce resources, 184
scatter, 170
school, xvii, xix
science, 40, 89, 203
scope, xv, xix, 57, 88, 172, 203, 204, 209, 229, 235, 236, 253, 258
SDRs, 73
seafood, 38
second generation, 202
secondary information, 163
semiconductors, 42
sensitivity, xvii, xviii, 246
service provider, 208
services, xiii, xv, xix, 7, 9, 14, 17, 50, 67, 120, 152, 183, 186, 189, 190, 191, 193, 194, 197, 198, 208, 238, 246, 248, 249
SES, 108
shadow economy, 158
shape, 22, 117
sheep, 249
shock, xiv, xv, xviii, 3, 4, 10, 12, 21, 24, 71, 104, 184, 187, 189, 190, 199, 237, 240, 241, 243, 246, 252, 253, 254, 255, 257, 258
shoots, 5
shores, 73
showing, 14, 23, 37, 43, 90, 140, 191, 221
SIC, 142
signalling, 238
signals, 238
signs, xiii, 13, 14, 17, 35, 36, 38, 64, 76, 104
silk, 249
simulation(s), xv, xvii, xviii, 104, 105, 184, 186, 189, 190, 193, 196, 200, 202, 204, 207, 215, 234, 237, 240, 243, 245, 249, 252, 257
Singapore, 49, 89, 91, 97, 148, 230, 232, 233
social capital, 69
society, xviii, 238
software, xiv, xvii, xix, xxi, 188, 206, 231, 233, 234, 238, 239, 249, 252, 253
solution, 153, 209, 238, 240, 242, 243, 244, 245, 246, 249, 252, 253
South Africa, 7, 61, 62, 65, 96, 103, 148, 224, 225, 233
South America, 125
South Asia, viii, xvi, 99, 108, 153, 161, 162, 163, 170, 172, 173, 180, 225, 226
South Korea, xiv, xv, xx, xxii, 27, 48, 56, 60, 68, 227, 233, 259
Southeast Asia, 29, 31, 39, 40, 41, 47, 57, 59, 60, 61, 62, 63, 64, 65, 67
Soviet Union, 88
Spain, xxii, xxiii, 5, 148
specialists, xix, 199, 213
specialization, xiii, xix, xxiii, xxiv, 56, 64, 65, 66, 69, 129, 130, 154, 214, 236, 248
species, 153
specifications, xviii, 112
specter, 37, 39
spending, 6, 12, 131
spillover effects, xiv
spillovers, xiii, 100, 258
Spring, 25
Sri Lanka, 89, 148, 163, 167, 168, 170, 171, 172, 230, 232
SS, 251, 252, 254, 258
SSA, 56, 62, 63, 64, 65, 250
stability, xiii, 5, 238
stakeholders, 172, 173
standard deviation, 120, 165, 167, 177
standard error, 145
state(s), xii, 29, 172, 199, 206, 221, 240, 242
state-owned enterprises, 29
statistics, 34, 42, 79, 91, 94, 101, 102, 123, 135, 142, 165, 166
steel, 34, 35, 36, 148, 184, 235
steel industry, 184
stimulus, 9, 21, 90, 183, 258
stock, 7, 9, 11, 17, 98, 128, 134, 185, 237, 241, 242, 243, 244, 245, 246, 247, 252
stock markets, 7, 9, 11
stock value, 134
storage, 50, 51, 54
strictures, 153
structural adjustment, 41

structural characteristics, 3
structural transformations, xiv
structure, xiii, xvii, xix, 24, 27, 29, 31, 32, 34, 37, 39, 40, 41, 47, 67, 82, 88, 107, 151, 152, 155, 156, 184, 186, 189, 190, 203, 213, 214, 215, 219, 220, 229, 239, 242, 246, 256, 258, 260
style, 64, 67, 200, 228
subjective weights, 163, 166
subjectivity, 178
sub-Saharan Africa, 62, 65
subsidy, 104
substitutes, 185, 216, 242
substitution, xviii, 29, 40, 63, 114, 194, 215, 233, 239, 256, 258
sugar beet, 249
supplier(s), xiv, 40, 88, 184
supply chain, 27, 43, 47, 48, 162
supply curve, 192
supply equations, 72
surplus, xiv, 14, 27, 28, 39, 42, 43, 47, 48, 60
survival, 154
sustainability, 28, 55, 56, 66
Sweden, 148, 233
Switzerland, 91, 97, 98, 148, 233, 259
symmetry, xix
syndrome, 81
Syria, 148

T

Taiwan, xiv, 27, 29, 31, 39, 41, 47, 56, 148, 232, 233
Tanzania, 148
target, 39, 40, 71, 220
tariff, xvi, 6, 96, 104, 151, 153, 154, 156, 157, 158, 161, 162, 184, 214, 215, 219, 223
tariff rates, 214
Task Force, 26
taxes, 153, 219
teams, xxiv, 206, 209
technical change, 66, 67, 190, 191, 192, 195, 218, 219, 253
techniques, xix, xx, 11, 21, 69, 183, 184, 220
technological advancement, 134
technological change, 60, 104, 237, 254
technological progress, xi, 55, 56, 57, 65, 67, 253
technology flows, xix, 228, 236, 237, 257
technology gap, 62, 235
technology transfer, xiv, xv, xvii, 62, 236
teeth, 203
telecommunications, 90
tension(s), 191, 192, 199, 204
tenure, 205
test statistic, 76
testing, xi, 206
textbook, 75
textiles, 57, 148, 219, 221, 235
Thailand, 42, 57, 60, 61, 64, 65, 148, 214, 224, 230, 232
thoughts, 129
threats, 28, 41
time frame, 91
time series, 71
time-frame, 245
tobacco, 249
Togo, 148
total factor productivity, xix, 195
tourism, xv, xxii, 111, 112, 113, 120, 121, 122, 124, 125
toys, 65
TPP, xii
tracks, 39
trade agreement, xiii
trade costs, 112, 113, 120, 121, 124
trade deficit, 28, 39, 42, 60, 88
trade facilitation, xi, xii, xv, xvii, 104, 105, 162, 248
trade liberalization, xii, xv, xvii, 10, 235
trade negotiations, xii, 88
trade pattern, xii, xvi, xix, xx, 31, 55, 56, 61, 62, 65, 67, 68, 231, 257
trade policy, xiii, xiv, xvii, xix, 29, 39, 40, 66, 88, 153, 158, 213, 214, 215, 231
trade-off, xx, 152
trading partners, 33, 43, 62, 74, 82, 87, 88, 89, 96, 103, 104, 126, 128, 134, 137, 138, 142, 144, 147
training, 206
transaction costs, 168, 170
transactions, xvii, 161, 236
Trans-Atlantic Trade and Investment Partnership, xii
transformation(s), xiii, xviii, xx, 22, 29, 31, 69, 122, 156, 215
transition period, 240
translation, 149
transmission, xiii, xv, 3, 4, 8, 186, 199, 236, 251, 253
Trans-pacific partnership, xii
transparency, xviii, 153
transport, xv, 6, 103, 107, 114, 115, 118, 119, 124, 163, 167, 168, 170, 171, 172, 185, 197, 198, 218, 235, 249
transport costs, xv, 119, 124
transportation, xv, 47, 60, 120, 149, 185, 198, 221
Treasury, 202, 206
treatment, 107, 215, 222, 228, 229, 237
trial, 238
Trinidad, 148
TTIP, xii
Turkey, 68, 148, 230

twist, 205

U

U.S. economy, xxiii, 184
Ukraine, 98
UNDP, xxi
unemployment rate, 5
UNESCO, 108
uniform, 190
unions, 112, 113
unit cost, 190
United Kingdom (UK), 91, 98, 101, 148, 203, 205, 233
United Nations (UN), xxii, 13, 18, 19, 20, 22, 23, 55, 63, 65, 67, 69, 108, 111, 121, 225
United States (USA), xix, xx, xxi, xvi, xvii, xxii, xxiv, 3, 4, 8, 25, 43, 90, 91, 92, 93, 95, 96, 97, 98, 100, 101, 103, 127, 128, 135, 139, 147, 148, 153, 200, 203, 223, 226, 227, 231, 232, 252, 254, 255, 256, 257, 258, 259, 260
updating, 207
up-skilling, 37
urban, 153
Uruguay, 40, 89, 125, 148
Uruguay Round, 40

V

variable costs, 112, 113, 118, 120
variations, 179, 214, 242
varieties, 56
vector, 141, 142, 178, 241
vegetables, 148
vehicles, 34, 149, 200, 202, 232, 234, 235, 249
vein, 172
Venezuela, 125, 148, 230
vertical integration, 41, 47
Vice President, 227
Vietnam, 57, 65
volatility, 7, 9, 10, 23, 24, 247
vulnerability, xiv, 6, 24

W

wage rate, 130, 131, 134, 197
wages, xvi, 29, 66, 107, 127, 128, 129, 134, 135, 137, 140, 141, 142, 143, 144, 145, 147, 185, 215
war, xi, 88
Washington, xx, xxi, xxii, xxiii, 150, 226, 260
watches, 57, 65
water, 29, 153
watershed, xii
weakness, 184
web, xii
welfare, xi, xvii, xviii, xix, 12, 104, 173, 215, 219, 220, 238
welfare loss, 173
Western Europe, 153
wholesale, 73, 79
wholesale price index, 73, 79
wood, 57, 148
wood products, 148
wool, 148
workers, xvi, 10, 127, 129, 131, 140, 142, 143, 145, 146, 147, 154, 204, 236
workforce, 37
World Bank, xi, xvii, xx, xxi, xxiv, 66, 90, 128, 134, 147, 150, 162, 163, 180, 225, 226, 227, 229, 231, 236, 260
World Development Report, 231, 236, 260
world economy, xi, xx, 3, 4, 5, 6, 7, 8, 10, 11, 13, 24, 28, 32, 40, 60, 67, 126, 152, 153
World Health Organization (WHO), 153
World Trade Organization (WTO), xii, xvii, 6, 28, 31, 43, 47, 48, 49, 96, 108, 156, 231
worldwide, 48, 162
worry, 39

Y

Yale University, 26
yarn, 65
yield, 113, 134, 242

Z

Zimbabwe, 148